ARCHITECT'S ROOM DESIGN DATA HANDBOOK

ARCHITECT'S ROOM DESIGN DATA HANDBOOK

Fred A. Stitt, Architect

Editor/Publisher, Guidelines

VNR VAN NOSTRAND REINHOLD
New York

Library of Congress Catalog Card Number
ISBN 0-442-00716-7

Van Nostrand Reinhold
115 Fifth Avenue
New York, New York 10003

Chapman and Hall
2-6 Boundary Row
London, SE1 8HN, England

Thomas Nelson Australia
102 Dodds Street
South Melbourne 3205
Victoria, Australia

Nelson Canada
1120 Birchmount Road
Scarborough, Ontario M1K 5G4, Canada

16 15 14 13 12 11 10 9 8 7 6 5 4 3 2 1

Library of Congress Cataloging-in-Publication Data

Stitt, Fred A.
  Architect's room design data handbook / Fred A. Stitt.
      p.   cm.
  ISBN 0-442-00716-7
  1. Architectural design.   I. Title.
NA2750.S73   1992
729--dc20   91-45899
                                                 CIP

There are a few thinkers and innovators who are devoted to improving the way we do things in this profession; people like Ned H. Abrams, FAIA, Ernest Burden, Morry Wexler, Weld Coxe, Frank Mascia, and a handful of others.

This book is gratefully dedicated to you and your kind.

ARCHITECT'S ROOM DESIGN DATA HANDBOOK

TABLE OF CONTENTS

PREFACE -- HOW TO USE THIS BOOK

For years designers have had to go to a dozen or more different sources to get basic technical data about every room they design. They had to look in one source for planning rules of thumb; other sources for finishes; still others for HVAC requirements, lighting, electrical needs, acoustical standards, etc.

Now all that data is condensed in this one volume and presented room by room, building by building in the most convenient format possible. This data has been gathered as part of years of research for our GUIDELINES publications on office design practices, prevailing practices in construction specifications and detailing, building codes, and standards of government agencies.

The standards presented are guides, not absolutes. It's always wise to exceed minimum standards wherever possible and there's no reason not to substitute your own judgement whenever it better serves your design intent. Just watch for our WARNING notes about common problems with various materials and practices.

To find the building type you're working on, look in the Table of Contents where all the most common building types are listed.

Find the design standards for the rooms of the building you're working on and photocopy the pages you need to use as checklist worksheets. Check off the applicable standards and write in any additions, changes, and questions as needed.

Your checklist worksheets will be room-by-room coordination guides for design development and working drawing production. They're handy for reviewing and confirming design requirements with clients. You can also use the worksheets as checklists for cost estimating, engineering coordination, and construction administration.

By using these sheets as reference guides throughout a project, you can avoid much of the duplication of effort, back-tracking, and coordination errors that otherwise crop up through the course of most design projects.

Where options are listed under MINIMUMS, the minimums are usually somewhat in excess of common handbook and building code standards. We exceed ordinary standards when there is evidence that they are inadequate, or only barely adequate to assure health, comfort, and safety.

The majority of rooms in the majority of buildings follow the well-established standards listed in this handbook. If there's no particular reason to deviate from the standards, you'll save considerable time and trouble by sticking with the norms.

For additional help during predesign, programming, and design development phases see the ROOM DESIGN CHECKLIST section starting on page 272. For detailed specification text for most materials and appurtenances covered in this manual, see the ROOM MATERIALS SPECIFICATIONS CHECKLIST starting on page 306.

If you have any suggestions on how we can make this book more useful in future editions, please write me at GUIDELINES, Box 456, Orinda, CA 94563.

Fred Stitt, Editor/Publisher, GUIDELINES. Director, San Francisco Institute of Architecture.

ACKNOWLEDGEMENTS

Marti Barrett, Linda Hinkle, Joy Massa, Ginnie Meyer, Patrick Nelson, Beverly Patterson, Cloude Porteous,
Robert Riddlemoser, Paige Salem, Anita Shrieve, Kathy Thompson,
and especially, the finest of editors -- Wendy Lochner --
thanks for all your extraordinary help and support on this very demanding project.

ARCHITECT'S ROOM DESIGN DATA HANDBOOK

BANKS
SAVINGS & LOAN OFFICES

DESIGN STANDARDS -- BANKS/SAVINGS & LOAN, PUBLIC LOBBY

GENERAL	Recommended Standards	Minimum Standards
__ Occupancies and Floor Area	__ As per program with allowance for varying occupancies and traffic loads	__ As per program
__ Ceiling Height	__ 12' - 16' __ Can include low (8') soffit at entrance vestibule	__ 10' - 12' in smaller branch offices
__ Special Plan Considerations	__ Centralized writing counter areas __ Double-door air lock vestibule in hot or cold climates __ Lobby lounge seating areas near officer's areas	__ As per Recommended Standards

FINISHES	Cost Categories		
	A	B	C
__ Floors WARNING: Smooth, hard surface materials sometimes used at entrances -- such as terrazzo, marble, smooth tile, or polished travertine are safety hazards -- even those treated to be non-slip are a problem when wet and when in contact with certain shoe sole materials	__ Recessed floor mat for rainy/ snowy climates at vestibule __ Non-slip rubber or vinyl tile at entry vestibule __ Nylon or other synthetic fabric carpet near entry should be rated for heavy wear, stain resistant and reasonably dark tone, glued to floor __ Carpet may be a different, complementary color and fabric at adjacent spaces to allow easier replacement of the more heavily trafficked entry floor area __ Avoid light-tone reflective floor surfaces	__ Vinyl or asphalt tile at entry vestibule __ Synthetic fabric carpet rated for heavy wear near entry, glued to floor __ Complementary heavy to medium wear carpet at adjacent areas __ Other flooring considerations as per Cost Category A	__ Non-slip rubber or vinyl at entry vestibule __ Synthetic fabric carpet, glued
__ Walls & Substructure	__ Full-height store-front entry with automatic door opener __ Marble/other polished stone __ Interior wall finish typically plaster or gypsum board with heavy duty vinyl, fabric, or hardwood __ Exit wall fire ratings as per code	__ Foyer and exit area wall fire ratings as per code __ Gypsum board with heavy weight vinyl or fabric __ Plaster with sound absorbant treatment	__ Fire ratings as per code __ Gypsum board, painted
__ Ceiling	__ Baffle, metal, wood or other decorative ceiling __ Gypsum board with acoustic treatment __ Suspended decorative acoustic tile	__ Suspended decorative acoustic tile __ Gypsum board	__ Suspended acoustic tile, exposed grid __ Gypsum board
__ Counters & Built-In Furnishings	__ Polished stone, hardwood __ Composite plastic	__ Plastic laminate or as per bank furniture manufacturer	__ Plastic laminate
__ Fixtures	__ Phones __ Clock __ Lighted fire exit signs __ Lighted displays __ Surveillance cameras	__ Fixtures as per Cost Category A and/or program	__ Fixtures as per Cost Category A and/or program

DESIGN STANDARDS -- BANKS/SAVINGS & LOAN, PUBLIC LOBBY

DOORS & WINDOWS	Recommended	Minimum
__ Doors	__ Automatic doors as needed for heavy traffic and for most convenient handicap access __ Heavy-duty, glazed public entry doors with quiet operating hardware and automatic closers __ Double door air-lock vestibule to control indoor-outdoor temperature differences and outside noise	__ Glazed public entry doors with quiet operating hardware and automatic closers
__ Frames	__ 14 gauge steel or as per storefront detailing	__ 16 gauge steel
__ Hardware	__ Quiet, concealed automatic closers __ Security locking system	__ Automatic closer __ Security locks
__ Related Fixtures	__ Lighted exit signs at exit doors as per code __ Controlled locking coordinated with security alarm system __ Side panel glazing or safety vision panels at non-glazed doors	
__ Windows	__ Floor to ceiling front glazing with glass entry doors __ Floor base barrier and mid-height bar or barrier to prevent people from walking into full-height glazing	__ Glazing for clear viewing between interior and exterior near entry

FIXTURES/EQUIPMENT	Recommended	Minimum
__ Special furnishings	__ Information and display counter __ Announcement boards __ Display and brochure cabinets __ Check and deposit writing counters __ Movable or built-in lounge seating area near officer's desks __ ATM machine and auxiliary fixtures, lighting, communications, and security equipment	__ As per program and Recommended

PLUMBING	Recommended	Minimum
__ Fixtures	__ Fire sprinklers as required by code __ Fire hose cabinet __ Building standpipes at exterior	__ As per Recommended

DESIGN STANDARDS -- BANKS/SAVINGS & LOAN, PUBLIC LOBBY

HVAC	Recommended	Minimum
__ Occupancies	__ As per program -- allowing for variations in traffic at different times	__ As per program
__ Ventilation	__ 20 - 30 cfm outdoor air per occupant __ Air lock vestibule to preserve air temperatures and buffer air pressure changes as people enter and leave the building	__ 20 cfm outdoor air per occupant
__ HVAC System & Controls	__ As per adjacent officer and teller spaces __ Localized heating may be provided in vestibule	__ As per main public areas

ELECTRICAL POWER	Recommended	Minimum
__ Power Outlets	__ Outlets at teller counters __ Wall clock outlet __ Outlets as required for janitorial service __ Lighted fire exit signs at exit doors __ Floor outlets for reading lamps in lobby lounge __ Outlets at officer's desks in or adjacent to lobby __ Emergency battery powered exit lights and alarm	__ Outlets at teller counters __ Outlets as required for janitorial service __ Lighted fire exit signs at exit doors __ As required by program and code

LIGHTING	Recommended	Minimum
__ Lamps	__ Overall incandescent and/or fluorescent ceiling fixtures __ Downlights or task lights at writing counters and other focal points __ Spotlights and wall wash lights for displays and art work	__ Fluorescent ceiling lights __ Down lights or task lights at writing counters and other focal points
__ Switching	__ Central control, dimmers, and timers near security office	__ Lockable light switch controls near entrance

ILLUMINATION	Recommended	Minimum
	__ 20 - 30 f.c. at entry vestibule __ 50 - 70 f.c. at conference areas __ 100 f.c. at teller workstations	__ 15 - 20 f.c. at entry vestibule __ 30 - 70 f.c. at conference areas __ 60 - 100 f.c. at teller workstations

COMMUNICATIONS	Recommended	Minimum
	__ Fire/security alarms __ Public phones and account access phones __ Computer wiring __ ATM wiring and emergency phone	__ As per program

4

DESIGN STANDARDS -- BANKS/SAVINGS & LOAN, TELLER SPACE

GENERAL	Recommended Standards	Minimum Standards
__ **Occupancies and Floor Area**	__ 90 to 120 sq. ft. for supervisors __ 80 to 100 sq. ft. for clerical workers __ 30 sq. ft. per teller work station	__ 80 - 100 sq. ft. for supervisors __ 60 - 75 sq. ft for clerical workers __ 24 sq. ft. per teller work station
__ **Ceiling Height**	__Varies depending on building construction (12' to 14' ceiling height is common in ground floor, public access buildings)	__ Minimum finish ceiling height is 8' in small branch financial offices, 10' is preferred
__ **Special Plan Considerations**	__ 5' x 5' module -- with work cubicles behind teller stations of 10' x 10', 10' x 15', etc. __ Other common modules are 2.5', 4' and 6' NOTE: Modules and dimensions may be determined by modular bank furniture and partition system, ceiling system, electrical power grid -- preferably an integration of all.	

FINISHES	Cost Categories A	B	C
__ **Floors**	__ Carpet rated for medium wear, non-static, padded	__ Carpet for medium wear, padded or glued	__ Carpet, medium, glued __ Vinyl
__ **Walls & Substructure**	FIXED WALLS: __ 1-hour fire rating or more, as per building code __ Finish material flame spread ratings as per code __ Gypsum wallboard with medium weight vinyl or fabric __ Plaster, tile, wood finishes for decorative walls MOVABLE WALLS: See OPEN OFFICE	FIXED WALLS: __ Fire ratings as per building code __ Gypsum board with fabric or vinyl __ Plaster MOVABLE WALLS: See OPEN OFFICE	FIXED WALLS: __ Fire ratings as per building code __ Gypsum board with fabric or vinyl MOVABLE WALLS: See OPEN OFFICE
__ **Ceiling**	__ Vaulted integrated ceiling system __ Integral ceiling -- suspended acoustic tile or gypsum board, with integrated lighting	__ Suspended acoustic tile with integrated lighting __ Gypsum board ceiling with acoustic treatment	__ Suspended acoustic tile, exposed grid __ Gypsum board with surface-mounted lighting
__ **Acoustics** WARNING: Sound absorption treatment such as acoustical tiles or acoustical plaster have no value for sound proofing between rooms.	__ Sound isolated substructure where confidential privacy is required __ Provide for speech privacy in private offices and conference areas __ NC 30, STC 40-50 __ Doors to private offices and conference rooms with sound proofing gaskets at all edges	__ Most provisions as per Cost Category A __ NC 30, STC 35-40	__ All provisions as much as possible as per Cost Categories A & B

DESIGN STANDARDS -- BANKS/SAVINGS & LOAN, TELLER SPACE

DOORS & WINDOWS	Recommended	Minimum
__ **Doors**	__ 1-3/4" solid core with gaskets for sound privacy __ 1-3/4" hollow core where sound privacy is not required __ Gate access with security system as per teller station unit manufacturer	__ 1-3/4" hollow core __ Gate access with security system as per teller station unit manufacturer
__ **Frames**	__ 16 gauge steel or extra-sturdy wood jambs and frames	__ 16 gauge steel or hardwood jambs and frames
__ **Hardware**	__ Security systems as per teller station and bank equipment manufacturer	__ As per Recommended
__ **Windows**	__ Windows are not normally allowable in bank or savings and loan teller areas	__ As per Recommended
__ **Natural light**	__ May be provided by glazing at adjacent public lobby area	__ None

FIXTURES/EQUIPMENT	Recommended	Minimum

__ **Furnishings & Equipment**	__ As per program with allowances for:
	  __ Record storage cabinets and shelving
	  __ Data processing input and output
	  __ Customer and transaction files
	  __ Tack boards
	  __ Copiers
	  __ Check transaction printers
		__ As per program

PLUMBING	Recommended	Minimum
__ **Fixtures**	__ Fire sprinklers as per code, generally 1 or more to cover every 200 sq. ft.	__ Fire sprinklers as per code

6

DESIGN STANDARDS -- BANKS/SAVINGS & LOAN, TELLER SPACE

HVAC	Recommended	Minimum
__ Occupancies	__ As per program, generally allow 120 sq. ft. office space per manager and per clerical employee	__ As per program, generally allow a minimum of 100 sq. ft. office space per manager and 80 sq. ft. per clerical employee
__ Ventilation	__ 35 - 50 cfm outdoor air per occupant	__ 30 cfm outdoor air per occupant
__ HVAC System & Controls	__ Temperature controlled by individual thermostat __ Central HVAC system	__ If climate is zone controlled, temperatures 68° to 72°F. __ Even at minimum construction cost, provide generous fresh air supply and individual room control

ELECTRICAL POWER	Recommended	Minimum
__ Power Outlets	__ As per program and bank equipment manu- turer's requirements __ Task lighting outlets near desks and work stations __ Floor and wall outlets for manager's office equipment: computer, dictation, personal copier, Fax, etc. __ Clerical workstation outlets for typewriter, computer & printer, copier, Fax, dictation playback, electric sharpener, task lamp, etc. __ Outlets as required for janitorial service __ Duplex outlet for desk __ Security system and closed circuit video	__ As per program and bank equipment manu- turer's requirements __ Floor and wall outlets for manager's and clerks' basic office equipment -- at least one outlet at each partition

LIGHTING	Recommended	Minimum
__ Lamps	__ Integrated ceiling fluorescent fixtures __ Incandescent down lights at teller and custo- mer writing counter areas __ Task lights at work counters, file storage areas, copier and other clerical workstations	__ Fluorescent ceiling lighting, recessed or sur- face mounted __ Task lighting at workstations
__ Switching	__ Dimmer controls at incandescent downlights	__ Standard room switch controls or zone control

ILLUMINATION	Recommended	Minimum
	__ 100 f.c. at teller work surfaces __ Minimal background dark to light contrast	__ 60 - 100 f.c. on work surfaces

COMMUNICATIONS	Recommended	Minimum
__ Communications	__ Multiple-line phones __ Computer net lines __ Fax lines __ Intercoms __ Security system, silent alarms, fire alarms	__ As per Recommended

DESIGN STANDARDS -- BANKS/SAVINGS & LOAN, OPEN OFFICE

GENERAL	Recommended Standards	Minimum Standards
__ Occupancies and Floor Area	__ 130 sq. ft. average floor space per employee __ 100 to 250 sq. ft. for middle managers & Jr. executives __ 90 to 120 sq. ft. for supervisors __ 100 - 150 sq. ft. for secretaries __ 80 to 100 sq. ft. for clerical workers	__ 100 sq. ft. average floor space per employee __ 150 - 300 sq. ft. for top executives __ 90 - 225 sq. ft. for middle management, Jr. executives, and supervisors __ 80 - 100 sq. ft. for executive secretaries __ 75 sq. ft for clerical workers NOTE: 75 sq. ft. per personal working area is considered minimum for acoustical reasons
__ Ceiling Height	__ Varies depending on building construction (12' to 12' floor to floor height is common) __ 10' is recommended	__ Floor to floor heights range from 10' to 14' __ Minimum finish ceiling height is 8' with occassional 7' or 7'-6" soffits
__ Special Plan Considerations	__ 5'x 5' module -- cubicle dimensions of 10'x10', 10 x15', 10'x20', 15'x15', 15'x20', 15'x25' etc. __ Other common modules are 2.5', 4' and 6' NOTE: Modules and dimensions may be determined by partition system, ceiling system, electrical power grid -- preferably an integration of all.	

FINISHES	Cost Categories A	B	C
__ Floors	__ Carpet rated for heavy wear, non-static, glued __ Raised access floors must be heavy duty, not subject to vibration or deflection	__ Carpet for heavy wear, glued __ Vinyl with backing	__ Carpet for heavy wear, glued __ Carpet tile __ Vinyl
__ Walls & Substructure	FIXED WALLS: __ 1-hour fire rating or more, as per building code __ Finish material flame spread ratings as per code __ Gypsum wallboard with heavy weight vinyl MOVABLE SCREENS: See FURNISHINGS next page	FIXED WALLS: __ Fire ratings as per building code __ Gypsum board with medium to heavy weight vinyl	FIXED WALLS: __ Fire ratings as per building code __ Gypsum board with medium weight vinyl __ Gypsum board, painted
__ Ceiling	__ Vaulted integrated ceiling system __ Integral ceiling -- suspended acoustic tile or gypsum board, with integrated lighting	__ Suspended acoustic tile with integrated lighting __ Gypsum board ceiling with acoustic treatment	__ Suspended acoustic tile, exposed grid __ Gypsum board with surface-mounted lighting
__ Acoustics WARNING: Sound control is the most important environmental consideration in making open office plans work and it requires the utmost cooperation and coordination among acoustic, HVAC, electrical, and interior design consultants	__ Noise masking is one of the most important factors __ Stabilize background noise level at 55 dB with "white noise" generator __ NC 30, STC 40-50 __ Doors to private offices and conference rooms with sound proofing gaskets at all edges __ Cover large columns and hard finish perimeter walls with sound absorbing treatment	__ Most provisions as per Cost Category A __ NC 30, STC 35-40	__ Provisions as much as possible as per Cost Category A

DESIGN STANDARDS -- BANKS/SAVINGS & LOAN, OPEN OFFICE

DOORS & WINDOWS	Recommended	Minimum
__ Doors	__ Steel clad doors with vision panels at primary entry and exits __ Steel clad interior doors to auxiliary spaces	__ 1-3/4" solid core doors with vision panels and entry and exits __ 1-3/4" solid core interior doors to auxiliary spaces
__ Frames	__ 16 gauge steel or extra-sturdy wood jambs and frames	__ 16 gauge steel or hardwood jambs and frames
__ Hardware	__ Quiet self closers __ Panic bars as required by code	__ Self closers __ Panic bars as required by code
__ Windows	__ Fixed, double-pane glazing (operable vents are not normally provided for large open office plans) __ Tinted glazing, shading, blinds to prevent direct sun glare and reduce heat gain	__ Fixed with operable vents
__ Natural light	WINDOW WALLS: __ 3" run of window per 10 sq. ft. of floor provides view and outside light for greatest number of employees __ 20% of total floor area and up	WINDOW WALLS: __ 10% of total floor area

FURNISHINGS	Recommended	Minimum
__ Furnishings & Fixtures	MOVABLE SCREENS: __ 5'-3" height recommended, 10' length typical __ 8" clearance at floor for air movement & cleaning unless this creates sound transfer problems __ Fire-retardant fabric cover over highly sound absorbant insulation __ Added sound absorbing screens, alcoves for noisy office equipment such as impact printers and copiers __ NIC / SPP noise isolation values -- coordinate with acoustic consultant	__ As per program

PLUMBING	Recommended	Minimum
__ Fixtures	__ Fire sprinklers as per code, generally 1 or more to cover every 200 sq. ft. __ Sprinklers recessed and unobtrusive	__ Fire sprinklers as per code

DESIGN STANDARDS -- BANKS/SAVINGS & LOAN, OPEN OFFICE

HVAC	Recommended	Minimum
__ Occupancies	__ As per program; generally allow 100 sq. ft. per employee	__ As per program, generally allow a minimum of 100 sq. ft. office space per manager and 80 sq. ft. per clerical employee
__ Ventilation	__ 35 - 50 cfm outdoor air per occupant	__ 30 cfm outdoor air per occupant
__ HVAC System & Controls	__ Zone controlled, temperatures 68° to 72°F. __ Relative humidity between 50% - 65%, lower or higher depending on room temperature __ Maximum air movement at head height of 30' per minute	__ Zone controlled, temperatures 68° to 74°F. __ Even at minimum construction cost, provide generous fresh air supply

ELECTRICAL POWER	Recommended	Minimum
__ Power Outlets NOTE: Lighting on 2 and 3-phase current can avoid lighting fluctuations from alternating current	__ Shell building, floor raceways, 1 outlet per 125 sq. ft. (1.5 watts per sq. ft.) __ Task lighting outlets near desks and work stations __ Extra outlets at special workstations for office equipment such as computer printer, copiers, Fax, etc. __ Outlets as required for janitorial service __ Duplex outlet for each desk	__ Shell building, floor raceways, 1 outlet per 125 sq. ft. (1.5 watts per sq. ft.)

LIGHTING	Recommended	Minimum
__ Lamps	__ Integrated ceiling fluorescent fixtures __ Incandescent down lights at special work or reading areas __ Task lights at work counters, file storage areas, copier and other clerical workstations	__ Fluorescent ceiling lighting, recessed or surface mounted
__ Switching	__ Master area or zone switching -- automatic with manual overide	__ Master area or zone switching
__ Illumination	__ 100 - 150 f.c. on work surfaces __ No brightness variations over 3:1 __ Ceiling reflectance factor minimum of 0.7 __ Reflectance factor of furnishings approx. 0.5	__ 80 - 100 f.c. on work surfaces __ No brightness variations over 3:1

COMMUNICATIONS	Recommended	Minimum
__ Communications	__ Phones per sq. ft. as per program __ Computer net lines __ Fax lines __ Intercoms __ Fire/smoke detectors and alarms	__ As per Recommended

DESIGN STANDARDS -- BANKS/SAVINGS & LOAN, EXECUTIVE OFFICES

GENERAL	Recommended Standards	Minimum Standards
__ Occupancies and Floor Area	__ 300 sq. ft. and up for top executives __ 100 to 300 sq. ft. for middle managers & Jr. executives __ 90 to 120 sq. ft. for supervisors __ 100 - 150 sq. ft. for executive secretaries __ 80 to 100 sq. ft. for clerical workers	__ 150 - 300 sq. ft. for top executives __ 90 - 225 sq. ft. for middle management, Jr. executives, and supervisors __ 80 - 100 sq. ft. for executive secretaries __ 60 - 75 sq. ft for clerical workers
__ Ceiling Height	__ Varies depending on building construction (12' to 12' floor to floor height is common) __ 8' to 10' high is average range	__ Floor to floor heights range from 10' to 14' __ Minimum finish ceiling height is 8' with occassional 7' or 7'-6" soffits
__ Special Plan Considerations	__ 5'x 5' module -- with offices of 10'x10', 10'x15', 10'x20', 15'x15', 15'x20', 15'x25' etc. __ Other common modules are 2.5', 4' and 6' NOTE: Modules and dimensions may be determined by partition system, ceiling system, electrical power grid -- preferably an integration of all.	

FINISHES	Cost Categories A	B	C
__ Floors	__ Carpet rated for medium wear, non-static, padded	__ Carpet for medium wear, padded or glued	__ Carpet, medium, glued
__ Walls & Substructure	FIXED WALLS: __ 1-hour fire rating or more, as per building code __ Finish material flame spread ratings as per code __ Gypsum wallboard with medium weight vinyl or fabric MOVABLE WALLS: See OPEN PLAN OFFICES	FIXED WALLS: __ Fire ratings as per building code __ Gypsum board with fabric or vinyl __ Plaster MOVABLE WALLS: See OPEN PLAN OFFICES	FIXED WALLS: __ Fire ratings as per building code __ Gypsum board with fabric or vinyl MOVABLE WALLS: See OPEN PLAN OFFICES
__ Ceiling	__ Vaulted integrated ceiling system __ Integral ceiling -- suspended acoustic tile or gypsum board, with integrated lighting	__ Suspended acoustic tile with integrated lighting __ Gypsum board ceiling with acoustic treatment	__ Suspended acoustic tile, exposed grid __ Gypsum board with surface-mounted lighting
__ Acoustics WARNING: Sound absorption treatment such as acoustical tiles or acoustical plaster have no value for sound proofing between rooms.	__ Sound isolated substructure where confidential privacy is required __ Provide for speech privacy in private offices and conference areas __ NC 30, STC 40-50 __ Doors to private offices and conference rooms with sound proofing gaskets at all edges	__ Most provisions as per Cost Category A __ NC 30, STC 35-40	__ All provisions as much as possible as per Cost Categories A & B

DESIGN STANDARDS -- BANKS/SAVINGS & LOAN, EXECUTIVE OFFICES

DOORS & WINDOWS	Recommended	Minimum
__ Doors	__ 1-3/4" solid core with gaskets for sound privacy __ 1-3/4" hollow core where sound privacy is not required	__ 1-3/4" hollow core
__ Frames	__ 16 gauge steel or extra-sturdy wood jambs and frames	__ 16 gauge steel or hardwood jambs and frames
__ Hardware	__ Lockable for top executives __ Standard tubular latch set or cylindrical lock set	__ Standard knob set
__ Windows	__ Fixed with operable sliders or hoppers	__ Fixed with operable vents

	Recommended	Minimum
__ Natural light	__ OFFICES AT EXTERIOR WALLS: __ 20% total floor area and up __ Operable window area = 10% total floor area	__ OFFICES AT EXTERIOR WALLS: __ 10% total floor area __ Operable window area = 5% total floor area

FIXTURES/EQUIPMENT	Recommended	Minimum
__ Furnishings & Equipment	__ As per program with mounting allowances for: __ Bookshelves __ Tack board __ Chalk board or white board __ Chart rail __ Picture hanging rail __ As per program with space allowances for: __ Personal computer and printer __ Fax __ Personal copier	__ As per program

PLUMBING	Recommended	Minimum
__ Fixtures	__ Fire sprinklers as per code, generally 1 or more to cover every 200 sq. ft. __ Sprinklers recessed and unobtrusive	__ Fire sprinklers as per code

DESIGN STANDARDS -- BANKS/SAVINGS & LOAN, EXECUTIVE OFFICES

HVAC	Recommended	Minimum
__ Occupancies	__ As per program, generally allow 120 sq. ft. office space per manager and per clerical employee	__ As per program, generally allow a minimum of 100 sq. ft. office space per manager and 80 sq. ft. per clerical employee
__ Ventilation	__ 35 - 50 cfm outdoor air per occupant	__ 30 cfm outdoor air per occupant
__ HVAC System & Controls	__ Temperature controlled by individual thermostat __ Central HVAC system	__ If climate is zone controlled, temperatures 68° to 72°F. __ Even at minimum construction cost, provide generous fresh air supply and individual room control

ELECTRICAL POWER	Recommended	Minimum
__ Power Outlets	__ Shell building, floor raceways, 1 outlet per 125 sq. ft. (1.5 watts per sq. ft.) __ Task lighting outlets near desks and work stations __ Floor and wall outlets for manager's office equipment: computer, dictation, personal copier, Fax, etc. __ Secretarial office outlets for typewriter, computer & printer, copier, Fax, dictation playback, electric sharpener, task lamp, etc. __ Outlets as required for janitorial service __ Duplex outlet for desk	__ Shell building, floor raceways, 1 outlet per 125 sq. ft. (1.5 watts per sq. ft.) __ Floor and wall outlets for manager's and secretary's basic office equipment -- at least one outlet at each fixed wall

LIGHTING	Recommended	Minimum
__ Lamps	__ Integrated ceiling fluorescent fixtures __ Incandescent down lights at special work or reading areas __ Task lights at work counters, file storage areas, copier and other clerical workstations	__ Fluorescent ceiling lighting (if standard size fluorescent fixtures are too large for smaller offices, use incandescents and/or provide for lighting by task lamps)
__ Switching	__ Dimmer controls at incandescent downlights	__ Standard room switch controls or zone control

ILLUMINATION	Recommended	Minimum
	__ 100 - 150 f.c. on work surfaces __ Minimal background dark to light contrast	__ 60 - 100 f.c. on work surfaces

COMMUNICATIONS	Recommended	Minimum
__ Communications	__ Multiple-line phones __ Computer net lines __ Fax lines __ Intercoms __ Alarms	__ As per Recommended

DESIGN STANDARDS -- BANK VAULT/SAFETY DEPOSIT AREA

GENERAL	Recommended Standards	Minimum Standards
__ Occupancies	__ As per program -- 10 is a typical maximum	__ All as per program and as much as possible as per Recommended Standards
__ Floor Areas	__ As per program, will vary considerably	
__ Ceiling Height	__ 8' to 10' depending on room proportions	
__ Features	__ Maximum fire protection __ Maximum seismic reinforcing as suited to the region __ Maximum security provisions as recommended by vault equipment manufacturer	

FINISHES	Cost Categories		
	A	B	C
__ Floors & Sub-structure	__ Concrete slab -- heavy-duty reinforcing __ Carpet, medium, direct glue __ Vinyl finish floor	__ Concrete slab __ Vinyl over slab __ Asphalt tile over slab	__ As per Cost Category B __ Exposed concrete slab
__ Walls & Substructure	__ Reinforced concrete __ Reinforced masonry units __ Plaster finish wall __ Furred gypsum board	__ Substructure as per Cost Category A __ Gypsum board	__ As per Cost Category B __ Minimums as required by bank equipment manufacturers
__ Ceiling & Sub-structure	__ Reinforced concrete __ Plaster finish ceiling __ Furred or suspended gypsum board	__ Substructure as per Cost Category A __ Furred or suspended gypsum board	__ Substructure as per Cost Category A __ Suspended acoustic tile, exposed grid
__ Acoustics	__ Provide for speech privacy in conference areas adjacent to safety deposit or vault areas __ NC 30, STC 45-50 __ Doors to conference space gasketed at all edges	__ Provisions for speech privacy	__ As per Cost Category B
__ Counters / Work Surfaces	__ Polished stone, metal frame	__ Laminated plastic, wood backing, metal frame	__ Laminated plastic, wood frame
__ Fixtures	__ Phones __ Clock __ Lighted fire exit signs __ Lighted displays __ Surveillance cameras	__ Fixtures as per Cost Category A and/or program	__ Fixtures as per Cost Category A and/or program

DESIGN STANDARDS -- BANK VAULT/SAFETY DEPOSIT AREA

DOORS & WINDOWS	Recommended	Minimum
__ Doors, Frames, and Hardware	NOTE: This highly specialized aspect of detailing will be thoroughly covered by requirements of bank equipment manufacturers -- designer must be especially alert to the interface problems of structural connections, anchors, fire safety and other issues not directly specified by bank equipment manufacturers or consultants __ Safety deposit and vault doors as per bank equipment manufacturers __ Frames, hardware, and related security and fire safety design provisions as per code and bank equipment manufacturer's requirements	__ As per program and as per Recommended
__ Windows / Glazing	__ Secure, bullet proof partition glazing NOTE: Conference rooms related to safety deposit and vault areas should be interior rooms in secure areas without windows	__ As per Cost Category A

FIXTURES/EQUIPMENT	Recommended	Minimum
__ Safety deposit and vault area equipment	__ Safety deposit boxes and locking systems __ Security doors to safety deposit and vault areas __ Bar gates __ Vault timer locking systems __ Area sensing security systems __ Built in desk, table, or counter	__ As per Recommended

PLUMBING	Recommended	Minimum
__ Fixtures	__ As required for fire safety NOTE: Plumbing and mechanical equipment chases have been used as access routes and escape routes by intruders to otherwise secure areas and should be avoided	__ As per Recommended

DESIGN STANDARDS -- BANK VAULT/SAFETY DEPOSIT AREA

HVAC	Recommended	Minimum
__ Occupancies	__ As per program -- usually intermittent with about six to ten people maximum	__ As per program
__ Ventilation	__ 35 - 50 cfm outdoor air per occupant or as per adjacent major spaces	__ 30 cfm outdoor air per occupant
__ HVAC System & Controls	__ Central HVAC system with zone control at 68 to 72 F. __ Provide for emergency ventilation in enclosed security areas in event of long-term power outage	__ If climate is zone controlled, temperatures 68 to 72 F.

ELECTRICAL POWER	Recommended	Minimum
__ Power Outlets	__ As required for building maintenance __ As required by bank equipment manufacturer __ Floor outlet for task lighting at table or counter	__ As per program and Recommended

LIGHTING	Recommended	Minimum
__ Lamps	__ Standard flourescent fixtures __ Task lighting at counting table or counter	__ As per Recommended
__ Switching	__ Security switch control	

ILLUMINATION	Recommended	Minimum
	__ 60 - 90 f.c. at tables, desks, or counters	__ 50 f.c. on work surfaces

COMMUNICATIONS	Recommended	Minimum
__ Communications	__ Intercom __ Security video __ Security systems as per bank equipment manufacturer's requirements	__ As per Recommended

CHURCHES

DESIGN STANDARDS -- CHURCH ENTRY LOBBY & VESTIBULE

GENERAL	Recommended Standards	Minimum Standards
__ Occupancies and Floor Area	__ As per program with allowance for varying occupancies and traffic loads	__ As per program
__ Ceiling Height	__ 10' - 12' __ Can include low (7'- 6" to 8') soffit at entrance	__ 8' - 9' in smaller centers
__ Special Plan Considerations	__ Double-door air lock vestibule in hot or cold climates __ Exterior canopy for weather protection at drive up entry __ Coat storage __ Lobby access to rest rooms, usher's office, and church administrative office	__ As per Recommended Standards

FINISHES	Cost Categories		
	A	B	C
__ **Floors** WARNING: Smooth, hard surface materials sometimes used at entrances -- such as terrazzo, marble, smooth tile, or polished travertine are safety hazards -- even those treated to be non-slip are a problem when wet and when in contact with certain shoe sole materials	__ Recessed floor mat for rainy/ snowy climates __ Non-slip rubber or vinyl tile at entry vestibule __ Nylon or other synthetic fabric carpet near entry should be rated for heavy wear, stain resistant and reasonably dark tone, glued to floor __ Carpet may be a different, complementary color an fabric at other spaces to allow easier replacement of the more heavily trafficked entry floor area __ Avoid light-tone reflective floor surfaces	__ Vinyl or asphalt tile at entry vestibule __ Synthetic fabric carpet rated for heavy wear near entry, glued to floor __ Complementary heavy to medium wear carpet at adjacent areas __ Other flooring considerations as per Cost Category A	__ Vinyl or asphalt tile __ Synthetic fabric carpet near entry, glued __ Non-slip rubber or vinyl at entry vestibule
__ **Fixtures**	__ Coat/umbrella racks __ Public phone __ Handicap access allowing for handicapped and elderly __ Lighted fire exit signs __ Displays, bulletin board	__ Fixtures as per Cost Category A and/or program	__ Fixtures as per Cost Category A and/or program
__ **Walls & Substructure**	__ Interior wall finish, typically plaster or gypsum board with heavy-duty vinyl or fabric __ Exit wall fire ratings as per code	__ Foyer and exit area wall fire ratings as per code __ Gypsum board with heavy-weight vinyl or fabric __ Plaster with sound absorbant treatment	__ Fire ratings as per code __ Gypsum board, painted
__ **Ceiling**	__ Decorative ceiling as complement to church auditorium __ Suspended acoustic tile __ Gypsum board with acoustic treatment or texture finish	__ Suspended acoustic tile __ Gypsum board	__ Suspended acoustic tile, exposed grid __ Gypsum board

DESIGN STANDARDS -- CHURCH ENTRY LOBBY & VESTIBULE

DOORS & WINDOWS	Recommended	Minimum
__ **Doors**	__ Heavy-duty, glazed public entry doors with quiet operating hardware and automatic closers __ Double door air-lock vestibule to control indoor-outdoor temperature differences and outside noise __ Automatic doors as needed for handicap access	__ Glazed public entry doors with quiet operating hardware and automatic closers
__ **Frames**	__ 14 gauge steel	__ 16 gauge steel
__ **Hardware**	__ Quiet, concealed automatic closers	
__ **Related Fixtures**	__ Lighted exit signs at exit doors as per code __ Controlled locking with security alarm system __ Side panel glazing or safety vision panels at non-glazed doors	
__ **Windows**	__ Floor to ceiling front glazing with glass entry doors __ Floor base barrier and mid-height bar or barrier to prevent people from walking into full-height glazing	__ No minimum requirements but views to the exterior are very desirable

FIXTURES/EQUIPMENT	Recommended	Minimum
__ **Special furnishings**	__ Information counter __ Bulletin and event announcement boards __ Display and exhibit cabinets __ Pamphlet racks __ Memorial plaques __ Coat racks __ Vestibule-related fixtures also listed on previous page	__ As per program and Recommended

PLUMBING	Recommended	Minimum
__ **Fixtures**	__ Drinking fountain near entry and/or near restrooms __ Fire sprinklers as required by code __ Fire hose cabinets as per code	__ As per Recommended

DESIGN STANDARDS -- CHURCH ENTRY LOBBY & VESTIBULE

HVAC	Recommended	Minimum
__ Occupancies	__ As per program -- allowing for large variations in occupancy at different times	__ As per program
__ Ventilation	__ 20 - 30 cfm outdoor air per occupant __ Air lock vestibule to preserve air temperatures and buffer air pressure changes as people enter and leave the building	__ 20 cfm outdoor air per occupant
__ HVAC System & Controls	__ As per primary adjacent public spaces __ Localized heating may be provided in waiting area of vestibule	__ As per main public areas

ELECTRICAL POWER	Recommended	Minimum
__ Power Outlets	__ Wall clock outlet __ Outlets as required for janitorial service __ Lighted fire exit signs at exit doors __ Lighted plaques, bulletin boards, pamphlet racks, & display cases __ Battery powered emergency exit lighting	__ Outlets at information desk __ Outlets as required for janitorial service __ Lighted fire exit signs at exit doors

LIGHTING	Recommended	Minimum
__ Lamps	__ Incandescent ceiling fixtures and downlights __ Wall wash lights __ Display case or plaque lighting	__ Incandescent ceiling fixtures
__ Switching	__ Central control near information desk	__ Standard room switch controls

ILLUMINATION	Recommended	Minimum
	__ 20 - 30 f.c.	__ 15 - 20 f.c.

COMMUNICATIONS	Recommended	Minimum
	__ Smoke, fire, & security alarms __ Public phone near entry	__ Alarms as required by code

DESIGN STANDARDS -- CHURCH AUDITORIUM

GENERAL	Recommended Standards	Minimum Standards
__ Occupancies & Floor Areas	__ 9 to 10 sq. ft. per person (includes aisles)	__ 8 sq. ft. per person
__ Depth of Auditorium	__ 40' maximum depth to see speaker clearly	__ 65' maximum to see gestures
__ Sight Lines	__ 45° horizontal angle of viewer sight line to speaker is recommended maximum	__ 60° horizontal angle of viewer sight line to speaker is maximum
__ Aisle Widths	__ Center aisle 7'-6" wide for weddings and funerals __ Side aisles, 4' to 5'	__ Center aisle 6' wide minimum for weddings, 7'-6" wide minimum for funerals __ Side aisles, 3'
__ Seats Per Row	__ 7 seats to aisle is maximum	__ As per code
__ Seat Spacing	__ 24" seating width per person __ 36" to 40" back-to-back	__ 20" seating width per person __ 32" minimum back-to-back, 42" maximum
__ Special Plan Considerations	__ Step rear seating and ramp aisles in longer auditoriums to assure good sight lines and visbility	

FINISHES	Cost Categories		
	A	B	C
__ Floors & Substructure	__ Hardwood on sleepers over concrete slab, carpet at aisles __ Concrete slab, steel trowel finish, integral color __ Heavy duty carpet at aisles, glued	__ Concrete slab	__ All finishes as per Cost Category B
__ Wainscot/Walls at Side Aisles	__ Sound reflective or absorbant walls as required for acoustic control __ Resistant to abrasion and damage by moving congregation	__ Materials to meet acoustic requirements as specified by consultant	
__ Seating	__ Pew seating recommended as most space efficient	__ Pews __ Movable seating for multi-purpose auditorium space	
__ Walls & Substructure	__ 1-hour fire rating or more, as per building code __ Finish material flame spread ratings as per code __ Sound-isolated construction __ Plaster or gypsum board with acoustic control structure and treatments	__ Materials and shaping to meet acoustic requirements as specified by consultant	
__ Ceiling & Substructure	__ Ceiling engineered for acoustic control -- partly reflective, partly absorbant	__ Materials and shaping to meet acoustic requirements as specified by consultants	
__ Acoustics -- Auditorium shaping, baffles, materials	__ As per professional acoustical engineer	__ As per professional acoustical engineer	

DESIGN STANDARDS -- CHURCH AUDITORIUM

DOORS & WINDOWS	Recommended	Minimum
__ Doors	__ 1-3/4" solid core auditorium doors, fire-rated assembly as required by local fire code __ Vision panels __ Sound proofing gaskets	NOTE: Quiet and effective door operation is so important to church services that all minimum door standards are as per Recommended.
__ Frames	__ 14 gauge steel at fire exit doors and doors to corridors __ Fire rated assembly as required by local code	
__ Hardware	__ Quiet, concealed automatic closers, sound gasketing __ Heavy duty panic bar and related exit hardware __ Quiet panic bar operation __ Wall or floor grabs to hold doors open during, before, and after services	
__ Windows/Glazing	__ Subdued glazing, shaded or with use of art glass to prevent direct sunlight glare __ Sound insulated glazing at walls at potential sources of exterior noise __ Operable glazing may be suitable for small chapels	__ As per Recommended

FIXTURES/EQUIPMENT	Recommended	Minimum
__ Audio-Visual	__ Sound control at pulpit __ Microphone at pulpit/lectern __ Electronic sound controls for choir, concerts, etc., as per recommendations of acoustic and audio consultant	__ As per program

PLUMBING	Recommended	Minimum
__ Fixtures	__ Recessed or concealed fire sprinklers __ Fire hose cabinets as required by fire code	__ As per code

DESIGN STANDARDS -- CHURCH AUDITORIUM

HVAC	Recommended	Minimum
__ Occupancies	__ As per program (programming for full use of these facilities requires expert consultation)	__ As per program
__ Ventilation	__ 25 - 30 cfm outdoor air per occupant	__ 20 cfm outdoor air per occupant
__ HVAC System & Controls	__ Central HVAC system __ Radiant heating __ Under-floor HVAC plenum for large auditorium volume, quiet heating and ventilation __ Allow for possible future church expansion in early planning of HVAC system	__ As per program or Recommended
__ Heating Temperature WARNING: A common source of complaints about church auditoriums is fluctuating temperatures and excessive air movement	__ Temperatures at seating levels controlled at 68° to 72° F with equipment adequate to quietly handle quick adjustment to rapidly changing occupancies	__ Temperatures at seating levels at 68° to 72°F. __ Even at minimum construction cost, provide generous fresh air supply and quiet, quick response system

ELECTRICAL POWER	Recommended	Minimum
__ Power Outlets	__ Concealed floor outlets for building maintenance __ Outlets at chancel as required for movable lectern or pulpit lights, concert sound amplification, etc. __ Power for exit lights at all exit doors __ Battery powered emergency exit lights	__ As per Recommended or as per program

LIGHTING	Recommended	Minimum
__ Lamps	__ Dimmer controlled ceiling house lighting __ Variable and decorative wall washer lighting __ Subdued floor lighting at aisles and all steps and ramps	__ As per Recommended
__ Switching	__ Controls at master panel near chancel and near auditorium main exit	
ILLUMINATION	Recommended __ 50 - 100 f.c. at pulpit and altar __ 15 - 30 f.c. at pews	Minimum __ As per Recommended

COMMUNICATIONS	Recommended	Minimum
__ Communications	__ Speakers as per acoustic and sound engineering consultants	__ As per Recommended or as per program

DESIGN STANDARDS -- CHURCH ALTAR AREA & CHOIR

GENERAL	Recommended Standards	Minimum Standards
__ Areas	__ As per program and requirements below	__ All items as per program and Recommended Standards
__ Chancel Floor	__ Raised floor, three 6" risers high	
__ Aisle	__ 6' wide clear aisle around chancel area	
__ Special Plan Consid-erations	__ All requirements vary depending on church denomination: __ Altar, 5' to 8' long x 30" deep x 4' wide -- may mount on 4" to 6" platform __ Pulpit with light and microphone, 2' to 3' wide x 16" deep, raised 1 to 3 steps __ Lectern with light and microphone, size as per pulpit (may be movable), 40" high __ Baptismal font as per program __ Communion rail, 30" high, 8" wide ledge	
__ Choir & Organ NOTE: Organ and choir locations must be decided before designing the main church auditorium	__ Location may be at rear or sides of chancel, rear or side of auditorium -- organ space and pipes as per organ manufacturer __ Allow 7 sq. ft. per person in choir	

FINISHES	Cost Categories A	B	C
__ Floors & Sub-structure	__ Wood frame platform with glued carpet over heavy plywood __ Concrete slab, steel trowel finish, integral color __ Carpet over raised concrete slab __ Tile, non-slip	__ Wood frame, carpet finish __ Raised concrete slab, steel trowel finish	__ All items as per Cost Category B
__ Walls & Substructure	__ Sound reflective or absor-bant walls as required for acoustic control __ 1-hour fire rating or more, as per building code __ Finish material flame spread ratings as per code __ Sound-isolated construction __ Plaster or gypsum board with acoustic control structure and treatments	__ Materials and shaping of space to meet acoustic requirements specified by acoustical consultant	
__ Ceiling & Sub-structure	__ Ceiling engineered for acoustic control -- partly reflective, partly absorbant	__ Materials and shaping to meet acoustic requirements as specified by consultants	
__ Acoustics -- room shaping, baffles, materials	__ As per professional acoustical consultant	__ As per professional acoustical consultant	
__ Organ NOTE: Consultation on organ and related acousti-cal items is required be-fore starting design of the auditorium space	__ Organ size, pipes, location, and surrounding space as per requirements of organ manufacturer	__ As per organ maker	

DESIGN STANDARDS -- CHURCH ALTAR AREA & CHOIR

DOORS & WINDOWS	Recommended	Minimum
__ **Doors**	__ Peripheral service doors, 1-3/4" solid core with fire rated assembly as required by fire code __ Vision panels __ Sound proofing gaskets	NOTE: Quiet and effective door operation is so important to church services that all minimum door standards are as per Recommended.
__ **Frames**	__ 14 gauge steel at fire exit doors and doors to corridors __ Fire rated assembly as required by local code	
__ **Hardware**	__ Quiet, concealed automatic closers, sound gasketing __ Heavy duty panic bar and related exit hardware at exit doors __ Quiet panic bar operation at exit doors	
__ **Windows/Glazing** WARNING: Glare and heat gain from side and rear glazing at altar/pulpit areas is a common problem -- even dark art glass can emit glare "hot spots" from low morning or afternoon sun	__ Subdued glazing, shaded or with careful use of art glass to prevent direct sunlight glare __ Sound insulated glazing at walls at potential sources of exterior noise	__ As per Recommended

FIXTURES/EQUIPMENT	Recommended	Minimum
__ **Audio-Visual**	__ Sound control at pulpit/lectern __ Microphone at pulpit/lectern __ Electronic sound controls for choir, concerts, etc., as per recommendations of acoustic and audio consultant	__ As per program

PLUMBING	Recommended	Minimum
__ **Fixtures**	__ Recessed or concealed fire sprinklers	__ As per code

DESIGN STANDARDS -- CHURCH ALTAR AREA & CHOIR

HVAC	Recommended	Minimum
__ Occupancies	__ As per overall auditorium	__ As per program
__ Ventilation	__ 25 - 30 cfm outdoor air per occupant	__ 20 cfm outdoor air per occupant

__ HVAC System & Controls	__ As per main church auditorium:
	  __ Central HVAC system
	  __ Radiant heating
		__ As per program or Recommended

__ Heating Temperature	__ Temperatures controlled at 68° to 72°F with equipment adequate to quietly handle quick adjustment to rapidly changing occupancies	__ Temperatures at seating levels at 68° to 72°F. __ Even at minimum construction cost, provide generous fresh air supply and quiet, quick response system

WARNING:
A common source of complaints about church auditoriums is fluctuating temperatures and excessive air movement

ELECTRICAL POWER	Recommended	Minimum
__ Power Outlets	__ Concealed floor outlets for building maintenance __ Outlets at chancel as required for movable lectern or pulpit lights, choir and concert sound amplification, etc. __ Power for organ	__ As per Recommended or as per program

LIGHTING	Recommended	Minimum
__ Lamps	__ Dimmer controlled ceiling house lighting __ Variable and decorative wall wash lighting __ Subdued floor lighting at steps	__ As per Recommended
__ Switching	__ Controls at master panel near chancel and near auditorium main exit	

ILLUMINATION	Recommended	Minimum
	__ 50 - 100 f.c. at pulpit and altar	__ As per Recommended

COMMUNICATIONS	Recommended	Minimum
__ Communications	__ Speakers as per acoustic and sound engineering consultants	__ As per Recommended or as per program

DESIGN STANDARDS -- CHURCH MINISTER'S STUDY

GENERAL	Recommended Standards	Minimum Standards
__ Occupancy	__ Minister and secretary __ Conference space for up to 6 people	__ Same
__ Floor Area	__ Office and conference, 380 sq. ft. __ Waiting, 140 sq. ft. (at secretary's space) __ Secretary, 180 sq. ft. __ Workspace & files, 200 sq. ft. __ Private lavatory & closet, 48 sq. ft.	__ Office and conference, 250 sq. ft. __ Waiting, 120 sq. ft.. (at secretary's space) __ Secretary, 120 sq. ft.. __ Workspace & files, 170 sq. ft.. __ Private lavatory, 40 sq. ft.
__ Ceiling Height	__ 9 - 12'	__ 9'
__ Plan features	__ Private and conducive to concentration	

FINISHES	Cost Categories A	B	C
__ Floors & Sub- structure	__ Padded carpet, wool or comparable fabric	__ Padded carpet for medium wear	__ Carpet, medium, glued
__ Wainscot	__ Wood paneling	__ Partial wood paneling __ Plaster __ Vinyl wall cover	__ If no wainscot, provide protective chair rail at conference space and waiting space
__ Counters & Built-in Furnishings	__ Custom hardwood finishes	__ Manufactured units, wood veneer __ Wood and plastic laminate combinations	__ Wood and plastic laminate combinations
__ Walls & Substructure	__ 1-hour fire rating or more, as per building code __ Finish material flame spread ratings as per code __ Sound-isolated construction __ Wood paneling __ Plaster __ Gypsum wallboard with fabric or vinyl	__ Fire ratings as per building code __ Gypsum board with fabric or vinyl __ Wood paneling at desk area	__ Fire ratings as per building code __ Gypsum board with fabric or vinyl __ Plaster
__ Ceiling & Sub- structure	__ Integral ceiling, plaster or gypsum board, with inte- grated lighting	__ Suspended acoustic tile with integrated lighting __ Suspended gypsum board ceiling with acoustic treat- ment	__ Suspended acoustic tile, exposed grid __ Gypsum board with acous- tic treatment
__ Acoustics	__ Provide for speech privacy with no sound transfer to or from outside or sur- rounding spaces __ NC 30, STC 45-50 __ Doors gasketed at all edges	__ Provisions as per Cost Cate- gory A	__ All provisions as much as possible as per Cost Category A

DESIGN STANDARDS -- CHURCH MINISTER'S STUDY

DOORS & WINDOWS	Recommended	Minimum
__ **Doors**	__ Doors 1-3/4" solid-core with sound proofing gaskets at all edges	__ 1-3/4" solid core doors are minimum for access to peripheral spaces __ No sound transfer from or to other rooms or outer corridor
__ **Frames**	__ 16 gauge steel	__ 16 gauge steel or extra-sturdy wood jamb and frame
__ **Hardware**	__ Quiet, concealed automatic closer __ Sound gasketing __ Security lock	__ Automatic closer __ Sound gasketing
__ **Windows**	__ Windows should provide views and ventilation conducive to concentrated work __ Double-pane for noise insulation from exterior	__ As per Cost Category A

FIXTURES/EQUIPMENT	Recommended	Minimum
__ **Special furnishings**	__ Work counter, reading shelf __ Built-in book shelves, from floor level to top of door height, most shelves 10" wide __ Tack board __ Chalk board or whiteboard	__ Bookshelves __ Tack board

PLUMBING	Recommended	Minimum
__ **Fixtures**	__ Lavatory with medicine cabinet, toilet, shower, and dressing area __ Drinking fountain accessible to reception waiting area	__ Toilet and lavatory with medicine cabinet

DESIGN STANDARDS -- CHURCH MINISTER'S STUDY

HVAC	Recommended	Minimum
__ Occupancy estimate	__ As per program, or allow for up to 6 occupants	__ As per program
__ Ventilation	__ 25 - 35 cfm	__ 25 cfm
__ HVAC System & Controls	__ Temperature controlled by individual thermostat __ Central HVAC system with individual room control	__ If climate is zone controlled, temperatures 68° to 72°F. __ Even at minimum construction cost, provide generous fresh air supply and individual room control

ELECTRICAL POWER	Recommended	Minimum
__ Power Outlets	__ Task lighting outlets near desk __ Outlets for office equipment: dictation machine, computer, etc. __ Outlet for VCR and video __ Secretarial office outlets for typewriter, computer, copier, Fax, dictation, etc. __ Waiting space or corridor outlet for janitor __ Wall clock at reception	__ Task lighting outlets near desk __ Standard office equipment outlets for minister and secretary

LIGHTING	Recommended	Minimum
__ Lamps	__ Diffused down lights, wall wash lights __ Variable overall incandescent ceiling lighting __ Spot lighting at book shelves __ Down lights at reading shelf __ Task lamps for minister __ Floor lamps in informal conference area	__ Ambient ceiling lighting __ Bright ceiling light or spots for book shelves and work areas
__ Switching	__ Dimmer controls for all fixed lights	__ Standard room switch controls __ Dimmer at conference area

ILLUMINATION	Recommended	Minimum
	__ 60 - 90 f.c. on work surfaces __ Minimal background dark to light contrast	__ 50 - 80 f.c. on work surfaces

COMMUNICATIONS	Recommended	Minimum
__ Telephone/Security	__ Multiple-line phone for minister and secretary __ Fax line	__ Phones

DESIGN STANDARDS -- CHURCH SACRISTY & ROBE ROOMS

GENERAL	Recommended Standards	Minimum Standards
__ Floor Areas:		
__ Ceremonial Vesting Room	__ Robe storage as per program __ Storage for vestments and ceremonial objects as per program	__ All items as per Recommended Standards except Choir Robing room space recommendations can be reduced by 20%
__ Altar Boys' Vesting Room	__ As per choir robing room (see below) __ Ceremonial object storage as per program	
__ Choir Robing Room	__ Allow 2' - 4" closet depth for robe hanging; 3" linear per robe __ 6" linear per person for coats __ Secure locker for purses and valuables __ 4' to 5' wide dressing corridor	
__ Ceiling Heights	__ 8' with 7' soffits (avoid high shelves if possible)	
__ Special Plan Considerations	__ Provide adjacent rest rooms __ Locate adjacent to church auditorium and chancel	

FINISHES	Cost Categories		
	A	B	C
__ Floor	__ Carpet, padded	__ Carpet, glued	__ Vinyl or asphalt tile
__ Base	__ Hardwood, Premium grade	__ Hardwood, paint grade	__ Hardwood, paint grade
__ Shelving, built-in storage units	__ Wood, Premium grade	__ Wood, Custom grade casework	__ Hardwood, paint grade
__ Counter tops	__ Wood, Premium grade __ Plastic laminate, HPDL grade	__ Plastic laminate	__ Plastic laminate
__ Walls	__ Hardboard or plywood paneling __ Gypsum board with vinyl or fabric	__ Gypsum board, painted	__ Gypsum board
__ Soffits & Ceiling	__ Gypsum board	__ Gypsum board	__ Gypsum board

DESIGN STANDARDS -- CHURCH SACRISTY & ROBE ROOMS

DOORS & WINDOWS	Recommended	Minimum
__ **Doors**	__ 1-3/4" solid-core __ Sound-proofing gaskets if rooms require sound isolation	__ 1-3/4" solid core doors are minimum for access to peripheral spaces __ No sound transfer allowable from or to the church chancel or auditorium
__ **Frames**	__ 16 gauge steel	__ 16 gauge steel or extra-sturdy wood frame
__ **Hardware**	__ Sound gasketing __ Security locks	__ Sound gasketing __ Standard locksets
__ **Wardrobe Doors**	__ Bifold, Premium grade	__ Bifold, economy or paint grade __ Sliding, #2 grade
__ **Window light**	__ Equal to 15% of floor area or more for dressing rooms with exterior walls	__ No minimum requirement
__ **Skylight**	__ 2' x 4' or larger for interior robing rooms or for light balance in robing rooms with outside light	

FIXTURES	Recommended	Minimum
__ **Built-ins**	__ Robe hanging rods __ Clothing hanging pole-and-shelf combination __ Hooks __ Full-length mirrors	__ Pole and shelf __ Hooks

FURNISHINGS		
__ **Storage & Work Space**	__ Sewing machine space in large robing rooms if not in work sacristy __ Ironing counter space in large robing rooms if not in work sacristy __ Drawer or bin storage units	__ No minimum requirements

PLUMBING	Recommended	Minimum

__ **Water supply & drainage**	__ Fire sprinklers as per code
	
	__ Lavatory at large robing room
	   __ 3/4" supply
	   __ 2" fixture drains
	
	__ Drinking fountain at large robing room
		__ Fire sprinklers as per code

DESIGN STANDARDS -- CHURCH SACRISTY & ROBE ROOMS

HVAC	Recommended	Minimum
__ Heating	__ 70° to 72° F temperature	__ 68° to 73° F heat at point 3'-0" above floor
__ Ventilation	__ 30 c.f. per minute per person in dressing area __ No noticeable air drafts	__ 20 c.f. per minute per person
__ HVAC System	__ Forced air __ Floor conducted radiant heat __ Radiator or fan coil unit in dressing areas	__ Forced air __ Radiator or fan coil unit
__ HVAC Controls	__ Thermostat, zone or room controls	__ Central thermostat

ELECTRICAL POWER	Recommended	Minimum

__ Power Outlets	__ Easily accessible grounded outlets for:
	   __ Iron and task lamp
	   __ Sewing machine
	
	__ All outlets with ground fault interrupt protection
		__ Easily accessible grounded outlets at average of every 10 linear feet

__ Circuits	__ Separate circuits for any fixtures rated at 20 amps or more	

LIGHTING	Recommended	Minimum
__ Lamps	__ Recessed incandescent __ Track lights for spots or floods __ Dressing mirror lights	__ Central recessed or surface mounted fixtures
__ Switching	__ 3-way switches if there is multiple room access __ Door activated light at enclosed wardrobes	__ Switches at main entry

ILLUMINATION	Recommended	Minimum
	__ 60 - 100 f.c.	__ 50 f.c. general light

COMMUNICATIONS	Recommended	Minimum
__ Communications	__ Smoke, fire, & security alarms __ Intercom	__ Alarms as required by code

DESIGN STANDARDS -- CHURCH COMMUNITY ROOM

GENERAL	Recommended Standards	Minimum Standards

__ Occupancies	__ As per program with allowance for varying types of occupancies:
	    __ Meetings
	    __ Receptions and parties
	    __ Hobby activities/classes
		__ As per program

__ Floor Area	__ 8 sq. ft. per person for social events __ 12 sq. ft. per person for meetings __ 20 sq. ft. per person for class and general activity use	__ 7 sq. ft. per person for social events __ 10 sq. ft. per person for meetings __ 15 sq. ft. per person for class and general activity use
__ Ceiling Height	__ 10' to 14'	__ 9' to 12'

FINISHES	Cost Categories		
	A	B	C
__ Floors & Sub-structure	__ Sound isolated substructure __ Nylon or acrylic carpet rated for heavy wear and glued to floor	__ Sound isolated substructure __ Carpet, heavy to medium, glued __ Vinyl	__ Carpet, medium, glued __ Vinyl or asphalt tile
__ Counters & Built-in Furnishings	__ Kitchenette tile or plastic laminate work counter with overhead and under-counter cabinets __ Lockable storage cabinets	__ Workspace for food and coffee preparation __ Cabinets under and above workspace counter	
__ Walls & Substructure	__ Fire ratings as per code __ Sound-isolated construction __ Gypsum board with heavy-weight vinyl or fabric __ Plaster __ Chair rail at exposed walls	__ Fire ratings as per code __ Gypsum board with medium to heavyweight vinyl, or fabric __ Gypsum board, painted __ Chair rail at exposed walls near movable seating	__ Fire ratings as per code __ Gypsum board, painted
__ Ceiling & Sub-structure	__ Sound isolated substructure __ Suspended acoustic tile with integrated lighting	__ Suspended acoustic tile __ Suspended gypsum board ceiling with acoustic treatment	__ Suspended acoustic tile, exposed grid __ Gypsum board with acoustic treatment
__ Acoustics	__ This room must be sound isolated from quiet areas of the building __ NC 30 - 35, STC 45 - 55 __ Doors solid core with sound gaskets at all edges __ Walls adjacent to quiet areas must extend from floor to roof slab above and be caulked and sound proofed at all edges and penetrations	__ NC 25 - 35, STC 45 - 55 __ As per Cost Category A	__ All provisions as much as possible as per Cost Category B

DESIGN STANDARDS -- CHURCH COMMUNITY ROOM

DOORS & WINDOWS	Recommended	Minimum
__ **Doors**	__ 1-3/4" solid core entry/exit doors __ Sound proofing gaskets at all edges unless room is located in non-sound sensitive part of the building __ Vision panel in door or beside it __ Doors to auxiliary rooms or corridors 1-3/4" solid core with sound-proofing gaskets at all edges __ Doors fire rated if opening onto fire exit corridors -- as per fire code	__ As per Recommended but door construction and finish may be of middle to economy grades
__ **Frames**	__ 16 gauge steel __ 14 gauge frames at fire-rated doors	__ 16 gauge steel or extra-sturdy wood jambs and frames __ 14 gauge frames at fire-rated doors
__ **Hardware**	__ Quiet, concealed automatic closers __ Panic bar exit hardware __ Controlled locking	__ Automatic closers, sound gasketing, and controlled locking systems
__ **Windows**	__ Window with blinds and blackout drapes __ Operable sash OK but allow for building security __ Orientation and blinds to prevent sun glare and heat gain	__ As per Recommended

FIXTURES/EQUIPMENT	Recommended	Minimum
__ **Special furnishings**	__ Kitchenette with sink, stove, mini-refrigerator, work counter and cabinets __ Display and exhibit cabinets __ Display shelves __ Video and VCR station __ Concealed chalk board or white board if there is a definite "front" presentation space in the room	__ Work sink and counter alcove __ As per program and Recommended
__ **Audio-Visual Equipment**	__ Provisions for slide, video, and audio presentations __ Built-in screen if presentation space is definite __ Storage and/or convenient access to portable screen and other equipment storage __ Space for rolling chalk or white boards, display boards, projector carts, movable lectern, etc.	__ Provisions as much as possible as per Recommended

PLUMBING	Recommended	Minimum
__ **Fixtures**	__ Drinking fountain at nearby corridor or near restrooms __ Sink with kitchenette __ Fire sprinklers __ Fire hose cabinet as per local fire code	__ As per Recommended __ Stainless steel or porcelain work sink __ Fire sprinklers and fire hose cabinet as required by code

DESIGN STANDARDS -- CHURCH COMMUNITY ROOM

HVAC	Recommended	Minimum
__ **Occupancies**	__ As per program -- allowing for variations in occupancy at different times __ Estimate 1 person per 8 sq. ft. at social events, 1 person per 10 sq. ft. at meetings	__ As per program __ For approximate estimating, maximum occupancy of 1 person per 7 sq. ft. at social events, 1 person per 10 sq. ft. at meetings
__ **Ventilation**	__ 20 - 30 cfm outdoor air per occupant	__ 20 cfm outdoor air per occupant
__ **HVAC System & Controls**	__ Temperature controlled by individual thermostat __ Central HVAC system with individual room control	__ If climate is zone controlled, temperatures 68° to 74°F. __ Central system with individual room or zone control

ELECTRICAL POWER	Recommended	Minimum
__ **Power Outlets**	__ Outlets at kitchenette countertop __ Power as required for kitchenette refrigerator and electric stove __ Outlets for presentation slide and film projectors, video, electrified lectern, overhead projector, video camera, etc. __ Wall base outlets or outlet strips for all contemplated future electric or electronic equipment __ Wall clock outlet __ Outlets as required for janitorial service __ Lighted fire exit signs at exit doors __ Emergency battery powered exit lights	__ Outlets as per program or required by code

LIGHTING	Recommended	Minimum
__ **Lamps**	__ Mixture of incandescent and fluorescent ceiling fixtures	__ Fluorescent ceiling lights, recessed or sur-face mounted __ Some ceiling lights dimable during audio/visual displays at lectures
__ **Switching**	__ Dimmer controls for incandescent lighting with standard switches near entry __ Alternative dimmer controls near speaker locations for A/V presentations	__ Dimmer controls for incandescent lighting and standard room switch controls at entry

ILLUMINATION	Recommended	Minimum
	__ 50 - 100 f.c.	__ 30 - 70 f.c.

COMMUNICATIONS	Recommended	Minimum
	__ Fire alarms __ Microphone jacks and ceiling speakers	__ Alarms as required by code

35

COMMUNITY CENTERS

DESIGN STANDARDS -- COMMUNITY CENTER ENTRY LOBBY

GENERAL	Recommended Standards	Minimum Standards
__ Occupancies and Floor Area	__ As per program with allowance for varying occupancies and traffic loads	__ As per program
__ Ceiling Height	__ 10' - 12' __ Can include low (7'- 6" to 8') soffit at entrance	__ 8' - 9' in smaller centers
__ Special Plan Considerations	__ Centralized information desk __ Double-door air lock vestibule in hot or cold climates __ Vestibule should provide waiting space and seating	__ As per Recommended Standards

FINISHES	Cost Categories		
	A	B	C
__ **Floors** WARNING: Smooth, hard surface materials some-times used at entrances -- such as terrazzo, marble, smooth tile, or polished travertine are safety haz-ards -- even those treated to be non-slip are a prob-lem when wet and when in contact with certain shoe sole materials	__ Recessed floor mat for rainy/ snowy climates __ Non-slip rubber or vinyl tile at entry vestibule __ Nylon or other synthetic fabric carpet near entry should be rated for heavy wear, stain resistan and reasonably dark tone, glued to floor __ Carpet may be a different, complementary color and fabric at other spaces to allow easier replacement of the more heavily trafficked entry floor area __ Avoid light-tone reflective floor surfaces	__ Vinyl or asphalt tile at entry vestibule __ Synthetic fabric carpet rated for heavy wear near entry, glued to floor __ Complementary heavy to medium wear carpet at adjacent areas __ Other flooring considerations as per Cost Category A	__ Vinyl or asphalt tile __ Synthetic fabric carpet near entry, glued __ Non-slip rubber or vinyl at entry vestibule
__ **Fixtures**	__ Coat/umbrella racks __ Public phone __ Handicap access allowing for handicap and elderly __ Lighted fire exit signs __ Displays, bulletin board	__ Fixtures as per Cost Category A and/or program	__ Fixtures as per Cost Category A and/or program
__ **Walls & Substructure**	__ Full-height store-front entry may include automatic door opener __ Interior wall finish typically plaster or gypsum board with heavy-duty vinyl or fabric __ Exit wall fire ratings as per code	__ Foyer and exit area wall fire ratings as per code __ Gypsum board with heavy weight vinyl or fabric __ Plaster with sound absorbant treatment	__ Fire ratings as per code __ Gypsum board, painted
__ **Ceiling**	__ Baffle or other decorative ceiling __ Suspended acoustic tile __ Gypsum board with acoustic treatment or texture finish	__ Suspended acoustic tile __ Gypsum board	__ Suspended acoustic tile, exposed grid __ Gypsum board

DESIGN STANDARDS -- COMMUNITY CENTER ENTRY

DOORS & WINDOWS	Recommended	Minimum
__ **Doors**	__ Heavy-duty, glazed public entry doors with quiet operating hardware and automatic closers __ Double door air-lock vestibule to control indoor-outdoor temperature differences and outside noise __ Automatic doors as needed for heavy traffic and for most convenient handicap access	__ Glazed public entry doors with quiet operating hardware and automatic closers
__ **Frames**	__ 14 gauge steel	__ 16 gauge steel
__ **Hardware**	__ Quiet, concealed automatic closers	
__ **Related Fixtures**	__ Lighted exit signs at exit doors as per code __ Controlled locking with security alarm system __ Side panel glazing or safety vision panels at non-glazed doors	
__ **Windows**	__ Floor to ceiling front glazing with glass entry doors __ Floor base barrier and mid-height bar or barrier to prevent people from walking into full-height glazing	__ No minimum requirements but views to the exterior are very desirable

FIXTURES/EQUIPMENT	Recommended	Minimum
__ **Special furnishings**	__ Information counter __ Bulletin and event announcement boards __ Display and exhibit cabinets __ See entry vestibule-related fixtures listed on previous page	__ As per program and Recommended

PLUMBING	Recommended	Minimum
__ **Fixtures**	__ Drinking fountain near entry and/or near restrooms __ Fire sprinklers as required by code	__ As per Recommended

DESIGN STANDARDS -- COMMUNITY CENTER ENTRY

HVAC	Recommended	Minimum
__ Occupancies	__ As per program -- allowing for large variations in traffic at different times	__ As per program
__ Ventilation	__ 20 - 30 cfm outdoor air per occupant __ Air lock vestibule to preserve air temperatures and buffer air pressure changes as people enter and leave the building	__ 20 cfm outdoor air per occupant
__ HVAC System & Controls	__ As per primary adjacent public spaces __ Localized heating may be provided in waiting area of vestibule	__ As per main public areas

ELECTRICAL POWER	Recommended	Minimum
__ Power Outlets	__ Outlets at information desk __ Wall clock outlet __ Outlets as required for janitorial service __ Lighted fire exit signs at exit doors	__ Outlets at information desk __ Outlets as required for janitorial service __ Lighted fire exit signs at exit doors

LIGHTING	Recommended	Minimum
__ Lamps	__ Overall incandescent and/or fluorescent ceiling fixtures __ Downlights or task lights at information desk	__ Fluorescent ceiling lights, recessed
__ Switching	__ Central control near information desk	__ Standard room switch controls

ILLUMINATION	Recommended	Minimum
	__ 20 - 30 f.c. at entry vestibule __ 50 - 70 f.c. at information desk area	__ 15 - 20 f.c. at entry vestibule __ 30 - 70 f.c.

COMMUNICATIONS	Recommended	Minimum
	__ PA system -- fire/security alarms __ Public phones near entry	__ Alarms as required by code

DESIGN STANDARDS -- COMMUNITY CENTER MULTIPURPOSE ROOM

GENERAL	Recommended Standards	Minimum Standards

__ Occupancies	__ As per program with allowance for varying types of occupancies:
	  __ Public lectures
	  __ Community organization meetings
	  __ Staff meetings and events
	  __ Receptions and parties
		__ As per program

__ Floor Area	__ 20 s.f. per person for general use __ 12 s.f. per person for lectures	__ 15 s.f. per person for general use __ 10 s.f. per person for lectures
__ Ceiling Height	__ 10' to 14'	__ 9' to 12'

FINISHES	Cost Categories		
	A	B	C
__ Floors & Sub-structure	__ Sound isolated substructure __ Nylon or acrylic carpet rated for heavy wear and glued to floor	__ Sound isolated substructure __ Carpet, heavy to medium, glued __ Vinyl	__ Carpet, median, glued __ Vinyl or asphalt tile
__ Counters & Built-in Furnishings	__ Kitchenette tile or plastic laminate work counter with overhead and under-counter cabinets __ Lockable storage cabinets	__ Workspace for food and coffee preparation __ Cabinets under and above workspace counter	
__ Walls & Substructure	__ Fire ratings as per code __ Sound-isolated construction __ Gypsum board with heavy weight vinyl or fabric __ Plaster __ Chair rail at exposed walls	__ Fire ratings as per code __ Gypsum board with medium to heavy weight vinyl, or fabric __ Gypsum board, painted __ Chair rail at exposed walls near movable seating	__ Fire ratings as per code __ Gypsum board, painted
__ Ceiling & Sub-structure	__ Sound isolated substructure __ Suspended acoustic tile with integrated lighting	__ Suspended acoustic tile __ Suspended gypsum board ceiling with acoustic treatment	__ Suspended acoustic tile, exposed grid __ Gypsum board with acoustic treatment
__ Acoustics	__ This room must be sound isolated from quiet areas of the building __ NC 30 - 35, STC 45 - 55 __ Doors solid core with sound gaskets at all edges __ Walls adjacent to quiet areas such as a reading lounge must extend from floor to roof slab above and be caulked and sound proofed at all edges and penetrations	__ NC 25 - 35, STC 45 - 55 __ As per Cost Category A	__ All provisions as much as possible as per Cost Category B

DESIGN STANDARDS -- COMMUNITY CENTER MULTIPURPOSE ROOM

DOORS & WINDOWS	Recommended	Minimum
__ **Doors**	__ 1-3/4" solid core entry/extit doors __ Sound proofing gaskets at all edges unless room is located in non-sound sensitive part of the building __ Vision panel in door __ Doors to auxiliary rooms or corridors 1-3/4" solid core with sound proofing gaskets at all edges __ Doors fire rated if opening onto fire exit corridors -- as per fire code	__ As per Recommended Standards but door construction and finish may be of middle to economy grades
__ **Frames**	__ 16 gauge steel __ 14 gauge frames at fire-rated doors	__ 16 gauge steel or extra-sturdy wood jambs and frames __ 14 gauge frames at fire-rated doors
__ **Hardware**	__ Quiet, concealed automatic closers __ Panic bar exit hardware __ Controlled locking	__ Automatic closers, sound gasketing, and controlled locking systems
__ **Windows**	__ Windows OK with blinds and blackout drapes __ Operable sash not accessible from the exterior __ Orientation and blinds to prevent sun glare and heat gain	__ As per Recommended

FIXTURES/EQUIPMENT	Recommended	Minimum
__ **Special furnishings**	__ Kitchenette with sink, stove, mini-refrigerator, work counter and cabinets __ Display and exhibit cabinets __ Display shelves __ Video and VCR station __ Concealed chalk board or white board if there is a definite "front" presentation space in the room	__ Work sink and counter alcove __ As per program and Recommended
__ **Audio-Visual Equipment**	__ Provisions for slide, video, and audio presentations __ Built-in screen if presentation space is definite __ Storage and/or convenient access to portable screen and other equipment storage __ Space for rolling chalk or white boards, display boards, projector carts, movable lectern, etc.	__ Provisions as much as possible as per the Recommended standards

PLUMBING	Recommended	Minimum
__ **Fixtures**	__ Drinking fountain at nearby corridor or near restrooms __ Sink with kitchenette __ Fire sprinklers	__ As per Recommended standards __ Stainless steel or porcelain work sink __ Fire sprinklers as required by code

DESIGN STANDARDS -- COMMUNITY CENTER MULTIPURPOSE ROOM

HVAC	Recommended	Minimum
__ Occupancies	__ As per program -- allowing for variations in occupancy at different times	__ As per program __ For approximate estimating, maximum occupancy of 1 person per 7 sq. ft. at social events, 1 person per 10 sq. ft. at lectures
__ Ventilation	__ 20 - 30 cfm outdoor air per occupant	__ 20 cfm outdoor air per occupant
__ HVAC System & Controls	__ Temperature controlled by individual thermostat __ Central HVAC system with individual room control	__ If climate is zone controlled, temperatures 68° to 74°F. __ Central system with individual room or zone control

ELECTRICAL POWER	Recommended	Minimum
__ Power Outlets	__ Outlets at kitchenette countertop __ Power as required for kitchenette refrigerator and electric stove __ Outlets for presentation slide and film projectors, video, electrified lecturn, overhead projector, video camera, etc. __ Wall base outlets or outlet strips for all contemplated future electric or electronic equipment __ Wall clock outlet __ Outlets as required for janitorial service __ Lighted exit signs at exit doors	__ Outlets as per program or required by code

LIGHTING	Recommended	Minimum
__ Lamps	__ Mixture of incandescent and fluorescent ceiling fixtures	__ Fluorescent ceiling lights, recessed or surface mounted __ Some ceiling lights dimable during audio/visual displays at lectures
__ Switching	__ Dimmer controls for incandescent lighting with standard switches near entry __ Alternative dimmer controls near speaker locations for A/V presentations	__ Dimmer controls for incandescent lighting and standard room switch controls at entry
ILLUMINATION	Recommended __ 50 - 70 ESI (f.c.) for reading and study	Minimum __ 30 - 70 ESI (f.c.) for reading and study

COMMUNICATIONS	Recommended	Minimum
	__ PA system -- fire/security alarms __ Ceiling speakers and microphone jacks	__ Alarms as required by code

DESIGN STANDARDS -- COMMUNITY CENTER LIBRARY & READING ROOM

GENERAL	Recommended Standards	Minimum Standards
__ Occupancies	__ As per program with allowance for varying types of occupant densities: __ Readers requiring privacy and extra space __ Communal tables for groups of four to six __ Lounge readers	__ As per program; see the introductory section on Libraries for rules of thumb for overall occupancies and spatial requirements
__ Floor Area	__ 40 s.f. per reader	__ 35 s.f. per reader
__ Ceiling Height	__ 8' to 9' -- reading areas less than 100 s.f. __ 10' to 14' main reading area __ 16' to 20' at room with mezzanine	__ 7'- 6" -- reading areas less than 100 s.f. __ 10' main reading area

FINISHES	Cost Categories		
	A	B	C
__ Floors & Sub- structure	__ Sound isolated substructure __ Nylon or acrylic carpet rated for heavy wear and glued to floor in heavy traffic areas __ Padded carpet may be provided in study area __ Tight weave, cut or loop pile __ Static removal is essential	__ Sound isolated substructure __ Carpet for heavy wear in traffic areas, medium wear elsewhere, glued __ Vinyl NOTE: Sound absorptive carpet flooring is preferred in virtually all areas of the library except utility spaces	__ Carpet, medium, glued __ Vinyl in reception areas __ Asphalt tile at adjacent reference or stack areas WARNING: Asphalt tile floors in combination with some types of movable chairs can cause extreme noise problems
__ Counters & Built-in Furnishings	__ Manufactured units, wood veneer, plastic laminate work surfaces	__ Manufactured wood and plastic laminate combinations	__ Plastic laminate
__ Walls & Substructure	__ Fire ratings as per code __ Sound-isolated construction __ Gypsum board with heavy weight vinyl or fabric __ Chair rail at exposed walls near movable seating	__ Fire ratings as per code __ Gypsum board with fabric or vinyl, medium weight __ Chair rail at exposed walls near movable seating	__ Fire ratings as per code __ Gypsum board with fabric or vinyl, medium
__ Ceiling & Sub- structure	__ Sound isolated substructure __ Suspended acoustic tile with integrated lighting	__ Suspended acoustic tile with integrated lighting __ Suspended gypsum board ceiling with acoustic treatment	__ Suspended acoustic tile, exposed grid __ Gypsum board with acoustic treatment
__ Acoustics WARNING: Exterior court-yards, atriums, and open stairs are common noise hazards for libraries -- noise levels are most acute at the upper floors affected by such elements	__ All surfaces sound absorptive __ 40-50 decibel electronic "white noise" recommended as background noise masking __ NC25 - 35, STC 45-55 __ Doors to adjacent offices and conference rooms solid core with sound gaskets at all edges	__ NC 25 - 35, STC 45 - 55 __ Doors to adjacent offices and conference rooms solid core with sound gaskets at all edges __ Sound barriers above adjacent floor-to-ceiling partitions	__ All provisions as much as possible as per Cost Category B

DOORS & WINDOWS	Recommended	Minimum
__ **Doors**	__ Heavy-duty public entry doors with quiet operating hardware and automatic closers __ Double door air-lock vestibule to control indoor-outdoor temperature differentiations and outside noise __ Doors to adjacent rooms 1-3/4" solid core with sound proofing gaskets at all edges	__ 1-3/4" solid core doors, gasketed at all edges __ Doors to adjacent rooms 1-3/4" solid core with sound proofing gaskets at all edges
__ **Frames**	__ 16 gauge steel	__ 16 gauge steel or extra-sturdy wood jambs and frames
__ **Hardware**	__ Quiet, concealed automatic closers __ Locking to control access to storage and maintenance areas	__ Automatic closers, sound gasketing, and controlled locking systems
__ **Windows**	__ Windows OK for restful views such as courtyard gardens or yard scenery, otherwise keep windows high for daylighting but not views __ Operable sash not accessible from the exterior __ Orientation and blinds to prevent sun glare and heat gain	__ Windows as will enhance reading room environment -- daylight and views

FIXTURES/EQUIPMENT	Recommended	Minimum
__ **Special furnishings**	__ Bulletin and announcement boards __ Display and exhibit cabinets __ Display shelves for periodicals, special publications __ Book shelves	__ As per program and Recommended standards
__ **Audio-Visual Equipment**	__ Video and VCR machines with headphones for sound -- located where not visually distracting to readers __ Headphone access for video, audio tapes, etc.	

PLUMBING	Recommended	Minimum
__ **Fixtures**	__ Drinking fountain near entry and/or restrooms __ Fire sprinklers as required by code	__ As per Recommended standards

DESIGN STANDARDS -- COMMUNITY CENTER LIBRARY & READING ROOM

HVAC	Recommended	Minimum
__ Occupancies	__ As per program -- allowing for variations in occupancy at different times	__ As per program __ For approximate estimating: 20 people per 1,000 s.f.
__ Ventilation	__ 20 - 30 cfm outdoor air per occupant __ Ventilation noise should be minimal in reading rooms __ Air speed at head level should not be greater than 40 f.p.m. __ For sound masking, use electronic "white noise" only	__ 20 cfm outdoor air per occupant
__ HVAC System & Controls	__ Central HVAC system with individual room control	__ If climate is zone controlled, temperatures 70° to 74°F. __ Central system with individual room or zone control __ Warm & cool forced air (zoned) __ Package systems not recommended

ELECTRICAL POWER	Recommended	Minimum
__ Power Outlets	__ Lamp outlets near fixed reading tables and work stations __ Outlets at control desk __ Floor and wall outlets for copier, headphone systems, video, etc. __ Wall base outlets or outlet strips for all contemplated future equipment __ Wall clock outlet __ Outlets as required for janitorial service __ Lighted exit signs at exit doors	__ As per program and/ or as required by code

LIGHTING	Recommended	Minimum
__ Lamps	__ Wall wash lights __ Downlights at reading areas or adjustable table and floor lamps __ Overall incandescent and/or fluorescent ceiling fixtures __ Book lighting fixtures at book shelves	__ Fluorescent ceiling lights, recessed or surface mounted __ Downlights at reading areas __ Book lighting fixtures at book shelves
__ Switching	__ Dimmer control fot incandescent downlights	__ Standard room switch controls

ILLUMINATION WARNING: Library lighting is commonly inadequate despite its obvious importance	Recommended	Minimum
	__ 60 - 80 ESI (f.c.) for reading __ If reading lamps are provided, 50 f.c. is OK for general lighting -- task lights non-glare __ 90% Visual Comfort Performance	__ 50 - 70 ESI (f.c.) for reading and study

COMMUNICATIONS	Recommended	Minimum
	__ PA system -- fire/security alarms __ Public phone near entry	__ Alarms as required by code

45

CONFERENCE CENTERS

CONTENTS

DESIGN STANDARDS -- CONFERENCE CENTER ENTRY LOBBY

GENERAL	Recommended Standards	Minimum Standards
__ Occupancies and Floor Area	__ As per program with allowance for varying occupancies and traffic loads	__ As per program
__ Ceiling Height	__ 10' - 20' __ Can include low (7'- 6" to 8') soffit at entrance	__ 10' - 12' in smaller centers
__ Special Plan Considerations	__ Centralized information/registration desk __ Double-door air lock vestibule in hot or cold climates __ Ample, clear signage to identify meeting room locations and event notices are crucial	__ As per Recommended Standards

FINISHES	Cost Categories		
	A	B	C
__ **Floors** WARNING: Smooth, hard surface materials sometimes used at entrances -- such as terrazzo, marble, smooth tile, or polished travertine are safety hazards -- even those treated to be non-slip are a problem when wet and when in contact with certain shoe sole materials	__ Recessed floor mat for rainy/ snowy climates at vestibule __ Non-slip rubber or vinyl tile at entry vestibule __ Nylon or other synthetic fabric carpet near entry should be rated for heavy wear, stain resistant and reasonably dark tone, glued to floor __ Carpet may be a different, complementary color an fabric at other spaces to allow easier replacement of the more heavily trafficked entry floor area __ Avoid light-tone reflective floor surfaces	__ Vinyl or asphalt tile at entry vestibule __ Synthetic fabric carpet rated for heavy wear near entry, glued to floor __ Complementary heavy to medium wear carpet at adjacent areas __ Other flooring considerations as per Cost Category A	__ Non-slip rubber or vinyl at entry vestibule __ Synthetic fabric carpet near entry, glued __ Vinyl or asphalt tile
__ **Fixtures**	__ Public phones __ Handicap access allowing for handicap and elderly __ Lighted fire exit signs __ Displays, bulletin board	__ Fixtures as per Cost Category A and/or program	__ Fixtures as per Cost Category A and/or program
__ **Walls & Substructure**	__ Full-height store-front entry with automatic door opener __ Interior wall finish typically plaster or gypsum board with heavy weight vinyl or fabric __ Exit wall fire ratings as per code	__ Foyer and exit area wall fire ratings as per code __ Gypsum board with heavy weight vinyl or fabric __ Plaster with sound absorbant treatment	__ Fire ratings as per code __ Gypsum board, painted
__ **Ceiling**	__ Plaster __ Baffle, metal, wood or other decorative ceiling __ Gypsum board with acoustic treatment __ Suspended decorative acoustic tile __ Fire resistive treated wood	__ Suspended decorative acoustic tile __ Gypsum board	__ Suspended acoustic tile, exposed grid __ Gypsum board

DESIGN STANDARDS -- CONFERENCE CENTER ENTRY

DOORS & WINDOWS	Recommended	Minimum
__ **Doors**	__ Automatic doors as needed for heavy traffic and for most convenient handicap access __ Heavy-duty, glazed public entry doors with quiet operating hardware and automatic closers __ Double door air-lock vestibule to control indoor-outdoor temperature differentiations and outside noise	__ Glazed public entry doors with quiet operating hardware and automatic closers
__ **Frames**	__ 14 gauge steel or heavy-duty aluminum store front detailing	__ 16 gauge steel or as per store front manufacturer
__ **Hardware**	__ Quiet, concealed automatic closers	
__ **Related Fixtures**	__ Lighted exit signs at exit doors as per code __ Controlled locking with security alarm system __ Side panel glazing or safety vision panels at non-glazed doors	
__ **Windows**	__ Floor to ceiling front glazing with glass entry doors __ Floor base barrier and conspicuous mid-height bar or barrier to prevent people from walking into full-height glazing	__ No minimum requirements but views to the exterior are very desirable __ Safety barriers at full-height glazing as per Recommended

FIXTURES/EQUIPMENT	Recommended	Minimum
__ **Special furnishings**	__ Information/registration counter __ Bulletin and event announcement boards __ Display and exhibit cabinets __ Event notice displays __ Ample signage and location map displays	__ As per program and Recommended standards

PLUMBING	Recommended	Minimum
__ **Fixtures**	__ Drinking fountain near entry and/or near restrooms __ Fire sprinklers as required by code __ Fire hose cabinets as required by code	__ As per Recommended standards

DESIGN STANDARDS -- CONFERENCE CENTER ENTRY

HVAC	Recommended	Minimum
__ Occupancies	__ As per program -- allowing for large variations in traffic	__ As per program
__ Ventilation	__ 20 - 30 cfm outdoor air per occupant __ Air lock vestibule to preserve air temperatures and buffer air pressure changes as people enter and leave the building	__ 20 cfm outdoor air per occupant
__ HVAC System & Controls	__ As per primary adjacent public spaces __ Localized heating may be provided in waiting area of vestibule	__ As per main public areas

ELECTRICAL POWER	Recommended	Minimum
__ Power Outlets	__ Outlets at information/registration desk __ Wall clock outlet __ Outlets as required for janitorial service __ Lighted fire exit signs at exit doors __ Battery powered emergency lights	__ Outlets at information desk __ Outlets as required for janitorial service __ Lighted fire exit signs at exit doors

LIGHTING	Recommended	Minimum
__ Lamps	__ Overall incandescent and/or fluorescent ceiling fixtures __ Downlights or task lights at information/registration desk and other focal points __ Spotlights and wall wash lights for displays and artwork	__ Fluorescent ceiling lights __ Down lights or task lights at information/registration desk and other focal points
__ Switching	__ Central control, dimmers, and timers near information/registration desk	__ Standard room switch controls near entry

ILLUMINATION	Recommended	Minimum
	__ 20 - 30 f.c. at entry vestibule __ 50 - 70 f.c. at information desk area	__ 15 - 20 f.c. at entry vestibule __ 30 - 70 f.c.

COMMUNICATIONS	Recommended	Minimum
	__ PA system -- fire/security alarms __ Generous number of public phones	__ Alarms as required by code __ Public phones

49

DESIGN STANDARDS -- CONFERENCE CENTER MEETING ROOMS

GENERAL	Recommended Standards	Minimum Standards
__ Occupancies & Floor Areas	__ 25 s.f. per person for up to 8 people __ 20 s.f. per person for 8 to 10 people __ 18 s.f. per person for 20 to 40 people	__ As per program
__ Ceiling Height	__ 10' to 12' depending on room proportions	__ 10'
__ Plan features	__ Maximum provision for conference room sound control and minimal acoustic, HVAC, and visual distractions	

FINISHES	Cost Categories		
	A	B	C
__ Floors & Sub-structure	__ Sound isolated substructure __ Carpet rated for heavy wear, glued	__ Sound isolated substructure __ Carpet for medium to heavy wear, glued	__ Carpet, medium, glued
__ Wainscot	__ Wood paneling at executive conference rooms	__ Partial wood paneling __ Plaster __ Heavy weight vinyl wall cover	__ If no wainscot, provide protective chair rail
__ Counters & Built-in Furnishings	__ Coffee service counter alcove -- plastic laminate, HPDL grade __ Built-in projector cabinet	__ Plastic laminate utility counter	
__ Walls & Substructure	__ 1-hour fire rating or more, as per building code __ Finish material flame spread ratings as per code __ Sound-isolated construction __ Wood paneling __ Plaster __ Gypsum wallboard with fabric or heavy grade vinyl	__ Fire ratings as per code __ Gypsum board with fabric or vinyl	__ Fire ratings as per code __ Gypsum board with fabric or vinyl
__ Ceiling & Sub-structure	__ Integral ceiling, plaster or gypsum board, with integrated lighting __ Sound isolated substructure __ Partial hard surface sound reflective areas at ceiling and walls	__ Suspended acoustic tile with integrated lighting __ Suspended gypsum board ceiling with acoustic treatment	__ Suspended acoustic tile, exposed grid __ Gypsum board with acoustic treatment
__ Acoustics	__ Provide for speech privacy in private conference meeting rooms __ NC 30, STC 60 __ Doors to conference rooms gasketed at all edges __ Sound reflecting surfaces at speaker's area	__ NC 30, STC 40 __ Other provisions as per Cost Category A	__ All provisions as much as possible as per Cost Category B

50

DESIGN STANDARDS -- CONFERENCE CENTER MEETING ROOMS

DOORS & WINDOWS	Recommended	Minimum
__ **Doors** CAUTION: No sound transfer allowable from or to other rooms or exterior corridor	__ Steel doors -- 18 to 16 gauge with sound proofing gaskets at all edges __ Fire-rated assembly __ 1-3/4" solid-core with sound proofing gaskets	__ Steel doors -- 18 gauge __ 1-3/4" solid core doors are minimum for access to peripheral spaces __ Fire-rated assembly
__ **Frames**	__ 16 gauge stee __ 14 gauge steel at fire exit doors and doors to corridor __ Corner guards for protection from service carts, moving furniture in and out, etc.	__ 16 gauge steel or extra-sturdy wood jambs and frames for smaller rooms
__ **Hardware**	__ Heavy-duty latchsets __ Quiet, concealed automatic closers, sound gasketing, and controlled locking systems __ Panic bars for meeting rooms for more than ten people or as per code __ Kickplates	__ Heavy-duty latchsets __ Automatic closers __ Panic bars as per code
__ **Windows**	__ Windows are generally not desired for conference rooms but, if used, provide: __ Double-pane for noise insulation from exterior __ Blinds and black out screens	__ As per Recommended

FIXTURES/EQUIPMENT	Recommended	Minimum
__ **Special furnishings**	__ Projector cabinet and/or counter __ A/V equipment storage cabinet	
__ **Audio-Visual/Meeting Equipment**	__ Any items built-in must be unobtrusive until required for use in meetings __ Projection screen __ Tack board __ White board	__ Ready access to projection screens, chalk boards, etc. from near-by storage

PLUMBING	Recommended	Minimum
__ **Fixtures**	__ Restrooms accessible __ Drinking fountains accessible __ Fire sprinklers as required by code	__ As per program

DESIGN STANDARDS -- CONFERENCE CENTER MEETING ROOMS

HVAC	Recommended	Minimum
__ Occupancies	__ As per program, or if not designated: __ 500 sq. ft. per 15 people	__ As per program
__ Ventilation	__ 35 - 50 cfm outdoor air per occupant	__ 30 cfm outdoor air per occupant
__ HVAC System & Controls	__ Temperature controlled by individual thermostat __ Central HVAC system	__ If climate is zone controlled, temperatures 68 to 72F. __ Central system with individual room or zone control __ Warm & cool forced air (zoned) __ Package systems not recommended __ Even at minimum construction cost, provide generous fresh air supply

ELECTRICAL POWER	Recommended	Minimum
__ Power Outlets	__ Outlets for audio visual equipment __ Floor and wall outlets for transcription, recording and playback equipment __ Floor and wall outlets for computer and video playback equipment __ Outlets for axiliary exhibit equipment __ Podium outlet and sound amplification	__ As per Recommended or as per program

LIGHTING	Recommended	Minimum
__ Lamps	__ Variable incandescent ceiling lighting __ Incandescent down lights for exhibits and/or note taking during A/V presentations __ Ambient fluorescent lighting, indirect preferred __ Wall wash lighting at tackboard wall	__ Standard fluorescent fixtures
__ Switching	__ Dimmer controls for incandescent lights __ Switch controls at entry and at rear wall	__ Standard room switch controls

ILLUMINATION	Recommended	Minimum
	__ 60 - 90 f.c. on exhibit or work table surfaces __ Minimal background dark to light contrast	__ 50 - 80 f.c. on exhibit or work table surfaces

COMMUNICATIONS	Recommended	Minimum
__ Communications	__ Microphone jacks and ceiling speakers __ Video and computer __ House phone and intercom __ Fire and smoke alarms	__ As per Recommended or as per program

DESIGN STANDARDS -- CONFERENCE CENTER LARGE LECTURE ROOMS

GENERAL	Recommended Standards	Minimum Standards
__ Occupancies & Floor Areas	__ 12 s.f. per person for 40 to several hundred people __ Spatial programming for these spaces requires great care	__ As per program
__ Ceiling Height	__ 12' to 16' depending on room proportions	__ 12'
__ Plan features	__ Maximum provision for conference room sound control and minimal acoustic, HVAC, and visual distractions __ Built-in low stage or platform with steps __ Built in projection room or rear-view projection room and screen	

FINISHES	Cost Categories		
	A	B	C
__ Floors & Sub-structure	__ Sound isolated substructure __ Carpet rated for heavy wear, glued	__ As per Cost Category A or as per program	__ Carpet, medium wear, glued
__ Wainscot	__ Hardwood paneling __ Plaster or as per main wall __ Heavy weight vinyl	__ Plaster or as per main wall __ Heavy weight vinyl wall cover	__ If no wainscot, and if seating is movable, provide protective chair rail
__ Counters & Built-in Furnishings	__ Fixed seating may be part of the client's program but should be considered carefully in terms of cost, flexibility and maintenance __ Coffee service counter alcove __ Built-in A/V cabinet, projection booth	__ Plastic laminate utility counter	
__ Walls & Substructure	__ 1-hour fire rating or more, as per building code __ Finish material flame spread ratings as per code __ Sound-isolated construction __ Plaster with acoustic control treatments __ Gypsum wallboard with fabric or heavy grade vinyl	__ Fire ratings as per code __ Gypsum board with fabric or vinyl	__ Fire ratings as per code __ Gypsum board with fabric or vinyl
__ Ceiling & Sub-structure	__ Integral ceiling, plaster or gypsum board, with integrated lighting __ Sound isolated substructure __ Partial hard surface above speaker's area	__ Suspended acoustic tile with integrated lighting __ Suspended gypsum board ceiling with acoustic treatment	__ Suspended acoustic tile, exposed grid __ Gypsum board with acoustic treatment
__ Acoustics	__ NC 30, STC 60 __ Double-door sound lock vestibule if room opens to public lobby or corridor __ Sound reflecting surfaces at speaker's area	__ NC 30, STC 40 __ Other provisions as per Cost Category A	__ All provisions as much as possible as per Cost Category B

DESIGN STANDARDS -- CONFERENCE CENTER LARGE LECTURE ROOMS

DOORS & WINDOWS	Recommended	Minimum
__ **Doors**	__ 1-3/4" solid-core with sound proofing gaskets at all edges __ Steel doors as required for fire safety	__ 1-3/4" solid core doors
__ **Frames**	__ 14 gauge steel at fire exit doors and doors to corridors __ 16 gauge steel at doors to storage closets or other peripheral spaces	__ As per Recommended
__ **Hardware**	__ Quiet, concealed automatic closers, sound gasketing, and controlled locking systems at entry doors __ Heavy duty panic bar and related exit hardware	__ Automatic closers at entry doors __ Panic bar and related exit hardware
__ **Windows**	__ Windows are not desired for large lecture rooms, especially auditorium settings	__ No windows

FIXTURES/EQUIPMENT	Recommended	Minimum
__ **Special furnishings**	__ Projector cabinet and/or counter __ A/V equipment storage cabinet	
__ **Audio-Visual/Meeting Equipment**	__ Any items built-in must be unobtrusive until required for use in presentations __ Rear projection room and screen __ Built-in projection screen __ Tack board __ White board	__ Ready access to projection screens, chalk boards, etc. from near-by storage

PLUMBING	Recommended	Minimum
__ **Fixtures**	__ Restrooms accessible __ Drinking fountains accessible __ Fire sprinklers as required by code, preferably in excess of code requirements	__ As per program

DESIGN STANDARDS -- CONFERENCE CENTER LARGE LECTURE ROOMS

HVAC	Recommended	Minimum
__ **Occupancies**	__ As per program (programming for full use of these facilities requires great care)	__ As per program
__ **Ventilation**	__ 35 - 50 cfm outdoor air per occupant	__ 30 cfm outdoor air per occupant
__ **HVAC System & Controls**	__ Locked individual thermostat __ Central HVAC system	__ If climate is zone controlled, temperatures 68 to 72F. __ Central system with individual room or zone control __ Warm & cool forced air (zoned) __ Package systems not recommended __ Even at minimum construction cost, provide generous fresh air supply

WARNING: A common source of complaint about ballrooms and large meeting room facilities is the quality of air and excessive variations in temperature

ELECTRICAL POWER	Recommended	Minimum
__ **Power Outlets**	__ Outlets for audio visual equipment __ Floor and wall outlets for transcription, recording and playback equipment __ Stage platform outlets for computer and video playback equipment __ Outlets for auxiliary exhibit equipment __ Podium outlet and sound amplification	__ As per Recommended or as per program

LIGHTING	Recommended	Minimum
__ **Lamps**	__ Variable incandescent ceiling lighting __ Incandescent down lights for exhibits and/or note taking during A/V presentations __ Ambient fluorescent lighting, indirect preferred __ Wall wash lighting	__ Standard fluorescent fixtures
__ **Switching**	__ Dimmer controls for incandescent lights __ Switch controls at entry and at stage platform area	__ Standard dimmer and room switch controls

ILLUMINATION	Recommended	Minimum
	__ 60 - 90 f.c. on exhibit or table surfaces __ Minimal background dark to light contrast	__ 50 - 80 f.c. on exhibit or table surfaces

COMMUNICATIONS	Recommended	Minimum
__ **Communications**	__ Microphone jacks; ceiling and front speakers __ Video and computer outlets __ House phone and intercom __ Fire and smoke alarms as per code	__ As per Recommended or as per program

DESIGN STANDARDS -- CONFERENCE CENTER TECH TRAINING ROOMS

GENERAL	Recommended Standards	Minimum Standards
__ **Occupancies & Floor Areas**	__ 25 s.f. per person for up to 8 people __ 20 s.f. per person for 8 to 10 people __ 18 s.f. per person for 20 to 40 people	__ As per program
__ **Ceiling Height**	__ 10' to 12' depending on room proportions	__ 10'
__ **Plan features**	__ Raised floor and extra deep suspended ceiling space to handle electrical and computer/ video/phone cables	

FINISHES	Cost Categories A	B	C
__ **Floors & Sub-structure**	__ Sound isolated substructure __ Raised computer room floor __ Vinyl sheet or tile floor __ Static safe flooring, (may require grounding)	__ As per Cost Category A	__ Vinyl tile
__ **Wainscot**	__ Wainscot, if any, may require special substructure and finish material, see program	__ As per Cost Category A __ If no wainscot, provide protective rail to protect walls from movable chairs and tables, carts, etc.	__ As per Cost Category B
__ **Counters & Built-in Furnishings**	__ Heavy duty work counters and tables __ Built-in audio/visual equipment and projection booth __ Lockable storage cabinets	__ Work counters as per program	__ As provided by client
__ **Walls & Substructure**	__ 1-hour to 2-hour fire rating as per program or code, whichever has highest standard __ Walls may require special substructure and finish materials, see program __ Sound-isolated construction __ Gypsum wallboard, painted or with heavy grade vinyl __ Grounds and supports for shelving, fixtures, and wall-mounted equipment __ Wall and corner guards	__ Fire ratings as per program or code, whichever has highest standard __ Gypsum board, painted	__ Fire ratings as per code __ Concrete block or gypsum board, painted
__ **Ceiling & Sub-structure**	__ Suspended ceiling; possible interstitial space for special cable and/or piping access __ Sound isolated substructure	__ Integrated or surface-mounted fluorescent light fixtures at ceiling	__ Suspended acoustic tile, exposed grid
__ **Acoustics**	__ NC 30, STC 50 __ Entry/exit doors gasketed	__ NC 30, STC 40	

56

DESIGN STANDARDS -- CONFERENCE CENTER TECH TRAINING ROOMS

DOORS & WINDOWS	Recommended	Minimum
__ **Doors**	__ 1-3/4" solid-core with sound proofing gaskets at all edges	__ 1-3/4" solid core doors are minimum for access to peripheral spaces
__ **Frames**	__ 16 gauge steel __ 14 gauge steel at fire exit doors and doors to corridor	__ 16 gauge steel or extra-sturdy wood jambs and frames for smaller rooms __ 14 gauge steel at fire exit doors and doors to corridor
__ **Hardware**	__ Quiet, concealed automatic closers, sound gasketing, and controlled locking systems __ Panic bars at exits for meeting rooms for more than ten people or as per code	__ Automatic closers __ Panic bars at exit doors as per code
__ **Windows**	__ Windows are generally not desired for technical training rooms but, if used, provide: __ Double-pane if exterior noise may be a problem __ Blinds	__ As per Recommended

FIXTURES/EQUIPMENT	Recommended	Minimum
__ **Special furnishings**	__ Projector cabinet and/or counter __ A/V equipment storage cabinet	
__ **Audio-Visual/Meeting Equipment**	__ Any items built-in must be unobtrusive until required for use in presentations __ Projection screen __ Tack board __ White board	__ Ready access to projection screens, white boards, etc. from near-by storage

PLUMBING	Recommended	Minimum
__ **Fixtures**	__ Wash sink __ Restrooms accessible __ Drinking fountains accessible __ Fire sprinklers as required by code or alternative dry fire suppression system __ Dry fire suppression system for electronic equipment and computer training rooms	__ As per program

DESIGN STANDARDS -- CONFERENCE CENTER TECH TRAINING ROOMS

HVAC	Recommended	Minimum
__ Occupancies	__ As per program, or if not designated: __ 500 sq. ft. per 15 people	__ As per program
__ Ventilation	__ 40 - 55 cfm outdoor air per occupant	__ 40 cfm outdoor air per occupant
__ HVAC System & Controls	__ Temperature controlled by individual thermostat __ Central HVAC system __ Allow for extra heat build-up from electronic equipment __ Humidify to avoid electrical static charge build-up	__ If climate is zone controlled, temperatures 68 to 72F. __ Central system with individual room or zone control __ Warm & cool forced air (zoned) __ Package systems not recommended __ Even at minimum construction cost, provide generous fresh air supply

ELECTRICAL POWER	Recommended	Minimum
__ Power Outlets	__ Outlets for audio visual equipment __ Floor and wall outlets for transcription, recording and playback equipment __ Floor and wall outlets for computer and video playback equipment __ Outlets for auxiliary exhibit equipment __ Podium outlet and sound amplification for formal presentations in larger training rooms __ Power and communications access may be through raised access floor or ceiling	__ As per Recommended or as per program

LIGHTING	Recommended	Minimum
__ Lamps	__ Variable incandescent ceiling lighting __ Incandescent down lights for work counters __ Ambient fluorescent lighting, indirect preferred __ Wall wash lighting at display walls	__ Standard fluorescent fixtures
__ Switching	__ Dimmer controls for incandescent lights __ Switch controls at entry and at instructor's station	__ Standard room switch controls

ILLUMINATION	Recommended	Minimum
	__ 60 - 90 f.c. on exhibit or work table surfaces __ Minimal background dark to light contrast	__ 50 - 80 f.c. on exhibit or work table surfaces

COMMUNICATIONS	Recommended	Minimum
__ Communications	__ Microphone jacks and ceiling speakers __ Video and computer __ House phone and intercom __ Fire and smoke alarms	__ As per Recommended or as per program

COURTHOUSES

DESIGN STANDARDS -- COURTHOUSE ENTRY & LOBBY

GENERAL	Recommended Standards	Minimum Standards
__ **Occupancies and Floor Area**	__ As per program with allowance for varying occupancies and traffic loads	__ As per program
__ **Ceiling Height**	__ 12' - 24' and more __ Can include low (8-10') soffit at entrance vestibule	__ 10' - 12' in smaller courthouses __ As per Recommended Standards
__ **Special Plan Considerations** CAUTION: Orientation and signage are major problems in many public buildings	__ Centralized security station/information desk __ Double-door air lock vestibule in hot or cold climates __ Metal dectector and package search station __ Seating alcoves for private conversations	

FINISHES	Cost Categories		
	A	B	C
__ **Floors** WARNING: Smooth, hard surface materials sometimes used at entrances -- such as terrazzo, marble, smooth tile, or polished travertine are safety hazards -- even those treated to be non-slip are a problem when wet and when in contact with certain shoe sole materials	__ Recessed floor mat for rainy/ snowy climates at vestibule __ Non-slip rubber or vinyl tile at entry vestibule __ Nylon or other synthetic fabric carpet near entry should be rated for heavy wear, stain resistant and reasonably dark tone, glued to floor __ Carpet may be a different, complementary color and fabric at other spaces to allow easier replacement of the more heavily trafficked entry floor area __ Avoid light-tone reflective floor surfaces	__ Vinyl or asphalt tile at entry vestibule __ Synthetic fabric carpet rated for heavy wear near entry, glued to floor __ Complementary heavy to medium wear carpet at adjacent areas __ Other flooring considerations as per Cost Category A	__ Non-slip rubber or vinyl at entry vestibule __ Synthetic fabric carpet, glued
__ **Walls & Substructure**	__ Full-height store-front entry with automatic door opener __ Marble/other polished stone __ Interior wall finish typically plaster or gypsum board with heavy duty vinyl, fabric, or hardwood __ Exit wall fire ratings as per code	__ Foyer and exit area wall fire ratings as per code __ Gypsum board with heavy weight vinyl or fabric __ Plaster with sound absorbant treatment	__ Fire ratings as per code __ Gypsum board, painted
__ **Ceiling**	__ Plaster __ Baffle, metal, wood or other decorative ceiling __ Gypsum board with acoustic treatment __ Suspended decorative acoustic tile	__ Suspended decorative acoustic tile __ Gypsum board	__ Suspended acoustic tile, exposed grid __ Gypsum board
__ **Counterts & Built-In Furnishings**	__ Polished stone, hardwood	__ Plastic laminate	__ Plastic laminate
__ **Fixtures**	__ Public phones in private booths __ Handicap access __ Lighted fire exit signs	__ Fixtures as per Cost Category A and/or program	__ Fixtures as per Cost Category A and/or program

60

DESIGN STANDARDS -- COURTHOUSE ENTRY & LOBBY

DOORS & WINDOWS	Recommended	Minimum
__ **Doors**	__ Automatic doors as needed for heavy traffic and for most convenient handicap access __ Heavy-duty, glazed public entry doors with quiet operating hardware and automatic closers __ Double door air-lock vestibule to control indoor-outdoor temperature differentiations and outside noise	__ Glazed public entry doors with quiet operating hardware and automatic closers
__ **Frames**	__ 14 gauge steel	__ 16 gauge steel
__ **Hardware**	__ Quiet, concealed automatic closers	
__ **Related Fixtures**	__ Lighted exit signs at exit doors as per code __ Controlled locking with security alarm system __ Side panel glazing or safety vision panels at non-glazed doors	
__ **Windows**	__ Floor to ceiling front glazing with glass entry doors __ Floor base barrier and mid-height bar or barrier to prevent people from walking into full-height glazing	__ Glazing for clear viewing between interior and exterior near entry

FIXTURES/EQUIPMENT	Recommended	Minimum
__ **Special furnishings**	__ Information desk __ Security desk (may be combined with Information desk) __ Tenant directory __ Elevator signage __ Location map __ Metal detectors and other security devices -- safety and security is a primay consideration	__ As per program and Recommended standards

PLUMBING	Recommended	Minimum
__ **Fixtures**	__ Drinking fountain near entry and/or near restrooms __ Fire sprinklers as required by code __ Fire hose cabinets as required by code	__ As per Recommended standards

DESIGN STANDARDS -- COURTHOUSE ENTRY & LOBBY

HVAC	Recommended	Minimum
__ Occupancies	__ As per program -- allowing for variations in traffic at different times	__ As per program
__ Ventilation	__ 20 - 30 cfm outdoor air per occupant __ Air lock vestibule to preserve air temperatures and buffer air pressure changes as people enter and leave the building	__ 20 cfm outdoor air per occupant
__ HVAC System & Controls	__ As per primary adjacent public spaces __ Localized heating may be provided in waiting area of vestibule	__ As per main public areas

ELECTRICAL POWER	Recommended	Minimum
__ Power Outlets	__ Outlets at information/securirty desk areas __ Wall clock outlet __ Outlets as required for janitorial service __ Lighted fire exit signs at exit doors __ Security video camera outlets	__ Outlets at information/securirty desk areas __ Outlets as required for janitorial service __ Lighted fire exit signs at exit doors

LIGHTING	Recommended	Minimum
__ Lamps	__ Iincandescent and/or fluorescent ceiling fixtures __ Downlights or spotlights at information and security desk, location map, directory, and other focal points __ Wall wash lights for displays and artwork	__ Fluorescent ceiling lights __ Down lights or task lights at registration/ cashier desk and other focal points
__ Switching	__ Central control, dimmers, and timers near security control area	__ Standard room switch controls near entry

ILLUMINATION	Recommended	Minimum
	__ 20 - 30 f.c. at entry vestibule __ 50 - 70 f.c. at information and security desk area and elevator lobby __ 10 - 20 f.c. at seating areas	__ 15 - 20 f.c. at entry vestibule __ 30 - 70 f.c. at information and security desk area

COMMUNICATIONS	Recommended	Minimum
	__ PA system -- fire/security alarms __ Public phones (ample number, private) __ Computer and video wiring at security desk	__ Alarms as required by code __ Public phones

DESIGN STANDARDS -- COURTHOUSE TRIAL COURTROOM

GENERAL	Recommended Standards	Minimum Standards
__ **Occupancy**	__ Potentially 20 to 30 or more in trial area __ 130 maximum in spectator seating	__ Allow minimum of 23 in trial area __ Minimum of 50 to 75 in spectator seating
__ **Plan Dimensions & Floor Area**	__ Approx. 2-to-1 length-to-width room propor- tions, w/ 40% to 60% of total for trial activitiy and the rest for public spectator seating __ 1,500 s.f.; small court, public seating up to 80 __ 2,400 s.f., average court w/ seating up to 125	__ 1,300 s.f.; small court, public seating up to 75 (800 s.f. for trial, 500 s.f. for public seating) __ 1,600 s.f., average court w/ seating up to 125 (900 s.f. for trial, 700 sq. ft for public seating)
__ **Ceiling Height**	__ 14' to 16'	__ 12' ceiling in smaller courts
__ **Plan features**	__ Up to ten adjacent auxiliary rooms and seven entry/egress points for varied court functions	__ Municipal courts at police stations are for cursory processing; have minimal facilities and may be multi-purpose meeting rooms

FINISHES	Cost Categories A	B	C
__ **Floors & Sub-structure**	__ Sound isolated substructure __ Carpet, heavy to medium wear, padded in trial area	__ Sound isolated substructure __ Carpet, medium, glue down	__ Carpet, medium, glued __ Vinyl or asphalt tile at public seating area
__ **Wainscot**	__ Wood paneling __ Marble/wood combination	__ Partial wood paneling __ Plaster __ Vinyl wall cover	__ If no wainscot and if seats are movable, provide protective chair rail
__ **Counters & Built-in Furnishings**	__ Custom hardwood finishes, brass accessories	__ Manufactured units, wood veneer __ Wood and plastic laminate combinations	__ Plastic laminate surfaces
__ **Walls & Substructure**	__ 1-hour fire rating or more, as per building code __ Finish material flame spread ratings as per code __ Sound-isolated construction __ Wood paneling __ Plaster __ Gypsum wallboard with fabric or vinyl	__ Fire ratings as per building code __ Gypsum wallboard with fab- ric or vinyl __ Wood paneling at judge's area	__ Fire ratings as per building code __ Gypsum board, painted __ Concrete block w/furred gypsum board __ Concrete block
__ **Ceiling & Sub-structure**	__ Suspended acoustic tile, concealed grid, integrated lighting or integral ceiling with acoustical treatment	__ Suspended acoustic tile with integrated lighting __ Suspended gypsum board with acoustic treament	__ Suspended acoustic tile, exposed grid __ Gypsum board w/ acoustic treatment
__ **Acoustics**	__ Reflective back panel to aid uniform sound distribution __ Sound isolated substructure __ Acoustical ceiling with re- flective surfaces as re- quired for uniform sound transmission __ 0.8 - 1.0 seconds revir- beration time __ NC 25, STC 45-50 __ Door gaskets at all edges __ Sound lock entry vestibule __ Ceiling speakers __ Noisy vents not allowable	__ Provide for speech clarity within the courtroom with- out sound transfer to or from surrounding spaces __ Other provisions as per Cost Category A	__ As per Cost Category B

DESIGN STANDARDS -- COURTHOUSE TRIAL COURTROOM

DOORS & WINDOWS	Recommended	Minimum
__ **Doors**	__ Double-doors at main entry with pivot hinges, panic bars, closers and stile locks or other secure locking when room not in use __ Sound lock entry vestibule w/pushplate operation for interior double doors -- entry doors must be handicap accessible __ Doors 1-3/4" solid-core with sound proofing gaskets at all edges (extra large doors for large courtrooms may be 2-1/4" thick) __ Security doors with vision panels, and locking apparatus at auxiliary doors such as at adjacent prisoner holding room	__ 1-3/4" solid core doors are minimum for access to peripheral spaces __ Entry must be convenient for handicapped __ Noise from exterior corridor must not intrude upon courtroom activity
__ **Frames**	__ 16 gauge steel frames, with extra reinforcing at wall and floor anchors	__ 16 gauge steel frames
__ **Hardware**	__ Quiet, concealed automatic closers __ Security locks to control access to and from peripheral areas -- locking controlled by bailiff and building security officers	__ All security doors with automatic closers, vision panels, sound gasketing, and controlled locking systems
__ **Windows**	__ Window light not recommended __ If daylighting is required, provide high windows to avoid distraction of outside events, __ Sound isolation double-glazing __ Blackout blinds for slide or film presentations of evidence __ Any glazing must be secure, without operable sash	__ Windows or daylighting not recommended, but if required, follow Recommended standards in the left column

FIXTURES/EQUIPMENT	Recommended	Minimum
__ **Special furnishings**	__ Portable lectern with light and microphone __ Secure space for storage of VCR, tape recorders, overhead and slide projector, projector stands, flip-charts, etc.	__ Secure storage accessible to courtroom for all A/V and presentation equipment and furnishings
__ **Audio-Visual**	__ Any items built-in must be unobtrusive until required for use __ Projection screen __ Tack board __ Chalk board __ Closed circuit video system for testimony and observation in rooms other than the courtroom	__ Ready access to projection screens, chalk boards, etc. from near-by storage
__ **Seating**	__ Built in swivel armchair seating for juries __ Padded pew seating for spectators __ Movable seating for judge, clerk, reporter, press, and attorneys	__ Movable furniture for court officers __ Pews or movable seats for jury and public

PLUMBING	Recommended	Minimum
__ **Water Supply**	__ Convenience sink accessible to courtroom __ Drinking fountain accessible to courtroom __ Public and other restrooms readily accessible to courtroom	N/A

DESIGN STANDARDS -- COURTHOUSE TRIAL COURTROOM

HVAC	Recommended	Minimum
__ Occupancy estimate	__ As per program, or allow for up to 30 occupants in trial area, a minimum of 50 and maximum of 150 in public seating and a possible separate area for news media in large courts	__ 60 per 1,000 s.f.
__ Heating	__ Temperatures 68° to 71°F.	__ Temperatures 68° to 71°F.
__ Ventilation	__ 25 - 35 cfm outdoor air per occupant	__ 25 cfm outdoor air per occupant
__ HVAC System & Controls	__ Central HVAC system with individual room control	__ Central system with individual room or zone control -- thermostat control at courtroom __ Warm & cool air forced air (zoned) __ Package systems not recommended
	CAUTIONS: __ Because of the tedious nature of court activity and the importance to all of remaining alert, stale, warm, or humid air is not allowable __ Clarity of spoken testimony is crucial, so noisy air supply or returns are not allowable __ Since ceilings are high, avoid dead air space or short- circuit of fresh air in ceiling air supply and exhausts	__ Even at minimum construction cost, provide generous fresh air supply and individual room temperature control

ELECTRICAL POWER	Recommended	Minimum
__ Power Outlets	__ Floor outlets at attorney's tables __ Outlet at front of jury box __ Outlets for clerk and court reporter __ Outlet at judge's station __ Outlets for movable lectern __ Audio visual outlets: projectors, video, X-ray viewer, sound amplifiers, tape players, etc. __ Outlets at press section or rear of seating for video cameras __ Other outlets as required for janitorial __ Wall clock outlet	__ Outlet at front of jury box __ Outlets for clerk and court reporter __ Outlet at judge's station __ Audio visual outlets: projectors, video, X-ray viewer, sound amplifiers, tape players, etc. __ Other outlets as required for janitorial

LIGHTING	Recommended	Minimum
__ Lamps	__ Diffused ambient lighting for public area __ Variable high level downlights at trial area __ Task lamps for judge, clerk, court reporter, attorneys, and at witness stand	__ Standard ceiling fixtures for trial and public seating areas __ Outlets for task lights as needed for judge, clerk, and court reporter
__ Switching	__ Dimmer for ambient lighting -- separate controls for seating and trial areas __ Dimmer and other switches controlled by bailiff	__ Switching at bailif's station

ILLUMINATION	Recommended	Minimum
	__ 70 - 80 f.c. in trial activity area __ 30 f.c. in public seating area	__ 70 f.c. in trial activity area __ 30 f.c. in public seating area

COMMUNICATIONS	Recommended	Minimum
__ Telephone/paging __ Sound system __ Security	__ Call signal system for witnesses, other paging __ Microphone for witnesses and ceiling speakers __ Phone and security alarm at judge's station __ Phone and security alarm at bailiff's station	__ Call signal system for calling witnesses __ Security alarm at judge's station

DESIGN STANDARDS -- COURTHOUSE JUDGE'S CHAMBERS

GENERAL	Recommended Standards	Minimum Standards
__ Occupancy	__ Judge and secretary __ Conference space for up to 12 people	__ Same
__ Floor Area	__ Office and conference, 380 s.f. __ Waiting, 140 s.f. (at secretary's space) __ Secretary, 180 s.f. __ Workspace & files, 240 s.f. __ Private lavatory & closet, 48 s.f.	__ Office and conference, 250 s.f. __ Waiting, 120 s.f. (at secretary's space) __ Secretary, 120 s.f. __ Workspace & files, 170 s.f. __ Private lavatory, 40 s.f
__ Ceiling Height	__ 9 - 12'	__ 9'
__ Plan features	__ Private, restricted access __ Comfortable and conducive to concentration	

FINISHES	Cost Categories		
	A	B	C
__ Floors & Sub-structure	__ Sound isolated substructure __ Padded carpet, wool or comparable fabric	__ Sound isolated substructure __ Padded carpet for medium wear	__ Carpet, medium, glued __ Vinyl in reception area and/or separate work area
__ Wainscot	__ Wood paneling __ Marble/wood combination	__ Partial wood paneling __ Plaster __ Vinyl wall cover	__ If no wainscot, provide protective chair rail at conference space and waiting space
__ Counters & Built-in Furnishings	__ Custom hardwood finishes, brass accessories	__ Manufactured units, wood veneer __ Wood and plastic laminate combinations	__ Wood and plastic laminate combinations
__ Walls & Substructure	__ 1-hour fire rating or more, as per building code __ Finish material flame spread ratings as per code __ Sound-isolated construction __ Wood paneling __ Plaster __ Gypsum wallboard w/ fabric or vinyl	__ Fire ratings as per building code __ Gypsum board with fabric or vinyl __ Wood paneling at judge's desk area	__ Fire ratings as per building code __ Gypsum board with fabric or vinyl __ Plaster
__ Ceiling & Sub-structure	__ Integral ceiling, plaster or gypsum board, with integrated lighting __ Sound isolated substructure	__ Suspended acoustic tile with integrated lighting __ Suspended gypsum board ceiling with acoustic treatment	__ Suspended acoustic tile, exposed grid __ Gypsum board with acoustic treatment
__ Acoustics	__ Provide for speech privacy with no sound transfer to or from outside or surrounding spaces __ NC 30, STC 45-50 __ Doors gasketed at all edges	__ Provisions as per Cost Category A	__ All provisions as much as possible as per Cost Category A

66

DESIGN STANDARDS -- COURTHOUSE JUDGE'S CHAMBERS

DOORS & WINDOWS	Recommended	Minimum
__ **Doors**	__ Doors 1-3/4" solid-core with sound proofing gaskets at all edges	__ 1-3/4" solid core doors are minimum for access to peripheral spaces __No sound transfer allowed from or to other rooms or exterior corridor
__ **Frames**	__ 16 gauge steel	__ 16 gauge steel or extra-sturdy wood jamb and frame
__ **Hardware**	__ Quiet, concealed automatic closers __ Security lock to control access to and from peripheral areas -- locking controlled by judge, bailiff, secretary, and building security officers	__ Automatic closers, sound gasketing, and controlled locking systems
__ **Windows**	__ Windows should provide views and ventilation conducive to concentrated work __ Double-pane for noise insulation from exterior __ Provide blinds and black out screens __ Operable sash not accessible from the exterior	__ As per Cost Category A

FIXTURES/EQUIPMENT	Recommended	Minimum
__ **Special furnishings**	__ Work counter, reading shelf __ Built-in book shelves, from floor level to top of door height, most shelves 10" wide __ Vault and secure, concealed storage space __ Barrier and gate between reception waiting space and secretarial buffer space	__ Bookshelves
__ **Audio-Visual/Meeting Equipment**	__ Any items built-in must be unobtrusive until required for use in meetings or pretrial hearings __ Projection screen __ Tack board __ Chalk board	__ Ready access to projection screens, chalk boards, etc. from near-by storage

PLUMBING	Recommended	Minimum
__ **Fixtures**	__ Lavatory with medicine cabinet, toilet, shower, and dressing area __ Drinking fountain accessible to reception waiting area	__ Toilet and lavatory with medicine cabinet

67

DESIGN STANDARDS -- COURTHOUSE JUDGE'S CHAMBERS

HVAC	Recommended	Minimum
__ Occupancy estimate	__ As per program, or allow for up to 16 occupants	__ As per program
__ Ventilation	__ 25 - 35 cfm outdoor air per occupant	__ 25 cfm outdoor air per occupant
__ HVAC System & Controls	__ Temperature controlled by individual thermostat __ Central HVAC system with individual room control	__ If climate is zone controlled, temperatures 68° to 72° F. __ Even at minimum construction cost, provide generous fresh air supply and individual room control

ELECTRICAL POWER	Recommended	Minimum
__ Power Outlets	__ Task lighting outlets near desk and work stations __ Outlets for office equipment: dictation machine, computer, etc. __ Outlet for VCR and video __ Audio visual outlets: projectors, video tape player, etc. at conference space __ Secretarial office outlets for typewriter, computer, copier, Fax, dictation, etc. __ Waiting space or corridor outlet for janitor __ Wall clocks, judge's office and reception	__ Standard office equipment outlets for judge and secretary __ Outlets at conference area for audio visual equipment

LIGHTING	Recommended	Minimum
__ Lamps	__ Diffused down lights, wall wash lights __ Variable overall incandescent ceiling lighting __ Spot lighting at book shelves __ Down lights at reading shelf __ Task lamps for judge __ Floor lamps in informal conference area	__ Ambient ceiling lighting __ Bright ceiling light or spots for bookshelves and work areas
__ Switching	__ Dimmer controls all fixed lights	__ Standard room switch controls __ Dimmer at conference area

ILLUMINATION		
	Recommended	Minimum
	__ 60 - 90 f.c. on work surfaces __ Minimal background dark to light contrast	__ 50 - 80 f.c. on work surfaces

COMMUNICATIONS	Recommended	Minimum
__ Telephone/Security	__ Multiple-line phone for judge and secretary __ Fax line __ Intercom __ Security alarm for judge and secretary	__ Phones and security alarms

68

DESIGN STANDARDS -- COURTHOUSE CONFERENCE ROOMS

GENERAL	Recommended Standards	Minimum Standards
__ **Occupancies**	__ As per program	__ As per program

__ **Floor Areas**	__ 250 s.f. for standard conference space
	__ 500 s.f. per 15 people
	__ Interior rooms are preferred
	__ Net s.f.. per person:
	   25 s.f. per person for up to 8 people
	   20 s.f. per person for 8 to 10 people
	   18 s.f. per person for 20 to 40 people
		__ 200 s.f. for standard conference spaces

__ **Ceiling Height**	__ 9' - 12'	
__ **Plan features**	__ Security controlled access to all rooms	

FINISHES	Cost Categories		
	A	B	C
__ **Floors & Sub-structure**	__ Sound isolated substructure __ Carpet rated for medium to heavy wear, padded	__ Sound isolated substructure __ Carpet, medium, padded __ Vinyl in separate secretarial and clerical work areas	__ Carpet, medium, direct glue __ Vinyl
__ **Wainscot**	__ Partial wood veneer paneling with chair rail	__ If no wainscot, provide protective chair rail at conference space and waiting space	__ As per Cost Category B
__ **Walls & Substructure**	__ 1-hour fire rating or more, as per building code __ Finish material flame spread ratings as per code __ Sound-isolated construction __ Wood paneling __ Plaster __ Gypsum wallboard w/ fabric or heavy grade vinyl	__ Fire ratings as per building code __ Gypsum board w/ fabric or vinyl	__ Fire ratings as per building code __ Gypsum board w/ fabric or vinyl
__ **Ceiling & Sub-structure**	__ Integral ceiling, plaster or gypsum board, with integrated lighting __ Sound isolated substructure	__ Suspended acoustic tile with integrated lighting __ Suspended gypsum board ceiling with acoustic treatment	__ Suspended acoustic tile, exposed grid __ Gypsum board with acoustic treatment
__ **Acoustics**	__ Provide for speech privacy in private offices and conference areas __ NC 30, STC 45-50 __ Doors to private offices and conference rooms gasketed at all edges	__ Provisions as per Cost Category A	__ All provisions as much as possible as per Cost Category A

DESIGN STANDARDS -- COURTHOUSE CONFERENCE ROOMS

DOORS & WINDOWS	Recommended Standards	Minimum Standards
__ Doors	__ 1-3/4" solid-core with sound proofing gaskets at all edges	__ 1-3/4" solid core doors are minimum for access to peripheral spaces __ No sound transfer allowed from or to other rooms or exterior corridor
__ Frames	__ 16 gauge steel	__ 16 gauge steel or extra-sturdy wood jambs and frames
__ Hardware	__ Quiet, concealed automatic closers __ Security locks to control access to and from peripheral areas	__ Automatic closers, sound gasketing, and controlled locking systems
__ Windows	NOTE: Courthouse conference rooms are usually interior rooms; windows are not desired, but if used: __ Double-pane for noise insulation from exterior __ Provide blinds and black-out screens __ Operable sash must not be accessible from the exterior	__ As per Cost Category A

FIXTURES/EQUIPMENT	Recommended	Minimum
__ Audio-Visual/Meeting Equipment	__ Any items built-in must be unobtrusive until required for use in meetings or pretrial hearings __ Projection screen __ Tack board __ Chalk board	__ Ready access to projection screens, chalk boards, etc. from near-by storage

PLUMBING	Recommended	Minimum
__ Fixtures	__ Restrooms in controlled access areas accessible to users of conference space __ Drinking fountains accessible	__ As per Recommended

70

DESIGN STANDARDS -- COURTHOUSE CONFERENCE ROOMS

HVAC	Recommended	Minimum
__ **Occupancies**	__ As per program	__ As per program
__ **Ventillation**	__ 35 - 50 cfm outdoor air per occupant	__ 30 cfm outdoor air per occupant
__ **HVAC System & Controls**	__ Temperature controlled by individual thermostat __ Central HVAC system with individual room control	__ If climate is zone controlled, temperatures 68 to 72F. __ Central system with individual room or zone control __ Warm & cool forced air (zoned) __ Package systems not recommended __ Even at minimum construction cost, provide generous fresh air supply and as much individual room temperature control as possible

ELECTRICAL POWER	Recommended	Minimum
__ **Power Outlets**	__ Outlets for audio visual equipment __ Floor and wall outlets for transcription, recording and playback equipment	__Outlets for transcription and audio visual equipment

LIGHTING	Recommended	Minimum
__ **Lamps**	__ Variable incandescent ceiling lighting	__ Standard flourescent fixtures
__ **Switching**	__ Dimmer controls for incandescent lights	__ Standard room switch controls

ILLUMINATION	Recommended	Minimum
	__ 60 - 90 f.c. on work surfaces __ Minimal background dark to light contrast	__ 50 - 80 f.c. on work surfaces

COMMUNICATIONS	Recommended	Minimum
__ **Communications**	__ Intercom __ Security alarms	__ As per program or as per Recommended

DESIGN STANDARDS -- COURTHOUSE OFFICES

GENERAL	Recommended Standards	Minimum Standards
__ Occupancies	__ As per program for Clerk of the Court, Magistrate, District Attorney, Public Defender, Counselors, Court Reporter, etc.	__ As per program
__ Floor Areas	As per program, generally: __ 300 s.f. or more for official's private offices __ 200 s.f. for secretaries __ 250 s.f. for conference spaces	As per program, otherwise minimums: __ 250 s.f. for official's offices __ 175 s.f. for secretaries __ 200 s.f. for conference spaces
__ Ceiling Height	__ 9' - 12'	__ 9'-0"
__ Plan features	__ Controlled access to all spaces	

FINISHES	Cost Categories		
	A	B	C
__ Floors & Sub- structure	__ Sound isolated substructure __ Carpet rated for medium to heavy wear, padded	__ Sound isolated substructure __ Carpet, medium, glued __ Vinyl in separate secretarial and clerical work areas	__ Carpet, glued __ Vinyl in reception areas __ Asphalt tile in separate work areas
__ Wainscot	__ Wood paneling at officials' desk areas	__ Partial wood paneling __ Plaster __ Vinyl wall cover	__ If no wainscot, provide protective chair rail at conference space and waiting space
__ Counters & Built-in Furnishings	__ Manufactured units, wood veneer	__ Manufactured wood and plastic laminate combinations	__ Plastic laminate
__ Walls & Substructure	__ 1-hour fire rating or more, as per building code __ Finish material flame spread ratings as per code __ Sound-isolated construction __ Wood paneling __ Plaster __ Gypsum wallboard with fabric or vinyl	__ Fire ratings as per building code __ Gypsum board with fabric or vinyl __ Wood paneling at officials' desk areas	__ Fire ratings as per building code __ Gypsum board with fabric or vinyl __ Plaster
__ Ceiling & Sub- structure	__ Integral ceiling, plaster or gypsum board, with integrated lighting __ Sound isolated substructure	__ Suspended acoustic tile with integrated lighting __ Suspended gypsum board ceiling with acoustic treatment	__ Suspended acoustic tile, exposed grid __ Gypsum board with/ acoustic treatment
__ Acoustics	__ Provide for speech privacy in private offices and conference areas __ NC 30, STC 45-50 __ Doors to private offices and conference rooms with sound proofing gaskets at all edges	__ Provisions as per Cost Category A	__ All provisions as much as possible as per Cost Category A

DESIGN STANDARDS -- COURTHOUSE OFFICES

DOORS & WINDOWS	Recommended	Minimum
__ **Doors**	__ Doors to officials' private offices 1-3/4" solid-core with sound proofing gaskets at all edges	__ 1-3/4" solid core doors are minimum for access to peripheral spaces __ No sound transfer allowed from or to other rooms or exterior corridor
__ **Frames**	__ 16 gauge steel	__ 16 gauge steel or extra-sturdy wood jambs and frames
__ **Hardware**	__ Quiet, concealed automatic closers __ Security locks to control access to and from peripheral areas	__ Automatic closers, sound gasketing, and controlled locking systems
__ **Windows**	__ Windows in private offices should provide views and ventilation conducive to concentrated work __ Double-pane for noise insulation from exterior __ Provide blinds and black out screens __ Operable sash not accessible from the exterior	__ As per Recommended

FIXTURES/EQUIPMENT	Recommended	Minimum
__ **Special furnishings**	__ Work counters __ Built-in book shelves, from floor level to top of door height	__ Bookshelves
__ **Audio-Visual/Meeting Equipment**	__ Any items built-in must be unobtrusive until required for use in meetings or pretrial hearings __ Projection screen __ Tack board __ Chalk board or white board	__ Ready access to projection screens, chalk boards, etc. from near-by storage

PLUMBING	Recommended	Minimum
__ **Fixtures**	__ Restrooms in controlled access areas accessible to personnel __ Drinking fountains accessible to office personnel __ Fire sprinklers at open work areas and other spaces as required by code	__ As per Recommended Standards

DESIGN STANDARDS -- COURTHOUSE OFFICES

HVAC	Recommended	Minimum
__ Occupancies	__ As per program for Clerk of the Court, Magistrate, District Attorney, Public Defender, Counselors, Court Reporter, etc.	__ As per program
__ Ventilation	__ 35 - 50 cfm outdoor air per occupant	__ 30 cfm outdoor air per occupant
__ HVAC System & Controls	__ Temperature controlled by individual thermostat __ Central HVAC system with individual room control	__ If climate is zone controlled, temperatures 68° to 72°F. __ Even at minimum construction cost, provide generous fresh air supply and individual room temperature control

ELECTRICAL POWER	Recommended	Minimum
__ Power Outlets	__ Task lighting outlets near desks and work stations __ Floor and wall outlets for court personnel office equipment: computers, dictation, etc. __ Secretarial office outlets for typewriters, computers, copiers, Faxes, dictation machines, etc. __ Outlets as required for janitorial service __ Wall clocks	__ Standard outlets for office equipment typewriters, computers, copier, Fax, etc. __ Outlets at conference spaces for audio visual equipment

LIGHTING	Recommended	Minimum
__ Lamps	__ Diffused down lights, wall wash lights at private offices __ Variable overall incandescent ceiling lighting __ Spot lighting at book shelves __ Spotlights or task lights at work counters, large file storage areas, copier and other clerical workstations	__ Standard office fluorescent ceiling lighting __ Bright ceiling light or spots for bookshelves and work areas
__ Switching	__ Dimmer controls at incandescent downlights	__ Standard room switch controls

ILLUMINATION	Recommended	Minimum
	__ 60 - 90 f.c. on work surfaces __ Minimal background dark to light contrast	__ 50 - 80 f.c. on work surfaces

COMMUNICATIONS	Recommended	Minimum
__ Communications	__ Multiple-line phones __ Fax lines __ Intercoms __ Security alarms	__ Phones, Fax, and intercom lines

GYMNASIUMS

DESIGN STANDARDS -- GYMNASIUM ATHLETIC SPACE

GENERAL	Recommended Standards	Minimum Standards

__ **Floor Areas**
 	
NOTE:
Other athletic rooms as per program: Exercise, Gymnastics, Dance, Weights, Wrestling -- most with construction requirements as per main gym space
	__ As per program, dependent on number of basketball courts and peripheral activity spaces -- typically:
	   __ 7,500 sq. ft high school
	   __ 8,000 sq. ft. college
	__ Basketball courts are primary size determinants of gym size and proportions:
	   __ 84' x 50' court sidelines, high school
	   __ 94' x 50' court sidelines, college
	__ 8' to 10' neutral zone around sidelines
		__ As per Recommended with 3' minimum neutral zone around sidelines
		__ Court sizes as per Recommended
		__ Total basketball gym sizes
		   __ 5,600 sq. ft high school minimum
		   __ 6,000 sq. ft. college minimum
		
		NOTE: Even minimal facilities should allow for cross court fold up practice backstops, volleyball, dancing, and other typical events and athletics

__ **Ceiling Height**	__ 28' clear height within 8' of court sidelines	__ 22' clear height within 3' of court sidelines
__ **Bleachers** NOTE: Typical seating rule of thumb: 3 sq. ft. per person; balcony seating is not recommended	__ 20" width per person __ 32" seat to seat __ 38" main aisles __ 8' from edge of seating to court side boundaries, 10 minimum to court end boundaries __ 18" seat height and 9-5/8" riser height typical	__ 18" width per person __ 28" seat to seat __ 36" main aisles __ 6' minimum from edge of seating to court side boundaries, 8' minimum to court end boundaries __ Seat heights and riser heights as per Recommended
__ **Support Spaces**	__ Lobby with vestibule, ticket booths, rest rooms __ Storage room with 6' wide access __ See Locker Rooms section for other spaces	

FINISHES	Cost Categories		
	A	B	C
__ **Floors**	__ Hardwood (Maple typical) T & G strip floor over 2x2 or larger sleepers over concrete slab	__ Hardwood	__ May be asphalt as per exterior courts
__ **Walls**	__ Ceramic tile to 8' __ Exposed concrete block above 6', painted light __ Provision for padding at walls of gymnastic and exercise rooms __ 1-hour fire rating or more, as per building code __ Finish material flame spread ratings as per code __ Exit corridor walls require protection from damage	__ Ceramic tile to 6' __ Exposed concrete block or cinder block above 6', painted light color __ Fire ratings of other materials as per building code	__ Concrete block or cinder block, painted glossy white __ Fire ratings of other materials as per building code
__ **Ceiling & Sub-structure** WARNING: Gymnasium roof failures during construction, in high winds, and in winter storms are excessively common	__ Exposed roof construction typically truss or glulam structural system __ Ceiling should be light color __ Baffles or diffusers as required to prevent lighting glare	__ Exposed roof, painted light color	__ Exposed structure and roof
__ **Acoustics**	__ Sound dampening is usually not a consideration unless musical sound system is to be of very high quality or finishes are so reflective that gym noise would be well beyond normal	__ As per Cost Category A	__ Acoustics not a consideration

DESIGN STANDARDS -- GYMNASIUM ATHLETIC SPACE

DOORS & WINDOWS	Recommended	Minimum
__ **Doors**	__ Large airlock vestibules at lobby in regions of extreme hot or cold climate __ 16 gauge steel exit doors with panic hardware __ Exit door sizes and locations as per local fire code -- and should be in excess of code __ Handicap access automatic doors	__ As per Recommended
__ **Frames**	__ 14 gauge steel	__ 16 gauge steel or comparable store-front assembly
__ **Hardware**	__ Panic bar hardware __ Exit alarms and security locks	__ As per Recommended
__ **Windows**	__ High windows OK if oriented to prevent glare and heat gain __ Skylights not recommended	__ As per Recommended

FIXTURES/EQUIPMENT	Recommended	Minimum
__ **Special Fixtures & Equipment**	__ As per program, athletic facilities consultant, and athletic equipment manufacturers __ Storage for instructional materials such as white boards or chalk boards, screens, VCR and monitor, etc. __ Folding or roll-out bleacher seating is usually required for most economical use of space __ Ticket booths and fixtures at lobby for paid athletics __ Trophy display cases at lobby/public areas __ Bulletin boards, display boards __ Directory	__ As per Recommended

PLUMBING	Recommended	Minimum
__ **Fixtures**	__ Fire sprinklers as per code __ Wet and dry standpipes, fire hose cabinets, etc. all as per code and preferably in excess of code minimums __ Drinking fountains and public restrooms __ Janitorial maintenance closet with mop sink	__ Fire sprinklers and other fire protection as per code __ Public restroom with janitor's sink

DESIGN STANDARDS -- GYMNASIUM ATHLETIC SPACE

HVAC	Recommended	Minimum
__ Occupancies	__ As per program or allow for 70 persons per 1,000 sq. ft of athletic area, 160 persons per 1,000 sq. ft. of bleacher and corridor area	__ As per program
__ Heating	__ Temperatures 58° to 65° F winter dry bulb	__ Temperatures 60° to 68° F winter dry bulb
__ Ventilation	__ 35 - 50 cfm outdoor air per occupant __ 50% relative humidity	__ Outside air: 30 cfm per occupant
__ HVAC System & Controls	__ Package HVAC units OK __ Positive air pressure to block outside air __ Air lock vestibule to preserve air temperatures and buffer air pressure changes as people enter and leave the gym __ Central thermostat control	__ As per Recommended

ELECTRICAL POWER	Recommended	Minimum
__ Power Outlets	__ Outlets as required for janitorial service __ Junction box outlets for clock __ Wiring for electric scoreboard __ Power for motorized bleachers __ Lighted exit signs at exit doors __ Outlets for video equipment, sports broadcasting if press area provided	__ As per Recommended and program

LIGHTING	Recommended	Minimum
__ Lamps	__ Hanging mercury vapor or flourescent lamps as per recommendations of lighting consultant __ Diffusion panels with flourescent lighting __ Recessed or surface mounted flourescent lamps at lobby and circulation spaces	__ As per Recommended
__ Switching	__ Lockable switches, lighting control panel	__ Standard switches and dimmers, central light control panel

ILLUMINATION	Recommended	Minimum
__ Sales areas	__ 20 to 60 f.c. at athletic areas __ 5 to 10 f.c. at bleachers and circulation areas	__ 20 to 40 f.c. at athletic areas __ 5 f.c. at bleachers and circulation areas

COMMUNICATIONS	Recommended	Minimum
__ Communications	__ Fire and smoke detectors and alarms __ Public announcement system __ Stereo music system __ Security alarms at exit doors __ Surveillance video at remote corridors/stairs __ Pay phones at lobby/public areas	__ As much per Recommended as possible

DESIGN STANDARDS -- GYMNASIUM SHOWER & LOCKER ROOMS

GENERAL	Recommended Standards	Minimum Standards
__ **Occupancies and Floor Areas**	__ As per program __ Recreational: 1 shower per each 8 to 10 lockers __ School: 1 shower per 1st. 25 users plus one shower for each additional 4 users __ Assume 16 sq. ft. shower room per shower head __ Bay plan, 16 lockers per bay, 5' circulation at end of each bay	__ As per program __ Recreational: 1 shower per each 10 to 12 lockers __ School: 1 shower per 1st 30 users plus one shower for each additional 5 users __ Assume 14 sq. ft. shower room per shower head __ Bay plan, 16 lockers per bay, 4' circulation at end of each bay
__ **Widths, Spacings, and Clearances** NOTE: Primary considerations are safety and convenience which require extra wide traffic areas, non-slip surfaces, good visibility, and rounded corners at edges of walls and fixtures	__ Dressing lockers typically 12" wide x 24" deep __ Storage lockers typically 12" x 12" __ Each locker aisle bay should have center aisle with benches and lockers each side, 10' total centerline distance locker to locker __ 3' aisle locker to bench and 4' bench to bench distance with center aisle __ Benches 1'-6" wide __ 12' - 16"	__ Dressing lockers 12" x 12" __ Storage lockers 12" x 12" __ Each locker aisle bay may have seating extended from locker base with 4' center aisle, 7'-6" total centerline distance locker to locker (one row of benches at center of aisle is not recommended even for a minimal facility) __ Benches 1'-6" wide __ 12'

FINISHES	Cost Categories		
	A	B	C
__ **Floor** WARNING: Leaks in shower room floors and drains are a major troublespot; provide expert detailing and careful jobsite attention	__ Ceramic tile, non-slip finish, sealed __ Quarry tile, non-slip, sealed __ Slope to floor drains WARNING: Terrazzo, sometimes specified as a "quality" flooring in portions of locker or shower rooms is vulnerable to staining and can be very slippery; not recommended	__ Ceramic tile, non-slip, sealed __ Vinyl sheet (may be OK in locker rooms and related areas but not for shower or drying areas; provide underlayment)	__ Polished concrete slab with hardener additive __ As per Cost Category B WARNING: Vinyl and asphalt tile are subject to moisture damage and maintenance problems and are not recommended for locker rooms
__ **Base**	__ As per floor with 6" to 12" high coves at recesses for ease of cleaning	__ As per floor	__ As per floor
__ **Wainscot**	__ Ceramic tile winscot or tile full height	__ Ceramic tile	__ Concrete block, painted __ Paint -- water and mildew resistant
__ **Walls**	__ Ceramic tile over concrete block or cinder block __ Waterproof plaster __ Gypsum board, type W at related spaces	__ Gypsum board, type W, with moisture resistant paint finish	__ As per Cost Category B
__ **Counter tops**	__ Plastic laminate, HPDL grade	__ Plastic laminate	__ As per Cost Category B
__ **Soffits & Ceiling**	__ Plaster, hard, smooth finish __ Gypsum board, type W __ Paint must be water and mildew resistant	__ Gypsum board, painted __ Paint -- water and mildew resistant	__ Gypsum board, painted __ Paint -- water and mildew resistant

DESIGN STANDARDS -- GYMNASIUM SHOWER & LOCKER ROOMS

DOORS & WINDOWS	Recommended	Minimum
__ Doors	__ 3'-6" steel doors, 16 gauge, corrosion resistant __ Visual barriers such as "S" entry __ Raised threshold where flooring changes	__ 3'-4" x 1-3/4" SC #2 grade with moisture resistant finish
__ Frames	__ 14 gauge steel	__ 16 gauge steel
__ Hardware	__ Automatic closers __ Steel or brass push plate __ Steel or brass kick plate __ Lockable where security is a consideration __ Handicapped accessible __ All hardware with corrosion resistant finishes	__ Brass or chrome plate __ Plated metal, standard grade
__ Window light	__ High windows OK equal to 20% of floor area or more __ 50% operable where not a security problem nor a hindrance to effective air conditioning	__ High windows OK equal to 10% of floor area or more, especially if will assist ventilation

FIXTURES	Recommended	Minimum
__ Fixtures & Fittings NOTE: Top quality fixtures may provide considerable long-term economies in maintenance	__ Full length mirrors __ Make-up mirrors at women's facilities __ Heavy duty towel bars in drying room __ Standard restroom fixtures and fittings at toilet rooms __ Auxiliary lav, toilet, urinal, towel and soap dis- pensers for convenient handicapped access __ Dressing cubicles with bench and robe hook __ Bulletin and announcement board at entry	__ As per Recommended; except most fixtures surface mounted instead of recessed and economy grade rather than top grade __ Surface-mounted fixtures must not be barriers to the handicapped
__ Support Area	__ Office and supervisory area; glazed and cen- trally located	

FURNISHINGS		
__ Built-ins	__ Tile or concrete foot shelf in drying room -- 18" high, 8" wide	

PLUMBING	Recommended	Minimum
__ Fixtures	__ Scald-proof, automatic setting hot water supply for shower __ Showers may be prefab, non-integral to walls __ Floor drains at showers, drying rooms, locker room and toilet rooms at least 20% in excess of plumbing handbook or code minimums __ Drinking fountain	__ As much per Recommended as possible

DESIGN STANDARDS -- GYMNASIUM SHOWER & LOCKER ROOMS

HVAC	Recommended	Minimum
__ Heating	__ 70° to 72° F temperature __ Radiator or fan coil unit	__ 68° to 73° F heat at point 3'-0" above floor
__ Ventilation	__ 45 c.f. per minute per estimated full occu- pancy	__ 35 c.f. per minute
__ HVAC System	__ Forced air	__ Forced air
__ HVAC Controls NOTE: The primary problem with shower/locker rooms is ventilation and the accumulations of odors, mildew, etc. that accompany uncon- trolled ventilation -- venti- lation should be designed well in excess of minimal staddndards	__ Thermostat, zone controls __ Dehumidifyer strongly recommended __ Natural cross ventilation of high windows or vents also recommended	__ Central thermostat

ELECTRICAL POWER	Recommended	Minimum
__ Power Outlets	__ Readily accessible grounded outlets for: __ Janitorial maintenance __ Junction box for built-in electrical fixtures such as hair dryers __ Clock outlet	__ As per Recommended
__ Circuits	__ All outlets with ground fault interrupt protec- tion	

LIGHTING	Recommended	Minimum
__ Lamps	__ Recessed fluorescent or incandescent __ Make-up mirror and full length mirror lights	__ Central recessed or surface mounted fixtures
__ Switching	__ Lockable standard switch at entry with control at central supervisory area or office	__ Switch at entry, lockable

ILLUMINATION	Recommended	Minimum
	__ 40 - 60 f.c.	__ 30 f.c. general light

COMMUNICATIONS	Recommended	Minimum
__ Communications	__ Smoke and fire alarms __ PA system	__ As per Recommended

HOTELS

DESIGN STANDARDS -- HOTEL ENTRY LOBBY

GENERAL	Recommended Standards	Minimum Standards
__ Occupancies and Floor Area	__ As per program with allowance for widely varying occupancies and traffic loads	__ As per program
__ Ceiling Height	__ 12' - 24' and more __ Can include low (8') soffit at entrance vestibule	__ 10' - 12' in smaller hotels
__ Special Plan Considerations CAUTION: Orientation and signage are major problems in many hotel lobbies	__ Centralized registration and cashier areas __ Double-door air lock vestibule in hot or cold climates; extra wide for baggage handling __ Bell captain, baggage storage, concierge, and other special spaces __ Lobby lounge seating areas	__ As per Recommended Standards

FINISHES	Cost Categories		
	A	B	C
__ **Floors** WARNING: Smooth, hard surface materials sometimes used at entrances -- such as terrazzo, marble, smooth tile, or polished travertine are safety hazards -- even those treated to be non-slip are a problem when wet and when in contact with certain shoe sole materials	__ Recessed floor mat for rainy/ snowy climates at vestibule __ Non-slip rubber or vinyl tile at entry vestibule __ Nylon or other synthetic fabric carpet near entry should be rated for heavy wear, stain resistant and reasonably dark tone, glued to floor __ Carpet may be a different, complementary color and fabric at other spaces to allow easier replacement of the more heavily trafficked entry floor area __ Avoid light-tone reflective floor surfaces	__ Vinyl or asphalt tile at entry vestibule __ Synthetic fabric carpet rated for heavy wear near entry, glued to floor __ Complementary heavy to medium wear carpet at adjacent areas __ Other flooring considerations as per Cost Category A	__ Non-slip rubber or vinyl at entry vestibule __ Synthetic fabric carpet, glued
__ **Walls & Substructure**	__ Full-height store-front entry with automatic door opener __ Marble/other polished stone __ Interior wall finish typically plaster or gypsum board with heavy duty vinyl, fabric, or hardwood __ Exit wall fire ratings as per code	__ Foyer and exit area wall fire ratings as per code __ Gypsum board with heavy weight vinyl or fabric __ Plaster with sound absorbant treatment	__ Fire ratings as per code __ Gypsum board, painted
__ **Ceiling**	__ Plaster __ Baffle, metal, wood or other decorative ceiling __ Gypsum board with acoustic treatment __ Suspended decorative acoustic tile	__ Suspended decorative acoustic tile __ Gypsum board	__ Suspended acoustic tile, exposed grid __ Gypsum board
__ **Counterts & Built-In Furnishings**	__ Polished stone, hardwood	__ Plastic laminate	__ Plastic laminate
__ **Fixtures**	__ Public phones __ Handicap access __ Lighted fire exit signs __ Displays, event notice board	__ Fixtures as per Cost Category A and/or program	__ Fixtures as per Cost Category A and/or program

DESIGN STANDARDS -- HOTEL ENTRY LOBBY

DOORS & WINDOWS	Recommended	Minimum
__ **Doors**	__ Automatic doors as needed for heavy traffic and for most convenient handicap access __ Heavy-duty, glazed public entry doors with quiet operating hardware and automatic closers __ Double door air-lock vestibule to control indoor-outdoor temperature differentiations and outside noise	__ Glazed public entry doors with quiet operating hardware and automatic closers
__ **Frames**	__ 14 gauge steel	__ 16 gauge steel
__ **Hardware**	__ Quiet, concealed automatic closers	
__ **Related Fixtures**	__ Lighted exit signs at exit doors as per code __ Controlled locking with security alarm system __ Side panel glazing or safety vision panels at non-glazed doors	
__ **Windows**	__ Floor to ceiling front glazing with glass entry doors __ Floor base barrier and mid-height bar or barrier to prevent people from walking into full-height glazing	__ Glazing for clear viewing between interior and exterior near entry

FIXTURES/EQUIPMENT	Recommended	Minimum
__ **Special furnishings**	__ Information/registration counter __ Bulletin and event announcement boards __ Display and exhibit cabinets __ Event notice displays __ Ample signage and location map displays	__ As per program and Recommended standards

PLUMBING	Recommended	Minimum
__ **Fixtures**	__ Drinking fountain near entry and/or near restrooms __ Fire sprinklers as required by code __ Fire hose cabinets as required by code __ Decorative fountain	__ As per Recommended standards

84

DESIGN STANDARDS -- HOTEL ENTRY LOBBY

HVAC	Recommended	Minimum
__ Occupancies	__ As per program -- allowing for large variations in traffic at different times	__ As per program
__ Ventilation	__ 20 - 30 cfm outdoor air per occupant __ Air lock vestibule to preserve air temperatures and buffer air pressure changes as people enter and leave the building	__ 20 cfm outdoor air per occupant
__ HVAC System & Controls	__ As per primary adjacent public spaces __ Localized heating may be provided in waiting area of vestibule	__ As per main public areas

ELECTRICAL POWER	Recommended	Minimum
__ Power Outlets	__ Outlets at registration/cashier desk area __ Wall clock outlet __ Outlets as required for janitorial service __ Lighted fire exit signs at exit doors __ Floor outlets for reading lamps in lobby lounge	__ Outlets at registration/cashier desk area __ Outlets as required for janitorial service __ Lighted fire exit signs at exit doors

LIGHTING	Recommended	Minimum
__ Lamps	__ Overall incandescent and/or fluorescent ceiling fixtures __ Downlights or task lights at registration/ cashier desk and other focal points __ Spotlights and wall wash lights for displays and artwork	__ Fluorescent ceiling lights __ Down lights or task lights at registration/ cashier desk and other focal points
__ Switching	__ Central control, dimmers, and timers near security area or registration desk	__ Standard room switch controls near entry

ILLUMINATION	Recommended	Minimum
	__ 20 - 30 f.c. at entry vestibule __ 50 - 70 f.c. at registration/cashier desk area __ 10 - 20 f.c. at lounge seating	__ 15 - 20 f.c. at entry vestibule __ 30 - 70 f.c. at registration/cashier desk area

COMMUNICATIONS	Recommended	Minimum
	__ PA system -- fire/security alarms __ Public phones and house phones __ Computer wiring at registration desk	__ Alarms as required by code __ Public phones and house phones

DESIGN STANDARDS -- HOTEL GUESTROOMS

GENERAL	Recommended Standards	Minimum Standards

__ Floor Area and Furniture Sizes	__ 12' x 18' median standard size
	__ 13' to 14' x 18' for more varied furniture plans
	__ 16' x 18' and up is best
	__ Furniture sizes
	  __ King size bed = 6'-6" wide x 6'-6" or 7' long
	  __ Queen size = 5' wide x 6'-6" or 7' long
	  __ Double = 4'-6" wide x 6'-6" or 7' long
	  __ Chest = 1'-6" to 1'-9" deep x 3' to 5' long
	  __ Nightstands = 1'-6" square
	  __ Chairs = 1'-6" to 2" square
	  __ TV = 1'-6" x 2'-10" (varies considerably)
	  __ Coffee table or desk = 1'-6" to 2' x 3' long
		__ 12' x 16' for double occupancy
		__ 12' x 14' for single occupancy
		__ Furniture sizes as per Recommended Standards

__ Widths and Clearances	__ Aisles at beds = 36" __ Aisle at dresser = 40" __ Aisle at closet = 42"	__ Aisles at beds = 30" __ Aisle at dresser = 36" __ Aisle at closet = 38"
__ Ceiling Height	__ 8' - 10' (more height in extra large rooms) __ 7' soffits or light coves OK	__ 8' __ 7' soffits

FINISHES	Cost Categories A	B	C
__ Floor	__ Carpet, padded, non-static, stain resistant, reasonably dark tone to hide staining __ Ceramic or marble tile (partial flooring at luxury rooms and in warm climates) __ Vinyl at suite kitchenettes	__ Carpet, padded or glued __ Hardwood, standard grade	__ Carpet, glued
__ Base	__ Hardwood, Premium Grade	__ Hardwood, paint grade	__ No base
__ Cabinets, Casework	__ Wood, Premium Grade casework standard	__ Wood, Custom Grade casework standard	__ Wood, paint grade
__ Counter tops	__ Plastic laminate, HPDL grade __ Plastic composite __ Ceramic tile	__ Wood, Custom Grade __ Plastic laminate	__ Plastic laminate
__ Wainscot	__ Plaster __ Fabric or heavy-duty decorative wall cover	__ Fabric or medium weight decorative wall cover __ Gypsum board, painted	__ Gypsum board, painted
__ Walls	__ Fabric or heavy-duty decorative wall cover __ Plaster __ Gypsum board __ Mirror	__ Fabric or medium weight decorative wall cover	__ Gypsum board, painted
__ Soffits & Ceiling	__ Plaster __ Gypsum board	__ Gypsum board, painted	__ Gypsum board, painted
__ Acoustics	__ Substructure with acoustical separation from floors above and below __ Walls at 48 STC	__ 40 STC	__ 30-35 STC

DESIGN STANDARDS -- HOTEL GUESTROOMS

DOORS & WINDOWS	Recommended	Minimum
__ **Doors**	__ 3'-0" x 1-3/4" 18 gauge steel or premium wood solid core __ Solid core, or SC with sound isolation gaskets	__ 2'-10" x 1-3/8" SC #2 grade
__ **Frames**	__ 14 gauge steel __ Wood -- custom or prehung	__ 16 gauge steel __ Wood prehung
__ **Hardware**	__ Premium hotel key set with deadbolt __ Electronic lock __ Automatic closer __ Peephole	__ Standard hotel key set with deadbolt __ Inside chain latch
__ **Window light**	__ Equal to 20% - 25% of floor area or more	__ Equal to minimum of 10% of floor area AND no less than 10 sq. ft.

FIXTURES	Recommended	Minimum
__ **Built-in** Also see: ROOM STANDARDS -- HOTEL GUEST ROOM DRESSING ROOMS	__ Wall mounted artwork __ TV -- cabinet-mounted or wall-mounted	__ No minimum requirements

FURNISHINGS		
__ **Space allowances for built-ins** Also see: **Floor Area and Furniture Sizes** on previous page	__ Built-in dresser: approx: 1'-9" deep x 4' to 5' long __ Built-in headboard with nightstands, nightstands approx 1'-6" square or 1'-2" deep by 2' wide	__ No minimum requirements

PLUMBING	Recommended	Minimum
__ **Water supply & drainage**	__ Wet bar -- 1/2" supply, 1-1/2" sink drain __ See ROOM STANDARDS -- HOTEL GUEST ROOM BATHROOMS	__ No minimum requirements

DESIGN STANDARDS -- HOTEL GUESTROOMS

HVAC	Recommended	Minimum
__ Heating	__ 68° to 72° heat	__ 67° to 72° heat at point 3'-0" above floor __ Forced air
__ Ventilation	__ Exterior opening for fresh air access, 10% to 20% of floor area and 8 sq. ft. __ 20 c.f. per minute __ No ventilation noise	__ Exterior opening, minimum 10% of floor area and 6 sq. ft. minimum __ 15 c.f. per minute
__ HVAC System	__ Forced air __ Radiator or fan coil unit	__ Forced air __ Radiator or fan coil unit
__ HVAC Controls	__ Thermostat	__ Thermostat

ELECTRICAL POWER	Recommended	Minimum

__ Power Outlets	__ Outlets at:
	   __ Nightstands
	   __ TV
	   __ Makeup mirror at dresser or dressing table
	   __ Perimeter wall at floor lampor swag lamp locations
	__ As required by code
		__ Outlets at 12' centers max. and adjacent to each side of bed(s)

LIGHTING	Recommended	Minimum
__ Lamps	__ Wall-mounted reading lights at bed(s) __ Entry hall ceiling or wall lamp __ Swag lamp	__ As per Recommended
__ Switching	__ Room and hall light switches at room entry __ Switched outlet for floor, swag or table lamp	__ Switches at room entry

ILLUMINATION	Recommended	Minimum
	__ 10 - 60 f.c. adjustable range (mainly determined by occupants and individual lamps)	__ 40 f.c. general light (mainly determined by occupants and individual lamps)

COMMUNICATIONS	Recommended	Minimum
__ Communications	__ Smoke and fire alarm __ TV cable __ Phone jacks at bedside and at work table or desk	__ Smoke and fire alarm __ TV cable __ Phone jacks at bedsid

DESIGN STANDARDS -- HOTEL BATHROOMS

GENERAL	Recommended Standards	Minimum Standards
__ **Floor Area**	__ Basic 3-fixture bath with extra lav counter space and/or built-in tub ledge, 9' x 6' = 54 sq. ft. __ Bath with compartmented toilet, and dressing space = 120 to 160 sq. ft.	__ Basic 3-fixture bathroom, 8' x 5' = 40 sq. ft.
__ **Widths and Clearances**	__ 5' to 7' wide dressing area __ Toilet front distance to lav or to wall = 2'-8" __ Toilet space width = 3' __ Clearance between edge of tub to wall or fixture = 3'-6" __ Lavs at counter = 1-'6" for each lav plus 2' to 3' counter space at one or both sides	__ 3' to 5' wide dressing area __ Toilet front distance to lav or to wall = 2'-2" __ Toilet space width = 2'-8" __ Clearance between edge of tub to wall or fixture = 3' __ Lav = 1-'6" to 2' width
__ **Ceiling Height**	__ 8' to 9'	__ 8'

FINISHES	Cost Categories		
	A	B	C
__ **Floor** WARNING: Bathroom flooring must have waterproof underlayment	__ Ceramic tile, non-slip finish __ Polished and sealed stone, non-slip finish __ Carpet	__ Ceramic tile __ Vinyl sheet	__ As per Cost Category B CAUTION: Vinyl tile is subject to moisture damage and mainte-nance problems and should not be used in bathrooms
__ **Base**	__ As per floor	__ As per floor	__ As per floor
__ **Wainscot**	__ Ceramic tile	__ Ceramic tile __ Gypsum board with moisture resistant paint finish	__ Gypsum board with moisture resistant paint finish
__ **Walls** WARNING: Waterproof backing board is required at walls of tubs and show-ers	__ Ceramic tile over waterproof gypsum board __ Waterproof plaster __ Gypsum board, water re-sistant	__ Gypsum board, water re-sistant	__ As per Cost Category B
__ **Counter tops**	__ Ceramic tile __ Polished and sealed stone __ Plastic laminate, HPDL grade	__ Ceramic tile __ Plastic laminate	__ Plastic laminate
__ **Soffits & Ceiling**	__ Plaster: hard, smooth finish __ Gypsum board, water re-sistant __ Paint, washable surface and must be water and midew resistant	__ Gypsum board, water re-sistant __ Paint -- water and mildew re-sistant	__ As per Cost Category B

DESIGN STANDARDS -- HOTEL BATHROOMS

DOORS & WINDOWS	Recommended	Minimum
__ **Doors**	__ 3'-0" x 1-3/4" HC premium to #2 grade, 7 ply __ Door may be undercut for air supply for fan exaust	__ 2'-10" x 1-3/8" HC #2 grade __ Door may be undercut for air supply for fan exaust
__ **Frames**	__ 16 gauge steel __ Wood, custom or prehung	__ 16 gauge steel __ Wood prehung
__ **Hardware**	__ Privacy, Bath Lock, BHMA standard __ Knobs/handles -- Brass, bronze, ceramic latchset	__ Privacy, Bath Lock, BHMA standard __ Brass or chrome plate __ Plated metal, standard grade
__ **Window light**	__ Equal to 20% of floor area or more for baths with exterior walls __ Most hotel baths are interior rooms with fan exahust ventilation	__ Most hotel baths are interior rooms with fan exaust ventilation

FIXTURES	Recommended	Minimum
__ **Built-ins**	__ Robe hooks __ Lighted shaving and makeup mirror __ Full-length dressing mirror, lighted __ Tub/shower grab bar, towel bars, low and high soap dishes	__ Robe hook __ Mirror __ Tub/shower towel bars, soap dish

FURNISHINGS		
__ **Built-ins**	__ Built-in makeup counter with large lighted mirror	__ No minimum requirements

PLUMBING	Recommended	Minimum
__ **Water supply & drainage**	__ 3/4" supply __ 2" fixture drains	__ 1/2" supply __ 1-1/2" fixture drains

DESIGN STANDARDS -- HOTEL BATHROOMS

HVAC	Recommended	Minimum
__ Heating	__ 70° to 72° temperature __ Ceiling heat lamp	__ 68° to 73° heat at point 3'-0" above floor __ Ceiling heat lamp
__ Ventilation	__ 45 c.f. per minute in dressing area __ Fan with exhaust vent to outside if room does not open to the exterior __ Minimal air drafts	__ 30 c.f. per minute
__ HVAC System	__ As per guest sleeping room	__ As per guest sleeping room
__ HVAC Controls	__ As per guest sleeping room	__ As per guest sleeping room

ELECTRICAL POWER	Recommended	Minimum

__ Power Outlets	__ Easily accessible grounded outlets for:
	   __ Dressing counter or table
	   __ Makeup and dressing mirror lights
	   __ Lav area and shaving mirror
	__ All outlets with ground fault interrupt protec-
	    tion
		__ Grounded outlets near lav and dressing or
		    make-up counter
		__ All outlets with ground fault interrupt protec-
		    tion

LIGHTING	Recommended	Minimum
__ Lamps	__ Recessed incandescent with heat lamp __ Lights over or beside medicine cabinet mirrors __ Lights at makeup mirror and full length dress- ing mirror	__ Central recessed or surface-mounted fixtures __ Light above medicine cabinet
__ Switching	__ 3-way switches if bath has multiple access __ Wall switch with timer for heat lamp __ Wall switch for vent fan if fan required	__ Switch at main entry __ Wall switch for vent fan if fan required

ILLUMINATION	Recommended	Minimum
	__ 60 - 100 f.c.	__ 50 f.c. general light

COMMUNICATIONS	Recommended	Minimum
__ Communications	__ Extension phone jack __ Smoke/fire alarm, if required by local code	__ As required by code

DESIGN STANDARDS -- HOTEL GUEST ROOM DRESSING ROOMS

GENERAL	Recommended Standards	Minimum Standards
__ Floor Area	__ Allow 2' width for clothing wardrobe space and 3 linear feet of closet storage per person __ 4' to 5' wide dressing area	__ 2' wide wardrobes and 3 linear feet minimum __ 5' wide dressing area
__ Furniture Sizes	__ Furniture sizes __ Dressers = 1'-9" deep x 4' to 5' long __ Make up table = 1'-10" deep x 3' to 4' long __ Chairs = 1'-6" to 2" square	__ Furniture sizes as per Recommended Standards
__ Widths and Clearances	__ Aisle at dresser = 3' __ Aisle in front of wardrobe entry = 4'	__ Aisle at dresser = 3' __ Aisle in front of wardrobe entry = 3'-4"
__ Ceiling Height	__ 8' with 7' soffits (avoid high shelves if possible)	__ 8' with 7" soffits

FINISHES	Cost Categories		
	A	B	C
__ Floor	__ Carpet, padded, non-static __ Ceramic tile (if to match bath) __ Polished and sealed stone (if to match stone bath floor)	__ Carpet __ Ceramic tile (if to match bath)	__ As per Cost Category B
__ Base	__ As per floor __ Hardwood, PremiumGrade	__ As per floor __ Hardwood, paint grade	__ As per floor
__ Shelving, built-in storage units	__ Wood, Premium Grade	__ Wood, Custom Grade casework	__ Hardwood, paint grade
__ Counter tops	__ Polished and sealed stone __ Ceramic tile (if makeup counter to match bath) __ Plastic laminate, HPDL grade	__ Plastic laminate	__ Plastic laminate
__ Walls	__ Plaster __ Gypsum board with heavy-duty decorative vinyl or fabric	__ Gypsum board __ Medium weight decorative vinyl or fabric wall covering	__ Gypsum board
__ Soffits & Ceiling	__ Plaster __ Gypsum board	__ Gypsum board __ Hardboard or plywood paneling	__ Gypsum board

DESIGN STANDARDS -- HOTEL GUEST ROOM DRESSING ROOMS

DOORS & WINDOWS	Recommended	Minimum
__ **Doors** NOTE: Most hotel dressing rooms are open plan, without doors	__ Bifold, wood premium grade	__ 3'-0" x 1-3/8" HC #2 grade __ Bifold, economy or paint grade __ Sliding, #2 grade
__ **Frames**	__ Wood -- custom or prehung	__ Wood prehung
__ **Hardware**	__ Knobs/handles -- Brass, bronze, ceramic latchset	__ Brass or chrome plate __ Plated metal, standard grade
__ **Window light**	__ Equal to 15% of floor area or more for dressing rooms with exterior walls	__ No minimum requirement
__ **Skylight**	__ 2' x 4' or larger for interior dressing rooms or for light balance in dressing rooms with outside light	

FIXTURES	Recommended	Minimum
__ **Built-ins** Also see: ROOM STANDARDS -- RESIDENTIAL CLOSETS	__ Clothing hanging rods, low and full-length __ Clothing hanging pole-and-shelf combination __ Robe hooks __ Shoe shelf or rack __ Tie racks __ Ironing board or counter for touchup ironing __ Full-length mirror, lighted	__ Pole and shelf __ Robe hook

FURNISHINGS		
__ **Built-ins** Also see: **Floor Area and Furniture Sizes** on previous page	__ Built in dresser: approx: 1'-9" deep x 4' to 5' long __ Built in makeup counter with large lighted adjustable mirror __ Sewing machine space if not in laundry room __ Clothes hampers __ Drawer or bin storage units	__ No minimum requirements

PLUMBING	Recommended	Minimum
__ **Water supply & drainage**	__ 3/4" supply __ 2" fixture drains	__ 1/2" supply __ 1-1/2" fixture drains

DESIGN STANDARDS -- HOTEL GUEST ROOM DRESSING ROOMS

HVAC	Recommended	Minimum
__ **Heating**	__ 70° to 72° temperature at dressing rooms (this standard is for forced air heat, not radiant heating)	__ 68° to 73° heat at point 3'-0" above floor __ Forced air
__ **Ventilation**	__ 20 c.f. per minute in dressing area __ No noticeable air drafts	__ 15 c.f. per minute
__ **HVAC System**	__ Forced air __ Floor conducted radiant heat __ Radiator or fan coil unit in dressing areas	__ Forced air __ Radiator or fan coil unit
__ **HVAC Controls**	__ Thermostat, zone or room controls	__ Central thermostat

ELECTRICAL POWER	Recommended	Minimum

__ **Power Outlets**	__ Easily accessible grounded outlets for:
	   __ Dressing counter or table
	   __ Makeup and dressing mirror lights
	   __ Iron and task lamp
	   __ Steamer
	   __ Shoe polisher
	   __ Vacuum
	   __ Sewing machine
		__ Easily accessible grounded outlets at average of every 10 linear feet

__ **Circuits**	__ All outlets with ground fault interrupt protection __ Separate circuits for any fixtures rated at 20 amps or more	

LIGHTING	Recommended	Minimum
__ **Lamps**	__ Recessed incandescent __ Track lights for spots or floods __ Make-up mirror and dressing mirror lights	__ Central recessed or surface mounted fixtures
__ **Switching**	__ 3-way switch at each room access __ Door activated light at enclosed wardrobes	__ Switches at main entry

ILLUMINATION	Recommended	Minimum
	__ 60 - 100 f.c.	__ 50 f.c. general light

COMMUNICATIONS	Recommended	Minimum
__ **Communications**	__ Smoke and fire alarm, concealed __ Extension phone jack	__ Smoke and fire alarm in dressing room or at bedroom

DESIGN STANDARDS -- HOTEL MEETING ROOMS

GENERAL	Recommended Standards	Minimum Standards
__ Occupancies & Floor Areas	__ 25 s.f. per person for up to 8 people __ 20 s.f. per person for 8 to 10 people __ 18 s.f. per person for 20 to 40 people	__ As per program
__ Ceiling Height	__ 9' to 14' depending on room proportions	__ 9'
__ Plan Features and Considerations WARNING: Noise from other events is the worst problem in hotel meeting rooms	__ Maximum provision for conference room sound control and minimal acoustic, HVAC, and visual distractions __ Avoid noise distractions from service corridors other hotel spaces	__ Avoid sound transfer between meeting rooms or between meeting rooms and other hotel spaces

FINISHES	Cost Categories A	B	C
__ Floors & Sub-structure	__ Sound isolated substructure __ Carpet rated for heavy wear, glued	__ Sound isolated substructure __ Carpet for medium to heavy-wear, glued	__ Carpet, medium, glued
__ Wainscot	__ Wood paneling at small "Boardroom" executive conference rooms	__ Partial wood paneling __ Plaster __ Heavy-duty vinyl wall cover	__ If no wainscot, provide protective chair rail
__ Counters & Built-in Furnishings	__ Coffee service or bar counter alcove __ Marble or other polished and sealed stone __ Plastic laminate, HPDL grade	__ Plastic laminate utility counter	
__ Walls & Substructure	__ 1-hour fire rating or more, as per building code __ Finish material flame spread ratings as per code __ Sound-isolated construction __ Wood paneling __ Plaster __ Gypsum wallboard with fabric or heavy grade vinyl	__ Fire ratings as per code, minimum 1-hour __ Gypsum board with fabric or vinyl	__ Fire ratings as per code, minimum 1-hour __ Gypsum board with fabric or vinyl
__ Ceiling & Sub-structure	__ Integral ceiling, plaster or gypsum board, with integrated lighting __ Sound isolated substructure __ Partial hard surface sound reflective areas at ceiling and walls	__ Suspended acoustic tile with integrated lighting __ Suspended gypsum board ceiling with acoustic treatment	__ Suspended acoustic tile, exposed grid __ Gypsum board w/ acoustic treatment
__ Acoustics	__ Provide for speech privacy in private conference meeting rooms __ NC 30, STC 60 __ Doors to conference rooms gasketed at all edges __ Sound reflecting surfaces at speaker's area	__ NC 30, STC 40 __ Other provisions as per Cost Category A	__ All provisions as much as possible as per Cost Category B

95

DESIGN STANDARDS -- HOTEL MEETING ROOMS

DOORS & WINDOWS	Recommended	Minimum
__ **Doors** CAUTION: No sound transfer allowable from or to other rooms or exterior corridor	__ Steel doors -- 18 to 16 gauge with sound proofing gaskets at all edges __ Fire-rated assembly __ 1-3/4" solid-core with sound proofing gaskets	__ Steel doors -- 18 gauge __ 1-3/4" solid core doors are minimum for access to peripheral spaces __ Fire-rated assembly
__ **Frames**	__ 16 gauge steel __ 14 gauge steel at fire exit doors and doors to corridor __ Corner guards for protection from service carts, moving furniture in and out, etc.	__ 16 gauge steel or extra-sturdy wood jambs and frames for smaller rooms
__ **Hardware**	__ Heavy-duty latchsets __ Quiet, concealed automatic closers, sound gasketing, and controlled locking systems __ Panic bars for meeting rooms for more than ten people or as per code __ Kickplates	__ Heavy-duty latchsets __ Automatic closers __ Panic bars as per code
__ **Windows**	__ Windows are generally not desired for conference rooms but, if used, provide: __ Double-pane for noise insulation from exterior __ Blinds and black out screens	__ As per Recommended

FIXTURES/EQUIPMENT	Recommended	Minimum
__ **Special furnishings**	__ Small conference rooms may include built-in screen and white board	
__ **Audio-Visual/Meeting Equipment**	__ Any items built-in must be unobtrusive until required for use in meetings __ Projection screen __ Tack board __ White board	__ Ready access to projection screens, chalk boards, etc. from near-by storage

PLUMBING	Recommended	Minimum
__ **Fixtures**	__ Restrooms accessible __ Drinking fountains accessible __ Fire sprinklers as required by code	__ As per program

DESIGN STANDARDS -- HOTEL MEETING ROOMS

HVAC	Recommended	Minimum
__ Occupancies	__ As per program, or if not designated: 　__ 500 sq. ft. per 15 people	__ As per program
__ Ventillation	__ 35 - 50 cfm outdoor air per occupant	__ 30 cfm outdoor air per occupant
__ HVAC System & 　Controls	__ Temperature controlled by individual room 　thermostat __ Central HVAC system	__ If climate is zone controlled, temperatures 　68 to 72F. __ Central system with individual room or zone 　control __ Warm & cool forced air (zoned) __ Package systems not recommended __ Even at minimum construction cost, provide 　generous fresh air supply

ELECTRICAL POWER	Recommended	Minimum
__ Power Outlets	__ Outlets for audio visual equipment __ Floor and wall outlets for transcription, record- 　ing and playback equipment __ Floor and wall outlets for computer and video 　playback equipment __ Outlets for axiliary exhibit equipment __ Podium outlets and sound amplification __ Outlets for janitorial equipment	__ As per Recommended or as per program

LIGHTING	Recommended	Minimum
__ Lamps	__ Variable incandescent ceiling lighting __ Incandescent down lights for exhibits and/or 　note taking during A/V presentations __ Ambient fluorescent lighting, indirect preferred __ Wall washer lighting at tackboard wall	__ Standard fluorescent fixtures __ Peripheral incandescent light or lights 　on dimmer
__ Switching	__ Dimmer controls for incandescent lights __ Switch controls at entry and at speaker loca- 　tions	__ Standard room switch controls
ILLUMINATION	Recommended __ 60 - 90 f.c. on exhibit or work table surfaces __ Minimal background dark to light contrast	Minimum __ 50 - 80 f.c. on exhibit or work table surfaces
COMMUNICATIONS	Recommended	Minimum
__ Communications	__ Microphone jacks and ceiling speakers __ Video and computer __ House phone and intercom __ Fire and smoke alarms	__ As per Recommended or as per program

DESIGN STANDARDS -- HOTEL BALLROOMS

GENERAL	Recommended Standards	Minimum Standards
__ Occupancies & Floor Areas	__ Extreme variations in occupancy depending on events to be accommodated -- programming requirements must be set with care	__ As per program
__ Ceiling Height	__ 14' to 24' depending on room proportions	__ 14'
__ Plan features	__ Maximum provision for acoustic control so that ballroom social events don't interfere with other guest and meeting activities	__ As much as possible as per Recommended Standards
WARNING: Fire hazard and fire exit considerations must have top priority consideration in planning large social spaces	__ Built-in low stage or platform or space and storage allowance for large portable stage __ Built in projection room __ Adjacent coat checkroom	

FINISHES	Cost Categories		
	A	B	C
__ Floors & Sub-structure	__ Sound isolated substructure __ Carpet rated for heavy wear, glued	__ As per Cost Category A or as per program	__ Carpet, medium wear, glued
__ Wainscot	__ Decorative panels which may include finishes of: __ Heavy-duty vinyl or fabric wall cover __ Marble or other polished stone __ Plaster	__ Plaster or as per main wall __ Heavy-duty decorative vinyl wall cover	__ If no wainscot provide protective chair rail
__ Counters	__ Bar service counter alcoves -- polished stone	__ Plastic laminate utility counters	__ No built-in counters required, all service can be portable
__ Walls & Substructure	__ 1-hour fire rating or more, as per building code __ Finish material flame spread ratings as per code __ Sound-isolated construction __ Plaster with acoustic control treatments __ Gypsum wallboard with fabric or heavy grade vinyl __ Mirrors, polished stone, other special decorative surfaces	__ Fire ratings as per code __ Gypsum board with heavy-weight fabric or vinyl	__ Fire ratings as per code __ Gypsum board with fabric or vinyl CAUTION: If medium weight or lightweight finish materials are used to reduce first costs, they will wear quickly and be a source of very high maintenance costs
__ Ceiling & Sub-structure	__ Decorative integral ceiling, plaster or gypsum board, with integrated lighting __ Sound isolated substructure	__ Suspended acoustic tile with integrated lighting __ Suspended gypsum board with acoustic treatment	__ Suspended acoustic tile, exposed grid __ Gypsum board w/ acoustic treatment
__ Acoustics	__ NC 30, STC 60 __ Double-door sound lock vestibule if room opens to public lobby or corridor __ Sound reflecting surfaces at band or speaker's platform areas (if balanced with sound amplification)	__ NC 30, STC 40 __ Other provisions as per Cost Category A	__ All provisions as much as possible as per Cost Category B

DESIGN STANDARDS -- HOTEL BALLROOMS

DOORS & WINDOWS	Recommended	Minimum
__ Doors	__ 1-3/4" solid-core with sound proofing gaskets at all edges __ Steel doors as required for fire safety	__ 1-3/4" solid core doors
__ Frames	__ 14 gauge steel at fire exit doors and doors to corridors __ 16 gauge steel at doors to storage closets or other peripheral spaces	__ As per Recommended
__ Hardware	__ Quiet, concealed automatic closers, sound gasketing, and controlled locking systems at entry doors __ Heavy duty panic bar and related exit hardware	__ Automatic closers at entry doors __ Panic bar and related exit hardware
__ Windows	__ Windows are not desired for ballrooms although high glazing or decorative skylighting is sometimes provided	__ No windows

FIXTURES/EQUIPMENT	Recommended	Minimum
__ Special furnishings	__ Projector cabinet and/or counter __ A/V equipment storage cabinet	
__ Audio-Visual/Meeting Equipment	__ Any items built-in must be unobtrusive until required for use in presentations __ Rear projection room and screen __ Built-in projection screen	__ Ready access to projection screens, chalk boards, etc. from near-by storage

PLUMBING	Recommended	Minimum
__ Fixtures	__ Restrooms accessible __ Drinking fountains accessible __ Fire sprinklers as required by code	__ As per program

DESIGN STANDARDS -- HOTEL BALLROOMS

HVAC	Recommended	Minimum
__ Occupancies	__ Extreme variations in occupancy; program-ming requires special care	__ As per program
__ Ventillation	__ 35 - 50 cfm outdoor air per occupant	__ 30 cfm outdoor air per occupant
__ HVAC System & Controls	__ Locked individual thermostat __ Central HVAC system	__ If climate is zone controlled, temperatures 68 to 72F. __ Central system with individual room or zone control __ Warm & cool forced air (zoned) __ Package systems not recommended __ Even at minimum construction cost, provide generous fresh air supply

WARNING: A common source of complaint about ballrooms and large meeting room facilities is the quality of air and excessive variations in temperature

ELECTRICAL POWER	Recommended	Minimum
__ Power Outlets	__ Outlets for audio visual equipment __ Floor and wall outlets for transcription, recording and playback equipment __ Stage platforml outlets for computer and video playback equipment __ Outlets for axiliary exhibit equipment __ Podium outlet and sound amplification	__ As per Recommended or as per program

LIGHTING	Recommended	Minimum
__ Lamps	__ Variable incandescent ceiling lighting __ Incandescent down lights for exhibits and/or note taking during A/V presentations __ Ambient fluorescent lighting, indirect preferred __ Wall washer lighting	__ Standard fluorescent fixtures
__ Switching	__ Dimmer controls for incandescent lights __ Switch controls at entry and at stage platform area	__ Standard dimmer and room switch controls

ILLUMINATION	Recommended	Minimum
	__ 60 - 90 f.c. on exhibit or table surfaces __ Minimal background dark to light contrast	__ 50 - 80 f.c. on exhibit or table surfaces

COMMUNICATIONS	Recommended	Minimum
__ Communications	__ Microphone jacks; ceiling and front speakers __ Video and computer outlets __ House phone and intercom __ Fire and smoke alarms as per code	__ As per Recommended or as per program

INDUSTRIAL BUILDINGS

DESIGN STANDARDS -- INDUSTRIAL, LIGHT MANUFACTURING

GENERAL	Recommended Standards	Minimum Standards
__ Occupancies	__ As per program	__ As per program
__ Floor Area and Spans	__ Floor area as per program but all planning should provide allowance for expansion __ One story clear spans from 80' to 120' __ Two-story construction -- heavy steel frame, concrete, or heavy timber depending on loads and required spans __ Rule of thumb for change and expansion: plan for 20 year building life, 5 year plan life	__ As per program __ Clear spans 40' to 80'
NOTE: One-story, long-span construction is almost universally preferred over two- or more story construction		
__ Storage Systems	__ Pallet rack and other systems as per warehouse planning engineer, consultants, and manufacturers' recommendations	__ Systems as per storage system manufacturer
__ Ceiling Height	__ 14' to 18' light manufacturing assembly __ Height of product or machinery plus100% __ Allow for 24" clear space under fire sprinklers	__ 10' to 14' light manufacturing assembly __ Height of product or machinery plus 75% __ Allow for 18" clear space under fire sprinklers
__ Loading Docks	__ Loading docks 18' wide with side ramps __ Floor height 4'-4" for truck loading docks __ Floor height 3'-7" for train loading docks __ Confirm heights, clearances, other specifics with local controlling transport agencies	__ Loading docks 16' wide __ Heights as per Recommended Standards

FINISHES	Cost Categories		
	A	B	C
__ Floors & Sub-structures	__ Industrial grade wood block __ Portland cement concrete __ Asphaltic concrete with light broom finish __ Trowel finish where applied must have non-slip surface __ Floor drainage slopes at 1/4" per lin. ft., 1/2" per lin. ft. to slab drains exposed to weather at loading doors	__ Concrete slab, light broom texture finish NOTE: __ Specialized manufacturing may entail special air cleaning, toxic waste storage and disposal, security, structural, and finish standards, but otherwise there won't be much basic construction cost differential between A, B, and C cost categories	__ Concrete slab
__ Walls & Structure	__ Concrete, tilt-up __ Concrete masonry units __ If clear spans not used, structural bays typically 20' to 40' __ Light color paint finish recommended to improve lighting and safety __ Interior fire walls as per fire code		__ Heavy duty sheet metal or manufactured insulated panel construction __ Metal or wood pole framing with corrugated sheet metal
__ Ceiling & Sub-structure	__ Exposed truss and joist or beam and joist system __ Corrugated metal		__ As per Cost Category A
__ Acoustics	__ As per OSHA and state industrial safety standards	__ As per OSHA and state industrial safety standards	__ As required by code

DESIGN STANDARDS -- INDUSTRIAL, LIGHT MANUFACTURING

DOORS & WINDOWS	Recommended	Minimum

__ **Doors**	__ 16 gauge steel entry/exit doors with panic bar hardware
	__ Steel roll-up doors
	__ Actual sizes as per program, otherwise:
	    __ 12' wide x 12' high nominal size
	    __ 18' to 20' wide x 18' high, motor operated for larger or unpredictable size storage items
		__ Steel entry/exit doors as required by code
		__ Horizontal sliding doors
		__ Vertical lift doors (if head room permits; see door manufacturer's literature)
		__ 10' wide x 10' to 12' high nominal size
		__ 16' x 16' for larger size storage items

__ **Frames**	__ Heaviest-gauge steel frames, channels and corner guards as recommended by door manufacturers	__ As per door manufacturer's requirements
__ **Hardware**	__ Door kickplates, bumpers, rails, etc. to guard against damage from carts and vehicles	__ As per door manufacturer's requirements
__ **Windows**	__ High side-wall windows OK __ High-level protected factory sash or fixed glass with small lights for easy replacement	__ None required except for administrative office space
__ **Skylighting**	__ Roof skylights -- pyramid wire glass or plastic bubble -- spaced for maximum utility and even distribution __ Monitors and sawtooth roofs if maximum interior daylight is required	__ None required if the required overall lighting--natural or artifical--is minimal

FIXTURES/EQUIPMENT	Recommended	Minimum

__ **Special Protective Fixtures**	__ Heaviest gauge corner guards at all interior corners, door frames, and columns
	__ Column guards to 5' height
	__ Guards, bollards, and mesh protection at:
	    __ Electrical panels and switchboards
	    __ Water or steam supply lines
	    __ Sprinkler risers
	    __ Plumbing valves
		__ Corner, wall guard, and utility protection in general as per Recommended

__ **Equipment Layout**	__ Selection as per industrial planning engineer, consultants, and manufacturers' recommendations; 5 year plan life is average	__ As per program

PLUMBING	Recommended	Minimum
__ **Fixtures**	__ Water as required for manufacturing process __ Sprinklers, gaseous fire extinquishing systems __ Fire hose cabinets __ Color code painting of major plumbing units __ Floor drains at each structural bay __ Floor drains or troughs at large loading dock doors to catch rain/melted snow __ Washroom cluster sink and other washroom fixtures as per program	__ Sprinklers and other fire protection equipment as per code

DESIGN STANDARDS -- INDUSTRIAL, LIGHT MANUFACTURING

HVAC	Recommended	Minimum

__ Ventilation	__ Roof ventilators:
	  __ Motorized rotary units
	  __ Continuous ridge ventilation
		__ Roof ventilators:
		  __ Wind powered rotary units
		  __ Ridge vents

__ HVAC System & Controls	__ Central system with thermostat controls as per climate and special requirements of materials in storage and in processing __ Single source HVAC facilities planning should allow for expansion of the manufacturing space and should be at a fixed perimeter location, not centralized in plan __ 68° F to 75° F range is typical, 40-50% relative but must depend on product needs	__ Unit heaters and ventilators, thermostat controlled __ Roof-mounted systems OK for 1-story and sometimes 2-story buildings

ELECTRICAL POWER	Recommended	Minimum

__ Power	__ Dependent on lighting and need for motor power for machinery
	  __ 480/277-volt, 4-wire -- for larger buildings, all-purpose service
	  __ 120/240-volt, 3-wire for basic lighting types
	  __ 208/120 3- phase for motor power and electrical heating
		__ 120/240-volt, 3 wire

__ Power Outlets	__ As per program:
	  __ Junction boxes for all power machinery
	  __ Building maintenance outlets
	  __ Battery recharge outlets for electric vehicles
	  __ Time clocks
		__ As per Recommended

LIGHTING	Recommended	Minimum
__ Lamps	__ Surface mounted or suspended fluorescent __ Suspended mercury vapor lamps __ Color-corrected lighting if necessary to read color-coded manufacturing elements __ Exterior mercury vapor lamps at loading docks, security lights at entrances and exits	__ Fluorescent or mercury vapor lamps __ Task lights at inspection and paperwork areas
__ Switching	__ Master switchboard near main entry and administration or maintenance office	__ As per Recommended

ILLUMINATION	Recommended	Minimum
	__ 40-60 foot-candles overall __ 60-100 foot-candles for office work, paper-work, supervisory areas __ 3-6 foot-candles loading dock night lights	__ 40 foot-candles overall __ 50 foot-candles for office work, paperwork, supervisory areas __ 1-3 foot candles loading dock night lights

COMMUNICATIONS	Recommended	Minimum
__ Communications	__ Intercoms __ Time buzzers for breaks, lunch, shift changes __ Fire alarms and fire department call __ Security systems and emergency call __ Computer terminals and printers __ Phones/Fax	__ As per program

DESIGN STANDARDS -- INDUSTRIAL TECHNICAL CENTER

GENERAL	Recommended Standards	Minimum Standards
__ **Occupancies & Floor Areas** NOTE: Provision for changes in partitioning, HVAC, and utilities is of utmost importance in these building types	__ This category includes high-tech industrial work and research labs -- actual occupancies will vary considerably from building to building and through the life of any particular building __ As per program; program analysis must be done with exceptional care to allow properly for immediate functions and later changes	__ As per program but investigate needs and allow for large engineering, maintenance, and construction support staff __ Minimal work space allowances for high-tech work and research: __ Work benches from 1'-6" to 3' width __ Work aisles from 3' for single person access to 4'-5" for double use aisle __ Work aisles 5' and wider for two mobile workers working back to back
__ **Ceiling Height**	__ 10' to 12' depending on room proportions	
__ **Plan features**	__ Generous utility corridors and interstitial spaces for utilities and services	

FINISHES	Cost Categories		
	A	B	C
__ **Floors & Sub-structure**	__ Sound isolated substructure __ Static safe flooring, (may require grounding) __ Raised access floor __ Vinyl sheet or tile floor __ Carpet tiles	__ As per Cost Category A	__ Vinyl tile
__ **Counters & Built-in Furnishings**	__ Heavy duty work counters and tables __ Built-in audio/visual equipment and projection booth __ Lockable storage cabinets	__ Work counters as per program __ As per Cost Category A	__ As provided by client
__ **Wainscot**	__ Wainscot, if any, may require special substructure and finish materials, see below and see program	__ If no wainscot, provide protective rail to protect exposed walls from movable chairs and tables, carts, etc.	__ As per Cost Category B
__ **Walls & Substructure**	__ 1-hour to 2-hour fire rating as per program or code, whichever has highest standard __ Relocatable walls may require special substructure and finish materials, see program __ Sound-isolated construction __ Gypsum wallboard, painted or with heavy grade vinyl __ Grounds and supports for shelving, fixtures, and wall-mounted equipment __ Wall and corner guards	__ Fire ratings as per program or code, whichever has highest standard __ Gypsum board, painted	__ Fire ratings as per code __ Concrete block or gypsum board, painted
__ **Ceiling & Sub-structure**	__ Suspended ceiling; possible interstitial space for special cable and/or piping access	__ Integrated or surface-mounted fluorescent light fixtures at ceiling	__ Suspended acoustic tile, exposed grid
__ **Acoustics**	__ NC 30, STC 50	__ NC 30, STC 40	__ As per program

DESIGN STANDARDS -- INDUSTRIAL TECHNICAL CENTER

DOORS & WINDOWS	Recommended	Minimum
__ Doors	__ 1-3/4" solid-core with sound proofing gaskets at all edges __ Most doors with vision panels	__ 1-3/4" solid core doors are minimum for access to peripheral spaces
__ Frames	__ 16 gauge steel __ 14 gauge steel at fire exit doors and doors to corridor	__ 16 gauge steel or extra-sturdy wood jambs and frames for smaller rooms __ 14 gauge steel at fire exit doors and doors to corridor
__ Hardware	__ Controlled security locking systems __ Easy open, latch hardware __ Quiet, concealed automatic closers, sound gasketing, and controlled locking systems __ Panic bars at exits for meeting rooms for more than ten people or as per code __ Kick plates and other protection from carts	__ Controlled locking __ Automatic closers __ Panic bars at exit doors as per code
__ Windows	__ Windows OK for research or high-tech asembly rooms, but work benches should not be parallel to the windows because of glare and light control problems __ Exterior window walls are often reserved for offices and meeting rooms __ Double-pane if exterior noise or climate require __ Careful orientation and shade control to prevent glare and heat gain __ No vents	__ As per Recommended
__ Skylights	__ Skylights not recommended except for diffused light in very high ceiling work space	

FIXTURES/EQUIPMENT	Recommended	Minimum
__ Special Furnishings	__ All as per program	__ Some furnishings can be of ecomomy grade rather than premium, but these facilities normally require top quality furnishings of all kinds

__ Meeting Equipment	__ Conference rooms:
	  __ Projection screen
	  __ Tack board
	  __ White write boards, often full height	

PLUMBING	Recommended	Minimum

__ Fixtures & Piped Utilities	__ Wash sinks, emergency sinks
	__ Drinking fountains
	__ Fire sprinklers as required by code or alternative dry fire suppression system for electronic and other water-sensitive areas
	__ Special piping:
	  __ Vacuum
	  __ Oxygen, other gases (protected from leaking gas accumulation
	  __ Comparessed air
		__ As per program

__ Drains	__ Acid-resistant piping and toxin collection basins	

DESIGN STANDARDS -- INDUSTRIAL TECHNICAL CENTER

HVAC	Recommended	Minimum
__ Occupancies	__ As per program, or for preliminary rule of thumb estimates: __ 500 sq. ft. per 15 people	__ As per program
__ Ventilation	__ 40 - 55 cfm outdoor air per occupant __ Fume hoods with generous allowance for relocating and adding fume hood exhausts	__ 40 cfm outdoor air per occupant
__ HVAC System & Controls WARNING: 30% to over 50% of the construction budget goes to mechanical services on many of these buildings -- yet such services are often made subservient to non-tecnical architectural considerations . . . this is the primary cause of the most complaints and failures in these buildings	__ Temperature controlled by computer master system __ Central HVAC system __ Allow for extra heat build-up from electronic equipment __ Humidify to avoid electrical static charge build-up	__ If climate is zone controlled,temperature fluc-tuations may have to be carefully controlled for highly specialized work or research __ Central system with individual room or zone control __ Warm & cool forced air (zoned) __ Package systems not recommended __ Even at minimum construction cost, provide generous fresh air supply

ELECTRICAL POWER	Recommended	Minimum
__ Power Outlets NOTE: Provide automatic backup power systems for emergencies	__ Outlets for research and manufacturing equipment __ Floor and wall outlets for computer and video playback equipment __ Power and communications access may be through raised floor or ceiling	__ As per Recommended or as per program
__ Electrical & Communication Utilities	__ All cabling readily accessible and relocatable	

LIGHTING	Recommended	Minimum
__ Lamps	__ Ambient fluorescent lighting __ Variable incandescent ceiling lighting __ Incandescent down lights for work counters	__ Standard fluorescent fixtures
__ Switching	__ Dimmer controls for incandescent lights __ Switch controls at entry and at instructor's station	__ Standard room switch controls

ILLUMINATION	Recommended	Minimum
	__ 60 - 120 f.c. on work bench surfaces __ Minimal background dark to light contrast	__ 50 - 100 f.c. on work bench surfaces

COMMUNICATIONS	Recommended	Minimum
__ Communications	__ Computer and video __ House phone and intercom __ Fire and smoke alarms	__ As per Recommended or as per program

LIBRARIES

DESIGN STANDARDS -- LIBRARY ENTRY & FOYER

GENERAL	Recommended Standards	Minimum Standards
__ Occupancies and Floor Area	__ As per program with allowance for varying occupancies and traffic loads	__ As per program; see the introductory section on Libraries for rules of thumb for overall occupancies and spatial requirements
__ Ceiling Height	__ Ceiling as per main public reading area __ Can include low (7'- 6" to 8') soffit at entrance	__ As per Recommended Standards
__ Special Plan Considerations	__ Double-door air lock vestibule in hot or cold climates __ Centralized circulation desk for controlling entry as well as monitoring reading area and open bookstacks __ Vestibule should provide waiting space	__ As per Recommended Standards

FINISHES	Cost Categories		
	A	B	C
__ Floors WARNING: Smooth, hard surface materials sometimes used at entrances -- such as terrazzo, marble, smooth tile, or polished travertine are safety hazards -- even those treated to be non-slip are a problem when wet and when in contact with certain shoe sole materials	__ Recessed floor mat for rainy/ snowy climates __ Rubber or vinyl tile at entry vestibule __ Nylon or other synthetic fabric carpet near entry should be rated for heavy wear, stain resistan and reasonably dark tone, glued to floor __ Carpet may be a different, complementary color and fabric at the public reading room to allow easier replacement of the more heavily trafficked entry and circulation desk floor areas __ Avoid light-tone reflective floor surfaces	__ Vinyl or asphalt tile at entry vestibule __ Synthetic fabric carpet rated for heavy wear near entry and in circulation desk area, glued to floor __ Complementary heavy to medium wear carpet at adjacent reading areas __ Complementary carpet or vinyl flooring at adjacent bookstack areas __ Other flooring considerations as per Cost Category A	__ Vinyl or asphalt tile at entry vestibule __ Synthetic fabric carpet near entry and in circulation desk area, glued __ Asphalt tile at adjacent reference or stack areas
__ Fixtures	__ Book return repository __ Electronic security exit __ Coat/umbrella racks __ Public phone __ Handicap access allowing for handicapped and elderly __ Lighted fire exit signs __ Displays, bulletin board	__ Fixtures as per Cost Category A and/or program	__ Fixtures as per Cost Category A and/or program
__ Walls & Substructure	__ Walls at entrance may be continuation of exterior wall __ Full-height store-front entry may include automatic opener __ Interior wall finish typically plaster or gypsum board with heavy weight vinyl or fabric __ Exit wall fire ratings as per code	__ Foyer and exit area wall fire ratings as per code __ Gypsum board with heavy weight vinyl or fabric __ Plaster with sound absorbant treatment	__ Fire ratings as per code __ Gypsum board, painted
__ Ceiling	__ Suspended acoustic tile __ Plaster with sound absorbant treatment	__ Suspended acoustic tile __ Gypsum board ceiling with acoustic treatment	__ Suspended acoustic tile, exposed grid __ Gypsum board, painted

DESIGN STANDARDS -- LIBRARY ENTRY & FOYER

DOORS & WINDOWS	Recommended	Minimum
__ **Doors**	__ Heavy-duty, glazed public entry doors with quiet operating hardware and automatic closers __ Double door air-lock vestibule to control indoor-outdoor temperature differentiations and outside noise __ Automatic doors as needed for heavy traffic and for most convenient handicap access	__ Glazed public entry doors with quiet operating hardware and automatic closers
__ **Frames**	__ 16 gauge steel	__ 16 gauge steel
__ **Hardware**	__ Quiet, concealed automatic closers	
__ **Related Fixtures**	__ Lighted exit signs at exit doors as per code __ Electronic security gates __ Controlled locking with security alarm system	__ Side panel glazing or safety vision panels at doors
__ **Windows**	__ Floor to ceiling front glazing with glass entry doors __ Floor base barrier and mid-height bar or barrier to prevent people from walking into full-height glazing __ Double-pane for noise insulation from exterior	

FIXTURES/EQUIPMENT	Recommended	Minimum
__ **Special furnishings**	__ Circulation desk or information counter __ Package and coat checking station __ Bulletin and announcement boards __ Display and exhibit cabinets __ Electronic security detector at exit __ See entry vestibule related fixtures listed on previous page	__ As per program and Recommended Standards

PLUMBING	Recommended	Minimum
__ **Fixtures**	__ Drinking fountain near entry and/or restrooms __ Fire sprinklers as required by code	__ As per Recommended Standards

DESIGN STANDARDS -- LIBRARY ENTRY & FOYER

HVAC	Recommended	Minimum
__ Occupancies	__ As per program -- allowing for variations in traffic at different times	__ As per program
__ Ventilation	__ 20 - 30 cfm outdoor air per occupant __ Air lock vestibule to preserve air temperatures and buffer air pressure changes as people enter and leave the building	__ 20 cfm outdoor air per occupant
__ HVAC System & Controls	__ As per circulation desk area and main reading room __ Localized heating may be provided in waiting area of vestibule in cold climates	__ As per main public areas of library

ELECTRICAL POWER	Recommended	Minimum
__ Power Outlets	__ Outlets at circulation desk __ Wall clock outlets __ Outlets as required for janitorial service __ Lighted fire exit signs at exit doors	__ Outlets at circulation desk __ Outlets as required for janitorial service __ Lighted fire exit signs at exit doors

LIGHTING	Recommended	Minimum
__ Lamps	__ Overall incandescent and/or fluorescent ceiling fixtures __ Downlights or task lights at circulation desk	__ Fluorescent ceiling lights, recessed or surface mounted
__ Switching	__ Central control at circulation desk	__ Standard room switch controls

ILLUMINATION	Recommended	Minimum
	__ 20 - 30 f.c. at entry vestibule __ 50 - 70 f.c. at circulation desk area	__ 15 - 20 f.c. at entry vestibule __ 30 - 70 f.c.

COMMUNICATIONS	Recommended	Minimum
	__ PA system -- fire/security alarms __ Public phone near entry	__ Alarms as required by code

DESIGN STANDARDS -- LIBRARY READING ROOM

GENERAL	Recommended Standards	Minimum Standards
__ Occupancies	__ As per program with allowance for varying types of occupant densities: __ Readers requiring privacy and extra space __ Communal tables for groups of four to six __ Lounge readers __ Visiting student groups	__ As per program; see the introductory section on Libraries for rules of thumb for overall occupancies and spatial requirements
__ Floor Area	__ 40 s.f. per reader	__ 35 s.f. per reader
__ Ceiling Height	__ 8' to 9' -- reading areas less than 100 s.f. __ 10' to 14' main reading area __ 16' to 20' at room with mezzanine	__ 7'- 6" -- reading areas less than 100 s.f. __ 10' main reading area

FINISHES	Cost Categories		
	A	B	C
__ Floors & Sub- structure	__ Sound isolated substructure __ Nylon or acrylic carpet rated for heavy wear and glued to floor in heavy traffic areas __ Padded carpet may be provided in study area __ Tight weave, cut or loop pile __ Static removal is essential	__ Sound isolated substructure __ Carpet for heavy wear in traffic areas, medium wear elsewhere, glued __ Vinyl NOTE: Sound absorptive carpet flooring is preferred in virtually all areas of the library except utility spaces	__ Carpet, medium, glued __ Vinyl in reception areas __ Asphalt tile at adjacent reference or stack areas WARNING: Asphalt tile floors in combination with some types of movable chairs can cause extreme noise problems
__ Counters & Built-in Furnishings	__ Manufactured units, wood veneer, plastic laminate work surfaces	__ Manufactured wood and plastic laminate combinations	__ Plastic laminate
__ Walls & Substructure	__ Fire ratings as per code __ Sound-isolated construction __ Gypsum board with heavy weight vinyl or fabric __ Chair rail at exposed walls near movable seating	__ Fire ratings as per code __ Gypsum board with fabric or vinyl, medium weight __ Chair rail at exposed walls near movable seating	__ Fire ratings as per code __ Gypsum board with fabric or vinyl, medium
__ Ceiling & Sub- structure	__ Sound isolated substructure __ Suspended acoustic tile with integrated lighting	__ Suspended acoustic tile with integrated lighting __ Suspended gypsum board ceiling with acoustic treatment	__ Suspended acoustic tile, exposed grid __ Gypsum board with acoustic treatment
__ Acoustics WARNING: Exterior court-yards, atriums, and open stairs are common noise hazards for libraries -- noise levels are most acute at the upper floors affected by such elements	__ All surfaces sound absorptive __ 40-50 decibel electronic "white noise" recommended as background noise masking __ NC25 - 35, STC 45-55 __ Doors to adjacent offices and conference rooms solid core with sound gaskets at all edges	__ NC 25 - 35, STC 45 - 55 __ Doors to adjacent offices and conference rooms solid core with sound gaskets at all edges __ Sound barriers above adjacent floor-to-ceiling partitions	__ All provisions as much as possible as per Cost Category B

DESIGN STANDARDS -- LIBRARY READING ROOM

DOORS & WINDOWS	Recommended	Minimum
__ Doors	__ Heavy-duty public entry doors with quiet operating hardware and automatic closers __ Double door air-lock vestibule to control indoor-outdoor temperature differentiations and outside noise __ Doors to adjacent rooms 1-3/4" solid core with sound proofing gaskets at all edges __ Side vision panels at doors, wire glass	__ 1-3/4" solid core doors, gasketed at all edges __ Doors to adjacent rooms 1-3/4" solid core with sound proofing gaskets at all edges
__ Frames	__ 16 gauge steel	__ 16 gauge steel or extra-sturdy wood jambs and frames
__ Hardware	__ Quiet, concealed automatic closers __ Locking to control access to storage and maintenance areas __ Panic exit hardware as required by code __ Lighted exit signs at exit doors as per code	__ Automatic closers, sound gasketing, and controlled locking systems __ Panic exit hardware as required by code
__ Windows	__ Windows OK for restful views such as courtyard gardens or yard scenery, otherwise use high windows for daylighting, not views __ Street front windows are recommended by some consultants to show off interior space and activities __ Double-pane for noise insulation from exterior __ Operable sash not accessible from the exterior __ Orientation and blinds to prevent sun glare and heat gain	__ Windows as will enhance reading room environment -- views (use windows to avoid closed or forbidding appearance of the exterior of the building)

FIXTURES/EQUIPMENT	Recommended	Minimum
__ Special furnishings	__ Circulation desk and files __ Package and coat checking station __ Card catalogs __ Bulletin and announcement boards __ Display and exhibit cabinets __ Display shelves for periodicals, special publications __ Microform readers __ Work counters for library reference __ Study carrels (See "Research & Reference") __ Book shelves (See "Stack Area") __ Electronic security detector at exit	__ As per program and Recommended standards NOTE: Book shelving is NOT recommended at walls -- walls are best utilized for special wall storage such as magazines, displays, and furniture placement, especially study carrels
__ Audio-Visual Equipment	__ Video and VCR machines with headphones for sound -- located where not visually distracting to readers __ Headphone access for video, audio tapes, etc. (See "Media Area")	

PLUMBING	Recommended	Minimum
__ Fixtures	__ Drinking fountain near entry and/or restrooms __ Fire sprinklers as required by code	__ As per Recommended standards

DESIGN STANDARDS -- LIBRARY READING ROOM

HVAC	Recommended	Minimum
__ Occupancies	__ As per program -- allowing for wide variations in occupancy at different times	__ As per program __ For approximate estimating: 20 people per 1,000 s.f.
__ Ventilation	__ 20 - 30 cfm outdoor air per occupant __ Ventilation noise is not allowable in reading rooms __ Air speed at head level should not be greater than 50 f.p.m. __ For sound masking, use electronic "white noise" only	__ 20 cfm outdoor air per occupant __ Ventilation noise is not allowable in reading rooms
__ HVAC System & Controls	__ Central HVAC system with individual room control	__ If climate is zone controlled, temperatures 68° to 74°F. __ Central system with individual room or zone control __ Warm & cool forced air (zoned) __ Package systems not recommended

ELECTRICAL POWER	Recommended	Minimum
__ Power Outlets	__ Task lighting outlets near fixed reading tables and work stations __ Outlets at circulation desk __ Floor and wall outlets for copiers, microform readers, microcomputers, headphone systems, etc. __ Wall base outlets or outlet strips for all contemplated future electric or electronic equipment __ Wall clock outlets __ Outlets as required for janitorial service __ Lighted exit signs at exit doors	__ As per program and/or as required by code

LIGHTING	Recommended	Minimum
__ Lamps	__ Diffused down lights, wall wash lights __ Overall incandescent and/or fluorescent ceiling fixtures __ Book lighting fixtures at book shelves __ Downlights or task lights at work counters, card catalog files, circulation desk	__ Fluorescent ceiling lights, recessed or surface mounted __ Downlights at reading areas __ Book lighting fixtures at book shelves __ Task lights at work areas and reference areas
__ Switching	__ Dimmer controls at incandescent downlights	__ Standard room switch controls

ILLUMINATION WARNING: Library lighting is commonly inadequate despite its obvious importance	Recommended	Minimum
	__ 50 - 70 ESI (f.c.) for reading and study __ If reading lights are provided, 50 f.c. is OK for general lighting -- task lights non-glare __ 90% Visual Comfort Performance	__ 30 - 70 ESI (f.c.) for reading and study

COMMUNICATIONS	Recommended	Minimum
	__ PA system -- fire/security alarms __ Public phone near entry	__ Alarms as required by code __ See "Media Room" for other communications

DESIGN STANDARDS -- LIBRARY BOOK STACK AREA

GENERAL	Recommended Standards	Minimum Standards
__ **Floor Area**	__ As per program -- based upon existing and projected future book collections __ Very roughly: 15 books per sq. ft. with double sided bookstacks and 3' aisles __ Modular design is predicated on runs of 3'-0" long book stack sections with 1'-6" columns or wider columns combined with duct work or other chases -- thus a 5' center-to-center stack plan allows five runs of 2' wide stacks with four 3' aisles centered within a 20' sq. structural bay	__ As per program; see the introductory section on Libraries for rules of thumb for overall minimum occupancies and spatial requirements
__ **Ceiling Height**	__ 8'-0" - 10'-0" (if using up-lights reflecting on ceiling, 9' is required)	__ 7'- 6" (with shelf lights built-in or ceiling lights parallel to stacks, otherwise 8'-6" minimum)

FINISHES & SUBSTRUCTURE	Cost Categories A	B	C
__ **Floors & Sub-structure**	__ Sound isolated substructure if noise of moving carts might intrude on spaces below __ Rubber or vinyl floor may be used at stack areas separated from the reading area __ Stacks which are part of public reading room -- use Nylon or acrylic carpet rated for heavy wear, glued to floor	__ If not part of reading room, floor may be rubber or vinyl, otherwise carpet for heavy wear, glued __ Stack areas for books in remote storage may have linoleum, asphalt tile, or concrete floors __ Slab floors on grade or below grade must not permit any infiltration of water or water vapor	__ As per Cost Category B
__ **Walls & Substructure**	__ Fire ratings as per code __ Finish material flame spread ratings as per code __ Wall construction may be concrete, masonry, plaster, gypsum board, etc. as per adjacent construction	__ Walls below grade must be totally water tight and must not permit any moisture or water vapor infiltration __ Fire ratings as per code __ Gypsum board, painted	__ Fire ratings as per code __ Gypsum board, painted
__ **Ceiling & Sub-structure**	__ Suspended acoustical tile	__ As per Cost Category A	__ Exposed substructure, painted for light reflection __ Suspended acoustic tile, exposed grid __ Gypsum board
__ **Acoustics**	__ Not a factor except where stacks are part of a reading or study space __ Reading room acoustic recommendations for construction are NC 25 - 35, STC 45 - 55	__ As per Cost Category A	__ As per Cost Category A

DESIGN STANDARDS -- LIBRARY BOOK STACK AREA

DOORS & WINDOWS	Recommended	Minimum
__ **Doors**	__ 1-3/4" solid core, metal clad fire doors for isolated book storage stacks __ Double-swinging, push-plate doors may be used to expedite movement of book carts __ Sound-proofing gaskets if stacks are open to quiet reading areas	__ Doors located, sized, and specified to allow free movement of book carts __ Doors may be optional if adjacent space is a secured area
__ **Frames**	__ 16 gauge steel	__ 16 gauge steel
__ **Hardware**	__ Quiet automatic closers __ Security locking system controlled by head librarian	__ Automatic closers __ Controlled locking
__ **Windows**	__ Windows not recommended for stack areas	__ As per Recommended Standards

FIXTURES/EQUIPMENT	Recommended	Minimum
__ **Furnishings**	__ Stack sections are 3' long with 1' wide shelves -- 2' wide for back to back __ 3'-9" - 4'-6" double-loaded aisle __ 7'-6" high top shelf maximum __ 15' to 18' maximum uninterrupted run __ 12" shelf-to-shelf height with 4" base; tall books need 14" shelf- to-shelf height __ Open pedestal base recommended for easier floor maintenance and air movement __ Bracket shelving for easier shelf changes __ Cross ties across tops of bookstacks recomended for lateral stability __ Study carrels are sometimes included within stack spaces __ Microform readers and computers are sometimes included within bookstack areas __ Work counters	__ Stack sections as per Recommended Standards except flat bottom units may be used rather than pedestal NOTE: Book shelving is NOT recommended at walls -- walls are best utilized for work tables or study carrels (carrels that require users to face walls with users' backs to aisles will be least used)

PLUMBING	Recommended	Minimum
__ **Fixtures**	__ Fire sprinklers as required by code WARNING: Plumbing above stack spaces are a hazard -- major and minor leaks from plumbing have damaged numerous book collections	__ As per Recommended Standards

DESIGN STANDARDS -- LIBRARY BOOK STACK AREA

HVAC	Recommended	Minimum
__ Occupancies	__ As per program -- allowing for varying occupancy	__ As per program
__ Ventilation	__ If stack area is in reading rooms or if study and reading will occur within stack areas, the air quality standards for those rooms will be applied -- otherwise, 20 cfm outdoor air per occupant	__ As per Recommended Standards
__ HVAC System & Controls	__ Dehumidification may be required for closed book stack spaces -- library consultant will advise __ Central HVAC system with individual room or automatic zone control	__ If climate is zone controlled, temperatures 68° to 72°F. __ Central system with zone control

ELECTRICAL POWER	Recommended	Minimum
__ Power Outlets	__ Task lighting and power outlets at fixed reading tables, work tables, and carrels __ Floor and wall outlets for copiers, microform readers, microcomputers, etc. __ Wall base outlets or outlet strips for all contemplated future electric or electronic equipment __ Outlets as required for janitorial service __ Power supply for built-in bookstack shelf lighting	__ Power outlets at fixed reading tables, work tables, and carrels __ Floor and wall outlets for copiers, microform readers, microcomputers, etc. __ Wall base outlets, junction box access for future electric or electronic equipment __ Outlets as required for janitorial service

LIGHTING	Recommended	Minimum
__ Lamps	__ Built-in stack unit shelf lighting with individual bookstack row switches __ Overall fluorescent ceiling lighting in a pattern coordinated with stack layout for best illumination of book titles __ Task lights or wall/ceiling down lights at work areas and reference areas	__ Overall fluorescent ceiling lighting in a pattern coordinated with stack layout for best illumination of book titles
__ Switching	__ Controlled room switching	__ Standard room switch controls

ILLUMINATION WARNING: Library stack area lighting is commonly inadequate despite its obvious importance	Recommended __ 50 - 70 f.c. at reading areas, 30 - 50 f.c. in stack aisles	Minimum __ 30 - 50 f.c.

COMMUNICATIONS	Recommended	Minimum
	__ PA system -- fire/security alarms __ See "Media Areas" for other communications	__ Alarms as required by code

DESIGN STANDARDS -- LIBRARY STUDY, RESEARCH, REFERENCE AREAS

GENERAL	Recommended Standards	Minimum Standards
__ Occupancies	__ Varies widely depending on library type -- assume a closed separate space with direct access to separate stacks, microforms, computers, and copier	__ As per program; see the introductory section on Libraries for rules of thumb for overall occupancies and spatial requirements
__ Floor Area	__ 48 s.f. per person	__ 40 s.f. per reader
__ Ceiling Height	__ 10' - 12'	__ 9'-0"

FINISHES	Cost Categories A	B	C
__ Floors & Sub-structure	__ Sound isolated substructure __ Nylon or acrylic carpet rated for heavy wear and glued to floor in heavy traffic areas __ Carpet static removal is essential	__ Sound isolated substructure __ Carpet rated for medium wear, glued	__ Carpet, medium, glued __ Rubber
__ Counters & Built-in Furnishings	__ Manufactured units, wood veneer, plastic laminate work surfaces	__ Manufactured wood and plastic laminate combinations	__ Plastic laminate
__ Walls & Substructure	__ 1-hour fire rating or more, as per building code __ Finish material flame spread ratings as per code __ Sound-isolated construction __ Gypsum board with heavy weight vinyl or fabric __ Chair rail at exposed walls near movable seating	__ Fire ratings as per code __ Gypsum board with medium to heavy weight vinyl or fabric __ Chair rail at exposed walls near movable seating	__ Fire ratings as per code __ Gypsum board, painted
__ Ceiling & Sub-structure	__ Sound isolated substructure __ Suspended acoustic tile with integrated lighting __ Sound barriers above partitions at adjoining rooms	__ Suspended acoustic tile with integrated lighting __ Suspended gypsum board ceiling with acoustic treatment	__ Suspended acoustic tile, exposed grid __ Gypsum board with acoustic treatment
__ Acoustics	__ All surfaces sound absorptive __ 40-50 decibel electronic "white noise" recommended as background noise masking __ NC 25 - 35, STC 45 - 55 __ Doors with sound gaskets __ Glazed partitions may require double glazing sound barrier if facing public area or corridor	__ NC 25 - 35, STC 45 - 55 __ Doors with sound gaskets __ Sound barriers above adjacent floor-to-ceiling partitions	__ All provisions as much as possible as per Cost Category B

DESIGN STANDARDS -- LIBRARY STUDY, RESEARCH, REFERENCE AREAS

DOORS & WINDOWS	Recommended	Minimum
__ **Doors**	__ 1-3/4" solid core __ Sound proofing gaskets if opening to corridor or potentially noisy public area	__ Door may be optional if adjacent space is not a noise area and room doesn't have to be secured
__ **Frames**	__ 16 gauge steel	__ 16 gauge steel or extra-sturdy wood jambs and frames
__ **Hardware**	__ Quiet automatic closer __ Non-locking unless includes equipment or materials vulnerable to theft	__ Automatic closer __ Controlled locking only if required for security
__ **Windows**	__ Windows OK for restful views such as courtyard gardens or yard scenery, otherwise keep windows high for daylighting but not views __ Double-pane for noise insulation from exterior __ Operable sash not accessible from the exterior	__ As per Recommended Standards

FIXTURES/EQUIPMENT	Recommended	Minimum
__ **Special furnishings**	__ Study carrels __ Work counters for library reference __ Microform readers __ Bulletin and announcement boards __ Display and exhibit cabinets NOTE: Study carrels smaller than 4' x 2.5' are not adequate for extended research and study -- 5' width is recommended with right and left hand drawer shelves and upper adjustable shelves -- 4.5' carrel wall height is adequate for privacy	__ As per program and Recommended Standards NOTE: Book shelving is NOT recommended at walls -- walls are best utilized for special wall storage such as magazines, displays, and furniture placement, especially study carrels
__ **Audio-Visual Equipment**	__ Video and VCR machines with headphones for sound -- located where not visually distracting to readers __ Headphone access for video, audio tapes, etc. (See "Media Area")	

PLUMBING	Recommended	Minimum
__ **Fixtures**	__ Drinking fountain near entry and/or restrooms __ Fire sprinklers as required by code	__ As per Recommended Standards

DESIGN STANDARDS -- LIBRARY STUDY, RESEARCH, REFERENCE AREAS

HVAC	Recommended	Minimum
__ Occupancies	__ As per program -- allowing for varying occupancy	__ As per program __ For approximate estimating: 50 s.f. per person
__ Ventilation	__ 20 - 30 cfm outdoor air per occupant __ Ventilation noise is not allowable in study rooms __ For sound masking, use electronic "white noise" only	__ 20 cfm outdoor air per occupant __ Ventilation noise is not allowable in study rooms
__ HVAC System & Controls	__ Central HVAC system with individual room control	__ If climate is zone controlled, temperatures 68° to 72°F. __ Central system with individual room or zone control

ELECTRICAL POWER	Recommended	Minimum
__ Power Outlets	__ Task lighting outlets at fixed reading tables and carrels __ Floor and wall outlets for copiers, microform readers, microcomputers, headphone systems, etc. __ Wall base outlets or outlet strips for all contemplated future electric or electronic equipment __ Wall clock outlet __ Outlets as required for janitorial service	__ Task lighting outlets at fixed reading tables and carrels __ Floor and wall outlets for copiers, microform readers, microcomputers, headphone systems, etc. __ Wall clocks __ Wall base outlets junction box access for future electric or electronic equipment __ Outlets as required for janitorial service

LIGHTING	Recommended	Minimum
__ Lamps	__ Overall incandescent and/or fluorescent ceiling fixtures __ Downlights or task lights at work counters	__ Fluorescent ceiling lighting, recessed or surface mounted __ Downlights at reading areas __ Book lighting fixtures at book shelves __ Task lights at work areas and reference areas
__ Switching	__ Individual study task light switching __ Standard room switch controls	__ Standard room switch controls

ILLUMINATION WARNING: Library lighting is commonly inadequate despite its obvious importance	Recommended	Minimum
	__ 50 - 70 ESI (f.c.) for reading and study __ Task lights non-glare -- page illumination not over 4 times brightness of background __ 90% Visual Comfort Performance rating	__ 30 - 70 ESI (f.c.) for reading and study

COMMUNICATIONS	Recommended	Minimum
	__ PA system -- fire/security alarms __ See "Media Areas" for other communications	__ Alarms as required by code

DESIGN STANDARDS -- LIBRARY MULTIPURPOSE ROOM

GENERAL	Recommended Standards	Minimum Standards
__ Occupancies	__ As per program with allowance for varying types of occupancies: __ Public lectures __ Community organization meetings __ Student groups on research field trips __ Staff meetings and events	__ As per program; see the introductory section on Libraries for rules of thumb for overall occupancies and spatial requirements
__ Floor Area	__ 20 s.f. per person for general use __ 12 s.f. per person for lectures	__ 15 s.f. per person for general use __ 10 s.f. per person for lectures
__ Ceiling Height	__ 10' to 14'	__ 9' to 12'

FINISHES	Cost Categories		
	A	B	C
__ Floors & Sub-structure	__ Sound isolated substructure __ Nylon or acrylic carpet rated for heavy wear and glued to floor	__ Sound isolated substructure __ Carpet, heavy to medium, glued __ Vinyl	__ Carpet, medium, glued __ Vinyl or asphalt tile WARNING: Asphalt tile floors, in combination with some types of movable chairs and tables, can cause extreme noise problems
__ Counters & Built-in Furnishings	__ Kitchenette tile or plastic laminate work counter with overhead and under-counter cabinets __ Lockable storage cabinets	__ Workspace for food and coffee preparation __ Cabinets under and above workspace counter	
__ Walls & Substructure	__ Fire ratings as per code __ Sound-isolated construction __ Gypsum board with heavy weight vinyl or fabric __ Plaster __ Chair rail at exposed walls	__ Fire ratings as per code __ Gypsum board with medium to heavy weight vinyl, or fabric __ Chair rail at exposed walls near movable seating	__ Fire ratings as per code __ Gypsum board, textured and/or smooth painted
__ Ceiling & Sub-structure	__ Sound isolated substructure __ Suspended acoustic tile with integrated lighting	__ Suspended acoustic tile __ Suspended gypsum board ceiling with acoustic treatment	__ Suspended acoustic tile, exposed grid __ Gypsum board with acoustic treatment
__ Acoustics NOTE: Unlike other main library areas, this space should not be "dead" in terms of sound reflectance -- some sound reverberation is desirable for meetings and lectures	__ This room must be sound isolated from the rest of the library -- especially from reading and study rooms __ NC 30 - 35, STC 45 - 55 __ Doors solid core with sound gaskets at all edges __ Walls adjacent to reading and study areas must extend to floor or roof slab above and be caulked and sound proofed at all edges and penetrations	__ NC 25 - 35, STC 45 - 55 __ As per Cost Category A, but acoustic requirements will not be so acute if the room is located away from reading and study areas	__ All provisions as much as possible as per Cost Category B

DESIGN STANDARDS -- LIBRARY MULTIPURPOSE ROOM

DOORS & WINDOWS	Recommended	Minimum
__ **Doors**	__ 1-3/4" solid core entry/extit doors __ Sound proofing gaskets at all edges unless room is located in non-sound sensitive part of the building __ Vision panel in door __ Doors to auxiliary rooms or corridors 1-3/4" solid core with sound proofing gaskets at all edges __ Doors fire rated if opening onto fire exit corridors -- as per fire code	__ As per Recommended Standards but door construction and finish may be of lesser grades
__ **Frames**	__ 16 gauge steel	__ 16 gauge steel or extra-sturdy wood jambs and frames
__ **Hardware**	__ Quiet, concealed automatic closers __ Panic bar exit hardware __ Controlled locking __ Lighted fire exit signs as per code	__ Automatic closers, sound gasketing, and controlled locking systems
__ **Windows**	__ Windows OK with blinds and blackout drapes __ Double-pane for noise insulation from exterior __ Operable sash not accessible from the exterior __ Orientation and blinds to prevent sun glare and heat gain	__ As per Recommended Standards

FIXTURES/EQUIPMENT	Recommended	Minimum
__ **Special furnishings**	__ Kitchenette with sink, stove, mini-refrigerator, work counter and cabinets __ Display and exhibit cabinets __ Display shelves __ Video and VCR station __ Concealed chalk board or white board if there is a definite "front" presentation space in the room	__ Work sink and counter alcove __ As per program and Recommended Standards
__ **Audio-Visual Equipment**	__ Provisions for slide, video, and audio presentations __ Built-in screen if presentation space is definite __ Storage and/or convenient access to portable screen and other equipment storage __ Space for rolling chalk or white boards, display boards, projector carts, movable lecturn, etc.	__ Provisions as much as possible as per the Recommended Standards

PLUMBING	Recommended	Minimum
__ **Fixtures**	__ Drinking fountain at nearby corridor or near restrooms __ Sink within kitchenette __ Fire sprinklers	__ As per Recommended Standards __ Stainless steel or porcelain work sink __ Fire sprinklers as required by code

DESIGN STANDARDS -- LIBRARY MULTIPURPOSE ROOM

HVAC	Recommended	Minimum
__ Occupancies	__ As per program -- allowing for variations in occupancy at different times	__ As per program __ For approximate estimating, maximum occupancy of 1 person per 7 sq. ft. at social events, 1 person per 10 sq. ft. at lectures
__ Ventilation	__ 20 - 30 cfm outdoor air per occupant	__ 20 cfm outdoor air per occupant
__ HVAC System & Controls	__ Temperature controlled by individual thermostat __ Central HVAC system with individual room control	__ If climate is zone controlled, temperatures 68° to 74°F. __ Central system with individual room or zone control

ELECTRICAL POWER	Recommended	Minimum
__ Power Outlets	__ Task lighting outlets at work counters __ Outlets at kitchenette countertop __ Power as required for kitchenette refrigerator and electric stove __ Outlets for presentation slide and film projectors, video, electrified lecturn, overhead projector, video camera, etc. __ Wall base outlets or outlet strips for all comtenplated future electric or electronic equipment __ Wall clock outlet __ Outlets as required for janitorial service __ Lighted exit signs at exit doors	__ Outlets at work counter __ Avoid outlets close to work sink __ Other outlets as per Recommended Standards

LIGHTING	Recommended	Minimum
__ Lamps	__ Mixture of incandescent and fluorescent ceiling fixtures __ Overhead task lighting at work counters	__ Fluorescent ceiling lights, recessed or sur-faced mounted __ Some ceiling lights dimable during audio/visual displays at lectures
__ Switching	__ Dimmer controls for incandescent lighting with standard switches near entry __ Alternative dimmer controls near likely speaker locations for A/V presentations	__ Dimmer controls for incandescent lighting and standard room switch controls at entry
ILLUMINATION	Recommended __ 50 - 70 ESI (f.c.) for reading and study	Minimum __ 30 - 70 ESI (f.c.) for reading and study

COMMUNICATIONS	Recommended	Minimum
	__ PA system -- fire/security alarms __ Ceiling speakers and microphone jacks	__ Alarms as required by code __ See "Media Room" for other communications

123

DESIGN STANDARDS -- LIBRARY CHILDREN'S ROOM

GENERAL	Recommended Standards	Minimum Standards
__ Occupancies	__ As per program with allowance for varying types of occupancies: __ Story telling __ Young student groups on research field trips __ A/V presentations for children	__ As per program; see the introductory section on Libraries for rules of thumb for overall occupancies and spatial requirements
__ Floor Area	__ 20 s.f. per person for general use __ 12 s.f. per person for lectures	__ 15 s.f. per person for general use __ 10 s.f. per person for lectures
__ Ceiling Height	__ 8' to 9'	__ 8'-0"

FINISHES	Cost Categories		
	A	B	C
__ Floors & Sub-structure	__ Sound isolated substructure __ Nylon or acrylic carpet rated for heavy wear and glued to floor	__ Sound isolated substructure __ Carpet rated for heavy to medium wear, glued __ Vinyl	__ Carpet, medium, glued __ Vinyl or asphalt tile WARNING: Asphalt tile floors, in combination with some types of movable chairs and tables, can cause extreme noise problems
__ Counters & Built-in Furnishings	__ Low display and book shelves __ Lockable storage cabinets for educational materials and A/V equipment	__ As per Cost Category A	
__ Walls & Substructure	__ Glazing at upper half of partitions so that room is visually open to other space __ Fire ratings as per code __ Sound-isolated construction __ Gypsum board with heavy duty vinyl __ Low chair rail at exposed walls near movable seating	__ Fire ratings as per code __ Gypsum board with vinyl __ Low chair rail at exposed walls near movable seating	__ Fire ratings as per code __ Gypsum board, textured and/or smooth painted
__ Ceiling & Sub-structure	__ Sound isolated substructure __ Suspended acoustic tile with integrated lighting	__ Suspended acoustic tile __ Suspended gypsum board ceiling with acoustic treatment	__ Suspended acoustic tile, exposed grid __ Gypsum board with acoustic treatment
__ Acoustics	__ This room requires some sound isolation from the rest of the library -- especially from reading and study rooms __ NC 30 - 35, STC 45 - 55 __ Doors solid core with sound gaskets at all edges	__ NC 25 - 35, STC 45 - 55 __ As per Cost Category A, but acoustic requirements will not be so acute if the room is located away from reading and study areas	__ All provisions as much as possible as per Cost Category B

DESIGN STANDARDS -- LIBRARY CHILDREN'S ROOM

DOORS & WINDOWS	Recommended	Minimum
__ **Doors**	__ 1-3/4" solid core entry/extit doors __ Sound proofing gaskets at all edges unless room is located in non-sound sensitive part of the building __ Vision panels in and beside door __ Doors fire rated if opening onto fire exit corridors -- as per fire code	__ As per Recommended Standards but door construction and finish may be of lesser grades
__ **Frames**	__ 16 gauge steel	__ 16 gauge steel or extra-sturdy wood jambs and frames
__ **Hardware**	__ Easy operating doors for children __ Low mounted hardware for children's access __ Quiet, concealed closer hardware	__ As per Recommended Standards
__ **Windows**	__ Windows OK with blinds and blackout drapes __ Double-pane for noise insulation from exterior __ Operable sash not accessible from the exterior __ Orientation and blinds to prevent sun glare and heat gain	__ As per Recommended Standards

FIXTURES/EQUIPMENT	Recommended	Minimum
__ **Special furnishings**	__ Wash sink and counter alcove __ Low height display and exhibit cabinets __ Low height display shelves __ Video and VCR station __ Low height and adult height exhibit boards	__ As per program and Recommended Standards
__ **Audio-Visual Equipment**	__ Provisions for slide, video, and audio presentations	__ Provisions as much as possible as per the Recommended Standards

PLUMBING	Recommended Standards	Minimum Standards
__ **Fixtures**	__ Wash sink __ Children's height drinking fountain __ Fire sprinklers	__ As per Recommended Standards __ Fire sprinklers as required by code

DESIGN STANDARDS -- LIBRARY CHILDREN'S ROOM

HVAC	Recommended	Minimum
__ Occupancies	__ As per program -- allowing for variations in occupancy at different times	__ As per program
__ Ventilation	__ 20 - 30 cfm outdoor air per occupant	__ 20 cfm outdoor air per occupant
__ HVAC System & Controls	__ Temperature controlled by individual thermostat __ Central HVAC system with individual room control __ No hot water heating units in areas accessible to children	__ If climate is zone controlled, temperatures 68° to 72°F. __ Central system with individual room or zone control

ELECTRICAL POWER	Recommended	Minimum
__ Power Outlets	__ Outlets for presentation slide and film projectors and video __ Outlets for computers __ Wall base outlets or outlet strips for all contemplated future electric or electronic equipment __ Wall clock outlet __ Outlets as required for janitorial service __ Lighted exit signs at exit doors	__ Outlets as much as possible as per Recommended Standards

LIGHTING	Recommended	Minimum
__ Lamps	__ Overall incandescent and fluorescent ceiling fixtures	__ Overall fluorescent ceiling lights __ Incandescent ceiling lights dimable during visual displays at lectures
__ Switching	__ Dimmer controls for incandescent lighting with standard switches near entry __ Alternative dimmer controls near likely speaker locations for A/V presentations	__ Dimmer controls for incandescent lighting and standard room switch controls at entry

ILLUMINATION	Recommended	Minimum
	__ 50 - 70 ESI (f.c.) for reading and study	__ 30 - 70 ESI (f.c.) for reading and study

COMMUNICATIONS	Recommended	Minimum
	__ PA system -- fire/security alarms __ Cable TV and computer network cabling	__ Alarms as required by code __ See "Media Room" for other communications

DESIGN STANDARDS -- LIBRARY MEDIA ROOM

GENERAL	Recommended Standards	Minimum Standards
__ Occupancies	__ As per program with allowance for varying types of occupancies: __ Public multi-media presentations __ Research and study __ Student groups on research field trips	__ As per program; see the introductory section on Libraries for rules of thumb for overall occupancies and spatial requirements
__ Floor Area	__ 20 s.f. per person for general use __ 12 s.f. per person for lectures	__ 15 s.f. per person for general use __ 10 s.f. per person for lectures
__ Ceiling Height	__ 10' to 14'	__ 9' to 12'

FINISHES	Cost Categories		
	A	B	C
__ Floors & Sub-structure	__ Sound isolated substructure __ Nylon or acrylic carpet rated for heavy wear, glued to floor, with total static proofing __ Cable networking for computers and video may require a raised floor and/or extra ceiling and wall wiring chases	__ Sound isolated substructure __ Carpet rated for heavy to medium wear, static proofed, glued __ Vinyl __ Accessible ceiling and wall chases for communications and power cable	__ Carpet, medium, glued, with added static proofing __ Vinyl or asphalt tile WARNING: Asphalt tile floors, in combination with some types of movable chairs and tables, can cause extreme noise problems
__ Counters & Built-in Furnishings	__ Plastic laminate work counters with lockable overhead and undercounter cabinets __ Heavy-duty lockable storage units for portable computers and A/V equipment	__ Work counters __ Cabinets under and above workspace counter __ Lockable storage	__ Lockable storage
__ Walls & Substructure	__ Fire ratings as per code __ Sound-isolated construction __ Gypsum board with heavy weight vinyl or fabric __ Plaster __ Chair rail at exposed walls	__ Fire ratings as per code __ Gypsum board with medium weight vinyl __ Chair rail at exposed walls near movable seating	__ Fire ratings as per code __ Gypsum board, textured and/or smooth painted
__ Ceiling & Sub-structure	__ Sound isolated substructure __ Suspended acoustic tile with integrated lighting	__ Suspended acoustic tile __ Suspended gypsum board ceiling with acoustic treatment	__ Suspended acoustic tile, exposed grid __ Gypsum board with acoustic treatment
__ Acoustics NOTE: Some sound reflection and reverberation is desirable for public presentations	__ This room must be sound isolated from the rest of the library -- especially from reading and study rooms __ NC 30 - 35, STC 45 - 55 __ Doors solid core with sound gaskets at all edges __ Walls adjacent to reading and study areas must extend from floor to floor or to roof slab above and be caulked and sound proofed at edges and penetrations	__ NC 25 - 35, STC 45 - 55 __ As per Cost Category A, but acoustic requirements will not be so acute if the room is located away from reading and study areas	__ All provisions as much as possible as per Cost Category B

DESIGN STANDARDS -- LIBRARY MEDIA ROOM

DOORS & WINDOWS	Recommended	Minimum
__ **Doors**	__ 1-3/4" solid core entry/extit doors __ Sound proofing gaskets at all edges unless room is located in non-sound sensitive part of the building __ Vision panels in doors __ Doors to auxiliary rooms or corridors 1-3/4" solid core with sound proofing gaskets at all edges __ Doors fire rated if opening onto fire exit corridors -- as per fire code	__ As per Recommended Standards but door construction and finish may be of lesser grades
__ **Frames**	__ 16 gauge steel	__ 16 gauge steel or extra-sturdy wood jambs and frames
__ **Hardware**	__ Quiet, concealed automatic closers __ Panic bar exit hardware __ Controlled locking __ Lighted fire exit signs as per code	__ Automatic closers, sound gasketing, and controlled locking systems
__ **Windows**	__ Windows OK with blinds and blackout drapes __ Double-pane for noise insulation from exterior __ Operable sash not accessible from the exterior __ Orientation and blinds to prevent sun glare and heat gain	__ As per Recommended Standards

FIXTURES/EQUIPMENT	Recommended	Minimum
__ **Special furnishings**	__ Display and exhibit cabinets __ Display shelves __ Computer workstations __ Video and VCR stations __ Concealed chalk board or white board if there is a "front" presentation space in the room	__ As per program and Recommended Standards
__ **Audio-Visual Equipment**	__ Provisions for computers, CD and video disk storage, slide library and viewing storage, video projection and audio equipment __ Built-in screen if presentation space is defined __ Storage and/or convenient access to portable screen and other equipment storage __ Space for rolling chalk or white boards, display boards, projector carts, movable lectern, etc.	__ Provisions as much as possible as per the Recommended Standards

PLUMBING	Recommended	Minimum
__ **Fixtures**	__ Stainless steel or porcelain work sink __ Fire sprinklers or non-water fire suppression system	__ As per Recommended Standards __ Fire sprinklers as required by code

128

DESIGN STANDARDS -- LIBRARY MEDIA ROOM

HVAC	Recommended	Minimum
__ Occupancies	__ As per program -- allowing for variations in occupancy at different times	__ As per program __ For approximate estimating, maximum occupancy of 1 person per 10 sq. ft. at lectures
__ Ventilation	__ 20 - 30 cfm outdoor air per occupant __ Allow for extra heat build-up from electronic equipment __ Humidify to avoid electrical static charge build-up	__ 20 cfm outdoor air per occupant
__ HVAC System & Controls	__ Temperature controlled by individual thermostat __ Central HVAC system with individual room controll	__ If climate is zone controlled, temperatures 68° to 72°F. __ Central system with individual room or zone control

ELECTRICAL POWER	Recommended	Minimum
__ Power Outlets	__ Outlet strips for individual work stations for computers, video, VCR/CD/Video disk and audio tape playback, and computer printers __ Outlet strips for presentation slide and film projectors, video, electrified lecturn, overhead projector, video camera, etc. __ Wall base outlets or outlet strips for all contemplated future electric or electronic equipment __ Wall clock outlet __ Outlets as required for janitorial service __ Lighted exit signs at exit doors	__ Outlets at work counter __ Other outlets as much as possible as per Recommended Standards

LIGHTING	Recommended	Minimum
__ Lamps	__ Overall incandescent and fluorescent ceiling fixtures __ Overhead task lighting at work counters	__ Fluorescent ceiling lights, recessed or surface mounted __ Wall or ceiling incandescent lights
__ Switching	__ Dimmer controls for incandescent lighting with standard switches near entry __ Alternative dimmer controls near likely speaker locations for A/V presentations	__ Dimmer controls for incandescent lighting and standard room switch controls at entry

ILLUMINATION	Recommended	Minimum
	__ 40 - 60 ESI (f.c.)	__ 30 - 50 ESI (f.c.)

COMMUNICATIONS	Recommended	Minimum
	__ PA system -- fire/security alarms __ Ceiling speakers and microphone jacks __ Telecommunications cable and outlets __ Computer networking, video networking cable	__ Alarms as required by code __ As per program for electronic networks

MEDICAL BUILDINGS

DESIGN STANDARDS -- MEDICAL SUITES

GENERAL	Recommended Standards
__ **Occupancies & Floor Areas, Ceiling Heights, & Plan Features**	NOTE: See MEDICAL SUITES -- ROOMS for specifics of each room type

FINISHES	Recommended

__ **Floors**	__ Ceramic tile (wet areas)
	__ Sheet vinyl (wet areas, minor sugery, sanitation concerns;
	     fewer seams than VCT)
	__ Cushion sheet vinyl
	__ VCT-Vinyl composition tile (must be waxed & buffed)
	__ Carpet:
	  __ Wool
	  __ Nylon
	  __ Polypropylene
	  __ Loop pile (high traffic areas)
	  __ Cut pile
	  __ Synthetic backing (wet areas)
	  __ Glued
	  __ Solution dyed nylon (resists caustics & bleaching)
	  __ Antimicrobial treatment
	  __ Flourochemical treatment (resists stains-the most common
	     reason for carpet replacement)

__ **Walls**	__ Vinyl covered wood veneer __ Commercial vinyl wallcovering __ Gypsum board substrate, non-textured __ Gypsum board, textured __ Gypsum board, painted __ Wood paneling __ Grasscloth __Woven fabrics (consultation & waiting rooms)
__ **Ceilings**	__ Suspended acoustic tile __ Plastic coated (if extreme sanitation is important)

__ **Acoustics**	__ Provide for speech privacy in private offices, exam, and con-
	    ference areas
	__ NC 25, STC 45-50
	__ Doors to private offices, exam, and conference rooms with
	    sound proofing gaskets at all edges

__ **Counters & Built-In Furnishings**	__ See MEDICAL SUITES -- ROOMS for specifics of each room type

131

DESIGN STANDARDS -- MEDICAL SUITES

DOORS & WINDOWS	Recommended	Minimum
__ **Doors**	__ 1-3/4" solid core w/gaskets for sound privacy	__ 1-3/4" solid core
__ **Frames**	__ 16 gauge steel or extra-sturdy wood jambs and frames	__ 16 gauge steel or hardwood jambs and frames
__ **Hardware**	__ Lockable __ Standard tubular latch set or cylindrical lock set __ Security locks as required for records storage and medicine storage	__ Lockable __ Standard knob set
__ **Windows**	__ Fixed with operable sliders or hoppers __ Security windows where accessible to street level	__ Fixed with operable vents

FIXTURES/EQUIPMENT	Recommended	Minimum
__ **Special Furnishings**	__ See MEDICAL SUITES -- ROOMS for specifics of each room type	__ See MEDICAL SUITES -- ROOMS

PLUMBING	Recommended	Minimum
__ **Fixtures**	__ See MEDICAL SUITES -- ROOMS for specifics of each room type	__ See MEDICAL SUITES -- ROOMS

DESIGN STANDARDS -- MEDICAL SUITES

HVAC	Recommended	Minimum
__ Occupancies	__ See MEDICAL SUITES -- ROOMS for specifics of each room type	
__ Ventilation	__ 35 - 50 cfm outdoor air per occupant	__ 30 cfm outdoor air per occupant
__ HVAC System & Controls	__ Temperature controlled by individual thermostat __ Central HVAC system	__ If climate is zone controlled, temperatures 68° to 72°F. __ Even at minimum construction cost, provide generous fresh air supply and individual room control

ELECTRICAL POWER	Recommended	Minimum
__ Power Outlets	__ See MEDICAL SUITES -- ROOMS for specifics of each room type	__ As per Recommended

LIGHTING	Recommended	Minimum
__ Lamps	__ Integrated ceiling fluorescent fixtures __ Incandescent down lights at special work or reading areas __ Task lights at work counters, file storage areas, copier and other clerical workstations	__ Fluorescent ceiling lighting CAUTION: Standard full-size flourescent fixtures may be out of proportion to office size
__ Switching	__ Standard room switch controls except where dimming required (see MEDICAL SUITES -- ROOMS)	__ Standard room switch controls

ILLUMINATION	Recommended	Minimum
__ Corridors	__ 20 f.c.	__ As per Recommended
__ Waiting room	__ 30-50 f.c.	
__ Consultation rooms	__ 50 f.c.	
__ Exam rooms	__ 100 f.c.	
__ Nurses station	__ 100 f.c.	
__ Minor surgery	__ 100-150 f.c.	

COMMUNICATIONS	Recommended	Minimum
__ Communications	__ Multiple-line phones __ Fax lines __ Intercoms __ Alarms	__ As per Recommended

133

SPACE PLANNING AND MEDICAL BUILDING ROOM SIZES

TYPICAL BUILDING AREAS:

__ 11-12,000 min. sq. ft. rentable space per floor

__ 4 ft. planning module

BAY DEPTHS	SUITE SIZES
__ 28'	500 - 1,500 sq. ft.
__ 32'	1,200 - 3,000 sq. ft.
__ 44'	1,800 - 4,000 sq. ft.
__ 60'	4,000 - 1,0000 sq. ft.

__ Average solo practioner is 1200 sq. ft.

__ Most medical suites are 1200 - 2500 sq. ft.

PLANNING CONSIDERATIONS

__ Window mullions @ 4' on centerwith 4' planning grid

__ 8' & 12' rooms typical

__ 2' partition module = more flexibilty at somewhat higher costs

__ Window sills start @ 42" off floor

CEILING HEIGHTS

__ 8' - 8'-6" ceiling heights typical offices and smaller rooms

__ 9' - 10' Radiology

__ 9' - 10' Outpatient surgery

__ 9' -10' Physical therapy

__ Acoustical ceilings laid out in each room with interior partitions extending above finished ceiling 6" - 9"

MEDICAL SUITES

MEDICAL BUILDING ROOM SIZES continued

MEDICAL SUITE:

Waiting Room
  __ 12' x 12' -- 12' x 14'
  __ Add 4' to each dimension for each additional physician

Business Office
  __ 12' x 12'
  __ Approximately double room area for each additional physician
  __ Includes insurance clerk, bookkeeper, office manager

Exam Rooms
  __ 8' x 12'
  __ Three for each physician

Minor Surgery
  __ 12' x 12'

X-Ray Room
  __ 12' x 18' - 12' x 22'
  __ Includes darkroom, control, film filing, dressing area

Consultation
  __ 12' x 12'
  __ One for each physician

Nurse Station
  __ 8' x 10'
  __ Add 2' to each dimension for each additional physician

Toilets
  __ 5' x 6'
  __ Two for one to two physicians, three for three or more physicians

Storage
  __ 4' x 6'
  __ Add 2' to each dimension for each additional physician

Staff Lounge
  __ 8' x 12' -- 12' x 12'

EKG
  __ 12' x 12'

Laboratory
  __ 8' x 10' -- 16' x 18'
  __ Includes lab, waiting, blood draw

Add 15% more overall interior space for circulation

135

MEDICAL SUITES

ROOMS:

See MEDICAL BUILDING ROOM SIZES data preceding this page for programming estimates of room sizes.

WAITING ROOM

ROOM SIZE
__ Approx. 18 sq. ft per person
__ Larger room for non-appointment practices
__ Accomodate at least one hour of patient waiting

FIXTURES & FURNISHINGS
__ Secure coat hanging space
__ Seating
__ Magazine rack

PLANNING CONSIDERATIONS
__ Plan and decor should convey direct relationship to doctor services
__ Patient can move directly to reception window without interference
__ Move quickly to exam area without disturbing others
__ Wheelchair access
__ 4 - 6 ft. wide clear window to reception area

RECEPTION AREA

ROOM SIZE
__ As per Waiting Room

FIXTURES & FURNISHINGS
(include space for file cabinets if not bu ilt in, typewriter, and computer)
__ 6 lin. ft. of counter space
__ 4 - 6 ft. window
__ Clear sliding reception window
__ Recess for typewriter
__ Phone & messages station

PLANNING CONSIDERATIONS
__ "L" shaped return for departing patients
__ Appointments & cashier station may be separate from reception
__ See patient on arrival & departure

MEDICAL SUITES

ROOMS:

PATIENT EDUCATION ROOM

ROOM SIZE
__ 8' x 10' suggested

FIXTURES & FURNISHINGS
__ 30" high counter
__ Television monitor
__ VCR
__ Shelves for tapes & VCR

PLANNING CONSIDERATIONS
__ Located in front of suite off of waiting room

BUSINESS/FRONT OFFICE

ROOM SIZE
__ Varies, see MEDICAL BUILDING ROOM SIZES chart; and dependent on:
__ Appointments scheduled
__ Patients billed
__ Medical records stored
__ Patients greeted
__ Routine insurance & bookkeeping

FIXTURES & FURNISHINGS
(include space for file cabinets if not bu ilt in, typewriter, and computer)
__ Lower gate door with shelf @ 42"
__ Box for files to be refiled
__ Alcove for door
__ Guest chair

PLANNING CONSIDERATIONS
__ Combine with reception area

BOOKKEEPING AREA

ROOM SIZE
__ Size varies depending on bookkeeping system and number of patients

FIXTURES & FURNISHINGS
(include space for file cabinets if not bu ilt in, typewriter, and computer)
__ Computer system:
__ Proper screen distance & height
__ Adjustable keyboard
__ Proper lighting to avoid screen glare

PLANNING CONSIDERATIONS
__ May be combined with insurance area

MEDICAL SUITES

ROOMS:

INSURANCE AREA

ROOM SIZE
__ Size varies depending on staffing, see MEDICAL BUILDING ROOM SIZES, Business Office

FIXTURES & FURNISHINGS
(include space for filing cabinets if not bu ilt in, typewriter, and computer)
__ Desk
__ Calculator
__ File cabinets
__ Open shelf storage
__ Guest chair

PLANNING CONSIDERATIONS
__ Access to medical records
__ Access to copy machine
__ Combined with bookkeeping

RELATED BUSINESS OFFICE SPACES AND CONSIDERATIONS:

MEDICAL TRANSCRIPTION AREA
__ Space for transcriptionist in seperate room from noisy printers
__ One Countertop @ 26"
__ Other methods to be incorporated

DICTATION AREA
__ May be niche in corridor central to exam rooms
__ Wall mounted telephone
__ X-ray view box
__ Open storage compartments

OFFICE MANAGER ROOM

ROOM SIZE
__ 10' x 10'

FIXTURES & FURNISHINGS
(include space for file cabinets if not bu ilt in, typewriter, and computer)
__ Desk
__ Lockable cabinet storage
__ Guest chair

PLANNING CONSIDERATIONS
__ Manager hires personnel, orders supplies & drugs, assists physicians in secretarial & business matters
__ Located to face business office with glass window @ 48" to oversee staff

MEDICAL SUITES

ROOMS:

MEDICAL RECORDS STORAGE

ROOM SIZE
   __ Dependent on patient load, requires separate analysis

FIXTURES & FURNISHINGS
   __ Standard file 8 1/2" x 11"
   __ Radiology file 14 1/2" x 17 1/2"
   __ Lateral file cabinets
   __ Doorless or retractable doors
   __ Charts to be accomodated for 3 to 5 years

PLANNING CONSIDERATIONS
   __ Located convenient to:
      __ Receptionists
      __ Nurses
      __ Bookkeeper
   __ Located in Business Office

EXAMINATION ROOM

ROOM SIZE
   __ 8' x 12' suggested

PLANNING CONSIDERATIONS
   __ Nurses station & exam rooms clustered together
   __ Exam rooms close to consultation room
      __ Preferable that patients do not pass consultation room
   __ Corridors arranged so patients pass business/front office when exiting
   __ All exam rooms shouldbe identical for ease of use
   __ Avoid connecting doors between exam rooms & consultation rooms

FIXTURES & FURNISHINGS
   __ Full exam table
   __ Built-in sink cabinet
   __ Storage above sink
   __ Small wall mounted writing desk
   __ Stool on casters
   __ Guest chair
   __ Treatment stand
   __ Small piece of portable medical equipment
   __ Stress testing
   __ EKG unit & treadmill

MEDICAL SUITES

ROOMS:

EXAMINATION ROOMS continued

__ Dressing area
    __ 3' x 3' cubicle with surface mounted drapery
    __ Built-in bench or chair
    __ Clothes hook
    __ Hangers
    __ Mirror
    __ Shelf for disposable gowns

__ Sink cabinet
    __ 12" x 12" stainless steel bar sink
    __ Single lever faucet
    __ Cabinet __ 48" long min. __ 24" deep __ 36" high
__ Built-in trash compartment
__ Upper cabinet __ 48" long __ 12" deep __ 36" high __ 60" above floor
__ Paper towel & soap dispenser
__ Electrical outlet in drawer for specula (obstetrians & gynecologists)
__ Wall hung writing shelf @ 30"

__ Cabinets clad with plastic laminate

__ Windows start at 42"
    __ Gray glass
    __ Metal window blinds

__ Exam table foot end angled away from door & wall
__ Entry door to open inward away from wall
__ Entry at right side of door
__ Sink located on wall to right

__ Electrical - 3 grounded duplex outlets per room
    __ Above cabinet counter top @ 44"
    __ Foot of table @ 12"
    __ Head of table @12"

__ Exam table
    __ 27" wide & 54" long
    __ 78" long (orthopedic)
    __ Stirrups (pelvic or urologic)

MEDICAL SUITES

ROOMS:

TREATMENT / MINOR SURGERY

ROOM SIZE
___ 12' x 12' suggested

FIXTURES & FURNISHINGS
___ Upper & lower cabinets 10' to 12' in length
___ Ceiling-mounted surgical light over treatment table

PLANNING CONSIDERATIONS
___ Direct entrance with buzzer lock

X-RAY ROOM

ROOM SIZE
___ 10' x 12' without dressing area & darkroom
___ 9' ceiling

FIXTURES & FURNISHINGS
___ 3' minimum lead-lined door with heavy duty closer
___ Filmprocessing
___ If control area is outside room
___ Lead lined 3' x 3' glass window
___ Electrical
___ One outlet per counter
___ One outlet for film storage bin
___ Vacuum breaker on piping to tanks
___ Acid resistant pipes
___ Exhaust fan with light seal
___ Light proof louver ventilation panel
___ 24" min. door to open inward with light seal
___ Red warning light for developing

PLANNING CONSIDERATIONS
___ Adjacent to dark room
___ 2 or more walls lead lined to protect passersby

MEDICAL SUITES

ROOMS:

DARK ROOM

ROOM SIZE
__ 4' x 6' min. wet & dry side

FIXTURES & FURNISHINGS
__ Two 4' to 5' counters parallel with aisle or at right angle to each other
__ Counters & cabinets @ __ 36" __ 42" height
__ All open shelves
__ Wet side
__ Sink
__ Automatic processor
__ Floor drain
__ Replenisher tanks
__ Dry side
__ Loading cassettes
__ Light proof metal storage bin under counter
__ Rack for storage of cassettes
__ Lead lined cassette pass box to radiology
__ Located in wall close to film storage bin
__ Wood blocking to support tube stand

__ Electrical
__ One outlet per counter
__ One outlet for film storage bin
__ Vacuum breaker on piping to tanks
__ Acid resistant pipes
__ Exhaust fan w/light seal
__ Light proof louver venilation panel
__ 24" min. door to open inward w/light seal
__ Red warning light for developing
__ 75 watt incandescent fixture
__ Surface mounted to ceiling
__ Safe light for exposed film
__ Outlet @ 60"-72" above floor
__ Pull chain __ Switch
__ Switch seperated from incandescent
__ Small viewing area outside room
__ Double panel view box
__ Recessed __ Wall mounted

PLANNING CONSIDERATIONS
__ Adjacent to X-Ray Room

MEDICAL SUITES

ROOMS:

CONSULTATION ROOM

ROOM SIZE
__ 10' x 12' minimum
__ 12' x 12' recommended

FIXTURES & FURNISHINGS
__ Desk
__ Credenza
__ Bookshelves
__ 2 guest chairs
__ Coat closet
__ Private bathroom
__ Optional
　__ Sofa large enough for sleep
　__ Reading lamp
　__ Refrigerator
　__ Shower

PLANNING CONSIDERATIONS
__ Natural light
__ Located at rear of suite for privacy
__ Private entrance
__ Rear entry to suite

MEDICAL SUITES

ROOMS:

LABORATORY / NURSE STATION

ROOM SIZE
__ 8' x 12' suggested
__ Station may be recessed in niche in corridor

FIXTURES & FURNISHINGS
__ 6' of counter space w/cabinets above & below
__ Scales w/writing shelf
__ 24" per scale
__ Recessed into floor
__ Sink
__ Under counter refrigerator
__ Knee space work area with telephone
__ Laboratory
__ Double compartment sink
__ Knee space for microscope
__ Full size refrigerator __ Under counter rfrig.
__ Facility for blood draw
__ Standard chair
__ Prefabricated tablet-arm blood draw chair
__ One toilet adjacent to room w/speciman pass through door

PLANNING CONSIDERATIONS
__ Shield blood draw patient from sight of others
__ Adjacent to exam rooms

STORAGE

ROOM SIZE AND FITTINGS
__ 6' x 6' min.
__ Adjustable shelves on 2 or more walls
__ Lockable storage

MEDICAL SUITES

ROOMS:

STAFF LOUNGE

ROOM SIZE
__ 10' x 12' suggested

FIXTURES & FURNISHINGS
__ Built-in sink cabinet
____ 4'-6' in length
__ Under-counter refrigerator
__ Microwave
__ Garbage disposal
__ Small table & chairs

PLANNING CONSIDERATIONS
__ May include private entry/exit for doctors and staff
__ Coat closet

NURSERIES, KINDERGARTEN, & DAY CARE

DESIGN STANDARDS -- NURSERY SCHOOL/DAYCARE

GENERAL	Recommended Standards	Minimum Standards
__ Occupancies & Floor Area	__ As per program with allowance for varying types of occupancies in different sections __ 20 sq. ft. pe child, 30 sq. ft. per adult	__ As per program __ 15 s.f. per child, 20 sq. ft. per adult
__ Ceiling Height	__ 8' + __ Low ceiling or soffit alcoves are desirable	__ 8'-0"
__ Special Plan Considerations	__ All spaces must be observable by supervisory instructors and assistants at all times __ Entrance must be secure against unauthorized entry	__ As per Recommended

FINISHES	Cost Categories		
	A	B	C
__ Floors & Sub-structure	__ Nylon or acrylic carpet tiles rated for heavy wear and glued to floor __ Washable carpet tiles recommended __ Tight weave, dense, low pile __ Tiles may be patterend to visually define special areas __ Floor colors neutral for contrast with toys and slightly patterned to conceal stains __ Wood with non-slip runners	__ Carpet rated for heavy to medium wear, glued __ Vinyl in areas not subject to floor play activities	__ Carpet, medium, glued __ Vinyl or asphalt tile
__ Counters & Built-in Furnishings	__ Low display and book shelves __ Storage cabinets for educational and play materials __ Lockable cabinets for special educational materials and A/V equipment	__ As per Cost Category A	
__ Walls & Substructure NOTE: Sound isolated substructure if building is connected to other types of facilities	__ Glazing at upper half of partitions so that room is visually open to other corridor and office space __ Fire and flame spread ratings as per code __ Gypsum board with heavy duty, washable vinyl __ Low chair rail at exposed walls near movable seating	__ Fire ratings as per code __ Gypsum board with vinyl __ Low chair rail at exposed walls near movable seating	__ Fire ratings as per code __ Gypsum board, textured and/or smooth, painted with non-toxic paint
__ Ceiling & Sub-structure	__ Suspended acoustic tile with integrated lighting	__ Suspended acoustic tile __ Suspended gypsum board ceiling with acoustic treatment	__ Suspended acoustic tile, exposed grid __ Gypsum board with acoustic treatment
__ Acoustics	__ This room may require some sound isolation from other spaces __ NC 30 - 35, STC 40 - 45	__ NC 25 - 35, STC 35 - 40	

DESIGN STANDARDS -- NURSERY SCHOOL/DAYCARE

DOORS & WINDOWS	Recommended	Minimum
__ Doors	__ 1-3/4" solid core entry/extit doors __ Vision panels in and beside doors __ Doors rated as per fire code __ Children's doors with washable surfaces	__ As per Recommended but door construction and finish may be of lesser grades __ 1-3/8" HC interior doors with washable surfaces
__ Frames	__ 16 gauge steel or solid wood frames	__ Wood frame, custom or prehung
__ Hardware	__ Easy operating doors for children __ Low mounted hardware for children's access __ Lever type door handles __ Controlled buzzer entry at main entrance	__ As per Recommended Standards
__ Windows	__ Windows with blinds and blackout drapes __ Low windows or "kid windows" at different low heights where there are suitable views __ Double-pane if noise insulation from exterior is desirable __ Operable sash desirable for natural ventilation if opens onto secure area __ Orientation and exterior blinds to prevent sun glare and heat gain	__ As per Recommended Standards

FIXTURES/EQUIPMENT	Recommended	Minimum
__ Special furnishings	__ Wash sink and counter alcove __ Low height display and exhibit cabinets and shelves -- 3'-6" for child access __ Low height display shelves __ Video and VCR station __ Low height and adult height exhibit boards __ Planter area __ Animal cage area	__ As per program and Recommended Standards __ Provisions as much as possible as per Recommended
__ Audio-Visual Equipment	__ Provisions for slide, video, musical and audio presentations	

PLUMBING	Recommended Standards	Minimum Standards
__ Fixtures	__ Wash sink at children's height __ Children's height drinking fountain __ Children's kitchen sink __ Adult's kitchen sink __ Fire sprinklers	__ As per Recommended Standards __ Fire sprinklers as required by code

148

DESIGN STANDARDS -- NURSERY SCHOOL/DAYCARE

HVAC	Recommended	Minimum
__ Occupancies	__ As per program	__ As per program
__ Ventilation	__ 20 - 30 cfm outdoor air per occupant	__ 20 cfm outdoor air per occupant
__ HVAC System & Controls	__ Temperature controlled by individual room thermostat __ Floor radiant heating highly recommended __ Central HVAC system with individual room control OK if temperatures are controlled at floor level __ No hot water room heater units in areas accessible to children	__ If climate is zone controlled, temperatures 68° to 72° F. at floor level up to 4' __ Central system with individual room or zone control

ELECTRICAL POWER	Recommended	Minimum
__ Power Outlets	__ Outlets located out of reach of children and with safety covers __ Outlets for presentation slide and film projectors and video __ Counter height outlets for all contemplated future electric or electronic equipment __ Wall clock outlet __ Outlets as required for janitorial service __ Outlets or junction boxes for surveliance video cameras	__ Outlets as much as possible as per Recommended Standards

LIGHTING	Recommended	Minimum
__ Lamps	__ Overall incandescent and fluorescent ceiling fixtures	__ As per recommended
__ Switching	__ Dimmer controls for incandescent lighting with standard switches near entry	

ILLUMINATION	Recommended	Minimum
	__ 50 - 70 f.c. for play, reading, and arts and crafts	__ 30 - 70 f.c.

COMMUNICATIONS	Recommended	Minimum
	__ PA system -- fire/security alarms __ Cable TV __ Surveilance video system (cameras are now used in most facilities to record all events as defense against criminal and civil charges)	__ Alarms as required by code

149

SPECIAL PURPOSE AREAS OR ROOMS

__ **Reading Alcove**
- __ 50 - 75 sq. ft.
- __ Book shelves
- __ Platforms and nooks at different floor heights to form private reading areas
- __ Reading table for 6 children
- __ Bulletin board for exhibits
- __ Sloping book display shelf
- __ Movable shelf storage unit, with brake

__ **Block Alcove**
- __ 50 - 75 sq. ft.
- __ Storage shelves, 3'-6" maximum height, 11" wide
- __ Protected alcove so work will not be disrupted

__ **Manipulative Toy Area**
- __ 50 - 75 sq. ft.
- __ Storage shelves, 3'-6" maximum height, 11" wide
- __ Sloping shelves for puzzles
- __ Table for 4 to 5 children
- __ Relatively quiet protected area conducive to concentrated private work

__ **Art Area**
- __ 100 - 150 sq. ft.
- __ Vinyl floor
- __ Share sink with House Play kitchen area
- __ 18" high table, 15 sq. ft.
- __ Open shelving for art paper
- __ Cabinet art supply storage

__ **Tutoring Booths**
- __ 45 - 50 sq. ft. each booth
- __ Screened booth with transparent panels for private instruction
- __ Near sink

__ **House Play Area**
- __ 100 - 150 sq. ft.
- __ Counter & sink at child height
- __ Refrigerator and dry food storage
- __ Vinyl floor
- __ Household utensil storage
- __ Adult height kitchen sink near by

__ **Children's Toilets**
- __ Standard residential bath room or public restroom finishes and fixtures
- __ Fixtures at child height

__ **Office**
- __ As per program
- __ Space for standard office furnishings and equipment

__ **Teachers Work Centers**
- __ Work counter and file storage
- __ Open observation to plan and learning areas

NURSING HOMES & ELDERCARE

DESIGN STANDARDS -- NURSING HOME PATIENT ROOMS

GENERAL	Recommended Standards	Minimum Standards

__ Floor Area and Furniture Sizes	__ 12' x 18' median standard size (18' wide with 4' to 6' aisle space between beds)
	__ 13' to 14' x 18' for more varied furniture plans
	__ Most common: 2-bed unit with adjoining bath; 10% to 30% of rooms for single patients with 1 to 3 rooms as isolation rooms
	__ Personal storage = 6 sq. ft.-- 42" clear at front
	__ Furniture sizes
	  __ Standard hospital bed = 3'-0" wide x 7' long with side rails
	  __ Bedside cabinet = 1'-6" x 1'-8"
	  __ Chairs = 1'-6" to 2" square
	  __ TVs = 1'-6" x 2'-10" (varies)
		__ Minimum of 100 sq. ft. per bed
		__ 10' x 10' for single occupancy
		__ 12' x 16' for double occupancy
		__ Personal storage = 5 sq. ft.
		__ Furniture sizes as per Recommended Standards

__ Widths and Clearances	__ Aisles between beds = 48" __ Aisles between bed and wall = 36"	__ Aisles between beds = 36" __ Aisles between bed and wall = 30"
__ Ceiling Height	__ 8' - 10' __ 7' soffits or light coves OK	__ 8' __ 7' soffits

FINISHES	Cost Categories		
	A	B	C
__ Floor	__ Vinyl sheet (light padding OK if room is as much residential as medical) __ Carpet OK in residential nursing units - low-pile, thin pad, non-static, stain resistant, patterned to hide staining	__ Vinyl sheet __ Carpet, glued, in residential type facilities	__ Vinyl tile
__ Base	__ Vinyl cove -- attention to detail for easy cleaning	__ As per floor	__ As per floor
__ Cabinets, Casework	__ Wood, Custom Grade casework standard __ Plastic laminate facing	__ Wood, Custom Grade casework standard	__ Wood, paint grade
__ Counter tops	__ Plastic laminate, HPDL grade __ Plastic composite	__ Plastic laminate	__ Plastic laminate
__ Walls	__ Heavy-duty vinyl wall cover, Class A fire rating __ Gypsum board __ Wall rails to stop abrasion	__ Partial decorative vinyl cover __ Gypsum board, washable paint	__ Gypsum board, painted
__ Soffits & Ceiling	__ Washable acoustical tile __ Gypsum board	__ Acoustical tile __ Gypsum board, painted	__ Suspended acoustical tile, exposed grid __ Gypsum board, painted
__ Acoustics	__ Walls at 48 STC __ If floors and walls are hard-surfaced for ease of maintenance, reflected noise may be a problem __ Open plans with central nursing stations cause noise problems that must be dealt with, especially at night __ Consider use of white noise	__ 40 STC	__ 30-35 STC

DESIGN STANDARDS -- NURSING HOME PATIENT ROOMS

DOORS & WINDOWS	Recommended	Minimum
__ **Doors**	__ 3'-4" to 3'-6" wide x 1-3/4" to accommodate wheel chairs, walkers, gurneys, etc. __ Premium wood solid core construction __ Finishes must be easy to clean and refinish because of ongoing damage from carts, moving beds, etc.	__ 3'-0" x 1-3/8" SC #2 grade
__ **Frames**	__ 14 gauge steel	__ 16 gauge steel
__ **Hardware**	__ Standard hospital lever and plate __ Kickplates __ Quiety automatic closer __ Vision panel __ Door hold	__ Standard economy hospital grade
__ **Windows**	__ Vent from top to protect patients from falls __ Equal to 20% - 25% of floor area or more __ Room plan angled for views from bed if practical and if justified by exterior scenery __ Orientation to block glare and heat gain __ Blackout drapes	__ Equal to minimum of 10% of floor area AND no less than 10 sq. ft.

FIXTURES	Recommended	Minimum
__ **Built-in**	__ TVs -- cabinet-mounted or wall- or ceiling-mounted (1 per bed) __ Cubicle curtains at ceiling to visually isolate the bed __ Storage closet for clothing, shoe rack, shelves 1'-8" wide x 1'-10" deep __ Sink counter __ Make up mirror at sink counter	__ Wall- or ceiling-mounted shared TV

FURNISHINGS		
__ **Special Planning Considerations** Also see: **Floor Area and Furniture Sizes** on previous page	__ Secure storage for personal items (vertical storage for ambulatory patients, horizontal for non-ambulatory) __ Space for small, round, non-tip table __ Reachable book or magazine rack, shelf, or headboard __ Space for rocking chair or recliner	__ As per General mimimum standards on preceeding page

PLUMBING	Recommended	Minimum
__ **Water supply & drainage**	__ Bedside toilet compartments for severely disabled __ Wash sink in room with drinking water faucet	__ No minimum requirements

DESIGN STANDARDS -- NURSING HOME PATIENT ROOMS

HVAC	Recommended	Minimum
__ Occupancy	__ 1 to 2 patients plus visitors & staff	__ As per Recommended
__ Heating	__ 70° F to 72° F heat at bed height __ Balanced to prevent uneven heating	__ 68° F to 72° F heat at bed height
__ Ventilation	__ Exterior opening for fresh air access, 10% to 20% of floor area and 8 sq. ft. __ 30 c.f. per minute (extra ventilation required to help deal with odors) __ No ventilation noise __ No drafts -- patients complain of drafts and too much cold air more than they do about being too warm	__ Exterior opening, minimum 10% of floor area and 6 sq. ft. minimum __ 20 c.f. per minute
__ HVAC System	__ Forced air __ Radiator or fan coil unit if will not overheat one bed unit, underheat the other	__ Forced air __ Radiator or fan coil unit
__ HVAC Controls	__ Room thermostat with lockable override	__ Thermostat

ELECTRICAL POWER	Recommended	Minimum
__ Power Outlets	__ Outlets at: __ Bedside table/cabinet __ TV __ Make-up mirror __ Perimeter wall at floor lamp or swag lamp location (lamps must be secure) __ As required by code __ Safety covers to protect outlets not in use __ Fused, ground fault protected near sink	__ Outlets as required by governing codes

LIGHTING	Recommended	Minimum
__ Lamps	__ Wall-mounted reading lights at bed(s) __ Entry hall ceiling or wall lamp __ Swag lamp	__ As per Recommended
__ Switching	__ Illuminated room switches at room entry __ Switches large and easy to manipulate	__ Switches at room entry

ILLUMINATION	Recommended	Minimum
	__ 60 - 90 f.c. adjustable range __ 50% color rendition index __ Extra lighing is required for elderly to see properly -- should be soft and varied, not uniform and bright -- include ambient/indirect	__ 40 f.c. general light (mainly determined by occupants and individual lamps)

COMMUNICATIONS	Recommended	Minimum
__ Communications	__ Smoke and fire detector __ TV and music cables __ Phone jacks at bedside and at work table or desk __ Nurses' call switch and intercom __ TV remote __ TV, radio, music earphones	__ Smoke and fire alarm __ TV and music cables __ Phone jack at bedside

DESIGN STANDARDS -- NURSING HOME PATIENT BATHROOMS

GENERAL	Recommended Standards	Minimum Standards
__ **Floor Area**	__ Basic 3-fixture bath with extra lav counter space and/or built-in tub ledge, 9' x 6' = 54 sq. ft. (tubs and showers may be in separate bathing facilities space and lavatory may be in patient's bedroom)	__ Basic 3-fixture bathroom, 8' x 5' = 40 sq. ft.
__ **Widths and Clearances**	__ Toilet front distance to lav or to wall = 2'-8" __ Toilet space width = 3' __ Clearance between edge of tub to wall or fixture = 3'-6" __ Lavs at counter = 1'-6" for each lav plus 2' to 3' counter space at one or both sides	__ Toilet front distance to lav or to wall = 2'-2" __ Toilet space width = 2'-8" __ Clearance between edge of tub to wall or fixture = 3' __ Lav = 1'-6" to 2' width
__ **Ceiling Height**	__ 8' to 9'	__ 8'

FINISHES	Cost Categories		
	A	**B**	**C**
__ **Floor** WARNING: Bathroom flooring must have waterproof underlayment	__ Vinyl sheet __ Ceramic tile, non-slip finish	__ Ceramic tile __ Vinyl sheet	__ As per Cost Category B CAUTION: Vinyl tile is subject to moisture damage and maintenance problems and should not be used in bathrooms
__ **Base**	__ As per floor	__ As per floor	__ As per floor
__ **Wainscot**	__ Ceramic tile	__ Ceramic tile __ Gypsum board with moisture resistant paint finish	__ Gypsum board with moisture resistant paint finish
__ **Walls** WARNING: Waterproof backing board is required at walls of tubs and showers	__ Ceramic tile over waterproof gypsum board __ Waterproof plaster __ Gypsum board, water resistant	__ Gypsum board, water resistant	__ As per Cost Category B
__ **Counter tops**	__ Ceramic tile __ Polished and sealed stone __ Plastic laminate, HPDL grade	__ Ceramic tile __ Plastic laminate	__ Plastic laminate
__ **Soffits & Ceiling**	__ Gypsum board, type W, water resistant __ Paint, washable surface and must be water and midew resistant	__ Gypsum board, water resistant __ Paint -- water and mildew resistant	__ As per Cost Category B

DESIGN STANDARDS -- NURSING HOME PATIENT BATHROOMS

DOORS & WINDOWS	Recommended	Minimum
__ Doors	__ 3'-0" x 1-3/4" HC premium to #2 grade, 7 ply __ Door may be undercut for air supply for fan exhaust	__ 2'-10" x 1-3/8" HC #2 grade __ Door may be undercut for air supply for fan exhaust
__ Frames	__ 16 gauge steel __ Wood, custom or prehung	__ 16 gauge steel __ Wood prehung
__ Hardware	__ Brass or chrome plate	__ Plated metal, standard grade
__ Window light	__ Equal to 20% of floor area or more for baths with exterior walls __ Most are interior rooms with fan exhaust ventilation	__ Most nursing home toilet rooms are interior rooms with fan exhaust ventilation

FIXTURES	Recommended	Minimum
__ Built-ins	__ Robe hooks __ Lighted shaving and make-up mirror __ Tub/shower grab bar, towel bars, low and high soap dishes __ Towel bars with grab-bar mountings __ Recessed soap dishes	__ Robe hook __ Mirror __ Tub/shower towel bars, soap dish

FURNISHINGS		
__ Built-ins	__ Make-up counter with lighted mirror __ Under-counter cabinet storage	__ No minimum requirements

PLUMBING	Recommended	Minimum
__ Fixtures	__ Lav sometimes included in bath, sometimes in bedroom __ Bed pan washer __ Bath tubs or showers with seats and grab bars may be provided for minimum care units, otherwise separate supervised patient bathing facilties are provided at 1 per 10 to 15 patient rooms	__ As per program

DESIGN STANDARDS -- NURSING HOME PATIENT BATHROOMS

HVAC	Recommended	Minimum
__ Heating	__ 70° F to 72° F temperature __ Ceiling heat lamp	__ 68° F to 73° F heat at point 3'-0" above floor __ Ceiling heat lamp
__ Ventilation	__ 35 c.f. per minute in dressing area __ Fan with exhaust vent to outside if room does not open to the exterior __ Minimal air drafts	__ 30 c.f. per minute
__ HVAC System	__ As per patient bedroom	__ As per patient bedroom
__ HVAC Controls	__ As per patient bedroom	__ As per patient bedroom

ELECTRICAL POWER	Recommended	Minimum
__ Power Outlets	__ Easily accessible grounded outlets for: __ Dressing counter or table __ Lav area and shaving mirror __ All outlets with ground fault interrupt protection	__ Grounded outlets near lav and dressing or make-up counter __ All outlets with ground fault interrupt protection

LIGHTING	Recommended	Minimum
__ Lamps	__ Recessed incandescent with heat lamp __ Light at lav or make-up mirror __ Lights at make-up mirror and full length dressing mirror	__ Central recessed or surface-mounted fixtures __ Light above mirror
__ Switching	__ Illuminated 3-way switches if bath has multiple access __ Wall switch with timer for heat lamp __ Separate switch for vent fan if fan required	__ Switch at main entry __ Wall switch for vent fan if fan required

ILLUMINATION	Recommended	Minimum
	__ 70 - 100 f.c.	__ 70 f.c. general light

COMMUNICATIONS	Recommended	Minimum
__ Communications	__ Smoke/fire alarm, if required by local code __ Nurse call and intercom	__ As required by code

DESIGN STANDARDS -- NURSING HOME NURSES' STATION

GENERAL	Recommended Standards	Minimum Standards
__ **Occupancies** May also be a general supervisory and observation area for the Common Room and Recreational Rehabilitation area	__ Central locaton for control of patients' room corridor(s), common room, entry and support spaces (a separate entry control and administration office may be provided at the main entry and waiting space)	__ As per program, 100 sq. ft. minimum
__ **Floor Area**	__ As per program to handle: __ 2 to 3 nurses plus visiting medical staff __ 8' counter (see Counters below) __ 120 to 200 sq. ft.	__ As per program to handle: __ 2 nurses plus visiting medical staff __ 6' counter (see Counters below) __ 100 - 140 sq. ft
__ **Ceiling Height**	__ 12' to 14'	__ 10'

| FINISHES | Cost Categories | | |
	A	B	C
__ **Floors & Sub-structure**	__ Nylon or acrylic carpet rated for heavy wear and glued to floor __ Vinyl with thin padding	__ Vinyl sheet	__ Vinyl or asphalt tile
__ **Counters & Built-in Furnishings**	__ As per program -- counter and storage for patient chart rack, records, writing desks, files etc. __ Plastic laminate, HPDL grade	__ As per program __ Minimum 6' long counter __ Cabinets under and above workspace counter -- pre-fab casework, median quality __ Plastic laminate, median grade	__ As per program __ Preassembled units
__ **Walls & Substructure**	__ Typically open all sides but if has walls: __ Fire ratings as per code __ Gypsum board with heavy weight vinyl or fabric __ Chair rail at exposed walls	__ As per fire code __ Gypsum board with washable vinyl	__ As per fire code __ Gypsum board, washable paint
__ **Ceiling & Sub-structure**	__ Suspended acoustic tile with integrated lighting __ Washable acoustic tile	__ Suspended acoustic tile __ Suspended gypsum board ceiling with acoustic treatment	__ Suspended acoustic tile, exposed grid __ Gypsum board with acoustic treatment
__ **Acoustics**	__ At wall shared with quiet room(s): __ NC 30 - 35, STC 45 - 55	__ At wall shared with quiet room(s): __ STC 30 - 40	__ As much per Cost Category B as possible

DESIGN STANDARDS -- NURSING HOME NURSES' STATION

DOORS & WINDOWS	Recommended	Minimum

__ **Doors**	__ Low swinging gate if some boundary wanted in open plan station
	__ If door provided to adjacent administration or storage rooms:
	  __ Double acting swinging door
	  __ Vision panel in door
	  __ Non-swinging doors to auxiliary spaces 1-3/4" solid core
	__ Doors fire rated if opening onto fire exit corridors -- as per fire code
		__ As per Recommended but door construction and finish may be of middle to economy grades

__ **Frames**	__ 16 gauge steel __ 14 gauge steel frames at fire-rated doors	__ 16 gauge steel or extra-sturdy wood jambs and frames __ 14 gauge frames at fire-rated doors
__ **Hardware**	__ Quiet, concealed automatic closers __ Controlled locking system	__ Automatic closers, sound gasketing, and controlled locking systems
__ **Windows**	__ Windows, operable sash, and exterior glass doors as per Common Room	__ As per Recommended

FIXTURES/EQUIPMENT	Recommended	Minimum

__ **Special furnishings**	__ Counter space and work furnishings for patient needs, administration, and record keeping:
	  __ Patient chart rack
	  __ Supplies
	  __ Prescriptions
	  __ Personal storage
	  __ Lockable cabinets
	  __ Writing desks
	  __ File drawers
	  __ Computer and printer
	  __ Fax
	  __ Typewriters
	  __ Copier
	__ Some administrative and office functions may be combined with the nurses' station in smaller facilities or confined to a separate administrative office
		__ Work sink and counter alcove
		__ As per program and as much per Recommended as possible

PLUMBING	Recommended	Minimum
__ **Fixtures**	__ Drinking fountain at nearby corridor or near restrooms -- wheelchair accessible __ Sink with kitchenette __ Fire sprinklers __ Fire hose cabinet as per local fire code	__ As per Recommended __ Stainless steel or porcelain work sink __ Fire sprinklers and fire hose cabinet as required by code

DESIGN STANDARDS -- NURSING HOME NURSES' STATION

HVAC	Recommended	Minimum
__ Occupancies	__ As per program -- often combined with corridor space and Common Room or Dayroom	__ As per program
__ Ventilation	__ 30 cfm outdoor air per occupant	__ 20 cfm outdoor air per occupant
__ HVAC System & Controls	__ Temperature controlled by individual thermostat __ Central HVAC system with individual room control	__ If climate is zone controlled, temperatures 68° to 74°F. __ Central system with individual room or zone control __ Radiator or fan-coil unit -- protected from access by patients

ELECTRICAL POWER	Recommended	Minimum
__ Power Outlets	__ Outlets for: __ Wall clock __ Janitorial service __ Task lights __ Computers __ Fax __ Copier __ Electric typewriters __ Nurse call system __ Other outlets to provide for future electric and electronic equipment __ Emergency battery powered exit lights	__ Outlets as per program or required by code

LIGHTING	Recommended	Minimum
__ Lamps	__ Mixture of incandescent and fluorescent ceiling fixtures __ Task lights at counter and desk areas	__ Fluorescent ceiling lights, recessed or surface mounted
__ Switching	__ Dimmer controls for incandescent lighting with standard switches near entry __ Dimmer controls for corridors and adjacent Common Room	__ Dimmer controls for incandescent lighting and standard room switch controls at entry

ILLUMINATION	Recommended	Minimum
	__ 70 - 100 f.c.	__ 60 - 90 f.c.

COMMUNICATIONS	Recommended	Minimum
__ Communications	__ PA system -- fire/security alarms __ Nurse call intercom room communication __ Public pay phone in hall or near waiting area __ Switchboard __ Paging system	__ Alarms as required by code __ Nurse call station

160

DESIGN STANDARDS -- NURSING HOME COMMON ROOM

GENERAL	Recommended Standards	Minimum Standards

__ **Occupancies**
May also provide space and facilities for exercise equipment and for arts and crafts equipment and supplies such as for sewing, drawing and painting, ceramics, leather, weaving, etc., -- such facilities might be separate areas
	__ Observation from nurse's station
	__ As per program with allowance for varying occupancies:
	   __ Social events, parties, sing-alongs
	   __ Group TV, films, lectures, sermons
	   __ Organized hobbies, recreational therapy
	   __ Exercise therapy
	   __ Group meals, games
	   __ Reading (or provide separate library)
		__ As per program

__ **Floor Area**	__ 35 sq. ft. per person	__ 30 sq. ft. per patient or at least 300 sq. ft.
__ **Ceiling Height**	__ 10' to 14'	__ 9' to 12'

FINISHES	Cost Categories A	B	C
__ **Floors & Sub-structure**	__ Nylon or acrylic carpet rated for heavy wear and glued to floor __ Wood strip __ Vinyl sheet with thin cushion	__ Sound isolated substructure __ Carpet, heavy wear, glued __ Vinyl	__ Carpet, median, glued __ Vinyl or asphalt tile
__ **Counters & Built-in Furnishings**	__ Kitchenette or snack bar -- tile or plastic laminate work counter with overhead and undercounter cabinets __ Lockable storage cabinets	__ Workspace for snacks and drinks preparation __ Cabinets under and above workspace counter	__ Preassembled units
__ **Walls & Substructure**	__ Sound isolated from patient rooms __ Fire ratings as per code __ Gypsum board with heavy weight vinyl or fabric __ Chair rail at exposed walls	__ Fire ratings as per code __ Gypsum board with medium to heavy weight vinyl __ Gypsum board, painted __ Chair rail at exposed walls near movable seating	__ Fire ratings as per code __ Gypsum board with washable paint
__ **Ceiling & Sub-structure**	__ Suspended acoustic tile with integrated lighting __ Washable acoustic tile	__ Suspended acoustic tile __ Suspended gypsum board ceiling with acoustic treatment	__ Suspended acoustic tile, exposed grid __ Gypsum board with acoustic treatment
__ **Acoustics**	__ This room must be sound isolated from quiet areas of the building __ NC 30 - 35, STC 45 - 55 __ Walls adjacent to quiet areas such as a reading lounge must extend from floor to roof slab above and be caulked and sound proofed at all edges and penetrations	__ NC 25 - 35, STC 45 - 55 __ As per Cost Category A	__ All provisions as much as possible as per Cost Category B

DESIGN STANDARDS -- NURSING HOME COMMON ROOM

DOORS & WINDOWS	Recommended	Minimum
__ Doors	__ 3'-6" x 1-3/4" solid core double entry/exit doors (or open plan if sound privacy OK for patient rooms) __ Sound proofing gaskets at all edges unless room is located in non-sound sensitive part of the building __ Vision panel in door __ Doors to auxiliary rooms or corridors 1-3/4" solid core __ Doors fire rated if opening onto fire exit corridors -- as per fire code	__ As per Recommended but door construction and finish may be of middle to economy grades
__ Frames	__ 16 gauge steel __ 14 gauge steel frames at fire-rated doors	__ 16 gauge steel or extra-sturdy wood jambs and frames __ 14 gauge frames at fire-rated doors
__ Hardware	__ Quiet, concealed automatic closers __ Panic bar exit hardware	__ Automatic closers, sound gasketing, and controlled locking systems
__ Windows	__ Windows OK with blinds and blackout drapes __ Operable sash not accessible to patients __ Operable sash not accessible from the exterior __ Orientation and blinds to prevent sun glare and heat gain __ Sliding doors to outdoor seating very desirable but provide ample safety barriers to prevent collisions with sliding doors	__ As per Recommended

FIXTURES/EQUIPMENT	Recommended	Minimum
__ Special furnishings	__ Space for couches, coffee tables, comfortable lounging chairs __ Any built-in seating, 20" above floor __ "Hard" furnishings with rounded corners to help avoid injuries __ Residential lamps secured to tables or floors __ Kitchenette with snack bar, work counter and cabinets __ Display and exhibit cabinets __ Display shelves __ Display and bulletin board walls __ Video and VCR station __ Bookshelves unless provided in separate study/library __ Provisions for slide, video, and audio presentations __ Built-in screen if presentation space is definite __ Storage and/or access to A/V equipment	__ Work sink and counter alcove __ As per program and as much per Recommended as possible

PLUMBING	Recommended	Minimum
__ Fixtures	__ Drinking fountain at nearby corridor or near restrooms -- wheelchair accessible __ Hobby sink and/or sink with kitchenette __ Fire sprinklers __ Fire hose cabinet as per local fire code	__ As per Recommended

DESIGN STANDARDS -- NURSING HOME COMMON ROOM

HVAC	Recommended	Minimum
__ Occupancies	__ As per program -- allowing for variations in occupancy at different times	__ As per program __ For approximate estimating, maximum occupancy of 1 person per 20 sq. ft. at social events
__ Ventilation	__ 30 cfm outdoor air per occupant	__ 20 cfm outdoor air per occupant
__ HVAC System & Controls	__ Temperature controlled by individual thermostat __ Central HVAC system with individual room control	__ If climate is zone controlled, temperatures 68° to 74°F. __ Central system with individual room or zone control __ Radiator or fan-coil unit -- protected from access by patients

ELECTRICAL POWER	Recommended	Minimum

__ Power Outlets	__ Outlets for:
	   __ Kitchenette and hobby counters
	   __ Slide projector, video, VCR, etc.
	   __ Wall clock
	   __ Janitorial service
	   __ Floor and table lamps
	   __ Hobby and work areas such as for sewing
	__ Outlets with safety guards
	__ Junction boxes for lighted exit signs at exit doors
	__ Emergency battery powered exit lights
		__ Outlets as per program or required by code

LIGHTING	Recommended	Minimum
__ Lamps	__ Mixture of incandescent and fluorescent ceiling fixtures	__ Fluorescent ceiling lights, recessed or surface mounted __ Some ceiling lights dimable during audio/visual displays at lectures
__ Switching	__ Dimmer controls for incandescent lighting with standard switches near entry	__ Dimmer controls for incandescent lighting and standard room switch controls at entry

ILLUMINATION	Recommended	Minimum
	__ 70 - 100 f.c.	__ 60 - 90 f.c.

COMMUNICATIONS	Recommended	Minimum
__ Communications	__ PA system -- fire/security alarms __ Ceiling speakers __ Nurse call station __ Public pay phone in adjacent hall	__ Alarms as required by code __ Nurse call station

163

ARCHITECT'S ROOM DESIGN DATA HANDBOOK

OFFICE BUILDINGS

DESIGN STANDARDS -- OFFICE BUILDING LOBBY

GENERAL	Recommended Standards	Minimum Standards
__ Occupancies and Floor Area	__ As per program with allowance for widely varying occupancies and traffic loads	__ As per program
__ Ceiling Height	__ 12' - 24' and more __ Can include low (8-10') soffit at entrance vestibule	_._ 10' - 12' in smaller office buildings
__ Special Plan Considerations	__ Centralized information desk __ Double-door air lock vestibule in hot or cold climates; extra wide for hand truck deliveries __ Lobby seating	__ As per Recommended Standards

FINISHES	Cost Categories A	B	C
__ Floors WARNING: Smooth, hard surface materials sometimes used at entrances -- such as terrazzo, marble, smooth tile, or polished travertine are safety hazards -- even those treated to be non-slip are a problem when wet and when in contact with certain shoe sole materials	__ Recessed floor mat for rainy/ snowy climates at vestibule __ Non-slip rubber or vinyl tile at entry vestibule __ Nylon or other synthetic fabric carpet near entry should be rated for heavy wear, stain resistant and reasonably dark tone, glued to floor __ Carpet may be a different, complementary color and fabric at other spaces to allow easier replacement of the more heavily trafficked entry floor area __ Avoid light-tone reflective floor surfaces	__ Vinyl or asphalt tile at entry vestibule __ Synthetic fabric carpet rated for heavy wear near entry, glued to floor __ Complementary heavy to medium wear carpet at adjacent areas __ Other flooring considerations as per Cost Category A	__ Non-slip rubber or vinyl at entry vestibule __ Synthetic fabric carpet, glued
__ Walls & Substructure	__ Full-height store-front entry with automatic door opener __ Marble/other polished stone __ Interior wall finish typically plaster or gypsum board with heavy duty vinyl, fabric, or hardwood __ Exit wall fire ratings as per code	__ Foyer and exit area wall fire ratings as per code __ Gypsum board with heavy weight vinyl or fabric __ Plaster with sound absorbant treatment	__ Fire ratings as per code __ Gypsum board, painted
__ Ceiling	__ Plaster __ Baffle, metal, wood or other decorative ceiling __ Gypsum board with acoustic treatment __ Suspended decorative acoustic tile	__ Suspended decorative acoustic tile __ Gypsum board	__ Suspended acoustic tile, exposed grid __ Gypsum board
__ Counterts & Built-In Furnishings	__ Polished stone, hardwood	__ Plastic laminate	__ Plastic laminate
__ Fixtures	__ Public phones __ Handicap access __ Lighted fire exit signs __ Displays, directory board	__ Fixtures as per Cost Category A and/or program	__ Fixtures as per Cost Category A and/or program

DESIGN STANDARDS -- OFFICE BUILDING LOBBY

DOORS & WINDOWS	Recommended	Minimum
__ **Doors**	__ Automatic doors as needed for heavy traffic and for most convenient handicap access __ Heavy-duty, glazed public entry doors with quiet operating hardware and automatic closers __ Double door air-lock vestibule to control indoor-outdoor temperature differentiations and outside noise	__ Glazed public entry doors with quiet operating hardware and automatic closers
__ **Frames**	__ 14 gauge steel	__ 16 gauge steel
__ **Hardware**	__ Quiet, concealed automatic closers	
__ **Related Fixtures**	__ Lighted exit signs at exit doors as per code __ Controlled locking with security alarm system __ Side panel glazing or safety vision panels at non-glazed doors	
__ **Windows**	__ Floor to ceiling front glazing with glass entry doors __ Floor base barrier and mid-height bar or barrier to prevent people from walking into full-height glazing	__ Glazing for clear viewing between interior and exterior near entry

FIXTURES/EQUIPMENT	Recommended	Minimum
__ **Special furnishings**	__ Information desk __ Security desk (may be combined with Information desk) __ Tenant directory __ Elevator signage __ Location map	__ As per program and Recommended standards

PLUMBING	Recommended	Minimum
__ **Fixtures**	__ Drinking fountain near entry and/or near restrooms __ Fire sprinklers as required by code __ Fire hose cabinets as required by code __ Decorative fountain	__ As per Recommended standards

166

DESIGN STANDARDS -- OFFICE BUILDING LOBBY

HVAC	Recommended	Minimum
__ Occupancies	__ As per program -- allowing for large variations in traffic at different times	__ As per program
__ Ventilation	__ 20 - 30 cfm outdoor air per occupant __ Air lock vestibule to preserve air temperatures and buffer air pressure changes as people enter and leave the building	__ 20 cfm outdoor air per occupant
__ HVAC System & Controls	__ As per primary adjacent public spaces __ Localized heating may be provided in waiting area of vestibule	__ As per main public areas

ELECTRICAL POWER	Recommended	Minimum
__ Power Outlets	__ Outlets at information/securirty desk areas __ Wall clock outlet __ Outlets as required for janitorial service __ Lighted fire exit signs at exit doors __ Security video camera outlets	__ Outlets at information/securirty desk areas __ Outlets as required for janitorial service __ Lighted fire exit signs at exit doors

LIGHTING	Recommended	Minimum
__ Lamps	__ Iincandescent and/or fluorescent ceiling fixtures __ Downlights or spotlights at information and security desk, location map, directory, and other focal points __ Wall wash lights for displays and artwork	__ Fluorescent ceiling lights __ Down lights or task lights at information and security desk desk and other focal points
__ Switching	__ Central control, dimmers, and timers near security control area	__ Standard room switch controls near entry

ILLUMINATION	Recommended	Minimum
	__ 20 - 30 f.c. at entry vestibule __ 50 - 70 f.c. at information and security desk area and elevator lobby __ 10 - 20 f.c. at seating area	__ 15 - 20 f.c. at entry vestibule __ 30 - 70 f.c. at information and security desk area

COMMUNICATIONS	Recommended	Minimum
	__ PA system -- fire/security alarms __ Public phones __ Computer and video wiring at security desk	__ Alarms as required by code __ Public phones

DESIGN STANDARDS -- OFFICE BUILDING, OPEN PLAN

GENERAL	Recommended Standards	Minimum Standards
__ **Occupancies and Floor Area** NOTE: Space for government offices is determined by the agency but will usually be as per Minimum Standards	__ The nominal range of open plan office sizes varies from 3,000 sq. ft. to 30,000 sq. ft. __ 200 - 350 sq. ft. for top executives __ 130 sq. ft. average floor space per employee __ 100 to 250 sq. ft. for middle managers & Jr. executives __ 90 to 120 sq. ft. for supervisors __ 100 - 150 sq. ft. for secretaries __ 80 to 100 sq. ft. for clerical workers	__ 100 sq. ft. average floor space per employee __ 150 - 300 sq. ft. for top executives __ 90 - 225 sq. ft. for middle management, Jr. executives, and supervisors __ 80 - 100 sq. ft. for executive secretaries __ 75 sq. ft for clerical workers NOTE: 75 sq. ft. per personal working area is considered minimum for acoustical reasons
__ **Ceiling Height**	__ Varies depending on building construction (12' to 12' floor to floor height is common) __ 10' is recommended	__ Floor to floor heights range from 10' to 14' __ Minimum finish ceiling height is 8' with occassional 7' or 7'-6" soffits
__ **Special Plan Considerations**	__ 5' x 5' module -- cubicle dimensions of 10'x10', 10' x15', 10'x20', 15'x15', 15'x20', 15'x25' etc. __ Other common modules are 2.5', 4' and 6' NOTE: Modules and dimensions may be determined by partition system, ceiling system, electrical power grid -- preferably an integration of all.	

FINISHES	Cost Categories		
	A	**B**	**C**
__ **Floors**	__ Carpet rated for heavy wear, non-static, glued __ Raised access floors must be heavy duty, not subject to vibration or deflection	__ Carpet for heavy wear, glued __ Vinyl with backing	__ Carpet for heavy wear, glued __ Carpet tile __ Vinyl
__ **Walls & Substructure**	FIXED WALLS: __ 1-hour fire rating or more, as per building code __ Finish material flame spread ratings as per code __ Gypsum wallboard with heavy weight vinyl MOVABLE SCREENS: See FURNISHINGS next page	FIXED WALLS: __ Fire ratings as per building code __ Gypsum board with medium to heavy weight vinyl	FIXED WALLS: __ Fire ratings as per building code __ Gypsum board with medium weight vinyl __ Gypsum board, painted
__ **Ceiling**	__ Vaulted integrated ceiling system __ Integral ceiling -- suspended acoustic tile or gypsum board, with integrated lighting	__ Suspended acoustic tile with integrated lighting __ Gypsum board ceiling with acoustic treatment	__ Suspended acoustic tile, exposed grid __ Gypsum board with surface-mounted lighting
__ **Acoustics** WARNING: Sound control is the most important environmental consideration in making open office plans work and it requires the utmost cooperaration and coordination among acoustic, HVAC, electrical, and interior design consultants	__ Noise masking is one of the most important factors __ Stabilize background noise level at 55 dB with "white noise" generator __ NC 30, STC 40-50 __ Doors to private offices and conference rooms with sound proofing gaskets at all edges __ Cover large columns and hard finish perimeter walls with sound absorbing treatment	__ Most provisions as per Cost Category A __ NC 30, STC 35-40	__ Provisions as much as possible as per Cost Category A

DESIGN STANDARDS -- OFFICE BUILDING, OPEN PLAN

DOORS & WINDOWS	Recommended Standards	Minimum Standards
__ **Doors**	__ Steel clad doors with vision panels at primary entry and exits __ Steel clad interior doors to auxiliary spaces	__ 1-3/4" solid core doors with vision panesl and entry and exits __ 1-3/4" solid core interior doors to auxiliary spaces
__ **Frames**	__ 16 gauge steel or extra-sturdy wood jambs and frames	__ 16 gauge steel or hardwood jambs and frames
__ **Hardware**	__ Quiet self closers __ Panic bars as required by code	__ Self closers __ Panic bars as required by code
__ **Windows**	__ Fixed, double pane glazing (operable vents are not normally povided for large open office plans) __ Tinted glazing, shading, blinds to prevent direct sun glare and reduce heat gain	__ Fixed with operable vents
__ **Natural light**	WINDOW WALLS: __ 3" run of window per 10 sq. ft. of floor provides view andoutside light for greatest number of employees __ 20% of total floor area and up	WINDOW WALLS: __ 10% of total floor area

FURNISHINGS	Recommended	Minimum
__ **Furnishings & Fixtures**	MOVABLE SCREENS: __ 5'-3" height recommended,10' length typical __ 8" clearance at floor for air movement & cleaning unless this creates sound transfer problems __ Fire-retardant fabric cover over highly sound absorbant insulation __ Added sound absorbing screens, alcoves for noisy office equipment such as impact printers and copiers __ NIC / SPP noise isolation values -- coordinate with acoustic consultant	__ As per program

PLUMBING	Recommended Standards	Minimum Standards
__ **Fixtures**	__ Fire sprinklers as per code, generally 1 or more to cover every 200 sq. ft. __ Sprinklers recessed and unobtrusive	__ Fire sprinklers as per code

DESIGN STANDARDS -- OFFICE BUILDING, OPEN PLAN

HVAC	Recommended Standards	Minimum Standards
__ **Occupancies**	__ As per program; generally allow 100 sq. ft. per employee	__ As per program, generally allow a minimum of 100 sq. ft. office space per manager and 80 sq. ft. per clerical employee
__ **Ventilation**	__ 35 - 50 cfm outdoor air per occupant	__ 30 cfm outdoor air per occupant
__ **HVAC System & Controls**	__ Zone controlled, temperatures 68° to 72°F. __ Relative humidity between 50% - 65%, lower or higher depending on room temperature __ Maximum air movement at head height of 30' per minute	__ Zone controlled, temperatures 68° to74°F. __ Even at minimum construction cost, provide generous fresh air supply

ELECTRICAL POWER	Recommended Standards	Minimum Standards
__ **Power Outlets** NOTE: Lighting on 2 and 3-phase current can avoid lighting fluctuations from alternating current	__ Shell building, floor raceways, 1 outlet per 125 sq. ft. (1.5 watts per sq. ft.) __ Task lighting outlets near desks and work stations __ Extra outlets at special workstations for office equipment such as computer printer, copiers, Fax, etc. __ Outlets as required for janitorial service __ Duplex outlet for each desk	__ Shell building, floor raceways, 1 outlet per 125 sq. ft. (1.5 watts per sq. ft.)

LIGHTING	Recommended Standards	Minimum Standards
__ **Lamps**	__ Integrated ceiling fluorescent fixtures __ Incandescent down lights at special work or reading areas __ Task lights at work counters, file storage areas, copier and other clerical workstations	__ Fluorescent ceiling lighting, recessed or surface mounted
__ **Switching**	__ Master area or zone switching -- automatic with manual overide	__ Master area or zone switching
__ **Illumination**	__ 100 - 150 f.c. on work surfaces __ No brightness variations over 3:1 __ Ceiling reflectance factor minimum of 0.7 __ Reflectance factor of furnishings approx. 0.5	__ 80 - 100 f.c. on work surfaces __ No brightness variations over 3:1

COMMUNICATIONS	Recommended Standards	Minimum Standards
__ **Communications**	__ Phones per sq. ft. as per program __ Computer net lines __ Fax lines __ Intercoms __ Fire/smoke detectors and alarms	__ As per Recommended Standards

DESIGN STANDARDS -- OFFICE BUILDING, MANAGERIAL OFFICES

GENERAL	Recommended Standards	Minimum Standards
__ **Occupancies and Floor Area** NOTE: Space for government offices is determined by the agency but will usually be as per Minimum Standards.	__ 300 sq. ft. and up for top executives __ 100 to 300 sq. ft. for middle managers & Jr. executives __ 90 to 120 sq. ft. for supervisors __ 100 - 150 sq. ft. for executive secretaries __ 80 to 100 sq. ft. for clerical workers	__ 150 - 300 sq. ft. for top executives __ 90 - 225 sq. ft. for middle management, Jr. executives, and supervisors __ 80 - 100 sq. ft. for executive secretaries __ 60 - 75 sq. ft for clerical workers
__ **Ceiling Height**	__ Varies depending on building construction (12' to 12' floor to floor height is common) __ 8' to 10' high is average range	__ Floor to floor heights range from 10' to 14' __ Minimum finish ceiling height is 8' with occassional 7' or 7'-6" soffits
__ **Special Plan Considerations**	__ 5' x 5' module -- with offices of 10'x10', 10'x15', 10'x20', 15'x15', 15'x20', 15'x25' etc. __ Other common modules are 2.5', 4' and 6' NOTE: Modules and dimensions may be determined by partition system, ceiling system, electrical power grid -- preferably an integration of all.	

FINISHES	Cost Categories		
	A	B	C
__ **Floors**	__ Carpet rated for medium wear, non-static, padded	__ Carpet for medium wear, padded or glued	__ Carpet, medium, glued
__ **Walls & Substructure**	FIXED WALLS: __ 1-hour fire rating or more, as per building code __ Finish material flame spread ratings as per code __ Gypsum wallboard with medium weight vinyl or fabric MOVABLE WALLS: See OPEN PLAN OFFICES	FIXED WALLS: __ Fire ratings as per building code __ Gypsum board with fabric or vinyl __ Plaster MOVABLE WALLS: See OPEN PLAN OFFICES	FIXED WALLS: __ Fire ratings as per building code __ Gypsum board with fabric or vinyl MOVABLE WALLS: See OPEN PLAN OFFICES
__ **Ceiling**	__ Vaulted integrated ceiling system __ Integral ceiling -- suspended acoustic tile or gypsum board, with integrated lighting	__ Suspended acoustic tile with integrated lighting __ Gypsum board ceiling with acoustic treatment	__ Suspended acoustic tile, exposed grid __ Gypsum board with surface-mounted lighting
__ **Acoustics** WARNING: Sound absorption treatment such as acoustical tiles or acoustical plaster have no value for sound proofing between rooms.	__ Sound isolated substructure where confidential privacy is required __ Provide for speech privacy in private offices and conference areas __ NC 30, STC 40-50 __ Doors to private offices and conference rooms with sound proofing gaskets at all edges	__ Most provisions as per Cost Category A __ NC 30, STC 35-40	__ All provisions as much as possible as per Cost Categories A & B

DESIGN STANDARDS -- OFFICE BUILDING, MANAGERIAL OFFICES

DOORS & WINDOWS	Recommended	Minimum
__ Doors	__ 1-3/4" solid core with gaskets for sound privacy __ 1-3/4" hollow core where sound privacy is not required	__ 1-3/4" hollow core
__ Frames	__ 16 gauge steel or extra-sturdy wood jambs and frames	__ 16 gauge steel or hardwood jambs and frames
__ Hardware	__ Lockable for top executives __ Standard tubular latch set or cylindrical lock set	__ Standard knob set
__ Windows	__ Fixed with operable sliders or hoppers	__ Fixed with operable vents
__ Natural light	__ OFFICES AT EXTERIOR WALLS: __ 20% total floor area and up __ Operable window area = 10% total floor area	__ OFFICES AT EXTERIOR WALLS: __ 10% total floor area __ Operable window area = 5% total floor area

FIXTURES/EQUIPMENT	Recommended	Minimum
__ Furnishings & Equipment	__ As per program with mounting allowances for: __ Bookshelves __ Tack board __ Chalk board or white board __ Chart rail __ Picture hanging rail __ As per program with space allowances for: __ Personal computer and printer __ Fax __ Personal copier	__ As per program

PLUMBING	Recommended	Minimum
__ Fixtures	__ Fire sprinklers as per code, generally 1 or more to cover every 200 sq. ft. __ Sprinklers recessed and unobtrusive	__ Fire sprinklers as per code

DESIGN STANDARDS -- OFFICE BUILDING, MANAGERIAL OFFICES

HVAC	Recommended	Minimum
__ Occupancies	__ As per program, generally allow 120 sq. ft. office space per manager and per clerical employee	__ As per program, generally allow a minimum of 100 sq. ft. office space per manager and 80 sq. ft. per clerical employee
__ Ventilation	__ 35 - 50 cfm outdoor air per occupant	__ 30 cfm outdoor air per occupant
__ HVAC System & Controls	__ Temperature controlled by individual thermostat __ Central HVAC system	__ If climate is zone controlled, temperatures 68° to 72°F. __ Even at minimum construction cost, provide generous fresh air supply and individual room control

ELECTRICAL POWER	Recommended	Minimum
__ Power Outlets	__ Shell building, floor raceways, 1 outlet per 125 sq. ft. (1.5 watts per sq. ft.) __ Task lighting outlets near desks and work stations __ Floor and wall outlets for manager's office equipment: computer, dictation, personal copier, Fax, etc. __ Secretarial office outlets for typewriter, computer & printer, copier, Fax, dictation playback, electric sharpener, task lamp, etc. __ Outlets as required for janitorial service __ Duplex outlet for desk	__ Shell building, floor raceways, 1 outlet per 125 sq. ft. (1.5 watts per sq. ft.) __ Floor and wall outlets for manager's and secretary's basic office equipment -- at least one outlet at each fixed wall

LIGHTING	Recommended	Minimum
__ Lamps	__ Integrated ceiling fluorescent fixtures __ Incandescent down lights at special work or reading areas __ Task lights at work counters, file storage areas, copier and other clerical workstations	__ Fluorescent ceiling lighting (if standard size fluorescent fixtures are too large for smaller offices, use incandescents and/or provide for lighting by task lamps)
__ Switching	__ Dimmer controls at incandescent downlights	__ Standard room switch controls or zone control

ILLUMINATION	Recommended Standards	Minimum Standards
	__ 100 - 150 f.c. on work surfaces __ Minimal background dark to light contrast	__ 60 - 100 f.c. on work surfaces

COMMUNICATIONS	Recommended	Minimum
__ Communications	__ Multiple-line phones __ Computer net lines __ Fax lines __ Intercoms __ Alarms	__ As per Recommended Standards

173

DESIGN STANDARDS -- OFFICE BUILDING CONFERENCE ROOMS

GENERAL	Recommended Standards	Minimum Standards

__ Occupancies & Floor Areas	__ 500 s.f. per 15 people
	__ 25 s.f. per person for up to 8 people
	__ 20 s.f. per person for 8 to 10 people
	__ 18 s.f. per person for 20 to 40 people
	__ Typical conference table dimensions:
	    3'x 7' for 6 to 8 people
	    4'x 8' for 8 to 10
	    4'x10' for 10 to 14
		__ As per program
		__ 200 s.f. for conference space

__ Ceiling Height	__ 9' to 12' depending on room proportions	__ 9'
__ Plan features	__ Interior rooms are preferred, without distraction of views and heat gain of windows	

FINISHES	Cost Categories A	B	C
__ Floors & Sub-structure	__ Sound isolated substructure __ Carpet rated for medium to heavy wear, padded	__ Sound isolated substructure __ Carpet for medium wear, glued	__ Carpet, medium, glued
__ Wainscot	__ Wood paneling at executive or board member conference rooms	__ Partial wood paneling __ Plaster __ Heavy weight vinyl wall cover	__ If no wainscot, provide protective chair rail
__ Counters & Built-in Furnishings	__ Coffee service counter alcove __ Built-in projector cabinet	__ Plastic laminate utility counter	
__ Walls & Substructure	__ 1-hour fire rating or more, as per building code __ Finish material flame spread ratings as per code __ Sound-isolated construction __ Wood paneling __ Plaster __ Gypsum wallboard with fabric or heavy grade vinyl	__ Fire ratings as per code __ Gypsum board with fabric or vinyl	__ Fire ratings as per code __ Gypsum board with fabric or vinyl
__ Ceiling & Sub-structure	__ Integral ceiling, plaster or gypsum board, with integrated lighting __ Sound isolated substructure __ Partial hard surface sound reflective areas at ceiling and walls	__ Suspended acoustic tile with integrated lighting __ Suspended gypsum board ceiling with acoustic treatment	__ Suspended acoustic tile, exposed grid __ Gypsum board w/ acoustic treatment
__ Acoustics	__ Provide for speech privacy in private offices and conference areas __ NC 30, STC 45-50 __ Doors to private offices and conference rooms gasketed at all edges __ Sound reflective surfaces	__Provisions as per Cost Category A	__ All provisions as much as possible as per Cost Category A

174

DESIGN STANDARDS -- OFFICE BUILDING CONFERENCE ROOMS

DOORS & WINDOWS	Recommended	Minimum
__ **Doors**	__ 1-3/4" solid-core with sound proofing gaskets at all edges	__ 1-3/4" solid core doors are minimum for access to peripheral spaces __ No sound transfer allowed from or to other rooms or exterior corridor
__ **Frames**	__ 14 gauge steel at doors to corridor	__ 16 gauge steel or extra-sturdy wood jambs and frames
__ **Hardware**	__ Quiet, concealed automatic closers, sound gasketing, and controlled locking systems	__ Automatic closers
__ **Windows**	__ Windows are generally not desired for office conference rooms but, if used, provide: __ Double-pane for noise insulation from exterior __ Blinds and black out screens	__ Private offices per Cost Category A

FIXTURES/EQUIPMENT	Recommended	Minimum
__ **Special furnishings**	__ Projector cabinet and/or counter __ A/V equipment storage cabinet	
__ **Audio-Visual/Meeting Equipment**	__ Any items built-in must be unobtrusive until required for use in meetings __ Projection screen __ Tack board __ Chalk board	__ Ready access to projection screens, chalk boards, etc. from near-by storage

PLUMBING	Recommended	Minimum
__ **Fixtures**	__ Restrooms accessible __ Drinking fountains accessible __ Fire sprinklers as required by code	__ As per program

175

DESIGN STANDARDS -- OFFICE BUILDING CONFERENCE ROOMS

HVAC	Recommended	Minimum
__ Occupancies	__ As per program, or if not designated: __ 500 sq. ft. per 15 people	__ As per program
__ Ventillation	__ 35 - 50 cfm outdoor air per occupant	__ 30 cfm outdoor air per occupant
__ HVAC System & Controls	__ Temperature controlled by individual thermostat __ Central HVAC system	__ If climate is zone controlled, temperatures 68 to 72F. __ Central system with individual room or zone control __ Warm & cool forced air (zoned) __ Package systems not recommended __ Even at minimum construction cost, provide generous fresh air supply

ELECTRICAL POWER	Recommended	Minimum
__ Power Outlets	__ Outlets for audio visual equipment __ Floor and wall outlets for transcription, recording and playback equipment __ Podium outlet and sound amplification	__Outlets for transcription and audio visual equipment

LIGHTING	Recommended	Minimum
__ Lamps	__ Variable incandescent ceiling lighting __ Ambient fluorescent lighting, indirect preferred	__ Standard fluorescent fixtures
__ Switching	__ Dimmer controls for incandescent lights	__ Standard room switch controls

ILLUMINATION	Recommended	Minimum
	__ 60 - 90 f.c. on work surfaces __ Minimal background dark to light contrast	__ 50 - 80 f.c. on work surfaces

COMMUNICATIONS	Recommended	Minimum
__ Communications	__ Microphone jacks and ceiling speakers in larger conference rooms __ Phone jacks and intercom __ Fire and smoke alarms	__ Fire and smoke alarms

DESIGN STANDARDS -- OFFICE BUILDING, EXECUTIVE OFFICES

GENERAL	Recommended Standards	Minimum Standards
__ Occupancies and Floor Area	__ 300 sq. ft. and up for top executives __ 100 - 150 sq. ft. for executive secretaries	__ 150 - 300 sq. ft. for top executives __ 80 - 100 sq. ft. for executive secretaries
__ Ceiling Height	__ Varies depending on building construction (12' to 12' floor to floor height is common) __ 8' to 10' high is average range	__ Floor to floor heights range from 10' to 14' __ Minimum finish ceiling height is 8' with occasional 7' or 7'-6" soffits
__ Special Plan Considerations	__ Common executive office dimensions are 15'x20', 15'x25' etc., as per 5'x5' module __ Other common modules are 2.5', 4' and 6' NOTE: Modules and dimensions may be determined by partition system, ceiling system, electrical power grid -- preferably an integration of all.	

FINISHES	Cost Categories A	B	C
__ Floors	__ Carpet rated for medium to heavy wear, non-static, padded	__ Carpet for medium wear, padded	__ Carpet, medium, glued

__ Walls & Substructure	__ FIXED WALLS:
	__ 1-hour fire rating or more, as per building code
	__ Finish material flame spread ratings as per code
	__ Wood veneer paneling
	__ Gypsum wallboard with heavy weight vinyl or fabric
	
	__ MOVABLE WALLS:
	    See OPEN OFFICE PLAN
		__ FIXED WALLS:
		__ Fire ratings as per building code
		__ Gypsum board with fabric or medium weight vinyl
		
		__ MOVABLE WALLS:
		    See OPEN OFFICE PLAN
			__ FIXED WALLS:
			__ Fire ratings as per building code
			__ Gypsum board with fabric or medium weight vinyl
			
			__ MOVABLE WALLS:
			    See OPEN OFFICE PLAN

__ Ceiling	__ Vaulted integrated ceiling system __ Integral ceiling -- suspended acoustic tile or gypsum board, with integrated lighting	__ Suspended acoustic tile with integrated lighting __ Gypsum board ceiling with acoustic treatment	__ Suspended acoustic tile, exposed grid __ Gypsum board with surface-mounted lighting
__ Acoustics	__ Sound isolated substructure where confidential privacy is required __ Provide for speech privacy in private offices and conference areas __ NC 25, STC 45-50 __ Doors to private offices and conference rooms with sound proofing gaskets at all edges	__ Most provisions as per Cost Category A __ NC 30, STC 35-40	__ All provisions as much as possible as per Cost Categories A and B

DESIGN STANDARDS -- OFFICE BUILDING, EXECUTIVE OFFICES

DOORS & WINDOWS	Recommended Standards	Minimum Standards
__ **Doors**	__ 1-3/4" solid core w/gaskets for sound privacy	__ 1-3/4" solid core
__ **Frames**	__ 16 gauge steel or extra-sturdy wood jambs and frames	__ 16 gauge steel or hardwood jambs and frames
__ **Hardware**	__ Lockable __ Standard tubular latch set or cylindrical lock set	__ Lockable __ Standard knob set
__ **Windows**	__ Fixed with operable sliders or hoppers	__ Fixed with operable vents

__ **Natural light**	__ OFFICES AT EXTERIOR WALLS: __ 20% total floor area and up __ Operable window area = 10% total floor area	__ OFFICES AT EXTERIOR WALLS: __ 10% total floor area __ Operable window area = 5% total floor area

FIXTURES/EQUIPMENT	Recommended	Minimum
__ **Furnishings &** **Equipment**	__ As per program with mounting allowances for: __ Bookshelves __ Tack board __ Chalk board or white board __ Chart rail __ Picture hanging rail __ As per program with space allowances for: __ Personal computer and printer __ Fax __ Personal copier	__ As per program

PLUMBING	Recommended Standards	Minimum Standards
__ **Fixtures**	__ Fire sprinklers as per code, generally 1 or more to cover every 200 sq. ft. __ Sprinklers recessed and unobtrusive as possible At top-level executive suite offices: __ Wet bar or kitchenette sink __ Washroom & toilet __ Shower	__ Fire sprinklers as per code, unobtrusive

178

DESIGN STANDARDS -- OFFICE BUILDING, EXECUTIVE OFFICES

HVAC	Recommended Standards	Minimum Standards
__ Occupancies	__ As per program, generally allow 300 sq. ft. office space per senior executive and 200 per executive secretary	__ As per program, generally allow a minimum of 200 sq. ft. office space per manager and 150 sq. ft. for executive secretary
__ Ventilation	__ 35 - 50 cfm outdoor air per occupant	__ 30 cfm outdoor air per occupant
__ HVAC System & Controls	__ Temperature controlled by individual thermostat __ Central HVAC system	__ If climate is zone controlled, temperatures 68° to 72°F. __ Even at minimum construction cost, provide generous fresh air supply and individual room control

ELECTRICAL POWER	Recommended Standards	Minimum Standards
__ Power Outlets	__ Task lighting outlets near desk, credenza, and work stations __ Floor and wall outlets for executive's office equipment: VCR/CD Rom & video playback, computer & printer, dictation, personal copier, Fax, etc. __ Secretarial office outlets for typewriter, computer & printer, copier, Fax, dictation playback, electric sharpener, task lamp, etc. __ Outlets as required for janitorial service __ Two duplex outlets for desk __ Allow extra outlet capacity for additional future equipment	__ Floor and wall outlets for executive's and secretary's basic office equipment with one to two outlets at each fixed wall __ As much as possible as per Recommended Standards

LIGHTING	Recommended Standards	Minimum Standards
__ Lamps	__ Integrated ceiling fluorescent fixtures __ Incandescent down lights at special work or reading areas __ Task lights at work counters, file storage areas, copier and other clerical workstations	__ Fluorescent ceiling lighting CAUTION: Standard full-size flourescent fixtures may be out of proportion to office size
__ Switching	__ Dimmer controls at incandescent downlights	__ Standard room switch controls

ILLUMINATION	Recommended Standards	Minimum Standards
	__ 100 - 150 f.c. on work surfaces __ Minimal background dark to light contrast	__ 60 - 100 f.c. on work surfaces

COMMUNICATIONS	Recommended Standards	Minimum Standards
__ Communications	__ Multiple-line phones __ Fax lines __ Intercoms __ Alarms	__ Phones, Fax, and intercom lines

PARKING GARAGES

DESIGN STANDARDS -- PARKING GARAGES

GENERAL	Recommended Standards	Minimum Standards
__ **Floor Area and Spans**	__ Number of stalls and garage height as per program and code restrictions	__ As per program and code __ 100' X 100' minimum lot size for ramp garages
NOTE: One-story, long-span construction is almost universally preferred over two- or more story construction	__ 14' width for driveway aisles __ 20' - 21' long parking stalls for standard cars __ 10' - 11' wide parking stalls for standard cars __ Construction will virtually always be reinforced concrete with spans determined by standard parking and driving aisle dimension requirements	__ 13' width for driveway aisles __ 19' long parking stalls __ 9' wide parking stalls
__ **Ceiling Height**	__ 9' - 12'	__ 8' (8' to inside of waffles with 7' high beams may be OK if as per local code requirements)
__ **Acoustics** NOTE: High frequency sound is highly reflective in these spaces which often causes loud "screeching" noise even when cars are not driven at high speed	__ As per OSHA and state safety standards __ High-frequency sound attenuation baffles or blanket insulation at ramp ceilings	__ As per OSHA and state safety standards

FINISHES	Cost Categories		
	A	B	C
__ **Floors**	__ Portland cement concrete __ Asphaltic concrete with light broom finish __ Trowel finish where applied must have non-slip surface __ Floor drainage slopes at 1/4" per lin. ft., 1/2" per lin. ft. to slab drains at loading doors	__ Concrete slab, light broom texture finish NOTE: __ Higher cost garages may include heat, bright lighting, light painted interiors, security features, etc.	__ Concrete slab __ Asphalt paving
__ **Walls, Structure, & Ceiling**	__ Reinforced concrete flat plate, waffle slab, or girder & beam system __ Concrete columns __ Concrete, tilt-up __ Concrete masonry units __ Interior fire walls as per fire code __ Color code painting __ Light color paint finish recommended to improve lighting and safety	__ As per cost Category A	__ As per Cost Categories A & B but with shorter structural spans -- as per minimal parking and driveway dimensions

DESIGN STANDARDS -- PARKING GARAGES

DOORS	Recommended	Minimum
__ **Doors**	__ Steel roll-up doors for secured garages __ Sizes as per program entry/exit sizes	__ Vertical lift doors (if head room permits; see door manufacturer's literature)
__ **Frames**	__ Heaviest-gauge steel frames, channels and corner guards as recommended by door manufacturers	__ As per door manufacturer's minimumrecommendations
__ **Hardware**	__ As per commercial garage door manufacturer's recommendations	__ As per door manufacturer's minimum requirements

FIXTURES/EQUIPMENT	Recommended	Minimum

__ **Special Fixtures**	__ Heaviest gauge corner guards at all interior corners, door frames, and columns
	__ Column guards to 5' height
	__ Guards, bollards, and mesh protection at:
	   __ Electrical panels and switchboards
	   __ Utility supply lines and roof drains
	   __ Sprinkler risers
	   __ Plumbing valves
	__ Parking directional signs
	__ Parking wall and car protective bumpers and guards rails
		__ Corner, wall guard, and utility protection in general as per Recommended

__ **Parking Equipment**	__ Parking gates and ticket vending machines __ Security video equipment __ Cashier's booths __ Traffic control tire spikes at exits	__ As per program

PLUMBING	Recommended	Minimum
__ **Fixtures**	__ Sprinklers __ Fire hose cabinets __ Floor drains at each structural bay __ Floor drains or troughs at entry/exit to catch rain/melted snow __ Washroom fixtures	__ Sprinklers and other fire protection equipment as per code

DESIGN STANDARDS -- PARKING GARAGES

HVAC	Recommended	Minimum
__ **Ventilation**	__ Open air ventilation __ Underground facilities require heavy-duty and carefully engineered exhaust removal and ventilation __ As per HVAC consultant	__ Open ventilation, otherwise as per Recommended Standards
__ **HVAC System & Controls**	__ Unit space heaters near attendants' workstations	__ Unit heaters as required

ELECTRICAL POWER	Recommended	Minimum
__ **Power**	__ 120/240-volt, 3 wire	__ 120/240-volt, 3 wire
__ **Power Outlets**	__ As per program: __ Office outlets __ Building maintenance outlets __ Emergency battery powered exit lights __ Security video cameras __ Electronic gate controls	__ As per Recommended

LIGHTING	Recommended	Minimum
__ **Lamps**	__ Suspended fluorescent __ Suspended mercury vapor lamps __ Exterior mercury vapor lampsat entrances and exits	__ Fluorescent or mercury vapor lamps __ Task lights at inspection and paperwork areas
__ **Switching**	__ Master switchboard near main entry and administration or maintenance office	__ As per Recommended

ILLUMINATION	Recommended	Minimum
	__ 10-15 f.c. overall __ 60 f.c. for office work __ 3-6 f.c. at exterior entry/exits	__ 5-10 f.c. overall __ 30 foot-candles for office work __ 1-3 f.c. at exterior entry/exits

COMMUNICATIONS	Recommended	Minimum
__ **Communications**	__ Intercoms __ Fire alarms and fire department call __ Security systems and police call	__ As per program

RESIDENTIAL

DESIGN STANDARDS -- RESIDENTIAL LIVING ROOMS

GENERAL	Recommended Standards	Minimum Standards
__ **Floor Area**	__ Recommended minimal width is 14'; 16' and up is preferred __ Recommended minimal length is 18'; 20' and up is most recommended	__ 13' widths and 16' lengths are minimal for small but workable living rooms for two or more people

__ **Furniture Sizes**	__ Basic approximate furniture sizes:
	  __ Couch = 3' wide x 7' long
	  __ Arm chair = 3' wide x 2'-10"
	  __ Occasional chair = 2'-6" x 2'-6"
	  __ Coffee table = 2' wide x 3'-6" long
	  __ TV = 3' wide x 2'
	  __ End tables = 2'-4" x 1'-6"
	  __ Book cases = 1'-6" wide x up to 5' long
		__ Furniture sizes as per Recommended Standards

__ **Widths and Clearances**	__ Traffic aisles = 44" __ Max. distance between facing seating = 6'	__ Traffic aisles = 40"
__ **Ceiling Height**	__ 8' - 12' __ 7' lighting cove soffits OK	__ 8'

FINISHES	Cost Categories		
	A	B	C
__ **Floor**	__ Carpet, padded, non-static __ Hardwood, 3/4" oak parquet or strip, Prime or #1 grade	__ Carpet, non-static __ Hardwood, standard grade	__ As per Cost Category B
__ **Base**	__ Hardwood, Premium Grade	__ Hardwood, paint grade	__ Hardwood, paint grade
__ **Cabinets, Casework**	__ Wood, Premium Grade casework standard	__ Wood, Custom Grade casework standard	__ Wood, paint grade
__ **Counter tops or mantle**	__ Wood, Premium Grade __ Marble or comparable polished and sealed stone __ Ceramic tile	__ Wood, Custom Grade built-in shelving or cabinets __ Plastic laminate built-in counters	__ Plastic laminate counters
__ **Wainscot**	__ Hardwood, Premium Grade __ Plaster __ Fabric or heavy duty decorative wall cover	__ Hardwood, Custom Grade __ Fabric or medium weight decorative wall cover __ Gypsum board, painted	__ Gypsum board, painted
__ **Walls**	__ Hardwood, Premium Grade __ Fabric or heavy duty decorative wall cover __ Plaster __ Gypsum board	__ Hardwood, Custom Grade __ Fabric or medium weight decorative wall cover	__ Gypsum board, painted
__ **Soffits & Ceiling**	__ Wood paneling, exposed beams, Premium Grade __ Plaster __ Gypsum board	__ Gypsum board, painted __ Plywood paneling	__ Gypsum board, painted
__ **Acoustics**	__ 35-40 STC	__ 25-35 STC	__ No required minimum

DESIGN STANDARDS -- RESIDENTIAL LIVING ROOMS

DOORS & WINDOWS	Recommended	Minimum
__ **Doors**	__ 3'-0" x 1-3/4" HC premium to #2 grade, 7 ply __ Solid core, or SC with gaskets if sound isolation required	__ 2'-10" x 1-3/8" HC #2 grade __ 2'-6" x 1-3/8" HC paint
__ **Frames**	__ Wood -- custom or prehung	__ Wood prehung
__ **Hardware**	__ Knobs/handles -- Brass, bronze, ceramic latchset	__ Brass or chrome plate __ Plated metal, standard grade
__ **Window light**	__ Equal to 20% - 25% of floor area or more	__ Equal to minimum of 10% of floor area AND no less than 20 sq. ft.

FIXTURES	Recommended	Minimum
__ **Built-in**	__ Picture hanging rail for artwork display __ Book shelves __ Shelf for artwork __ Display cabinets	__ No minimum requirements

FURNISHINGS

__ **Space allowances for built-ins**
 	
Also see:
Floor Area and Furniture Sizes on previous page
	__ Fireplace hearth (sizes vary, but minimum hearth dimensions are 24" x 36")
	__ Wet bar with cabinets above and/or below
	    __ 4' to 6' long
	    __ 1'-10" to 2' deep
	    __ 2'-10" to 3' high
	
	__ Built-in seating -- see nominal furniture sizes on previous page
		__ Fireplace hearth minimums as per code

PLUMBING	Recommended	Minimum

__ **Water supply & drainage**	__ Recessed and concealed fire sprinklers
	__ As required for wet bar:
	    __ 1/2" supply to wet bar sink
	    __ 1-1/2" wet bar fixture drain
		__ Plumbing not required

DESIGN STANDARDS -- RESIDENTIAL LIVING ROOMS

HVAC	Recommended	Minimum
__ Heating	__ 68° to 72° heat (this standard is for forced air heat, not radiant heating)	__ 67° to 72° heat at point 3'-0" above floor __ Forced air
__ Ventilation	__ Exterior opening for fresh air access, 10% to 20% of floor area and 8 sq. ft. __ 20 c.f. per minute __ No ventilation noise	__ Exterior opening, minimum 10% of floor area and 6 sq. ft. minimum __ 15 c.f. per minute
__ HVAC System	__ Forced air __ Floor conducted radiant heat __ Radiator or fan coil unit	__ Forced air __ Radiator or fan coil unit
__ HVAC Controls	__ Thermostat, zone or room controls	__ Central thermostat

ELECTRICAL POWER	Recommended	Minimum

__ Power Outlets	__ Grounded outlets, average spacing 8"
	__ Outlets at:
	   __ Seating and end table locations for lamps
	   __ TV
	   __ Stereo cabinet location
	   __ Wet bar
		__ Grounded duplex outlets at 12' centers max. and within 6' of doorways

__ Circuits	__ All outlets with ground fault interrupt protection __ Separate circuits for any fixtures rated at 20 amps or more	

LIGHTING	Recommended	Minimum
__ Lamps	__ Recessed incandescent __ Track lights or wall wash lights for artwork	__ Central recessed or surface mounted fixture __ Switch to table or floor lamp outlet
__ Switching	__ 3-way switch at each room access __ Dimmers for hanging or recessed fixtures, or wall wash lights __ Master household switching system	__ Switch at main entry

ILLUMINATION	Recommended	Minimum
	__ 30 - 100 f.c. adjustable range (mainly determined by occupants and individual lamps)	__ 50 f.c. general light (mainly determined by occupants and individual lamps)

COMMUNICATIONS	Recommended	Minimum
__ Communications	__ Smoke and fire alarm, concealed __ TV cable __ Phone jacks	__ Smoke and fire alarm __ Phone jacks

DESIGN STANDARDS -- RESIDENTIAL KITCHENS

GENERAL	Recommended Standards	Minimum Standards
__ **Minimum Floor Area**	__ Minimum determined by appliances and spaces listed below; 22 linear ft. is maximum length for total sink-stove-refrigerator triangle	__ No legally required minimum
__ **Minimum Widths and Clearances**	__ Minimum 2' wide counters, 4' to 5' aisles, 24" to 36" counter space between major appliances __ 4' to 7' between sink and refrigerator __ 4' to 6' between sink and range __ 4' to 9' between range and refrigerator	__ 1'-10" wide counters, 3' to 4' aisles __ 18" to 24" minimum counter space between major appliances __ 24" to 36" food preparation space
__ **Ceiling Height**	__ 9' and higher ceilings recommended for air flow and easy exhaust; 7' soffits OK	__ 8'-0" except for soffits __ 7'-0" soffits / dropped beams

| FINISHES | Cost Categories | | |
	A	B	C
__ **Floor**	__ Non-slip ceramic tile or quarry tile __ Solid vinyl sheet or tile __ Hardwood, 3/4" oak parquet or strip, Prime or #1 grade	__ Vinyl sheet or tile __ Hardwood, standard grade	__ Asphalt tile
__ **Base**	__ Ceramic or quarry tile __ Vinyl __ Hardwood	__ Vinyl __ Rubber __ Hardwood, standard grade	__ Vinyl __ Hardwood, paint grade
__ **Counters**	__ Ceramic tile over 3/4" exterior plywood __ Polished and sealed stone __ Composite __ Plastic laminate	__ Plastic laminate __ Composite	__ Plastic laminate
__ **Cabinets, Casework**	__ Wood, Premium Grade	__ Wood, Custom Grade	__ Wood, Paint Grade
__ **Walls**	__ Ceramic tile __ Plaster __ 5/8" Gypsum board (Type W at areas exposed to moisture or if backing for ceramic tile) __ Decorative heavy duty wall cover	__ Gypsum board __ Decorative medium weight vinyl wall cover	__ Gypsum board
__ **Soffits**	__ Wood panel with gypsum wallboard underlay __ Plaster __ Gypsum board	__ Gypsum board __ Plywood panel	__ Gypsum board
__ **Ceiling**	__ Wood, exposed beam __ Wood panel w/ gypsum wallboard underlay __ Plaster __ Gypsum board	__ Gypsum board	__ Gypsum board
__ **Acoustics**	__ 35-40 STC if sound protection for adjacent rooms is required	__ 25-35 STC if sound protection for adjacent rooms is required	__ No STC requirement or recommendation

DESIGN STANDARDS -- RESIDENTIAL KITCHENS

DOORS & WINDOWS	Recommended	Minimum
__ **Doors**	__ 3'-0" x 1-3/4" HC premium to #2 grade, 7 ply __ Traffic door: double acting with push plate and view panel __ Solid core, or SC with gaskets if sound isolation required	__ 2'-10" x 1-3/8" HC #2 grade __ 2'-6" x 1-3/8" HC paint
__ **Frames**	__ Wood -- custom or prehung	__ Wood, prehung
__ **Hardware**	__ Knobs/handles -- brass, bronze, ceramic latchset	__ Brass or chrome plated __ Plated metal, standard
__ **Window light**	__ Equal to 25% of floor area or more	__ Equal to minimum of 10% of floor area AND no less than 10 sq. ft.
__ **Skylights**	__ To balance light from windows and reduce window contrast glare	__ No required minimums

FIXTURES/EQUIPMENT		
__ **Sink**	__ Three-part insulated stainless steel or porcelain	__ Two-section light-gauge stainless
__ **Range**	__ Six-burner range top (preferred: 4 at one station, 2 near serving area) __ Built-in or hood exhaust	__ Four-burner stove or range top __ Hood exhaust
__ **Oven**	__ Double oven plus separate broiler	__ Double oven
__ **Refrigerator**	__ 48" combination or separate freezer and refrigerator units, 36" each	__ 30" wide, 10 cu. ft.
__ **Compactor**	__ 15", 6.5 amp motor; sound insulated cabinet	
__ **Garbage disposal**	__ 1/2 horsepower, heavy-duty	__ 1/3 horsepower
__ **Microwave oven**	__ 1800 watts	
__ **Dishwasher**	__ Premium grade, energy/water saver cycles	__ Standard
__ **Stand-alone freezer**	__ 36", 500 Watts	

PLUMBING	Recommended	Minimum
__ **Water heater**	__ 40 gal plus 10 for each bedroom (extra water heaters for distant bathrooms, or use continuous loop hot water supply)	__ 20 gal plus 10 for each bedroom
__ **Water supply**	__ 1" or 3/4" supply - Type K copper tubing	__ Hot & cold, 1/2" supply
__ **Water drainage**	__ 2" fixture drains __ 4" house drain	__ 1-1/2" fixture drains __ 3" house drain

DESIGN STANDARDS -- RESIDENTIAL KITCHENS

HVAC	Recommended	Minimum
__ Heating	__ Uniform 68 - 70° heat at all heights (this standard is for forced air heat, not radiant heating)	__ 70° heat at point 3'-0" above floor __ Forced air __ Unit heater
__ Ventilation	__ Exterior opening for fresh air access, 10% to 20% of floor area and 8 sq. ft. __ 30 c.f. per minute __ Exhaust fans at stove and oven __ Overload emergency exhaust fan	__ Exterior opening, minimum 10% of floor area and 5 sq. ft. minimum __ 25 c.f. per minute __ Exhaust fans at stove and oven
__ HVAC System & Controls	__ Forced air __ Floor conducted radiant heat __ Thermostat, zone or room controls	__ Forced air __ Central thermostat

ELECTRICAL POWER	Recommended	Minimum
__ Power Outlets	__ Grounded outlets at all counters, average spacing 2' to 3' __ Separate power outlet for every appliance __ All outlets with ground fault interrupt protection __ Wall clock outlet	__ Grounded duplex outlets at every counter space over 12" wide __ Ground fault interruption protected outlets within reach of sinks or faucets __ Separate kitchen circuit
__ Circuits	__ Separate circuits for all appliances rated at 20 amps or more	

LIGHTING	Recommended	Minimum
__ Lamps	__ Task-specific lights: Spots / track / recessed __ Balanced spot light and ambient lighting __ Recessed incandescent	__ Single fixture, fluorescent or incandescent
__ Switching	__ 3- or 4-way switch at each room access __ Dimmers for spots __ Dimmers for ambient __ Integrated central house control system	__ Single switch at main entry

ILLUMINATION	Recommended	Minimum
	__ 150 f.c. task lighting __ 50 - 75 f.c. general light	__ 100 f.c. task light __ 50 f.c. general light

COMMUNICATIONS	Recommended	Minimum
__ Communications	__ Phone jack near recipe desk or at counter near refrigerator __ Smoke and fire alarm	__ Phone jack __ Smoke and fire alarm

DESIGN STANDARDS -- RESIDENTIAL FAMILY AND BREAKFAST ROOMS

GENERAL	Recommended Standards	Minimum Standards
__ **Floor Area**	__ Size ranges are from 5' x 6' for a small dining nook to dining room or living room size __ This space may be an extension of the kitchen, or adjacent and directly accessible to the kitchen	__ As per Recommended Standards
__ **Minimum Widths and Clearances**	__ Width per dining place setting = 32" __ Aisle access behind chairs = 36" __ Service aisle = 40" - 48"	__ Minimum width per place setting = 28" __ Minimum aisle access behind chairs = 24" __ Minimum service aisle = 36"
__ **Ceiling Height**	__ 8' - 10' __ 7' soffits OK	__ 8' __ 7' soffits

FINISHES	Cost Categories		
	A	B	C
__ **Floor**	__ Solid vinyl sheet or tile __ Hardwood, 3/4" oak parquet or strip, Prime or #1 grade __ Non-slip ceramic tile or quarry tile	__ Vinyl sheet or tile __ Hardwood, standard grade	__ Asphalt tile
__ **Base**	__ Vinyl __ Hardwood __ Ceramic tile or quarry tile	__ Vinyl __ Rubber	__ Vinyl
__ **Cabinets, Casework**	__ Wood, Premium Grade	__ Wood, Custom Grade	__ Wood, paint grade
__ **Counter tops**	__ Ceramic tile over 3/4" exterior plywood __ Polished and sealed stone __ Plastic laminate	__ Plastic laminate __ Composite	__ Plastic laminate
__ **Wainscot**	__ Plaster __ Ceramic tile __ Gypsum board (Type W at areas exposed to moisture or if backing for ceramic tile) __ Decorative heavy duty wall cover	__ Gypsum board __ Decorative medium weight wall cover	__ Gypsum board
__ **Walls**	__ Wood panel with gypsum wallboard underlay __ Plaster __ Gypsum board	__ Gypsum board __ Plywood panel	__ Gypsum board
__ **Soffits & Ceiling**	__ Wood, exposed beam __ Wood panel w/ gypsum wallboard underlay __ Plaster __ Gypsum board	__ Gypsum board	__ Gypsum board
__ **Acoustics**	__ 35-40 STC if sound protection for adjacent rooms is required	__ 25-35 STC if sound protection for adjacent rooms is required	__ No STC requirement or recommendation

DESIGN STANDARDS -- RESIDENTIAL FAMILY AND BREAKFAST ROOMS

DOORS & WINDOWS	Recommended	Minimum
__ Doors	__ 3'-0" x 1-3/4" HC premium to #2 grade, 7 ply __ Traffic door: double acting with push plate and view panel __ Solid core, or SC with gaskets if sound isolation required	__ 2'-10" x 1-3/8" HC #2 grade __ 2'-6" x 1-3/8" HC paint
__ Frames	__ Wood -- custom or prehung	__ Wood, prehung
__ Hardware	__ Knobs/handles -- brass, bronze, ceramic latchset	__ Brass or chrome plate __ Plated metal, standard grade
__ Window light	__ Equal to 20% - 25% of floor area or more	__ Equal to minimum of 10% of floor area AND no less than 10 sq. ft.

FIXTURES	Recommended	Minimum

__ Built-in	__ Picture hanging rail for artwork display
	__ Shelving or cabinet for artwork display
	
	__ Wet bar with cabinets above and/or below
	    __ 4' to 6' long
	    __ 1'-10" to 2' deep
	    __ 2'-10" to 3' high
		__ No minimum requirements

FURNISHINGS		

__ Space allowances for built-ins	__ Built-in sideboard or buffet:
	    __ 4' to 6' long
	    __ 1'-6" to 2' deep
	    __ 2'-9" to 3' high
	
	__ Built-in china cabinet:
	    __ 2'-10" to 4' wide
	    __ 1'-4" to 1'-10" deep
	    __ 4' to 6' high
		__ No minimum requirements

PLUMBING	Recommended	Minimum
__ Water supply	__ 1/2" supply to wet bar sink	__ As per Recommended if wet bar is provided
__ Water drainage	__ 1-1/2" wet bar fixture drain	

DESIGN STANDARDS -- RESIDENTIAL FAMILY AND BREAKFAST ROOMS

HVAC	Recommended	Minimum
__ Heating	__ Uniform 70° heat at all heights (this standard is for forced air heat, not radiant heating)	__ 70° heat at point 3'-0" above floor __ Forced air
__ Ventilation	__ Exterior opening for fresh air access, 10% to 20% of floor area __ 20 c.f. per minute __ Drafts must be avoided at seating height __ Exhaust fan system in kitchen to prevent odors from penetrating dining room	__ Exterior opening, minimum 10% of floor area __ 15 c.f. per minute __ Exhaust fans at stove and oven
__ HVAC System & Controls	__ Forced air __ Floor conducted radiant heat __ Thermostat, zone or room controls	__ Forced air __ Radiator or fan coil unit __ Central thermostat and or manual controls at radiator or fan coil units

ELECTRICAL POWER	Recommended	Minimum

__ Power Outlets	__ Grounded outlets:
	  __ At 8' centers at wall
	  __ Two at wainscot height at sideboard and/ or buffet for food warmers, other appliances
	  __ Behind lighted china cabinet
	__ All outlets with ground fault interrupt protection
		__ Grounded duplex base outlets at 10' centers
		__ Outlets at sideboard and/or buffet counter locations
		__ Ground fault interruption protected outlets within reach of wet bar sink

__ Circuits	__ Separate circuits for all appliances rated at 20 amps or more	

LIGHTING	Recommended	Minimum
__ Lamps	__ Chandelier centered over dining table __ Recessed incandescent __ Track lights or wall wash lights for artwork	__ Central recessed or surface mounted fixture __ Switches at main entry
__ Switching	__ 3- or 4-way switch at each room access __ Dimmer for chandelier __ Dimmers for hanging or recessed fixtures, or wall wash lights	

ILLUMINATION	Recommended	Minimum
	__ 5 to 30 f.c. adjustable lighting	__ 30 f.c. general light

COMMUNICATIONS	Recommended	Minimum
__ Communications	__ Smoke and fire alarm, concealed	__ Smoke and fire alarm

DESIGN STANDARDS -- RESIDENTIAL DINING ROOMS

GENERAL	Recommended Standards	Minimum Standards
__ Floor Area	__ Most commonly recommended total floor space for dining: __ 6 diners = 160 sq. ft. __ 8 diners = 180 sq. ft. __ 10 - 12 diners = 248 sq. ft.	__ Minimum floor space for: __ 4 diners = 136 sq. ft. __ 6 diners = 150 sq. ft. __ 8 diners = 172 sq. ft. __ 10 - 12 diners = 210 sq. ft.
__ Minimum Widths and Clearances	__ Width per place setting = 32" __ Aisle access behind chairs = 36" __ Service aisle = 40" - 48"	__ Minimum width per place setting = 28" __ Minimum aisle access behind chairs = 24" __ Minimum service aisle = 36"
__ Ceiling Height	__ 8' - 10' __ 7' soffits OK	__ 8' __ 7' soffits

FINISHES	Cost Categories		
	A	B	C
__ Floor	__ Carpet, padded, non-stain synthetic, wool not recommended __ Hardwood, 3/4" oak parquet or strip, Prime or #1 grade __ Non-slip ceramic tile, stone tile, or quarry tile	__ Carpet, non-stain __ Hardwood, standard grade	__ As per Cost Category B __ Vinyl floor at combination dining/family rooms
__ Base	__ Hardwood __ Ceramic or quarry tile to match floor	__ Hardwood	__ Hardwood, paint grade __ Vinyl
__ Cabinets, Casework	__ Wood, Premium Grade casework	__ Wood, Custom Grade casework	__ Wood, paint grade
__ Counter tops	__ Wood, Premium Grade __ Polished and sealed stone __ Ceramic tile __ Plastic laminate, HPDL grade	__ Wood, Custom Grade __ Plastic laminate	__ Plastic laminate
__ Wainscot	__ Hardwood, Premium Grade __ Plaster __ Fabric or heavy duty decorative wall cover	__ Hardwood, Custom Grade __ Fabric or medium weight decorative wall cover __ Gypsum board, painted	__ Gypsum board, painted
__ Walls	__ Hardwood, Premium Grade __ Fabric or heavy duty decorative wall cover __ Plaster __ Gypsum board	__ Hardwood, Custom Grade __ Fabric or medium weight decorative wall cover	__ Gypsum board, painted
__ Soffits & Ceiling	__ Wood paneling, exposed beams, Premium Grade __ Plaster __ Gypsum board	__ Gypsum board, painted __ Plywood paneling	__ Gypsum board, painted
__ Acoustics	__ 35-40 STC if sound protection for adjacent rooms is required	__ 25-35 STC if sound protection for adjacent rooms is required	__ No minimum STC requirement or recommendation

DESIGN STANDARDS -- RESIDENTIAL DINING ROOMS

DOORS & WINDOWS	Recommended	Minimum
__ **Doors**	__ 3'-0" x 1-3/4" HC premium to #2 grade, 7 ply __ Traffic door: double acting with push plate and view panel __ Solid core, or SC with gaskets if sound isolation required	__ 2'-10" x 1-3/8" HC #2 grade __ 2'-6" x 1-3/8" HC paint
__ **Frames**	__ Wood -- custom or prehung	__ Wood, prehung
__ **Hardware**	__ Knobs/handles -- brass, bronze, ceramic latchset	__ Brass or chrome plate __ Plated metal, standard grade
__ **Window light**	__ Equal to 20% - 25% of floor area or more	__ Equal to minimum of 10% of floor area AND no less than 10 sq. ft.

FIXTURES	Recommended	Minimum

__ **Built-in**	__ Picture hanging rail for artwork display
	__ Shelving or cabinet for artwork display
	
	__ Wet bar with cabinets above and/or below
	   __ 4' to 6' long
	   __ 1'-10" to 2' deep
	   __ 2'-10" to 3' high
		__ No minimum requirements

FURNISHINGS		

__ **Space allowances for built-ins**	__ Built-in sideboard or buffet:
	   __ 4' to 6' long
	   __ 1'-6" to 2' deep
	   __ 2'-9" to 3' high
	
	__ Built-in china cabinet:
	   __ 2'-10" to 4' wide
	   __ 1'- 4" to 1'-10" deep
	   __ 4' to 6' high
		__ No minimum requirements

PLUMBING	Recommended	Minimum
__ **Water supply**	__ 1/2" supply to wet bar sink	__ As per Recommended if wet bar is provided
__ **Water drainage**	__ 1-1/2" wet bar fixture drain	

DESIGN STANDARDS -- RESIDENTIAL DINING ROOMS

HVAC	Recommended	Minimum
__ Heating	__ Uniform 70° heat at all heights (this standard is for forced air heat, not radiant heating)	__ 70° heat at point 3'-0" above floor __ Forced air
__ Ventilation	__ Exterior opening for fresh air access, 10% to 20% of floor area and 8 sq. ft. __ 20 c.f. per minute __ Drafts must be avoided at seating height __ Exhaust fan system in kitchen to prevent odors from penetrating dining room	__ Exterior opening, minimum 10% of floor area and 6 sq. ft. minimum __ 15 c.f. per minute __ Exhaust fans at stove and oven
__ HVAC System & Controls	__ Forced air __ Floor conducted radiant heat __ Thermostat, zone or room controls	__ Forced air __ Radiator or fan coil unit __ Central thermostat and or manual controls at radiator or fan coil units

ELECTRICAL POWER	Recommended	Minimum

__ Power Outlets	__ Grounded outlets:
	  __ At 8' centers at wall
	  __ Two at wainscot height at sideboard and/or buffet for food warmers, other appliances
	  __ Behind lighted china cabinet
	__ All outlets with ground fault interrupt protection
		__ Grounded duplex base outlets at 10' centers
		__ Outlets at sideboard and/or buffet counter locations
		__ Ground fault interruption protected outlets within reach of wet bar sink

__ Circuits	__ Separate circuits for all appliances rated at 20 amps or more	

LIGHTING	Recommended	Minimum
__ Lamps	__ Chandelier centered over dining table __ Recessed incandescent __ Track lights or wall wash lights for artwork	__ Central recessed or surface mounted fixture
__ Switching	__ 3- or 4-way switch at each room access __ Dimmer for chandelier __ Dimmers for hanging or recessed fixtures, or wall wash lights	__ Switches at main entry

ILLUMINATION	Recommended	Minimum
	__ 5 to 30 f.c. adjustable lighting	__ 30 f.c. general light

COMMUNICATIONS	Recommended	Minimum
__ Communications	__ Smoke and fire alarm, concealed	__ Smoke and fire alarm

DESIGN STANDARDS -- RESIDENTIAL BEDROOMS

GENERAL	Recommended Standards	Minimum Standards

__ Floor Area and Furniture Sizes	__ 12' x 12' to 14' x 16' and up double occupancy
	__ 9' x 12' and up for single occupancy
	__ Furniture sizes
	   __ King size bed = 6'-6" wide x 6'-6" or 7' long
	   __ Queen size = 5' wide x 6'-6" or 7' long
	   __ Double = 4'-6" wide x 6'-6" or 7' long
	   __ Twin beds = 3'-3" wide x 6'-6" or 7' long
	   __ Dresser = 1'-9" deep x 4' to 5' long
	   __ Chests = 1'-6" deep x 3' to 4" long
	   __ Nightstands = 1'-6" square
	   __ Chair = 1'-6" to 2" square
	   __ TV = 1'-6" x 2'-10" (varies considerably)
		__ 11' x 12' for double occupancy
		__ 8' x 12' for single occupancy
		__ Furniture sizes as per Recommended Standards

__ Widths and Clearances	__ Aisles at beds = 36" __ Aisle at dresser = 40" __ Aisle at closet = 42"	__ Aisles at beds = 30" __ Aisle at dresser = 36" __ Aisle at closet = 38"
__ Ceiling Height	__ 8' - 10' __ 7' soffits OK	__ 8' __ 7' soffits

FINISHES	Cost Categories A	B	C
__ Floor	__ Carpet, padded, non-static __ Hardwood, 3/4" oak parquet or strip, Prime or #1 grade __ Hardwood, PremiumGrade	__ Carpet __ Hardwood, standard grade	__ As per Cost Category B
__ Base	__ Wood, Premium Grade casework standard	__ Hardwood, paint grade	__ Hardwood, paint grade __ Vinyl
__ Cabinets, Casework	__ Wood, Premium Grade	__ Wood, Custom Grade casework standard	__ Wood, paint grade
__ Counter tops	__ Polished and sealed stone __ Ceramic tile __ Plastic laminate, HPDL grade	__ Wood, Custom Grade __ Plastic laminate	__ Plastic laminate
__ Wainscot	__ Wood, Premium Grade __ Plaster __ Fabric or heavy duty decorative wall cover	__ Wood, Custom Grade __ Fabric or medium weight decorative wall cover __ Gypsum board, painted	__ Gypsum board, painted
__ Walls	__ Hardwood, Premium Grade __ Fabric or heavy duty decorative wall cover __ Plaster __ Gypsum board	__ Hardwood, Custom Grade __ Fabric or medium weight decorative wall cover	__ Gypsum board, painted
__ Soffits & Ceiling	__ Wood paneling, exposed beams, Premium Grade __ Plaster __ Gypsum board	__ Gypsum board, painted __ Plywood paneling	__ Gypsum board, painted
__ Acoustics	__ 35-40 STC	__ 25-35 STC	__ 20-30 STC

197

DESIGN STANDARDS -- RESIDENTIAL BEDROOMS

DOORS & WINDOWS	Recommended	Minimum
__ Doors	__ 3'-0" x 1-3/4" HC premium to #2 grade, 7 ply __ Solid core, or SC with gaskets if sound isolation required	__ 2'-10" x 1-3/8" HC #2 grade __ 2'-6" x 1-3/8" HC paint
__ Frames	__ Wood -- custom or prehung	__ Wood, prehung
__ Hardware	__ Knobs/handles -- brass, bronze, ceramic latchset	__ Brass or chrome plate __ Plated metal, standard grade
__ Window light	__ Equal to 20% - 25% of floor area or more	__ Equal to minimum of 10% of floor area AND no less than 10 sq. ft.

FIXTURES	Recommended	Minimum
__ Built-in	__ Picture hanging rail for artwork display __ Book shelves __ Shelf for artwork	__ No minimum requirements

Also see:
ROOM STANDARDS --
RESIDENTIAL CLOSETS

FURNISHINGS		
__ Space allowances for built-ins	__ Built-in dresser: approx: 1'-9" deep x 4' to 5' long	__ No minimum requirements

Also see:
Floor Area and Furniture Sizes on previous page

__ Built-in headboard with nightstands; nightstands approx 1'-6" square or 1'-2" deep by 2' wide

PLUMBING	Recommended	Minimum
__ Water supply & drainage	__ See ROOM STANDARDS -- RESIDENTIAL BATHROOMS	__ No minimum requirements

DESIGN STANDARDS -- RESIDENTIAL BEDROOMS

HVAC	Recommended	Minimum
__ Heating	__ 68° to 72° heat (this standard is for forced air heat, not radiant heating)	__ 67° to 72° heat at point 3'-0" above floor __ Forced air
__ Ventilation	__ Exterior opening for fresh air access, 10% to 20% of floor area and 8 sq. ft. __ 20 c.f. per minute __ No ventilation noise	__ Exterior opening, minimum 10% of floor area and no less than 6 sq. ft. __ 15 c.f. per minute
__ HVAC System	__ Forced air __ Floor conducted radiant heat __ Radiator or fan coil unit	__ Forced air __ Radiator or fan coil unit
__ HVAC Controls	__ Thermostat, zone or room controls	__ Central thermostat

ELECTRICAL POWER	Recommended	Minimum

__ Power Outlets	__ Grounded outlets, average spacing 4' to 5'
	__ Outlets at:
	    __ Nightstands
	    __ TV
	    __ Stereo cabinet
	    __ Makeup mirror at dresser or dressing table
		__ Grounded duplex outlets at 12' centers max. and adjacent to each side of bed locations

__ Circuits	__ All outlets with ground fault interrupt protection __ Separate circuits for any fixtures rated at 20 amps or more	

LIGHTING	Recommended	Minimum
__ Lamps	__ Recessed incandescent __ Track lights or wall wash lights for artwork	__ Central recessed or surface mounted fixture __ Switch to table lamp outlet
__ Switching	__ 3-way switch at each room access __ Dimmers for hanging or recessed fixtures, or wall wash lights __ Master household switching and secuirty system with control board at bedside	__ Switch at main entry

ILLUMINATION	Recommended	Minimum
	__ 10 - 60 f.c. adjustable range (mainly determined by occupants and individual lamps)	__ 40 f.c. general light (mainly determined by occupants and individual lamps)

COMMUNICATIONS	Recommended	Minimum
__ Communications	__ Smoke and fire alarm, concealed __ TV cable __ Phone jacks at bedside	__ Smoke and fire alarm

DESIGN STANDARDS -- RESIDENTIAL DRESSING ROOMS

GENERAL	Recommended Standards	Minimum Standards
__ Floor Area	__ Allow 2' width for clothing wardrobe space and 12 linear feet of closet storage per person __ 5' to 7' wide dressing area (a two-person combined wardrobe and dressing room would thus be 12' long and 10' wide -- larger spaces may be desirable, especially if dressing-wardrobe connects to a bath)	__ 2' wide wardrobes and 8 linear feet minimum per person __ 5' wide dressing area
__ Furniture Sizes	__ Furniture sizes __ Dressers = 1'-9" deep x 4' to 5' long __ Makeup table = 1'-10" deep x 3' to 4' long __ Chairs = 1'-6" to 2" square	__ Furniture sizes as per Recommended Standards
__ Widths and Clearances	__ Aisle at dresser = 3' __ Aisle in front of wardrobe entry = 4'	__ Aisle at dresser = 3' __ Aisle in front of wardrobe entry = 3'-4"
__ Ceiling Height	__ 8' with 7' soffits (avoid high shelves if possible)	__ 8' with 7' soffits

FINISHES	Cost Categories		
	A	B	C
__ Floor	__ Carpet, padded, non-static __ Hardwood, 3/4" oak parquet or strip, Prime or #1 grade __ Ceramic tile (if to match bath) __ Polished and sealed stone (if to match stone bath floor)	__ Carpet __ Hardwood, standard grade __ Ceramic tile (if to match bath)	__ As per Cost Category B
__ Base	__ Hardwood, Premium Grade	__ Hardwood, paint grade	__ Hardwood, paint grade
__ Shelving, built-in storage units	__ Wood, Premium Grade	__ Wood, Custom Grade casework	__ Wood, paint grade
__ Counter tops	__ Wood, Premium Grade __ Polished and sealed stone __ Ceramic tile (if makeup counter to match bath) __ Plastic laminate, HPDL grade	__ Wood, Custom Grade __ Plastic laminate	__ Plastic laminate
__ Walls	__ Cedar for combination dressing room and wardrobe __ Plaster __ Gypsum board	__ Hardwood, Custom Grade __ Gypsum board	__ Gypsum board
__ Soffits & Ceiling	__ Plaster __ Gypsum board	__ Gypsum board __ Hardwood or plywood paneling	__ Gypsum board

DESIGN STANDARDS -- RESIDENTIAL DRESSING ROOMS

DOORS & WINDOWS	Recommended	Minimum
__ **Doors**	__ 3'-0" x 1-3/4" HC premium to #2 grade, 7 ply __ Bifold, wood premium grade __ Sliding, wood premium grade	__ 3'-0" x 1-3/8" HC #2 grade __ Bifold, economy or paint grade __ Sliding, #2 grade
__ **Frames**	__ Wood -- custom or prehung	__ Wood prehung
__ **Hardware**	__ Knobs/handles -- Brass, bronze, ceramic latchset	__ Brass or chrome plate __ Plated metal, standard grade
__ **Window light**	__ Equal to 15% of floor area or more for dress- ing rooms with exterior walls	__ No minimum requirement
__ **Skylight**	__ 2' x 4' or larger for interior dressing rooms or for light balance in dressing rooms with outside light	

FIXTURES	Recommended	Minimum
__ **Built-ins** Also see: DESIGN STANDARDS -- RESIDENTIAL CLOSETS	__ Clothing hanging rods, low and full-length __ Clothing hanging pole-and-shelf combination __ Robe hooks __ Shoe shelf or rack __ Tie racks __ Ironing board or counter for touchup ironing __ Full-length mirror, lighted	__ Pole and shelf __ Robe hook

FURNISHINGS		
__ **Built-ins** Also see: **Floor Area and Furni- ture Sizes** on previous page	__ Built in dresser: approx: 1'-9" deep x 4' to 5' long __ Built in makeup counter with large lighted adjustable mirror __ Sewing machine space if not in laundry room __ Clothes hampers __ Drawer or bin storage units	__ No minimum requirements

PLUMBING	Recommended	Minimum
__ **Water supply & drainage**	__ See DESIGN STANDARDS -- RESIDENTIAL BATHROOMS	__ As per Recommended

DESIGN STANDARDS -- RESIDENTIAL DRESSING ROOMS

HVAC	Recommended	Minimum
__ Heating	__ 70° to 72° temperature at dressing rooms (this standard is for forced air heat, not radiant heating)	__ 68° to 73° heat at point 3'-0" above floor __ Forced air
__ Ventilation	__ 20 c.f. per minute in dressing area __ No noticeable air drafts	__ 15 c.f. per minute
__ HVAC System	__ Forced air __ Floor conducted radiant heat __ Radiator or fan coil unit in dressing areas	__ Forced air __ Radiator or fan coil unit
__ HVAC Controls	__ Thermostat, zone or room controls	__ Central thermostat

ELECTRICAL POWER	Recommended	Minimum
__ Power Outlets	__ Easily accessible grounded outlets for: __ Dressing counter or table __ Makeup and dressing mirror lights __ Iron and task lamp __ Steamer __ Shoe polisher __ Vacuum __ Sewing machine	__ Easily accessible grounded outlets at average of every 10 linear feet
__ Circuits	__ All outlets with ground fault interrupt protection __ Separate circuits for any fixtures rated at 20 amps or more	

LIGHTING	Recommended	Minimum
__ Lamps	__ Recessed incandescent __ Track lights for spots or floods __ Makeup mirror and dressing mirror lights	__ Central recessed or surface mounted fixtures
__ Switching	__ 3-way switch at each room access __ Door activated light at enclosed wardrobes	__ Switches at main entry

ILLUMINATION	Recommended	Minimum
	__ 60 - 100 f.c.	__ 50 f.c. general light

COMMUNICATIONS	Recommended	Minimum
__ Communications	__ Smoke and fire alarm, concealed __ Extension phone jack	__ Smoke and fire alarm in dressing room or at bedroom

DESIGN STANDARDS -- RESIDENTIAL BATHROOMS

GENERAL	Recommended Standards	Minimum Standards
__ Floor Area	__ Basic 3-fixture bath with extra lav counter space and/or built-in tub ledge, 9' x 7' = 63 sq. ft. __ Bath with compartmented toilet, and dressing space = 120 to 160 sq. ft. __ Two-fixture guest bath or powder room with toilet and lav = 30 sq. ft. and up	__ Basic 3-fixture bathroom` = 40 sq. ft. __ Two-fixture guest bath or powder room with toilet and lav = 20 to 30 sq. ft.
__ Widths and Clearances	__ 5' to 7' wide dressing area __ Toilet front distance to lav or to wall = 2'-8" __ Toilet space width = 3' __ Clearance between edge of tub to wall or fixture = 3'-6" __ Lavs at counter = 1-'6" for each lav plus 2' to 3' counter space at one or both sides	__ 3' to 5' wide dressing area __ Toilet front distance to lav or to wall = 2'-2" __ Toilet space width = 2'-8" __ Clearance between edge of tub to wall or fixture = 3' __ Lav = 1-'6" to 2' width
__ Ceiling Height	__ 8' to 9' with 7' soffits	__ 8' with 7' soffits

| FINISHES | Cost Categories | | |
	A	B	C
__ Floor WARNING: Bathroom flooring must have moisture barrier underlayment	__ Ceramic tile, non-slip finish __ Polished and sealed stone, non-slip finish __ Carpet	__ Ceramic tile __ Vinyl sheet	__ As per Cost Category B CAUTION: Vinyl tile is subject to moisture damage and mainte-nance problems andand should not be used in bathrooms
__ Base	__ As per floor	__ As per floor	__ As per floor __ Hardwood, paint grade
__ Wainscot	__ Ceramic tile	__ Ceramic tile __ Gypsum board with moisture resistant paint finish	__ Gypsum board with moisture resistant paint finish
__ Walls ' WARNING: Waterproof backing board underlay-ment is required at tubs and showers	__ Ceramic tile over waterproof gypsum board __ Waterproof plaster __ Gypsum board, water re-sistant	__ Gypsum board, water re-sistant	__ As per Cost Category B
__ Built-in cabinets, linen and bath storage	__ Wood, Premium Grade	__ Wood, Custom Grade case-work	__ Wood, paint grade
__ Counter tops	__ Ceramic tile __ Polished and sealed stone __ Plastic laminate, HPDL grade	__ Ceramic tile __ Wood, Custom Grade __ Plastic laminate	__ Plastic laminate
__ Soffits & Ceiling	__ Plaster: hard, smooth finish __ Gypsum board, water re-sistant __ Paint must be water and mil-dew resistant	__ Gypsum board, water re-sistant __ Paint -- water and mildew re-sistant	__ As per Cost Category B

DESIGN STANDARDS -- RESIDENTIAL BATHROOMS

DOORS & WINDOWS	Recommended	Minimum
__ **Doors**	__ 3'-0" x 1-3/4" HC premium to #2 grade, 7 ply	__ 3'-0" x 1-3/8" HC #2 grade __ Bifold, economy or paint grade __ Sliding, #2 grade
__ **Frames**	__ Wood, custom or prehung	__ Wood, prehung
__ **Hardware**	__ Privacy, Bath Lock, BHMA standard __ Knobs/handles -- brass, bronze, ceramic latchset	__ Privacy, Bath Lock, BHMA standard __ Brass or chrome plate __ Plated metal, standard grade

__ **Window light**	__ Equal to 20% of floor area or more for baths
	    with exterior walls
		__ Equal to 10% of floor area or more for baths
		    with exterior walls

__ **Skylight**	__ 2' x 2' or larger for for interior bathrooms
	    or for light balance for bathrooms with
	    outside light	

FIXTURES	Recommended	Minimum
__ **Built-ins**	__ Retractable clothes drying rod __ Robe hooks __ Double-size, or dual medicine cabinets __ Lighted shaving and makeup mirror __ Full-length dressing mirror, lighted __ Hamper or hamper chute to lower floor laundry room __ Tub/shower grab bar, towel bars, soap dishes __ Towel warmer __ Jaccuzi	__ Medicine cabinet with mirror __ Robe hook __ Tub/shower towel bars, soap dishes

FURNISHINGS		

__ **Built-ins**	__ Built in makeup counter with large lighted
	    adjustable mirror
	__ Bathroom storage: Shelf cabinet and drawers
	    or bin storage units
		__ Cabinet storage under lav

PLUMBING	Recommended	Minimum

__ **Water supply &**
    drainage
	__ 3/4" supply
	__ 2" fixture drains
	
	__ 20 gallon water heater for bathrooms distant
	    from primary water heater or use continuous
	    loop hot water supply
		__ 1/2" supply
		__ 1-1/2" fixture drains

DESIGN STANDARDS -- RESIDENTIAL BATHROOMS

HVAC	Recommended	Minimum
__ Heating	__ 70° to 72° temperature (this standard is for forced air heat, not radiant heating) __ Radiator or fan coil unit in dressing areas __ Wall pane lheater for auxilary heat __ Ceiling heat lamp	__ 68° to 73° heat at point 3'-0" above floor __ Forced air
__ Ventilation	__ 45 c.f. per minute in dressing area __ Fan with exhaust vent to outside if room does not open to the exterior __ Minimal air drafts	__ 30 c.f. per minute
__ HVAC System	__ Forced air __ Floor conducted radiant heat	__ Forced air __ Radiator or wall panel
__ HVAC Controls	__ Thermostat, zone or room controls	__ Central thermostat

ELECTRICAL POWER	Recommended	Minimum

__ Power Outlets	__ Easily accessible grounded outlets for:
	    __ Dressing counter or table
	    __ Makeup and dressing mirror lights
	    __ Lav area and shaving mirror
	    __ Jacuzzi pump motor outlet
	    __ Radio and/or small TV
	 __ All outlets with ground fault interrupt protection
		__ Grounded outlets near lav and at bathroom dressing or make-up counters

__ Circuits	__ Separate circuits for any fixtures rated at 20 amps or more such as built-in hot tub Jacuzzi	

LIGHTING	Recommended	Minimum
__ Lamps	__ Recessed incandescent with heat lamp __ Lights over or at sides of medicine cabinet mirrors __ Lights at makeup mirror and full length dressing mirror	__ Central recessed or surface-mounted fixtures __ Light above medicine cabinet
__ Switching	__ 3-way switches if bath has multiple access __ Wall switch for heat lamp __ Wall switch for vent fan if fan required	__ Switch at main entry __ Wall switch for vent fan if fan required

ILLUMINATION	Recommended	Minimum
	__ 60 - 100 f.c.	__ 50 f.c. general light

COMMUNICATIONS	Recommended	Minimum
__ Communications	__ Extension phone jack	

DESIGN STANDARDS -- RESIDENTIAL LAUNDRY

GENERAL	Recommended Standards	Minimum Standards
__ **Floor Area**	__ 5' x 8' and up	__ 5' x 6'
__ **Fixtures and Funish-ings Sizes**	__ Furniture sizes: __ Washer / Dryer = 2'-1" wide x 2' deep to 2'-7" wide x 2'-4" deep __ Laundry sink = 1 or two tray, 2' deep x 1'-6' wide to 3'-4" wide __ Storage cabinets = 1' deep x 3' to 6' long __ Sewing table = 1'-4" x 2'-4" __ Sorting counter = 1'-8" - 2' wide x 8' long and up __ Ironing board = 1'-3" x 4'-6"	__ Fixture and furniture sizes as per Recommended Standards
__ **Clearances**	__ 3' walking aisles __ 4' working space at front of washer / dryer	__ 2'-6" walking aisles __ 3" at front of washer / dryer
__ **Ceiling Height**	__ 8' - 9'	__ 8'

FINISHES	Cost Categories		
	A	B	C
__ **Floor** CAUTION: Laundry floor should have moisture barrier under-layment	__ Vinyl sheet __ Vinyl or rubber tile __ Non-slip ceramic tile __ Quarry tile	__ Vinyl tile	__ Vinyl tile
__ **Base**	__ To match floor	__ To match floor	__ To match floor
__ **Cabinets**	__ Wood, Custom Grade	__ Wood, paint grade	__ Wood, paint grade
__ **Counters**	__ Ceramic tile __ Plastic laminate	__ Plastic laminate	__ Plastic laminatel
__ **Walls**	__ Gypsum board with heavy duty vinyl wall cover __ Gypsum board, smooth finish with water resistant paint	__ Gypsum board	__ Gypsum board
__ **Ceiling**	__ Gypsum board with acoustic treatment if reflected sound may be a nuisance	__ Gypsum board	__ Gypsum board
__ **Acoustics**	__ Separation pad under washer / dryer to inhibit transfer of vibration from machines to floor __ Added soundproofing at plumbing wall if wall is common to an adjacent room __ Gasketing and caulking to inhibit airbore sound transfer through common plumbing wall __ Doors with sound gasketing if noise transfer to adjacent room may be a nuisance __ 40-45 STC	__ Provide some noise transfer controls as per Cost Recommendation A where location of laundry room might create serious noise problems __ 40-45 STC	__ No minimum requirement, but recommend 40-45 STC

DESIGN STANDARDS -- RESIDENTIAL LAUNDRY

DOORS & WINDOWS	Recommended	Minimum
__ **Doors**	__ For work convenience it's often preferable to have no door or to use a sliding pocket door __ A double-swinging door may be used for convenience where visual privacy is required	__ 3'-0" x 1-3/8" HC #2 grade
__ **Frames**	__ Wood -- custom or prehung, heavy duty	__ Wood prehung
__ **Hardware**	__ Brass or chrome plate	__ Brass or chrome plate __ Plated metal, standard grade
__ **Window light**	__ Equal to 20% of floor area or more, 1/2 of which is operable for outside air	__ Equal to minimum of 10% of floor area, 1/2 operable for air
__ **Skylight**	__ 2' x 4' or larger for interior laundry rooms or for light balance in rooms with outside light	

FIXTURES	Recommended	Minimum
__ **Built-in**	__ Pull-out clothes drying rod __ Clothes hanging rod __ Storage cabinets, storage wall __ Laundry tray __ Work counter __ Sound isolation pad at washer/dryer	__ No minimum requirements

FURNISHINGS

	Recommended	Minimum
__ **Space allowances for built-ins** Also see: **Fixture and Furniture Sizes** on previous page	__ Built in work counter, approx: 2' deep x 8' or longer __ Storage cabinets = 1 'x 3' or longer	__ No minimum requirements

PLUMBING	Recommended	Minimum

__ **Water supply & drainage**	__ Washer
	  __ 1/2" hot and cold supply
	  __ 1-1/2" drain
	__ Laundry sink:
	  __ 1/2" hot and cold supply
	  __ 1-1/2" drain
		__ As per Recommended

DESIGN STANDARDS -- RESIDENTIAL LAUNDRY

HVAC	Recommended	Minimum
__ Heating	__ 67° to 70° heat (this standard is for forced air heat, not radiant heating)	__ 67° to 70° heat at point 3'-0" above floor __ Forced air
__ Ventilation	__ Exterior opening for fresh air access, 10% to 20% of floor area __ 20 c.f. per minute __ Floor or wall exhuast for dryer __ Roof or wall exhaust for dryer gas heat __ Fresh air source for gas dryer __ Fresh air intake and exhaust for water heater	__ 50% of window operable for air __ 15 c.f. per minute __ Fresh air intakes and exhaust vent outlets as per Recommended
__ HVAC System	__ Forced air __ Floor conducted radiant heat	__ Forced air __ Radiator or electric wall heater
__ HVAC Controls	__ Thermostat, zone or room controls	__ Central thermostat

ELECTRICAL POWER	Recommended	Minimum

__ Power Outlets	__ Grounded outlets, average spacing 4' to 5'
	__ Strip outlet at work counter
	__ Outlets at:
	  __ Washer and dryer
	  __ Sewing table
	  __ Task lighting for sorting
		__ Grounded duplex outlets at 10' centers max.
		__ Strip outlet at work counter

__ Circuits	__ All outlets with ground fault interrupt protection __ Separate circuits for any fixtures rated at 20 amps or more	

LIGHTING	Recommended	Minimum
__ Lamps	__ Surface mounted incandescent or fluorescent __ Track lights __ Task light at work counter	__ Surface mounted or hanging incandescent or fluorescent __ Task light at work counter
__ Switching	__ 3-way switch if there is dual room access	__ Switch at main entry

ILLUMINATION	Recommended	Minimum
	__ 100 to150 f.c. adjustable range	__ 100 f.c.

COMMUNICATIONS	Recommended	Minimum
__ Communications	__ Smoke and fire alarm __ Phone jack __ Intercom	__ Smoke and fire alarm

DESIGN STANDARDS -- RESIDENTIAL WORKSHOP

GENERAL	Recommended Standards	Minimum Standards
__ **Floor Area**	__ 10' x 12' and up	__ 8' x 10'

__ **Furniture Sizes**	__ Furniture sizes:
	  __ Storage cabinets = 2'x 4' to 6'
	  __ Filing cabinet = 1'-4" x 2'-4"
	  __ Work bench = 1'-8" - 2'x8' and up
	  __ Drafting table = 3' x 4' and up
	  __ Shop tools (table saw, drill press, lathe, etc. as required by program)
		__ Furniture sizes as per Recommended Standards

__ **Clearances**	__ 3' walking aisles __ 4' working space at front of work bench and around major bench tools or floor mounted power tools	__ 2'-6" walking aisles __ 3" at front of work bench and major tools __ 3' at front of drawer filing cabinet
__ **Ceiling Height**	__ 3'-6" at front of drawer filing cabinet __ 8' - 10'	__ 8'

FINISHES	Cost Categories		
	A	B	C
__ **Floor**	__ Vinyl or rubber tile __ Wood block shop flooring __ Quarry tile, grounded	__ Concrete slab, steel trowel finish __ Vinyl tile	__ As per Cost Category B
__ **Base**	__ To match floor	__ No base	__ No base
__ **Cabinets, Casework**	__ Wood, paint grade	__ Wood, pressboard	__ Cabinets optional
__ **Counters**	__ Wood block __ Plastic laminate (for light hobby work only)	__ Wood, plank	__ Counters optional
__ **Walls**	__ Gypsum board, Type X or double layer for extra fire resistance __ Peg-board or other mounting board storage walls	__ Gypsum board	__ Gypsum board
__ **Ceiling**	__ Gypsum board with acoustic treatment	__ Gypsum board	__ Gypsum board
__ **Acoustics**	__ 50-70 STC for heavy duty shop use with loud power tools, otherwise as per Cost Category B	__ 45-55 STC	__ 40-45 STC

DESIGN STANDARDS -- RESIDENTIAL WORKSHOP

DOORS & WINDOWS	Recommended	Minimum
__ **Doors**	__ 3'-0" x 1-3/4" SCor steel door with sound isolation gaskets	__ 3'-0" x 1-3/8" HC #2 grade
__ **Frames**	__ 18 gauge steel with steel door, otherwise 16 gauge __ Wood, custom or prehung	__ Wood prehung
__ **Hardware**	__ Brass or chrome plate __ Security lock	__ Brass or chrome plate __ Plated metal, standard grade __ Lockable
__ **Window light**	__ Equal to 20% - 25% of floor area or more, 1/2 operable for outside air	__ Equal to minimum of 10% of floor area , 1/2 operable
__ **Skylight**	__ 4' x 4' or larger for interior workshop rooms or for light balance in shops with outside light	

FIXTURES	Recommended	Minimum
__ **Built-in**	__ Storage cabinets, storage wall __ Wood or metal shelves __ Worksink __ Central shop vacuum system	__ No minimum requirements

FURNISHINGS		
__ **Space allowances for built-ins** Also see: **Floor Area and Furniture Sizes** on previous page	__ Built in work counter, approx: 2' deep x 8' or longer __ Storage cabinets = 2'x 4' or longer	__ No minimum requirements

PLUMBING	Recommended	Minimum
__ **Water supply & drainage**	__ Worksink: __ 1/2" hot and cold supply __ 1-1/2" drain	__ No minimum requirements

DESIGN STANDARDS -- RESIDENTIAL WORKSHOP

HVAC	Recommended	Minimum
__ Heating	__ 67° to 70° heat (this standard is for forced air heat, not radiant heating)	__ 67° to 70° heat at point 3'-0" above floor __ Forced air
__ Ventilation	__ Exterior opening for fresh air access, 10% to 20% of floor area . __ 20 c.f. per minute	__ 50% of exterior window operable __ 15 c.f. per minute
__ HVAC System	__ Forced air __ Floor conducted radiant heat __ Radiator or electric wall heater	__ Forced air __ Radiator or electric wall heater
__ HVAC Controls	__ Thermostat, zone or room controls	__ Central thermostat

ELECTRICAL POWER	Recommended	Minimum

__ Power Outlets	__ Grounded outlets, average spacing 4' to 5'
	__ Outlets at 2' spacing at workbench or counter
	__ Outlets for:
	    __ Floor-mounted tools (floor outlets or ceiling-hung)
	    __ Ceiling for pull-down lamps
	    __ Shop vacuum
		__ Grounded duplex outlets at 10' centers max.
		__ Strip outlet at workbench or work counter wall

__ Circuits	__ All outlets with ground fault interrupt protection __ Circuit for built-in shop vacuum system __ Separate circuits for any fixtures rated at 20 amps or more	

LIGHTING	Recommended	Minimum
__ Lamps	__ Surface mounted incandescent or flourescent __ Track lights	__ Surface mounted or hanging flourescent
__ Switching	__ 3-way switch at each room access __ Master household switching and secuirty system with control board at bedside	__ Switch at main entry

ILLUMINATION	Recommended	Minimum
	__ 100 to150 f.c. adjustable range	__ 100 f.c.

COMMUNICATIONS	Recommended	Minimum
__ Communications	__ Smoke and fire alarm __ Phone jacks __ Intercom	__ Smoke and fire alarm

DESIGN STANDARDS -- RESIDENTIAL OFFICE

GENERAL	Recommended Standards	Minimum Standards
__ Floor Area	__ 12' x 12' to 14' x 14' and up double occupancy __ 10' x 12' and up for single occupancy	__ 10' x 14' for double occupancy __ 8' x 12' for single occupancy

__ Furniture Sizes	__ Furniture sizes:
	  __ Desk chair = 2' x 2'
	  __ Credenza storage cabinet = 2' x 4' to 6'
	  __ Filing cabinet = 1'-4" x 2'-4"
	  __ Computer printer and Fax counter or table
	    = 1'-8" x 4' and up
	  __ Drafting table = 3' x 4' and up
		__ Furniture sizes as per Recommended Standards

__ Clearances	__ 3' walking aisles __ 3' working space behind desk __ 3'-6" to use front drawer filing cabinet	__ 2'-6" walking aisles __ 2'-6" behind desk __ 3' to use front drawer file cabinet
__ Ceiling Height	__ 8' - 10'	__ 8'

FINISHES	Cost Categories		
	A	B	C

__ Floor	__ Carpet, padded or glued,
	    non-static
	__ Hardwood, 3/4" oak parquet
	    or strip
		__ Carpet
		__ Hardwood, standard grade
		__ Vinyl
			__ As per Cost Category B

__ Base	__ Hardwood, Custom Grade	__ Hardwood, paint grade	__ Hardwood, paint grade __ Vinyl
__ Cabinets, Casework	__ Wood, Premium Grade casework	__ Wood, Custom Grade casework	__ Wood, paint grade
__ Counter tops	__ Wood, Premium Grade __ Plastic laminate, HPDL grade	__ Wood, Custom Grade __ Plastic laminate	__ Plastic laminate
__ Wainscot	__ Hardwood, Premium Grade __ Plaster __ Fabric or heavy duty decorative wall cover	__ Hardwood, Custom Grade __ Fabric or medium weight decorative wall cover __ Gypsum board, painted	__ Gypsum board, painted
__ Walls	__ Hardwood, Premium Grade __ Fabric or heavy duty decorative wall cover __ Plaster __ Gypsum board	__ Hardwood, Custom Grade __ Fabric or medium weight decorative wall cover	__ Gypsum board
__ Soffits & Ceiling	__ Plaster __ Gypsum board with acoustic treatment	__ Gypsum board	__ Gypsum board
__ Acoustics	__ 35-50 STC	__ 30-40 STC	__ No minimum, but if office will be in heavy use, 30-40 STC is recommended

DESIGN STANDARDS -- RESIDENTIAL OFFICE

DOORS & WINDOWS	Recommended	Minimum
__ **Doors**	__ 3'-0" x 1-3/4" HC premium to #2 grade, 7 ply __ Solid core, or SC with gaskets if sound isolation required	__ 3'-0" x 1-3/8" HC #2 grade
__ **Frames**	__ Wood -- custom or prehung	__ Wood, prehung
__ **Hardware**	__ Knobs/handles -- brass, bronze, ceramic latchset __ Security lock	__ Brass or chrome plate __ Plated metal, standard grade __ Lockable
__ **Window light**	__ Equal to 20% - 25% of floor area or more	__ Equal to minimum of 10% of floor area AND no less than 10 sq. ft.

FIXTURES	Recommended	Minimum
__ **Built-in**	__ Book and storage shelves __ Shelf for artwork	__ No minimum requirements

FURNISHINGS		
__ **Space allowances for built-ins**	__ Built in work counter, approx: 2' deep x 4' to 10' long	__ No minimum requirements

Also see:
Floor Area and Furniture Sizes on previous page

PLUMBING	Recommended	Minimum
__ **Water supply & drainage**	__ Worksink: __ 1/2" hot and cold supply __ 1-1/2" drain	__ No minimum requirements

DESIGN STANDARDS -- RESIDENTIAL OFFICE

HVAC	Recommended	Minimum
__ Heating	__ 68° to 70° heat (this standard is for forced air heat, not radiant heating)	__ 67° to 72° heat at point 3'-0" above floor __ Forced air
__ Ventilation	__ Exterior opening for fresh air access, 10% to 20% of floor area and 8 sq. ft. minimum __ 20 c.f. per minute	__ Exterior opening, minimum 10% of floor area and 6 sq. ft. minimum __ 15 c.f. per minute
__ HVAC System	__ Forced air __ Floor conducted radiant heat __ Radiator or fan coil unit	__ Forced air __ Radiator or fan coil unit
__ HVAC Controls	__ Thermostat, zone or room controls	__ Central thermostat

ELECTRICAL POWER	Recommended	Minimum

__ Power Outlets	__ Grounded outlets, average spacing 4' to 5'
	__ Outlets at:
	  __ Desk
	  __ Computer station(s)
	  __ Computer printer(s)
	  __ Fax
	  __ Copier
	  __ Answering machine
		__ Grounded duplex outlets at 10' centers max.

__ Circuits	__ All outlets with ground fault interrupt protection __ Separate circuits for any fixtures rated at 20 amps or more	

LIGHTING	Recommended	Minimum
__ Lamps	__ Recessed incandescent __ Track lights or wall wash lights for artwork	__ Central recessed or surface mounted fixture
__ Switching	__ 3-way switch at each room access __ Master household switching	__ Switch at main entry

ILLUMINATION	Recommended	Minimum
	__ 100 to150 f.c. adjustable range (mainly determined by occupants and individual lamps)	__ 100 f.c. general light (mainly determined by occupants and individual lamps)

COMMUNICATIONS	Recommended	Minimum
__ Communications	__ Smoke and fire alarm, concealed __ Phone jacks	__ Smoke and fire alarm

RESTAURANTS

DESIGN STANDARDS -- RESTAURANT FOYER

GENERAL	Recommended Standards	Minimum Standards
__ Floor Area	__ As per program. __ Waiting area for up to 12 to 16 people at 15 sq. ft. per person for seating, 8 sq. ft. per person for stand-up waiting __ Waiting area for over 16 people not recommended, use bar or other space as waiting area	__ As per program. __ Waiting area for up to 12 to 16 people at 10 sq. ft. per person for seating, 6 sq. ft. per person for stand-up waiting
__ Ceiling	__ 10' - 14' __ 8' soffit OK	__ 8' OK in foyers for smaller restaurants __ 7' soffits OK
__ Special Plan Considerations	WARNINGS AND CAUTIONS FOR ALL RESTAURANT DESIGN: __ Never design a one or two step-down entry from foyer to dining area unless they are extremely well lit, clearly marked, and with handrails -- such steps are a very common cause of falls __ Restaurant foyers and waiting areas are often described by patrons as cramped, smoky, noisy, drafty from the front door opening and closing, and generally unpleasant. __ Intercoms are often inadquate for calling patrons for seating in a noisy waiting area __ Built-in seating and booth seating is often poorly designed and uncomfortable in size -- too high or two low -- so give such seating extra care in design	

FINISHES, DOORS, FIXTURES, HVAC, ETC. AS PER DINING ROOMS -- see next page

DESIGN STANDARDS -- RESTAURANT DINING ROOM

GENERAL	Recommended Standards	Minimum Standards
__ **Floor Area**	__ Recommended seating areas for dining: __ 4 diners = 130 sq. ft. __ 6 diners = 160 sq. ft. __ 8 diners = 180 sq. ft. __ 10 - 12 diners = 248 sq. ft.	__ Minimum floor space for: __ 4 diners = 90 sq. ft. __ 6 diners = 150 sq. ft. __ 8 diners = 172 sq. ft. __ 10 - 12 diners = 210 sq. ft.
__ **Minimum Widths and Clearances**	__ Width per place setting = 32" __ Aisle access behind chairs = 36" __ Service aisle = 40" - 48"	__ Minimum width per place setting = 28" __ Minimum aisle access behind chairs = 24" __ Minimum service aisle = 36"
__ **Ceiling Height**	__ 10' - 14' __ 7'-6" soffits OK	__ 9' __ 7' soffits
__ **Special Plan Considerations**	__ 4-person tables set at 45° provides maximum seating room and greatest planning flexibility (36" table, 18" seats, 18" aisle per module)	

FINISHES	Cost Categories		
	A	B	C
__ **Floor**	__ Carpet, glued, non-stain synthetic, static proof (wool not recommended) __ Non-slip ceramic tile, stone tile, or quarry tile __ Hardwood, 3/4" oak parquet or strip, Prime or #1 grade	__ Carpet, glued, non-stain __ Hardwood, standard grade	__ As per Cost Category B __ Vinyl floor OK in family convenience restaurants
__ **Base**	__ Hardwood __ As per floor	__ Hardwood	__ Hardwood, paint grade __ Vinyl
__ **Cabinets, Casework**	__ Wood, Premium grade casework	__ Wood, Custom grade casework	__ Wood, paint grade
__ **Counter tops**	__ Wood, Premium Grade __ Polished and sealed stone __ Ceramic tile __ Plastic laminate, HPDL grade	__ Wood, Custom Grade __ Plastic laminate	__ Plastic laminate
__ **Wainscot**	__ Hardwood, Premium grade __ Plaster __ Fabric or heavy duty decorative wall cover	__ Hardwood, Custom grade __ Fabric or medium weight decorative wall cover __ Gypsum board, painted	__ Gypsum board, painted
__ **Walls**	__ Hardwood, Premium grade __ Fabric or heavy duty decorative wall cover __ Plaster __ Gypsum board	__ Hardwood, Custom grade __ Fabric or medium weight decorative wall cover	__ Gypsum board, painted
__ **Soffits & Ceiling**	__ Wood paneling, exposed beams, Premium Grade __ Plaster __ Gypsum board	__ Gypsum board, painted __ Plywood paneling	__ Gypsum board, painted
__ **Acoustics**	__ 35-40 STC if sound protection between dining space and adjacent rooms is required	__ 25-35 STC if sound protection between dining space and adjacent rooms is required	__ No minimum STC requirement or recommendation

DESIGN STANDARDS -- RESTAURANT DINING ROOM

DOORS & WINDOWS	Recommended	Minimum
__ **Doors**	__ 3'-0" to 3'-6" x 1-3/4" SC premium to #2 grade, 7 ply __ Traffic door: double acting with push plate and view panel __ Solid core, or SC with gaskets if sound isolation required	__ 3'-0" x 1-3/8" HC #2 grade
__ **Frames**	__ Wood -- custom or prehung	__ Wood, prehung
__ **Hardware**	__ Knobs/handles -- brass, stainless steel __ Kickplates -- brass, stainless steel	__ Brass plate or chrome __ Plated metal, standard grade
__ **Window light**	__ Equal to 25% to 30% of floor area or more	__ Equal to minimum of 20% of floor area

FIXTURES	Recommended	Minimum
__ **Built-in**	__ Picture hanging rail for artwork display __ Shelving or cabinets for display __ Cashier's station __ Maitre d' station __ Wait stations with storage, water, and ice supply	__ No minimum requirements

FURNISHINGS		
__ **Space allowances for built-ins**	__ Dining booths = 5'-6" long x 3'-6" deep __ Counter seating = 20" deep x 24" per diner with 4'-6" for work aisle behind counter __ Built-in bench seating for booth and waiting area = 24" x 24" per person	__ Dining booths = 5'-6" long x 4' deep __ Counter seating = 18" deep x 20" per diner with 4' for work aisle behind counter __ Built-in bench seating for booth and waiting area = 18" deep x 20"wide per person

PLUMBING	Recommended	Minimum
	__ Supply to ice machine and water station sink __ 1-1/2" drains at water station drains __ Sprinklers, concealed __ Fire hose cabinets as per fire code	__ As per Recommended

DESIGN STANDARDS -- RESTAURANT DINING ROOM

HVAC	Recommended	Minimum
__ Occupancy	__ As per program and restaurant consultant -- density of seating will depend on restaurant type and turnover rate	__ As per program
__ Heating	__ Uniform 70° F heat at all heights	__ 70° F heat at point 3'-0" above floor
__ Ventilation WARNING: Drafts near air supply and exhausts, kitchen door, and entry are a common cause of diner discomfort and complaints	__ 25 - 35 c.f. per minute __ Drafts must be avoided at seating height __ Exhaust fan system in kitchen must prevent odors from reaching dining room	__ 20 c.f. per minute
__ HVAC System & Controls	__ Forced air __ Floor conducted radiant heat __ Thermostat, zone or room controls	__ Forced air __ Radiator or fan coil unit __ Central thermostat and or manual controls at radiator or fan coil units

ELECTRICAL POWER	Recommended	Minimum

__ Power Outlets	__ Grounded outlets:
	  __ As required for janitorial maintenance
	  __ Strip outlets at wainscot height at side board and/or buffet for food warmers, other appliances
	  __ At wait station
	  __ At maitre d' station for podium light
	  __ At cashier station
	  __ For artwork
	__ All outlets with ground fault protection
		__ Grounded duplex base outlets at 10' centers
		__ Outlets at sideboards and wait station locations
		__ Ground fault interruption protected outlets

__ Circuits	__ Separate circuits for appliances rated at 20 amps or more	

LIGHTING	Recommended	Minimum
__ Lamps	__ Downlights or accent lights centered over dining tables __ Recessed incandescent __ Track lights or wall wash lights for artwork	__ Central recessed or surface mounted fixture
__ Switching	__ 3- or 4-way switch at each room access __ Dimmer for chandeliers __ Dimmers for hanging or recessed fixtures, and/or wall wash lights	__ Switches at main entry __ Some dimmer control is very desirable

ILLUMINATION	Recommended	Minimum
	__ 5 to 30 f.c. adjustable lighting	__ 30 f.c. general light

COMMUNICATIONS	Recommended	Minimum
__ Communications	__ Smoke and fire alarms, concealed __ Phone and intercom communication at cashier __ Public phone near waiting area or restrooms __ Intercoms at wait and maitre d' stations for kitchen communication	__ Smoke and fire alarms __ Phone and intercom at cashier station __ Public phone near waiting area or restrooms

219

DESIGN STANDARDS -- RESTAURANT KITCHENS

GENERAL	Recommended Standards	Minimum Standards
__ Floor Area	__ Restaurants serving 100 to 400 meals per day generally require 5 to 7 sq. ft. per meal __ Restaurants serving over 500 meals per day may require a maximum of 6 sq. ft per meal __ Approx. 33% of floor space for equipment, remainder for work tables and aisles __ Alternate rule of thumb: 8 to 11 sq. ft. of kitchen per dining seat	__ Restaurants serving 100 to 400 meals per day require minimum 4 to 5 sq. ft. per meal __ Restaurants serving over 500 meals per day require minimum 5 sq. ft. per meal __ Approx. 30% of floor space for equipment, remainder for work tables and aisles
__ Work table sizes	__ 30" wide tables (36" if storage at back) __ 42" work tables with workers both sides __ 4' to 8' length for single worker, 8' to 12' length for two adjacent workers	__ 24" wide tables (36" if storage at back) __ 40" work tables with workers both sides __ 4' to 6' length for single worker, 6' to 10' length for two adjacent workers
__ Aisle widths	__ 38" aisles and wider for single worker __ 44" and wider for two-way worker traffic __ 56" and wider for cart traffic __ 66" for heavy two-way cart or tray traffic	__ 36" for single worker __ 40" for two-way worker traffic __ 50" for cart traffic __ 60" for heavy two-way cart or tray traffic
__ Ceiling Height	__ 12' and higher ceilings recommended for air flow and easy exhaust; 7' soffits with exhaust fans OK	__ 10' minimum __ 7' soffits with exhaust fans OK
__ Special Plan Considerations	__ Work counters and aisles at right angles to main traffic aisles	

FINISHES	Cost Categories		
	A	B	C
__ Floor NOTE: Provide floor slopes to drains and depress floor slabs for insulation at walk-in refrigerators WARNING: Terrazzo and rubber are damaaged by kitchen products	__ Seamless poured floor __ Non-slip ceramic tile or quarry tile __ Solid vinyl sheet -- heavy grade with backing __ Vinyl tile	__ Quarry tile __ Vinyl sheet or vinyl tile WARNING: Terrazzo and rubber are damaged by kitchen products	__ Asphalt tile __ Concrete slab, steel trowel finish
__ Base & Coves NOTE: Provide high base and curbs, coves, and toe spaces for easy cleaning	__ As per floor __ Concrete curbs for floor-mounted equipment	__ As per floor	__ As per floor
__ Counters & Back-splashes	__ Stainless steel __ Ceramic tile or sealed quarry tile __ Butcher block sections	__ Stainless steel __ Plastic laminate	__ Plastic laminate
__ Walls	__ Ceramic tile __ Keenes cement plaster __ Plastic laminate __ 5/8" Gypsum board (Type W) with water- & mildew-resistant glossy paint	__ Gypsum board with water-resistant and mildew resistant glossy paint	__ Gypsum board with washable paint
__ Soffits & Ceiling	__ Keenes cement plaster __ 5/8" Gypsum board (Type W)	__ Gypsum board with water- & mildew-resistant paint	__ Gypsum board with washable paint
__ Acoustics	__ 52-58 STC	__ 48-55 STC	__ 45-50 STC

DESIGN STANDARDS -- RESTAURANT KITCHENS

DOORS & WINDOWS	Recommended	Minimum

__ **Doors**
 	
NOTE: Provide service vestibule buffers between kitchen and serving areas
	__ Traffic doors -- double-acting with large push plates, kick plates, and view panel
	__ Other doors:
	   __ Heavy-duty steel finish or heavy-duty push plates and kick plates
	   __ Sound isolation gasket
	
	__ Exit doors with panic bars, fire rated assembly as required by fire code
		__ Traffic doors -- as per Recommended
		
		__ Other doors:
		   __ 1-3/4" solid core with push plates and kick plates
		
		__ Exit doors with panic bars, fire rated assembly as required by fire code

__ **Frames**	__ 14 gauge steel	__ 16 gauge steel
__ **Hardware**	__ Brass or chrome plated	__ Brass plated and stainless steel
__ **Skylights**	__ As needed to augment daytime artifical light and balance and reduce window contrast glare	__ No required minimums

FIXTURES/EQUIPMENT	Recommended	Minimum

NOTE:
 	
There are wide variations in types and sizes of kitchen equipment that might be selected -- coordinate closely with the chef, kitchen planning consultant, and consulting engineers . . . equipment and size notes here are only for the most preliminary consideration.
 	
City codes are often strict regarding hood design, exhaust, and safety features and must be consulted early in the design process.
	__ Rule of thumb, cold storage area relative to total kitchen area =
	__ Total food storage = 20% of kitchen
	__ Rules of thumb on refrigeration, of total cold storage space:
	   __ 33% meats
	   __ 33% produce
	   __ 20% dairy products
	   __ 15% - 25% frozen foods
	   __ 5% - 10% for salads, breads, prepared meals
	__ Walk-in refrigerators (usually required for service of over 400 or more meals daily)
	__ Dishwasher area -- 2' or 3' wide x 5' to 10' (or longer conveyor type systems)
	__ Range -- six- to twelve-burner range tops
	__ Hood exhaust as per local code
	__ Ovens -- 2' to 3' wide x 2' deep
	__ Sinks -- food prep, pot washing, etc., as per program -- generally 2' to 3' long x 2' wide
	__ Compactor
	__ Microwave oven
		__ As per recommended

PLUMBING	Recommended	Minimum
__ **Water heater**	__ As per program and kitchen planning consultant	__ As per program
__ **Water supply**	__ 1" or 3/4" supply - Type K copper tubing __ Fire sprinklers (dry fire extinquishers at stoves)	__ Hot & cold, 3/4" supply
__ **Water drainage**	__ 2" fixture drains __ 4" house drains __ 4" floor drains	__ 1-1/2" fixture drains __ 3" house drain

DESIGN STANDARDS -- RESTAURANT KITCHENS

HVAC	Recommended	Minimum
__ **Heating** NOTE: kitchens provide most of their own heat and HVAC engineering is largely for removal of heat and exhaust	__ 68° - 72° F uniform at all levels __ Forced air if required __ Radiator or fan coil unit if localized heating required	__ 70° - 74° F at 3'-0" above floor __ Unit heaters
__ **Ventilation**	__ Exhaust fans at stove, oven, dishwasher areas plus overload emergency exhaust fans __ Outside exhausts for refrigeration equipment __ 50 c.f.m. outdoor air per person __ Operable windows are desirable for smaller kitchens -- 20% or more of floor area	__ 4 air changes per hour w/20% of air supply from outside __ 35 - 40 c.f.m. __ Exhaust fans at cooking and dishwashing equipment __ Outside exhausts for refrigeration equipment
__ **HVAC System & Controls**	__ Thermostat, zone or room controls	__ Room thermostat

ELECTRICAL POWER	Recommended	Minimum
__ **Power Outlets** NOTE: Kitchen consultant and electrical engineer must work in close coordination throughout kitchen planning, particularly in the earliest decision-making phases and in the latter phases when last-minute changes may be made	__ Grounded outlets at all wall counters and work tables, average spacing 2' to 3' __ Separate power outlet for every appliance __ All outlets with ground fault interrupt protection	__ Grounded duplex outlets spaced at 4' at every counterspace over 12" wide __ Ground fault interruption protection within reach of sinks or faucets
__ **Circuits**	__ Separate circuits for all appliances rated at 20 amps or more	__ Separate circuit for kitchen electrical equipment

LIGHTING	Recommended	Minimum
__ **Lamps**	__ Overall flourescent work lighting, surface mounted or pendant __ Task-specific lights: Spots/track/recessed	__ Single fixture, fluorescent or incandescent
__ **Switching**	__ 3- or 4-way switch at each kitchen access __ Central panel for all switches	__ Single switch at main entry __ Individual soffit task light switches

ILLUMINATION	Recommended	Minimum
	__ 200 f.c. task lighting __ 50 - 60 f.c. general lighting	__ 150 f.c. task lighting __ 50 f.c. general lighting

COMMUNICATIONS	Recommended	Minimum
__ **Communications**	__ Phone at kitchen office, recipe desk, receiving desk, and cashier station __ Intercom connect with manager's office, cashier, etc. __ Smoke and fire alarms	__ Phone jacks as per program __ Smoke and fire alarms

RESTROOMS

DESIGN STANDARDS -- RESTROOMS

PRIMARY FIXTURES

MINIMUM ALLOCATION OF FIXTURES BY BUILDING TYPE

For higher quality facilities, increase the fixture count by 15% to 25%

	WATER CLOSETS	LAVATORIES	URINALS
__ **Auditoriums & Other Assembly Buildings**	__ 1 per 100 occupancy __ For occupancies over 400, add 1 for each additional 500 males and 1 for each additional 100 females	__ 1 per 100 occupancy __ Occupancy over 750, add 1 per each 500 persons	__ 1 per each 100 males up to 500; add one for each additional 300 males
__ **Dormatory Housing**	__ Males: 1 per 8 __ Females: 1 per 4	__ 1 per 15 persons	__ 1 per 15 males (not provided in smaller housing units)
__ **Office Buildings**	__ Males: 1 per 15 persons up to 50; 1 per 20 persons up to 100; 1 per 40 additional persons __ Females: Multiply preceding estimates by 1.5	__ 1 per 15 persons for occupancy up to 60; 1 per 25 persons for occupancy up to 125; 1 for each additional 45 persons	__ 1 per 25 males
__ **Industrial Plants, Labs, Workshops**	__ Males: 1 per 10 persons up to 50 occupants; 1 per 20 persons up to 100; 1 for each additional 30 persons __ Females: Multiply above estimates by 1.5	__ 1 per 10 persons	__ 1 per 25 males
__ **Schools**	__ Males: 1 per 100 __ Females: 1 per 20	__ 1 per 75 persons	__ 1 per 25 males
__ **Institutional Buildings (public restrooms)**	__ Males: 1 per 20 occupancy up to 100; 1 per each additional 50 __ Females: Multiply preceding estimates by 1.5	__ 1 per 15 persons for occupancy up to 60; 1 per 25 persons for occupancy up to 125; 1 for each additional 45 persons	__ 1 per 25 males

NOTE:
The number of women's restroom fixtures required by most building codes is inadequate

DESIGN STANDARDS -- RESTROOMS

GENERAL	Recommended Standards	Minimum Standards
__ Occupancies and Floor Areas	__ Assume 50 sq. ft. of total toilet room space per water closet (see preceding page for water closet estimates)	__ Basic 3-fixture bathroom = 40 sq. ft. __ Two-fixture guest bath or powder room with toilet and lav = 20 to 30 sq. ft.
__ Fixture Widths, Spacings, and Clearances	__ Toilet stalls = 3' x 5' __ Toilet front distance to stall door = 2'-8" __ Lavs = 3' o.c. __ Lavs at counter = 1'-6" for each lav plus 2' to 3' counter space at one or both sides __ Handicapped toilet stall = 3'-8" wide fcr front entry, 4'-0" wide for side entry with 4' clear space in front of toilet __ Door to handicapped toilet stall = 3'-6" front entry, 4'-0" side entry with 6'-0" turn around space __ Passageways = 4'+ wide	__ 3' to 5' wide dressing area __ Toilet front distance to lav or to wall = 2'-2" __ Toilet space width = 2'-8" __ Clearance between edge of tub to wall or fixture = 3' __ Lav = 1'-6" to 2' width
__ Ceiling Height	__ 8' to 9' with 7' soffits	__ 8' with 7' soffits

FINISHES	Cost Categories A	B	C
__ Floor WARNING: Bathroom flooring must have moisture barrier under-layment, and floors on upper levels require complete waterproof seal	__ Ceramic tile, non-slip finish __ Polished and sealed stone, non-slip finish __ Slope to drain WARNING: Terrazzo, sometimes specified as a "quality" flooring in restrooms, is vulnerable to chemical staining and is not recommended	__ Ceramic tile __ Vinyl sheet	__ As per Cost Category B WARNING: Vinyl or asphalt tile are subject to moisture damage and maintenance problems and are not recommended for restrooms
__ Base	__ As per floor	__ As per floor	__ As per floor
__ Wainscot	__ Ceramic tile	__ Ceramic tile __ Gypsum board with vinyl finish __ Gypsum board with water resistant paint finish	__ As per walls __ Gypsum board, painted
__ Walls	__ Ceramic tile over waterproof gypsum board __ Waterproof plaster __ Gypsum board, type W	__ Gypsum board, water resistant	__ Concrete block, painted
__ Counter tops	__ Ceramic tile, sealed __ Composite __ Plastic laminate, HPDL grade	__ Ceramic tile, sealed __ Plastic laminate	__ No counters
__ Soffits & Ceiling	__ Plaster: hard, smooth finish __ Gypsum board, type W __ Paint must be water and mildew resistant	__ Gypsum board, painted __ Paint -- water and mildew resistant	__ Gypsum board, painted

DESIGN STANDARDS -- RESTROOMS

DOORS & WINDOWS	Recommended	Minimum
__ Doors	__ 3'-6" steel door, 16 gauge __ 3'-6" x 1-3/4" SC premium to #2 grade, 7 ply __ Restrooms in high-use locations such as transit terminals should provide unobstructed "S" entry without doors __ Raised threshold	__ 3'-4" x 1-3/4" SC #2 grade
__ Frames	__ 14 gauge steel __ Wood, extra-heavy duty	__ 16 gauge steel __ Wood prehung (for low-use restrooms)
__ Hardware	__ Automatic closers __ Steel or brass push plate __ Steel or brass kick plate __ Lockable where security is a consideration __ Handicapped accessible	__ Brass or chrome plate __ Plated metal, standard grade
__ Window light	__ Equal to 20% of floor area or more for restrooms at exterior walls __ 50% operable where not a security problem nor a hindrance to effective air conditioning	__ Equal to 10% of floor area or more for restrooms at exterior walls

FIXTURES	Recommended	Minimum

__ Fixtures & Fittings
 	
NOTE: Top quality fixtures may provide considerable long-term economies in maintenance
	__ Recessed waste receptacle
	__ Recessed paper towel dispenser
	__ Recessed soap dispenser
	__ Lav mirrors
	__ Full length mirror
	__ Toilet partition mounted:
	   __ Seat cover dispenser
	   __ Toilet tissue dispenser
	   __ Feminine napkin disposal
	   __ Coat hook
	   __ Package shelf
	__ Handicapped stall includes above listed fittings, plus:
	   __ Grab bars as per code
	   __ Recessed multi-roll toilet tissue dispenser
	__ Grab bar, towel bars, soap dishes
	__ Auxiliary lav, urinal, towel and soap dispensers for convenient handicapped access
		__ As per Recommended except most fixtures surface mounted instead of recessed and economy grade rather than top grade
		__ Surface-mounted fixtures must not be barriers to the handicapped

FURNISHINGS

__ Built-ins	__ Built-in make-up counter with large lighted mirrors	

PLUMBING	Recommended	Minimum
__ Fixtures NOTE: Water supply and drains should be larger than code minimums to avoid maintenance problems	__ Wall-mounted urinals and toilets, top grade __ Countertop mounted lavs __ Automatic sensor lav water supply __ Automatic urinal flush control __ Floor drain for mopping and to control overflows	__ Wall or floor-mounted urinals/toilets __ Wall-mounted lavs __ Standard flush mounts

DESIGN STANDARDS -- RESTROOMS

HVAC	Recommended	Minimum
__ Heating	__ 70° to 72° F temperature (this standard is for forced air heat, not radiant heating) __ Radiator or fan coil unit	__ 68° to 73° F heat at point 3'-0" above floor __ Forced air
__ Ventilation	__ 45 c.f. per minute per estimated full occupancy __ Fan with exhaust vent to outside	__ 30 c.f. per minute
__ HVAC System	__ Forced air	__ Forced air
__ HVAC Controls	__ Thermostat, zone controls	__ Central thermostat

ELECTRICAL POWER	Recommended	Minimum
__ Power Outlets	__ Easily accessible grounded outlets for: __ Electric shave at mirror __ Jjanitorial maintenance __ Vending machines such as shoe polisher __ Junction box for built-in electrical fixtures such as electric hand dryers	__ As per Recommended
__ Circuits	__ All outlets with ground fault interrupt protection __ Separate circuits for any fixtures rated at 20 amps or more	

LIGHTING	Recommended	Minimum
__ Lamps	__ Recessed fluorescent or incandescent __ Make-up mirror and full length mirror lights	__ Central recessed or surface mounted fixtures
__ Switching	__ Lockable standard switch at entry	__ Switch at entry, non lockable for small restrooms in secure buildings __ Fan exhaust combined with light switch in smaller restrooms without direct outside ventilation

ILLUMINATION	Recommended	Minimum
	__ 40 - 60 f.c.	__ 30 f.c. general light

COMMUNICATIONS	Recommended	Minimum
__ Communications	__ Smoke and fire alarms __ PA where public announcements might be made, such as at theaters or transit terminals	__ As per Recommended

227

SCHOOLS

Note:

Data provided here for classrooms and related spaces are equally applicable to elementary schools, junior high schools, and high schools. Some requirements will vary depending on local school boards and state boards of education standards.

DESIGN STANDARDS -- SCHOOL CLASSROOM

GENERAL	Recommended Standards	Minimum Standards
__ Occupancies	__ As per the overall Educational Plan and design program __ For predesign and schematic planning estimate assume 30 sq. ft. per pupil	__ As per program __ Code exit minimums may allow planning for 15 sq. ft. per pupil but this is inadequate __ Allow 20 to 25 sq. ft. per pupil
__ Floor Area	__ As per program -- 784 sq. ft. to 900 sq. ft. is a common range of floor areas for classrooms (28' x 28' to 30' x 30')	__ As per program but 625 sq. ft. (25 students with 25 sq. ft. each) would normally be minimum
__ Ceiling Height	__ 10' to 12' high __ Sloping ceilings up to 14' are desirable	__ 9'-6" in smaller classrooms
__ Plan Considerations	__ Access to outdoors is desirable	__ Safety is of primary concern in all facilities, even if low cost

FINISHES	Cost Categories		
	A	B	C
__ **Floors & Sub-structures** CAUTION: Avoid carpet near exterior entrances, sinks, and other sources of wetting, staining, or soiling	__ Sound isolated substructure __ Nylon or acrylic carpet rated for heavy wear and glued to floor; static proofed __ Vinyl tile	__ Sound isolated substructure __ Carpet, heavy wear, glued __ Vinyl tile	__ Carpet, medium, glued __ Vinyl or asphalt tile WARNING: Asphalt tile floors, in combination with some types of movable chairs and tables, can cause extreme noise problems
__ **Walls & Substructure**	__ Top grade wall writing surfaces and tack boards __ Gypsum board or plaster, painted; heavyweight vinyl or fabric OK where surface is not vulnerable to damage __ Fire ratings and material flame spread ratings as per code __ Complete sound separation between rooms __ Complete thermal insulation at exterior walls	__ Top grade wall writing surfaces recommended to reduce school maintenance and operating costs __ Gypsum board, painted	__ Chalk boards or marker boards along one wall __ Tack board at one wall __ Gypsum board over stud construction __ Concrete block, painted __ Fire ratings as per code
__ **Ceiling**	__ Sound isolated substructure __ Vaulted or coffered ceiling __ Suspended acoustic tile with integrated lighting	__ Suspended acoustic ceiling with integrated lighting	__ Suspended ceiling with exposed grid __ Surface mounted or pendant fixtures
__ **Counters & Built-In Fixtures & Furnishings**	__ Cabinetry as per educational design program __ Map rails, chart rails, projection screens, etc. __ Chair rails at walls in rooms with movable chairs __ Bookshelves and cabinets as per program __ Instructor's locker/cabinet	__ As much as possible as per Cost Category A	__ Economy grade fixtures and furnishings; higher grades recommended where important to save building operating costs
__ **Acoustics**	__ NC 30 - 35, STC 45 - 55 __ Acoustical consultant to optimize acoustic performance of all rooms __ Acoustic separation of all substructures	__ NC 25 - 35, STC 40 - 45	__ STC 35 - 45 __ Sound isolated construction as required by program in specific spaces

DESIGN STANDARDS -- SCHOOL CLASSROOM

DOORS & WINDOWS	Recommended	Minimum
__ Doors	__ 1-3/4" solid core entry/exit doors __ Sound proofing gaskets at all edges unless room is located in non-sound sensitive part of the building __ Vision panel in or beside door __ Doors fire rated if opening onto fire exit corridors -- as per fire code	__ As per fire code
__ Frames	__ 14 gauge steel	__ 16 gauge steel
__ Hardware NOTE: Heavy-duty hardware saves maintenance costs and is very desirable	__ Quiet, concealed automatic closers __ Panic bar exit hardware as required by code __ Controlled locking __ Handicapped access hardware	__ As per Recommended
__ Windows	__ Double pane for noise insulation from exterior __ Sound insulating gaskets on operable sash __ Blinds and blackout drapes __ Orientation and exterior shades to prevent sun glare and heat gain	__ As per code for light requirements __ Operable sash as per code __ Blinds and blackout drapes __ Design orientation and fixtures to prevent sun glare and heat gain will greatly decrease school building operating costs
__ Skylights	__ Skylights not recommended without ready controls of heat gain and blackout	

FIXTURES/EQUIPMENT	Recommended	Minimum
__ Special Furnishings	__ As per Educational Plan, program and special classroom uses, such as laboratories and art rooms	__ As per Recommended
__ Audio-Visual/Meeting Equipment	__ Computer network __ Television and VCR __ Overhead projector __ Provisions for slide and film presentations __ Built-in screen if presentation area is defined __ Storage and/or convenient access to portable screen and other equipment storage	__ As much per Recommended as possible

PLUMBING	Recommended	Minimum
__ Fixtures	__ As required by program for special classroom functions such as labs, art classes, etc. __ For lower grades and younger children: stainless steel sink with bubbler __ Sprinklers	__ As per code

DESIGN STANDARDS -- SCHOOL CLASSROOM

HVAC	Recommended	Minimum
__ Occupancies	__ As per program -- up to 30 per classroom, 30 sq. ft. per student	__ As per program -- up to 36 per classroom or 20 to 25 sq. ft. per student
__ Ventilation	__ 20 to 30 cfm outside air per occupant during hot or cold weather, otherwise operable windows will provide most ventilation	__ 20 cfm outdoor air per occupant
__ HVAC System & Controls NOTE: If later expansion of the school is anticipated, provide for expansion of the HVAC system	__ Energy monitoring sensors connecting to central computerized control system __ Central HVAC system with individual room control __ If climate is zone controlled, temperatures 68° to 70° F __ Relative humidity between 50% - 65%, lower or higher depending on room temperature __ Maximum air movement at head height of 30' per minute	__ If climate is zone controlled, temperatures 68° to 72° F __ Air conditioning if required by climate __ Fan coil units __ Individual room thermostats

ELECTRICAL POWER	Recommended	Minimum
__ Power Outlets	__ Outlets for each computer and other instructional equipment required by overall Education Plan __ Task lighting outlets at instructor's station and all work or display counters __ Outlets for presentation slide and film projectors, video, overhead projector, video monitor, video projector, etc. __ Wall base outlets or outlet strips for all contemplated future electric or electronic equipment __ Outlets as required for janitorial service __ For clock and communication systems	__ Instructor's station __ As required for maintenance __ Outlets for audio/visual equipment __ For clock and communication systems

LIGHTING	Recommended	Minimum
__ Lamps	__ Integrated ceiling fluorescent fixtures __ Fluorescent high output with low glare __ Task lights or downlights as per program __ No brightness variations over 3:1 __ Ceiling reflectance factor minimum of 0.7 __ Reflectance factor of furnishings approx. 0.5	__ Fluorescent ceiling lights, recessed or surface mounted __ Some ceiling lights dimmable for audio/visual presentations
__ Switching	__ Bank light switching with dimmer lights for audio/visual presentations	__ Standard wall switches near instructor's station

ILLUMINATION	Recommended	Minimum
	__ 70 - 100 f.c. for reading and study, with primary dependence on natural light	__ 50 - 70 f.c.

COMMUNICATIONS	Recommended	Minimum
__ Communications	__ Outside telephone line __ Fire and smoke alarms __ Intercom and PA system __ Centrally controlled clock and signal bell __ Computer lines __ Video cable	__ As much as possible as per Recommended

DESIGN STANDARDS -- SECONDARY SCHOOL LIBRARY/STUDY HALL

GENERAL	Recommended Standards	Minimum Standards
__ Occupancies	__ As per Education Master Plan and school design program	__ As per program; see the introductory section on Libraries for rules-of-thumb for overall occupancies and spatial requirements
__ Floor Area	__ 50 sq. ft. per reader	__ 35 sq. ft.
__ Ceiling Height	__ 8' to 9' -- reading alcoves less than 100 sq. ft. __ 10' to 14' main reading area __ 16' to 20' at room with mezzanine	__ 7'- 6" -- reading areas less than 100 sq. ft. __ 10' main reading area

FINISHES	Cost Categories		
	A	B	C
__ Floors & Sub-structure	__ Sound isolated substructure __ Nylon or acrylic carpet rated for heavy wear and glued to floor in heavy traffic areas __ Tight weave, cut or loop pile __ Static removal is essential	__ Sound isolated substructure __ Carpet for heavy wear in traffic areas, medium wear elsewhere, glued __ Vinyl NOTE: Sound absorptive carpet flooring is preferred in virtually all areas of a library except utility spaces	__ Carpet, medium, glued __ Vinyl in reception areas __ Asphalt tile at adjacent reference or stack areas WARNING: Asphalt tile floors in combination with some types of movable chairs can cause extreme noise problems
__ Walls & Substructure	__ Fire ratings as per code __ Sound-isolated construction __ Gypsum board with heavy-weight vinyl or fabric __ Chair rail at exposed walls near movable seating __ Large tackboard walls	__ Fire ratings as per code __ Gypsum board with fabric or vinyl, medium weight __ Chair rail at exposed walls near movable seating	__ Fire ratings as per code __ Gypsum board, painted
__ Ceiling & Sub-structure	__ Sound isolated substructure __ Suspended acoustic tile with integrated lighting	__ Suspended acoustic tile with integrated lighting __ Suspended gypsum board	__ Suspended acoustic tile, exposed grid __ Gypsum board with acoustic treatment
__ Counters & Built-in Furnishings	__ Manufactured units, wood veneer, plastic laminate work surfaces	__ Manufactured wood and plastic laminate combinations	__ Plastic laminate
__ Acoustics	__ All surfaces sound absorptive __ 40-50 decibel electronic "white noise" recommended as background noise masking __ NC25 - 35, STC 45 - 55 __ Doors to adjacent offices and conference rooms solid core with sound gaskets at all edges	__ NC 25 - 35, STC 45 - 55 __ Doors to adjacent offices and conference rooms solid core with sound gaskets at all edges __ Sound barriers above adjacent floor-to-ceiling partitions	__ All provisions as much as possible as per Cost Category B

DESIGN STANDARDS -- SECONDARY SCHOOL LIBRARY

DOORS & WINDOWS	Recommended	Minimum
__ Doors	__ Heavy-duty entry doors with quiet operating hardware and automatic closers __ Doors to adjacent rooms 1-3/4" solid core with sound proofing gaskets at all edges	__ 1-3/4" solid core doors, gasketed at all edges __ Doors to adjacent rooms 1-3/4" solid core with sound proofing gaskets at all edges
__ Frames	__ 14 gauge steel	__ 16 gauge steel or extra-sturdy wood jambs and frames
__ Hardware	__ Quiet, concealed automatic closers __ Locking to control after hours access	__ Automatic closers, sound gasketing, and controlled locking systems
__ Windows	__ Windows OK for views and natural light __ North light preferred, avoid windows facing low easterly morning sun and westerly afternoon sun __ Operable sash OK but should be controlled by librarian, not students __ Orientation and blinds to prevent sun glare and heat gain	__ Windows as will enhance reading room environment -- daylight and views
__ Skylights	__ Skylighting desirable if heat gain is controlled	__ No skylights

FIXTURES/EQUIPMENT	Recommended	Minimum
__ Special furnishings	__ Bulletin and announcement boards __ Display and exhibit cabinets __ Display shelves for periodicals, special publications __ Book shelves	__ As per program and Recommended
__ Audio-Visual Equipment	__ Video and VCR machines with headphones for sound -- located where not visually distracting to readers __ Headphone access for video, audio tapes, etc.	

PLUMBING	Recommended	Minimum
__ Fixtures	__ Drinking fountain near entry and/or restrooms __ Fire sprinklers as required by code __ Fire hose cabinet __ Sink in library work room	__ As per Recommended

DESIGN STANDARDS -- SECONDARY SCHOOL LIBRARY

HVAC	Recommended	Minimum
__ Occupancies	__ As per program -- allowing for variations in occupancy at different times __ Approximate max. of 1 person per 40 sq. ft.	__ As per program __ Maximum of 1 person per 30 sq. ft.
__ Ventilation	__ 20 - 30 cfm outdoor air per occupant __ Ventilation noise should be minimal in reading rooms __ Air speed at head level should not be greater than 40 f.p.m. __ For sound masking, use electronic "white noise" only	__ 20 cfm outdoor air per occupant
__ HVAC System & Controls	__ Central HVAC system with individual room control __ Temperatures at 68° to 72° F __ Relative humidity 50% maximum	__ If climate is zone controlled, temperatures 68° to 72° F __ Central system with individual room or zone control __ Warm & cool forced air (zoned) __ Package systems/fan coil units OK if don't create noise problems

ELECTRICAL POWER	Recommended	Minimum
__ Power Outlets	__ Lamp outlets near fixed reading tables and work stations __ Outlets at control desk __ Floor and wall outlets for copier, headphone systems, video, etc. __ Wall base outlets or outlet strips for all contemplated future equipment __ Wall clock outlet __ Outlets as required for janitorial service __ Lighted exit signs at exit doors	__ As per program and/or as required by code

LIGHTING	Recommended	Minimum
__ Lamps	__ Wall wash lights __ Downlights at reading areas or adjustable table and floor lamps __ Overall incandescent and/or fluorescent ceiling fixtures __ Book lighting fixtures at book shelves	__ Fluorescent ceiling lights, recessed or surface mounted __ Downlights at reading areas __ Book lighting fixtures at book shelves
__ Switching	__ Dimmer control for incandescent downlights __ Bank light switches	__ Standard room switch controls

ILLUMINATION WARNING: Library lighting is commonly inadequate despite its obvious importance	Recommended	Minimum
	__ 60 - 100 f.c. for reading and study __ If reading lamps are provided, 50 f.c. is OK for general lighting -- task lights non-glare __ 90% Visual Comfort Performance	__ 50 - 70 f.c. for reading and study

COMMUNICATIONS	Recommended	Minimum
__ Communications	__ Outside telephone line __ Fire and smoke alarms __ Intercom and PA system __ Centrally controlled clock and signal bell __ Computer lines __ Video cable	__ As much as possible as per Recommended

DESIGN STANDARDS -- SCHOOL AUDITORIUM

GENERAL	Recommended Standards	Minimum Standards
__ Occupancies & Floor Areas	__ 8 to 9 sq. ft. per person for average 300 to 400 pupil occupancy (includes aisles)	__ 7.5 sq. ft. per person
__ Depth of Auditorium __ Depth to Width Ratio __ Sight Lines	__ 60' __ Depth of auditorium = 3 x proscenium width __ 60° angle of viewer sight line to screen or subject on stage is maximum for horizontal viewing __ 30° is maximum vertically from center of screen or head height of performers, which determines lowest front row seating	__ 80' maximum __ Depth of auditorium = 3.5 x proscenium width __ Sight line angles as per Recommended Standards with some seats at up to 65° horizontal and 35° vertical viewing angles if absolutely necessary
__ Aisle Widths __ Seats Per Row	__ As per Code, typically start at 36" and widen 1-1/2" per 5' to 45" at cross aisles __ 7 seats to aisle is maximum unless there is generous space in front of each seat (follow seating company recommendations)	__ As required by code __ As required by code
__ Seat Spacing	__ Conventional = 14" clear at front of seats __ 36"+ for back-to-back, conventional seating __ 22"+ o.c. side-by-side spacing	__ Conventional = 13" clear at front of seats __ 32"+ for back-to-back, conventional seating __ 20" o.c. side-by-side spacing

FINISHES	Cost Categories A	B	C
__ Floors & Sub-structure	__ Concrete slab, raised above HVAC plenum at ground floor, stepped at balconies __ Heavy duty carpet at aisles, stain resistant, glued	__ Concrete slab	__ Small schools may use gymnasiums or convertable cafeterias for auditorium space NOTE: All as much as possible as per Cost Category B
__ Wainscot/Walls at Side Aisles	__ Sound reflective or absorbant walls as required for acoustic control __ Highly resistant to abrasion and damage	__ Materials to meet acoustic requirements as specified by consultants	
__ Seating	__ As per requirements and recommendations of seating manufacturer	__ As per program	
__ Walls & Substructure	__ 1-hour fire rating or more, as per building code __ Finish material flame spread ratings as per code __ Sound-isolated construction __ Plaster or gypsum board with acoustic control structure and treatments	__ Materials and shaping to meet acoustic requirements as specified by consultants	
__ Ceiling & Sub-structure	__ Theater ceiling engineered for acoustic control, stage lighting supports, and fire and seismic safety	__ Materials and shaping to meet acoustic requirements as specified by consultants	
__ Acoustics -- Auditorium shaping, baffles, materials	__ As per professional theater acoustical engineer	__ As per professional theater acoustical engineer	

DESIGN STANDARDS -- SCHOOL AUDITORIUM

DOORS & WINDOWS	Recommended	Minimum
__ **Doors**	__ 1-3/4" solid core steel auditorium doors, fire rated as required by local fire code __ Vision panels __ Sound proofing gaskets	NOTE: Quiet and effective door operation is so important to proper theater operation that all minimum door standards are as per Recommended.
__ **Frames**	__ 14 gauge steel at fire exit doors and doors to corridors __ Fire rated assembly as required by local code	
__ **Hardware**	__ Quiet, concealed automatic closers, sound gasketing __ Heavy duty panic bar and related exit hardware __ Quiet panic bar operation __ Wall or floor grabs to hold doors open during intermissions and exiting	
__ **Glazing**	__ Glazing at projection and spotlight and sound control booths __ Projection or control booth glazing must be as approved by acoustic consultant in materials, location, and angular orientation	__ As per Recommended

FIXTURES/EQUIPMENT	Recommended	Minimum
__ **Audio-Visual**	__ Projection, lighting, and sound control equipment all as per program and as recommended or required by engineering and theater consultants __ Locked security access to all control rooms and spaces	__ As per program

PLUMBING	Recommended	Minimum
__ **Fixtures**	__ Sprinklers as required by local fire code __ Fire hose cabinets as required by local fire code	__ As per code

DESIGN STANDARDS -- SCHOOL AUDITORIUM

HVAC	Recommended	Minimum
__ **Occupancies**	__ As per program (programming for full use of these facilities requires expert consultation)	__ As per program
__ **Ventilation**	__ 20 - 25 cfm outdoor air per occupant	__ 15 - 20 cfm outdoor air per occupant
__ **HVAC System & Controls**	__ Central HVAC system __ Under floor HVAC plenum recommended for large volume, slow air speed heating and ventilation	
__ **Heating Temperature**	__ Temperatures at seating levels controlled at 68° to 72° F with equipment adequate to quietly handle quick adjustment to rapidly changing occupancies	__ Temperatures at seating levels at 68° to 72° F __ Even at minimum construction cost, provide generous fresh air supply and quiet, quick response system

ELECTRICAL POWER	Recommended	Minimum
__ **Power Outlets**	__ Concealed floor outlets for building maintenance __ All stage and control booth outlets as per theater consultant and electrical engineer __ Power for exit lights at all exit doors __ Battery powered emergency exit lights	__ As per Recommended or as per program

LIGHTING	Recommended	Minimum
__ **Lamps**	__ Variable ceiling house lighting __ Variable and decorative wall washer lighting __ Subdued floor lighting at aisles and at steps and ramps	__ As per Recommended
__ **Switching**	__ Controls at secure master switch control room	

ILLUMINATION	Recommended	Minimum
	__ Totally variable as per theater consultant recommendations __ 10 f.c. during intermissions	__ As per Recommended

COMMUNICATIONS	Recommended	Minimum
__ **Communications**	__ Speakers as per acoustic and sound engineering consultants	__ As per Recommended or as per program

DESIGN STANDARDS -- SCHOOL AUDITORIUM STAGE & BACKSTAGE

GENERAL	Recommended Standards	Minimum Standards
__ Floor Areas	__ As per program; 1,000 - 1,200 sq. ft. common to secondary schools with 300 enrollment	NOTE: All stage requirements for schools are highly variable; review design program and/or theater consultant
__ Sizes of Stage Areas	__ Proscenium and stage widths, depths, and heights are highly variable in school auditoriums; review design program and/or theater consultant	
__ Gridiron	__ If provided, gridiron as per program and theater consultant	
__ Sight Lines	__ Allow for 60° angle of audience sight line to screen or subject on stage as maximum for horizontal viewing __ Allow for 30° as maximum vertically from center of screen or head height of performers, which determines lowest front row seating and highest balcony seating	__ Sight lines as per Recommended
__ Other backstage areas for school -- auditorium-theater 300 to 400 audience NOTE: These space sizes are highly variable in school auditoriums; sizes noted here are for tentative and preliminary consideration only	__ Workshop = 800 sq. ft. __ Scenery storage = 1,000 sq. ft. __ Costume sewing and storage = 400 sq. ft. __ Green room = 144 sq. ft. __ Two group dressing rooms = 300 sq. ft. each __ Restrooms = 140 sq. ft. each __ Auditorium and stage manager's office = 160 sq. ft.	__ Workshop = 400 to 600 sq. ft. __ Scenery storage = 800 sq. ft. __ Costume sewing and storage = 300 sq. ft. __ Conference room = 400 sq. ft. __ Green room = 140 sq. ft. __ Two group dressing rooms = 240 sq. ft. each __ Restrooms = 120 sq. ft. each __ Stage manager = 120 sq. ft.

FINISHES	Cost Categories A	B	C
__ Floors & Sub-structure NOTE: All finishes as approved by professional theater design and acoustic consultants and fire marshall	__ Concrete slab ground floor support for stage structure __ Traps beneath stage as per theater consultant __ Effective stage area: hardwood floor on sleepers __ Surface for mounting neoprene cushioned dance floor, if required __ Concrete slab at work areas __ Vinyl at occupied spaces	__ Concrete slab base floor with sleepers and hardwood floor above __ Concrete slab at work and storage areas __ Vinyl or asphalt tile at occupied backstage rooms such as dressing rooms	NOTE: Theater auditorium and stage requirements are so important to successful utilization of the building that the lowest cost economies of construction, materials, and fixtures should not normally be considered
__ Walls NOTE: Dressing room mirrors with makeup lights	__ Backstage utility space walls: gypsum board, etc. -- 2-hour fire rating	__ Backstage utility space walls: concrete block, unfinished gypsum board	
__ Ceiling	__ Stage and fly loft ceiling engineered for acoustic control, lighting supports, and fire and seismic safety __ Equipment and fixtures as per stage equipment manufacturer	__ As per theater consultant and equipment manufacturer	

238

DESIGN STANDARDS -- SCHOOL AUDITORIUM STAGE & BACKSTAGE

DOORS & WINDOWS	Recommended	Minimum
__ **Doors**	__ 10' x 14' exterior wall door for moving scenery, traveling show sets, etc. __ 8' x 12' to 10' x 14' stage workshop door __ Security entry door for cast and crew __ 1-3/4" solid core steel doors to backstage rooms, fire rated as required by local fire code __ Vision panels __ Sound proofing gaskets at all edges of back-stage doors	__ 8' x 12' scenery and equipment access doors __ 8' x 12' stage workshop door __ 1-3/4" solid core doors
__ **Frames**	__ 14 gauge steel at fire exit doors and doors to corridors __ Fire rated assembly as required by local code	__ As per Recommended
__ **Hardware**	__ Quiet, concealed automatic closers, sound gasketing __ Heavy duty panic bar and related exit hardware	__ Automatic closers at entry doors __ Panic bar and related exit hardware
__ **Windows/Glazing**	__ Glazing as per theater consultant or equipment manufacturer details at projection, spotlight, and sound control booths __ Projection or control booth glazing must be as approved by acoustic consultant in materials, location, and angular orientation __ No exterior wall glazing except in peripheral backstage rooms such as the workshop and stage director's office	__ As per Recommended

FIXTURES/EQUIPMENT	Recommended	Minimum
__ **Audio-Visual**	__ Projection, lighting, and sound control equipment all as per program and as recommended or required by engineering and theater consultants __ Locked security access to all lighting, switching, and sound control rooms	__ As per program and Recommended -- primarily a factor of elaboration and sophistication of staging and lighting effects, and programmed variable uses of the theater

PLUMBING	Recommended	Minimum

__ **Fixtures**	__ Sprinklers as required by local fire code
	__ Fire hose cabinets as required by fire code
	__ Janitor's closet with mop sink
	__ Work sink in workshop
	__ Three lavatories in each group dressing room
	__ Rest rooms:
	   __ Men -- 2 lavs, 2 toilets, 2 urinals
	   __ Women -- 3 lavs, 4 toilets
		__ As per program and fire code

239

DESIGN STANDARDS -- SCHOOL AUDITORIUM STAGE & BACKSTAGE

HVAC	Recommended	Minimum
__ Occupancies	__ As per program	__ As per program
__ Ventilation	__ Shared with auditorium __ Large smoke vent and emergency vent fan at roof above fly loft	__ As per Recommended
__ HVAC System & Control	__ Central HVAC system, shared with auditorium __ Because of the critical nature of thermal and air comfort for performers and audience, this work requires expert theater and HVAC engineering consulting	__ As per Recommended
__ Temperature	__ Temperature range 68° to 70° F -- lower range in stage area for dance performances	__ Temperature range 68° to 72° F

ELECTRICAL POWER	Recommended	Minimum
__ Power Outlets	__ Outlets at columns and perimeter walls for building maintenance __ All stage and control booth outlets as per theater consultant and electrical engineer	__ As per Recommended and/or as per program

LIGHTING	Recommended	Minimum
__ Lamps	__ Spot and flood lighting as per theater and electrical engineering consultants __ Emergency exit lights __ Battery operated emergency exit lamps	__ As per Recommended and/or as per program
__ Switching	__ Master control room and spotlight booth consoles as per theater and electrical engineering consultants	__ As per Recommended and/or as per program

ILLUMINATION	Recommended	Minimum
	__ Stage lighting as per theater consultants and stage production designers	__ As per Recommended and/or as per program

COMMUNICATIONS	Recommended	Minimum
__ Communications	__ Cross-stage and stage to spot booth and control booth intercoms __ Outside phone lines __ Fire call system	__ As per Recommended and/or as per program

DESIGN STANDARDS -- HOME ECONOMICS CLASSROOM

GENERAL	Recommended Standards	Minimum Standards
__ Occupancies	__ As per the overall Education Plan and design program -- typically 20 - 25 students per class	__ As per program
__ Floor Area	__ 40 sq. ft. per pupil	__ Allow 30 to 35 sq. ft. per pupil __ As per program but 750 sq. ft. (25 students with 30 sq. ft. each) would normally be minimum space
__ Ceiling Height	__ 10' to 14' high	__ 9'-6" in smaller classrooms
__ Plan Considerations	__ Safety features are high priority in the kitchen setting	__ As per Recommended

FINISHES	Cost Categories		
	A	B	C
__ Floors & Sub-structures	__ Sound isolated substructure __ Non-slip ceramic tile __ Quarry tile __ Vinyl sheet, heavy duty	__ Vinyl tile, heavy duty	__ Vinyl or asphalt tile WARNING: Asphalt tile floors, in combination with some types of movable chairs and tables, can cause extreme noise problems
__ Walls & Substructure	__ Top grade wall writing surfaces and tack boards __ Ceramic tile __ Gypsum board or plaster, painted __ Fire ratings and flame spread ratings as per code __ Complete sound separation between rooms __ Complete thermal insulation at exterior walls	__ Top grade wall writing surfaces recommended to reduce school maintenance and operating costs __ Gypsum board, painted	__ Chalk boards or marker boards along one wall __ Tack board at one wall __ Gypsum board over stud construction __ Concrete block, painted __ Fire ratings as per code
__ Ceiling	__ Vaulted or coffered ceiling __ Suspended acoustic tile with integrated lighting	__ Suspended acoustic ceiling with integrated lighting	__ Suspended ceiling with exposed grid __ Surface mounted or pendant fixtures
__ Counters & Built-In Fixtures & Furnishings	__ Plastic laminate or composite __ Cabinetry as per educational design program __ Kitchen style base and overhead cabinets at all available wall and overhead space -- metal, premium __ Pantry __ Instructor's locker/cabinet __ Chart rails, pull down screen __ Chair rails at walls in rooms with movable chairs	__ As much as possible per Cost Category A	__ Economy grade fixtures and furnishings -- higher grades recommended for saving building operating costs
__ Acoustics	__ NC 30 - 35, STC 45 - 55 __ Acoustical consultant to optimize acoustic performance of all rooms __ Acoustic separation of all substructures	__ NC 25 - 35, STC 40 - 45	__ STC 35 - 45 __ Sound isolated construction as required by program in specific spaces

DESIGN STANDARDS -- HOME ECONOMICS CLASSROOM

DOORS & WINDOWS	Recommended	Minimum
__ **Doors**	__ 1-3/4" solid core entry/exit doors __ Sound proofing gaskets at all edges unless room is located in non-sound sensitive part of the building __ Vision panel in or beside door __ Doors fire rated if opening onto fire exit corridors -- as per fire code	__ As per fire code
__ **Frames**	__ 14 gauge steel	__ 16 gauge steel
__ **Hardware** NOTE: Heavy-duty hardware saves maintenance costs and is very desirable	__ Quiet, concealed automatic closers __ Panic bar exit hardware as required by code __ Controlled locking __ Handicapped access hardware	__ As per Recommended
__ **Windows**	__ Double pane for noise insulation from exterior __ Sound insulating gaskets on operable sash __ Blinds and blackout drapes __ Orientation and exterior shades to prevent sun glare and heat gain	__ As per code for light requirements __ Operable sash as per code __ Blinds and blackout drapes __ Design orientation and fixtures to prevent sun glare and heat gain will greatly decrease school building operating costs
__ **Skylights**	__ Skylights not recommended without ready controls of heat gain and blackout	

FIXTURES/EQUIPMENT	Recommended	Minimum

__ **Special Furnishings**
CLEARANCES:
__ Minimum 2' wide counters, 4' to 5' aisles, 24" to 36" counter space between major appliances
__ 4' to 7' between sink and refrigerator
__ 4' to 6' between sink and range
__ 4' to 9' between range and refrigerator
	__ As per Education Plan and program
	__ Residential kitchen fixtures for student use and demonstration kitchen with demonstration viewing mirror
	__ Kitchen work islands as per program with:
	  __ Two-bowl kitchen sink
	  __ Range
	  __ Oven
	  __ Garbage disposal
	  __ Microwave oven
	__ Equipment usually shared by work stations:
	  __ Dishwasher
	  __ Refrigerator
	  __ Freezer
		__ As per Recommended

__ **Audio-Visual/Meeting Equipment**	__ Television and VCR __ Overhead projector __ Provisions for slide and film presentations __ Built-in screen if presentation area is defined __ Storage and/or convenient access to portable screen and other equipment storage	__ As much per Recommended as possible

PLUMBING	Recommended	Minimum
__ **Fixtures**	__ Sprinklers and dry or gaseous fire extinguishers __ 1" or 3/4" supply - Type K copper tubing __ 2" fixture drains __ 4" house drain	__ As per code __ Hot & cold, 1/2" supply __ 1-1/2" fixture drains __ 3" house drain

DESIGN STANDARDS -- HOME ECONOMICS CLASSROOM

HVAC	Recommended	Minimum
__ Occupancies	__ As per program -- up to 25 per classroom, 40 sq. ft. per student	__ As per program -- up to 25 per classroom at 25 sq. ft. minimum per student
__ Ventilation	__ 30 to 35 cfm outside air per occupant during hot or cold weather, otherwise operable windows will provide most ventilation __ Exhaust fans at all workstations	__ 25 cfm outdoor air per occupant
__ HVAC System & Controls NOTE: If later expansion of the school is anticipated, provide for expansion of the HVAC system	__ Energy monitoring sensors connecting to central computerized control system __ Central HVAC system with individual room control __ If climate is zone controlled, temperatures 68° to 70° F __ Relative humidity between 50% - 65%, lower or higher depending on room temperature	__ If climate is zone controlled, temperatures 68° to 72° F __ Air conditioning if required by climate __ Fan coil units __ Individual room thermostats

ELECTRICAL POWER	Recommended	Minimum
__ Power Outlets	__ Outlets for each computer and other instructional equipment required by overall Education Plan __ Countertop appliance outlets at 3' o.c. approx. __ Task lighting outlets at instructor's station and all work or display counters __ Outlets for presentation slide and film projectors, video, overhead projector, video monitor, video projector, etc. __ Wall base outlets or outlet strips for all contemplated future kitchen appliances __ Outlets as required for janitorial service __ For clock and communication systems	__ Instructor's station __ Countertop appliance outlets at 6' o.c. __ As required for maintenance __ Outlets for audio/visual equipment __ For clock and communication systems

LIGHTING	Recommended	Minimum
__ Lamps	__ Integrated ceiling fluorescent fixtures __ Fluorescent high output with low glare __ Task lights or downlights as per program __ No brightness variations over 3:1 __ Ceiling reflectance factor minimum of 0.7 __ Reflectance factor of furnishings approx. 0.5	__ Fluorescent ceiling lights, recessed or surface mounted __ Some ceiling lights dimmable for audio/visual presentations
__ Switching	__ Bank light switching with dimmer lights for audio/visual presentations	__ Standard wall switches near instructor's station

ILLUMINATION	Recommended	Minimum
	__ 80 - 100 f.c. with ample natural light	__ 70 - 90 f.c.

COMMUNICATIONS	Recommended	Minimum
__ Communications	__ Outside telephone line __ Fire and smoke alarms __ Intercom and PA system __ Centrally controlled clock and signal bell __ Video cable	__ As much per Recommended as possible

DESIGN STANDARDS -- SCHOOL SCIENCE LABS

GENERAL	Recommended Standards	Minimum Standards
__ **Occupancies &** **Floor Area** NOTE: Smaller schools will usually combine chemistry, biology, and physics, in general science rooms such as specified here	__ As per the overall Education Plan and design program -- typically 20 students per class __ Individual labs -- chemistry, physics, and biology will all have unique features and equipment -- these should be reviewed in detail with faculty and the education consultant __ 40 sq. ft. per pupil	__ As per program but 750 sq. ft. (25 students with 30 sq. ft. each) would normally be minimum space __ Allow 30 to 35 sq. ft. per pupil
__ **Ceiling Height**	__ 10' to 14' high	__ 9'-6" in smaller classrooms
__ **Plan Considerations**	__ Safety planning is of highest priority	__ As per Recommended

FINISHES	Cost Categories		
	A	**B**	**C**
__ **Floors & Sub-** **structures**	__ Sound isolated substructure __ Lab grade rubber tile __ Quarry tile __ Vinyl sheet, heavy duty	__ Vinyl tile, heavy duty, lab grade	__ Vinyl or asphalt tile
__ **Walls & Substructure**	__ Top grade wall writing surfaces and tack boards __ Ceramic tile __ Gypsum board or plaster, painted with washable paint __ Fire ratings and flame spread ratings as per code __ Complete sound separation between rooms	__ Top grade wall writing surfaces recommended to reduce school maintenance and operating costs __ Gypsum board, painted	__ Chalk boards or marker boards along one wall __ Tack board at one wall __ Gypsum board over stud construction __ Concrete block, painted __ Fire ratings as per code
__ **Ceiling**	__ Vaulted or coffered ceiling __ Suspended acoustic tile with integrated lighting __ Cleanable ceiling surfaces	__ Suspended acoustic ceiling with integrated lighting	__ Suspended ceiling with exposed grid __ Surface mounted or pendant fixtures

__ **Counters & Built-In**
Fixtures & Furnishings
	__ Plastic laminate or composite
	__ Laboratory cabinetry as per educational design program
	   __ Glass lockable display cabinets
	   __ Secure lockable metal storage cabinets
	__ Instructor's locker/cabinet
	__ Chart rails, pull down screen
	__ Chair rails at walls in rooms with movable chairs
		__ As much as possible per Cost Category A	__ Economy grade fixtures and furnishings -- higher grades recommended where possible to save on building operating costs

__ **Acoustics**	__ NC 30 - 35, STC 45 - 55 __ Acoustic separation of all substructures	__ NC 25 - 35, STC 40 - 45	__ STC 35 - 45 __ Sound isolated construction as required by program in specific spaces

DESIGN STANDARDS -- SCHOOL SCIENCE LABS

DOORS & WINDOWS	Recommended	Minimum
__ **Doors**	__ 1-3/4" solid core entry/exit doors __ Sound proofing gaskets at all edges unless room is located in non-sound sensitive part of the building __ Vision panel in or beside door __ Doors fire rated if opening onto fire exit corridors -- as per fire code	__ As per fire code
__ **Frames**	__ 14 gauge steel	__ 16 gauge steel
__ **Hardware** NOTE: Heavy-duty hardware saves maintenance costs and is very desirable	__ Quiet, concealed automatic closers __ Panic bar exit hardware as required by code __ Controlled locking __ Handicapped access hardware	__ As per Recommended
__ **Windows**	__ Double pane for noise insulation from exterior __ Sound insulating gaskets on operable sash __ Blinds and blackout drapes __ Orientation and exterior shades to prevent sun glare and heat gain	__ As per code for light requirements __ Operable sash as per code __ Blinds and blackout drapes __ Design orientation and fixtures to prevent sun glare and heat gain will greatly decrease school building operating costs
__ **Skylights**	__ Skylights not recommended	

FIXTURES/EQUIPMENT	Recommended	Minimum
__ **Special Furnishings**	__ As per Education Plan and program __ Instructor's demonstration table with overhead presentation mirror __ Laboratory counters and cabinets with acid resistant laboratory grade counter tops __ Acid resistant sinks __ Exhaust hoods __ Acid resistant back splash and wall protection __ Wall-mounted utility connections __ Refrigerator	__ As much per Recommended as possible
__ **Audio-Visual/Meeting Equipment**	__ Computer network __ Television and VCR __ Overhead projector __ Provisions for slide and film presentations __ Built-in screen if presentation area is defined __ Storage and/or convenient access to portable screen and other equipment storage	__ As much per Recommended as possible

PLUMBING	Recommended	Minimum
__ **Fixtures**	__ Sprinklers and dry or gaseous fire extinquishers __ Lab sinks and first-aid sink as per program __ 3/4" supply __ 2" fixture drains __ Natural gas lines	__ As per code __ Hot & cold, 1/2" supply __ 1-1/2" fixture drains

245

DESIGN STANDARDS -- SCHOOL SCIENCE LABS

HVAC	Recommended	Minimum
__ Occupancies	__ As per program -- up to 25 per classroom, 40 sq. ft. per student	__ As per program -- up to 25 per classroom at 25 sq. ft. minimum per student
__ Ventilation	__ 30 to 35 cfm outside air per occupant during hot or cold weather, otherwise operable windows will provide most ventilation __ Laboratory grade ventilation hood	__ 25 cfm outdoor air per occupant
__ HVAC System & Controls NOTE: If later expansion of the school is anticipated, provide for expansion of the HVAC system	__ Energy monitoring sensors connecting to central computerized control system __ Central HVAC system with individual room control __ If climate is zone controlled, temperatures 68° to 70° F __ Relative humidity between 50% - 65%, lower or higher depending on room temperature	__ If climate is zone controlled, temperatures 68° to 72° F __ Air conditioning if required by climate __ Individual room thermostats

ELECTRICAL POWER	Recommended	Minimum
__ Power Outlets	__ Outlets for each computer and other instructional equipment required by overall Education Plan __ Countertop equipment outlets -- 1 per station __ Task lighting outlets at instructor's station and all work or display counters __ Outlets for presentation slide and film projectors, video, overhead projector, video monitor, video projector, etc. __ Wall base outlets or outlet strips for planned future powered laboratory equipment __ Outlets as required for janitorial service __ For clock and communication systems	__ Instructor's station __ Countertop appliance outlets at 6' o.c. __ As required for maintenance __ Outlets for audio/visual equipment __ For clock and communication systems

LIGHTING	Recommended	Minimum
__ Lamps	__ Integrated ceiling fluorescent fixtures __ Fluorescent high output with low glare __ Task lights or downlights as per program __ No brightness variations over 3:1 __ Ceiling reflectance factor minimum of 0.7 __ Reflectance factor of furnishings approx. 0.5	__ Fluorescent ceiling lights, recessed or surface mounted __ Some ceiling lights dimmable for audio/visual presentations
__ Switching	__ Bank light switching with dimmer lights for audio/visual presentations	__ Standard wall switches near instructor's station

ILLUMINATION	Recommended	Minimum
	__ 80 - 100 f.c. with ample natural light	__ 70 - 90 f.c.

COMMUNICATIONS	Recommended	Minimum
__ Communications	__ Outside telephone line __ Fire and smoke alarms __ Intercom and PA system __ Centrally controlled clock and signal bell __ Video cable	__ As much per Recommended as possible

246

DESIGN STANDARDS -- SCHOOL VOCATIONAL SHOPS

GENERAL	Recommended Standards	Minimum Standards
__ Occupancies & Floor Area NOTE: Smaller schools will often combine shop courses in one general workshop	__ As per the overall Education Plan and design program -- typically 20 students per class __ Individual shops -- wood, metal, auto, machine, electronics, and welding -- will all have unique features and equipment to review in detail with faculty and with the education consultant __ 40 sq. ft. per pupil	__ As per program or allow 30 to 35 sq. ft. per pupil plus shop tables, counters, and power tools
__ Ceiling Height	__ 10' to 14' high	__ 9'-6" in smaller shops
__ Plan Considerations	__ Safety planning is of highest priority	__ As per Recommended

FINISHES	Cost Categories		
	A	B	C
__ Floors & Sub-structures	__ Sound isolated substructure __ Asphalt tile, heavy duty	__ Concrete slab, integral color	__ Concrete slab
__ Walls & Substructure	__ Wall writing surfaces and tack boards __ Gypsum board __ Fire ratings and flame spread ratings as per code __ Complete sound separation from other departments	__ Top grade wall writing surfaces recommended to reduce school maintenance and operating costs __ Gypsum board, painted	__ Chalk boards or marker boards along one wall __ Tack board at one wall __ Gypsum board over stud construction __ Concrete block, painted __ Fire ratings as per code
__ Ceiling	__ Suspended acoustic tile with integrated lighting __ Cleanable ceiling surfaces	__ Suspended acoustic ceiling with integrated lighting	__ Suspended ceiling with exposed grid __ Surface mounted or pendant fixtures
__ Counters & Built-In Fixtures & Furnishings	__ Plastic laminate or composite __ Shop cabinetry as per education design program __ Secure lockable metal storage cabinets __ Instructor's locker/cabinet __ Chart rails, pull down screen	__ As much as possible per Cost Category A	__ Economy grade fixtures and furnishings -- higher grades recommended where possible to save on building operating costs
__ Acoustics	__ NC 30 - 35, STC 45 - 55 __ Acoustic separation of all substructures	__ NC 25 - 35, STC 40 - 45	__ STC 35 - 45 __ Sound isolated construction as required by program in specific spaces

DESIGN STANDARDS -- SCHOOL VOCATIONAL SHOPS

DOORS & WINDOWS	Recommended	Minimum
__ **Doors**	__ 1-3/4" solid core entry/exit doors __ Sound proofing gaskets at all edges unless room is located in non-sound sensitive part of the building __ Vision panel in or beside door __ Doors fire rated if opening onto fire exit corridors -- as per fire code	__ As per fire code
__ **Frames**	__ 14 gauge steel	__ 16 gauge steel
__ **Hardware** NOTE: Heavy-duty hardware saves maintenance costs and is very desirable	__ Automatic closers __ Panic bar exit hardware as required by code __ Controlled locking __ Handicapped access hardware	__ As per Recommended
__ **Windows** __ **Skylights**	__ Blinds and blackout drapes __ Orientation and exterior shades to prevent sun glare and heat gain __ Skylights recommended if oriented not to add unduly to heat gain	__ As per code for light requirements __ Operable sash as per code __ Blinds and blackout drapes __ Design orientation and fixtures to prevent sun glare and heat gain will greatly decrease school building operating costs

FIXTURES/EQUIPMENT	Recommended	Minimum

__ **Special Furnishings**	__ As per Education Plan and program
	__ Specialized counters and equipment for
	    __ Wood working
	    __ Metal working
	    __ Auto repair
	__ Dust collection system in wood working areas
	__ Auto emissions extraction system
	__ Instructor's demonstration table with overhead presentation mirror
	__ Washup sinks
	__ Exhaust hoods
	__ Wall-mounted utility connections
		__ As much per Recommended as possible

__ **Audio-Visual/Meeting Equipment**	__ Computer network __ Television and VCR __ Overhead projector __ Provisions for slide and film presentations __ Built-in screen if presentation area is defined __ Storage and/or convenient access to portable screen and other equipment storage	__ As much per Recommended as possible

PLUMBING	Recommended	Minimum
__ **Fixtures**	__ Sprinklers and dry or gaseous fire extinguishers __ Wash-up sinks as per program __ 3/4" supply __ 2" fixture drains __ Gas lines as per program	__ As per code __ Hot & cold, 1/2" supply __ 1-1/2" fixture drains

DESIGN STANDARDS -- SCHOOL VOCATIONAL SHOPS

HVAC	Recommended	Minimum
__ Occupancies	__ As per program -- up to 25 per classroom, 40 sq. ft. per student	__ As per program -- up to 25 per classroom at 25 sq. ft. minimum per student
__ Ventilation	__ 30 to 35 cfm outside air per occupant during hot or cold weather, otherwise operable windows will provide most ventilation __ Ventilation hood as per program	__ 25 cfm outdoor air per occupant __ Wood dust exhaust in wood shop __ Vehical emissions exhaust removal in auto shop __ Gas exhausts in welding or other gaseous work areas
__ HVAC System & Controls NOTE: If later expansion of the school is anticipated, provide for expansion of the HVAC system	__ Energy monitoring sensors connecting to central computerized control system __ Central HVAC system with individual room control __ If climate is zone controlled, temperatures 68° to 70° F	__ If climate is zone controlled, temperatures 68° to 72° F __ Air conditioning if required by climate __ Individual room thermostats

ELECTRICAL POWER	Recommended	Minimum
__ Power Outlets	__ Outlets for each power tool required by overall Education Plan __ Countertop equipment outlets -- 1 per station __ Task lighting outlets at instructor's station and all work or display counters __ Outlets for presentation slide and film projectors, video, overhead projector, video monitor, video projector, etc. __ Wall base outlets or outlet strips for all contemplated future shop power tools __ Outlets as required for janitorial service __ For clock and communication systems	__ Instructor's station __ Countertop appliance outlets at 6' o.c. __ As required for maintenance __ Outlets for audio/visual equipment __ For clock and communication systems

LIGHTING	Recommended	Minimum
__ Lamps	__ Integrated ceiling fluorescent fixtures __ Fluorescent high output with low glare __ Task lights or downlights as per program	__ Fluorescent ceiling lights, recessed or surface mounted __ Some ceiling lights dimmable for audio/visual presentations
__ Switching	__ Bank light switching with dimmer lights for audio/visual presentations	__ Standard wall switches near instructor's station

ILLUMINATION	Recommended	Minimum
	__ 80 - 100 f.c. with ample natural light	__ 70 - 90 f.c.

COMMUNICATIONS	Recommended	Minimum
__ Communications	__ Outside telephone line __ Fire and smoke alarms __ Intercom and PA system __ Centrally controlled clock and signal bell __ Video cable	__ As much per Recommended as possible

DESIGN STANDARDS -- ART & CRAFTS CLASSROOMS

Note: Most standards and requirements other than finishes and furnishings will be as per standard Classroom

GENERAL	Recommended Standards	Minimum Standards
__ Occupancies & Floor Area	__ As per the overall Education Plan and design program-- typically 20 - 25 students per class __ 30 sq. ft. per pupil	__ 25 sq. ft. per pupil __ As per program but 625 sq. ft. (25 students with 25 sq. ft. each) would normally be minimum space
__ Ceiling Height	__ 10' to 14' high (sloping ceiling with high north light preferred	__ 9'-6" in smaller classrooms
__ Plan Considerations	__ Lighting, mobility, and generous work table and storage space __ Direct access to the outside is desirable	__ As per Recommended

FINISHES	Cost Categories		
	A	B	C
__ Floors & Sub-structures	__ Sound isolated substructure __ Vinyl sheet, heavy duty	__ Vinyl tile, heavy duty	__ Vinyl or asphalt tile WARNING: Asphalt tile floors, in combination with some types of movable chairs and tables, can cause ex-treme noise problems
__ Walls & Substructure	__ Writing boards and tack boards __ All walls either for storage or display space: __Tack display __ Hanging display __ Shelf display __ Gypsum board or plaster, painted -- light color __ Fire ratings and flame spread ratings as per code __ Complete sound separation between rooms	__ As per Cost Category A __ Gypsum board, painted	__ Marker boards along one wall __ Tack board at one wall __ Gypsum board over stud construction __ Concrete block, painted __ Fire ratings as per code
__ Ceiling	__ Vaulted or coffered ceiling __ Suspended acoustic tile with integrated lighting	__ Suspended acoustic ceiling with integrated lighting	__ Suspended ceiling with exposed grid __ Surface mounted or pendant fixtures
__ Counters & Built-In Fixtures & Furnish-ings	__ Wood worktops and plastic laminate __ Cabinetry as per educational design program __ Base cabinets at all available low wall space -- wood or metal, premium __ Instructor's locker/cabinet __ Projection screen __ Chair rails at walls in rooms with movable chairs	__ As much as possible as per Cost Category A	__ Economy grade fixtures and furnishings -- higher grades recommended for saving building operat-ing costs
__ Acoustics	__ NC 30 - 35, STC 45 - 55 __ Acoustic separation of all substructures	__ NC 25 - 35, STC 40 - 45	__ STC 35 - 45 __ Sound isolated construc-tion as required by pro-gram in specific spaces

RETAIL STORES &
SUPERMARKETS

DESIGN STANDARDS -- RETAIL SHOPS

GENERAL	Recommended Standards	Minimum Standards
__ Floor Areas & Clearances	__ Single aisle shop: 14' to 20' wide x 50' to 90' long __ Main public aisles, 5'-6" to 8' wide __ Clerk aisles 2'-6" to 3'-6" wide	__ Single aisle shop: 12' to 18' wide x 50' to 60' long __ Main public aisles, 4'-6" __ Clerk aisles 2'-4"
__ Ceiling Height	__ 10' to 16' in shop space, 12' is typical __ 8' minimum under and at mezzanines __ 9' basement areas	__ 8' minimum in primary space __ 7' minimum in adjacent service areas __ 8' basement areas
__ Plan Features	__ Smaller shops need attention-getting design -- generally in contrast with neighboring stores __ Merchandise should contrast with decor __ Security should be evident but low-key	

FINISHES	Cost Categories		
	A	B	C
__ Floors	__ Carpet rated for heavy wear, non-static, padded __ Nylon or acrylic carpet rated for heavy wear, glued __ Carpet tile, heavy duty __ Heavy-duty vinyl sheet or tile in convenience shops such as grocery or drug stores __ Specialty shops and botiques may use any floor material: wood, marble, tile, stone, terrazzo, etc.	__ Nylon or acrylic carpet rated for heavy wear, glued __ Heavy-duty vinyl sheet or tile in convenience shops	__ Carpet, glued __ Carpet tile, heavy duty __ Vinyl or asphalt tile
__ Counters & Built-In Furnishings	__ Manufactured units, wood Premium Grade, safety glass __ Plastic laminate	__ Manufactured units, wood veneer, plastic laminate, safety glass	__ As per Cost Category B
__ Walls & Substructure	__ 1-hour fire rating or more, as per building code __ Finish material flame spread ratings as per code __ Gypsum wallboard with heavy-weight vinyl or fabric (where finish wall isn't a packaged display wall) __ Mirror walls, especially in smaller shops __ Exit wall fire ratings as per code	__ Fire ratings as per building code __ Gypsum board with heavy weight vinyl or fabric __ Wall finishes may be dominated by packaged display units such as slot walls, prefab shelving, cubes, display cabinets, etc.	__ Gypsum board, painted __ Manufactured wall panels and display units
__ Ceiling & Sub-structure	__ Integral ceiling, plaster or gypsum board, with integrated lighting __ Gypsum board ceiling with acoustic treatment __ Luminous or egg crate __ Custom designed baffles	__ Suspended acoustic tile with integrated lighting __ Gypsum board ceiling with acoustic treatment __ Manufactured	__ Suspended acoustic tile, exposed grid __ Gypsum board with surface-mounted lighting
__ Acoustics	__ NC 25 - 35, STC 45 - 55	__ NC 25 - 35, STC 45 - 55	

252

DESIGN STANDARDS -- RETAIL SHOPS

DOORS & WINDOWS	Recommended	Minimum
__ **Doors**	__ Store-front entrances with automatic door (see RETAIL SHOW WINDOWS in the next section) __ Heavy-duty public entry doors with quiet operating hardware and automatic closers __ Automatic doors as needed for heavy traffic and for convenient handicap access	__ Outward swinging push activated door with automatic closer __ Vestibule to avoid door swings into public walkways __ Glazed public entry doors with quiet operating hardware and automatic closers
__ **Frames**	__ 14 gauge steel at fire walls and labeled doors	__ 16 gauge steel
__ **Hardware**	__ Store Door Lock, preassembled or integral type lock and latch __ Store security locking system with alarm	__ Automatic closers __ Controlled locking system
__ **Windows**	__ See RETAIL SHOW WINDOWS in the next section __ Windows for light or view are rarely used or desirable __ Skylighting is desirable in apparel and fabric stores for most accurate display of actual colors	__ See RETAIL SHOW WINDOWS in the next section

FIXTURES/EQUIPMENT	Recommended	Minimum
__ **Special Furnishings**	__ As per program -- most retail clients will have a selection of furnishings customarily used for their retailing specialty __ Most retail shop counters, racks, display cases, etc. are modular package units, not custom designed or permanently built-in __ Custom designed units must be engineered with care, and pre-tested for wearability	__ As per Recommended

PLUMBING	Recommended	Minimum
__ **Fixtures**	__ Fire sprinklers as per code, generally 1 or more to cover every 200 sq. ft. __ Sprinklers recessed and unobtrusive as possible __ Wet and dry standpipes, fire hose cabinets, etc. all as per code and preferably in excess of code minimums __ Drinking fountain and restroom fixtures in customer service area of larger retail spaces	__ Fire sprinklers and other fire protection as per code __ Rest room near customer service area

DESIGN STANDARDS -- RETAIL SHOPS

HVAC	Recommended	Minimum
__ Occupancies	__ As per program	__ As per program
__ Ventilation	__ 35 - 50 cfm outdoor air per occupant __ Extra ventilation at high-heat lighting, displays, and equipment	__ Outside air: 15 - 30 cfm per occupant
__ HVAC System & Controls CAUTION: Lack of fresh air is considered a major factor in "shoppers fatigue." Stores in larger buildings that are minimally designed in terms of air conditioning should provide alternative air filter and air freshener sources wherever possible.	__ Package HVAC units ok for small stores, central HVAC with zone control for malls and department store __ Positive air pressure to block outside air __ Humidity control to prevent static electricity __ Air speed at head level should not be greater than 50 f.p.m. __ Air lock vestibule to preserve air temperatures and buffer air pressure changes as people enter and leave the building __ If climate is zone controlled, temperatures 68° to 72°F __ Central system with individual room or zone control	__ As much as possible per Cost Category A

ELECTRICAL POWER	Recommended	Minimum
__ Power Outlets	__ At interior columns: 2 duplex outlets at opposite sides above base, 1 at 12" below ceiling __ At exterior wall columns: 1 duplex outlet each __ Wall base outlet strips with outlets at 3' centers __ Lighted exit signs at exit doors __ Additional outlets as required for janitorial service __ Generous junction box outlets for changing ceiling, wall, and display case lighting	__ At interior columns: 1 duplex outlet above base, 1 at 12" below ceiling __ Wall base outlets junction box access for future electric or electronic equipment __ Janitorial outlets __ Lighted fire exit signs at exit doors __ Junction boxes to allow for fixture and lighting changes

LIGHTING	Recommended	Minimum
__ Lamps	__ Surface mounted, recessed, or flush recessed fluorescent fixtures for general illumination (4'x4' units at 12' spacing is common) __ Supplementary display lights: Stage lights, track lights, swivel spots, pin spots, cove lights, display case and accent lights	__ As per Recommended CAUTION: Even at low budget, the primary rule is to concentrate on lighting the merchandise, not the store
__ Switching	__ Maximum flexibility and variability, lockable switches	__ Standard switches and dimmers, central light controll panel

ILLUMINATION	Recommended	Minimum
__ Sales areas	__ Self service areas 150-200 f.c., assisted, 90 f.c.	__ 70 f.c.
__ Product displays	__ 100 to 500 f.c. (highest light on small items)	__ 300 f.c.
__ General merchandise	__ 100 f.c. minimum, higher in showcases	__ 70 f.c.
__ Non display space	__ 30-40 f.c. (showcase light 2 x ambient lighting)	__ 20 f.c.

COMMUNICATIONS	Recommended	Minimum
__ Communications	__ Fire and smoke detectors and alarms __ Cash register area phone lines __ Security alarms __ Surveilance systems, remote controlled video cameras and monitors	__ As per Recommended

254

DESIGN STANDARDS -- SUPERMARKETS

GENERAL	Recommended Standards	Minimum Standards

__ Floor Areas	__ Square footage ranges are 20,000 sq. ft. to 36,000 sq. ft.
	 __ Space divisions:
	     __ 80% of store space for merchandise and checkout stands
	     __ 20% of store space for storage and maintenance
		__ As per Recommended

__ Aisle spacings	__ 8' shopping aisles, 4' wide shelf units	__ 7' shopping aisles, 4' wide shelf units
__ Ceiling Height	__ 14' to 20' __ 8' minimum under mezzanines or soffits __ 9' in stock rooms	__ 12' __ 7'-6" minimum under mezzanines or soffits __ 8' in stock rooms
__ Special Planning Considerations	__ Plan shape usually rectangular, such as a 2-to-3 ratio with all checkout stands across the front entry level, shelves and aisles at right angle to the front, receiving and storage in the back or side, and produce and frozen foods at each side __ The structural grid should be designed to match the aisle and display shelving module so there are no columns in the aisles -- multiples of 11' or 12' are common	__ As per Recommended

FINISHES	Cost Categories		
	A	B	C
__ Floors	__ Heavy-duty vinyl sheet or tile over concrete slab	__ Vinyl sheet or tile over slab	__ Vinyl or asphalt tile over slab
__ Counters & Built-In Furnishings	__ Manufactured units, wood with plastic laminate	__ Manufactured units, wood veneer, plastic laminate	__ As per Cost Category B
__ Walls & Substructure	__ 5/8" gypsum wallboard __ 1-hour fire rating or more, as per building code __ Finish material flame spread ratings as per code __ Work room and corridor walls require protection from abrasion __ Corner guards	__ Gypsum board __ Fire ratings as per building code __ Wall finishes may be dominated by packaged display units such as prefab shelving, display cabinets, etc. __ Corner guards	__ Gypsum board, painted __ Fire ratings as per building code __ Manufactured wall panels and display units
__ Ceiling & Sub-structure	__ Integral ceiling, plaster or gypsum board, with integrated lighting __ Gypsum board ceiling with acoustic treatment __ Luminous or egg crate __ Custom designed baffles over specialty shops or boutiques such as florist, bakery, deli, etc.	__ Suspended acoustic tile with integrated lighting __ Gypsum board ceiling with surface-mounted lighting or hanging fixtures	__ Exposed structure and roof slab with hanging light fixtures
__ Acoustics	__ Provide for sound privacy between office or work-spaces and the main store __ NC 25 - 35, STC 45 - 55 __ Sound isolation pads and insulation for refrigeration and HVAC equipment	__ As per Cost Category A	__ Sound insulation or isolation for employee work rooms and heavy-duty refrigeration and HVAC equipment

DESIGN STANDARDS -- SUPERMARKETS

DOORS & WINDOWS	Recommended	Minimum
__ **Doors**	__ Store-front entrances with automatic sliding doors (swinging automatic doors not recommended) __ Additional automatic controls as needed for convenient handicapped access __ Large airlock vestibules with automatic door openers in regions of extreme hot or cold climate __ Steel interior workroom doors with kickplates	__ Store-front entrances with automatic doors __ Solid core interior workroom doors with kickplates
__ **Frames**	__ 14 gauge steel or comparable store-front assemblies	__ 16 gauge steel or comparable store-front assembly
__ **Hardware**	__ Store security locking system with alarm	__ Controlled locking system
__ **Windows**	__ Large storefront windows are typical across front street or parking lot entrance __ Windows are not recommended for work and storage spaces __ Skylights are not recommended	__ As per Recommended

FIXTURES/EQUIPMENT	Recommended	Minimum
__ **Special Fixtures & Equipment**	__ As per program -- most supermarket clients will provide their own fixtures and equipment __ Most supermarket counters, racks, display cases, etc. are modular package units, not custom designed or permanently built-in __ If any display units are custom designed, they must be engineered with care and tested for wearability	__ As per Recommended

PLUMBING	Recommended	Minimum
__ **Fixtures**	__ Fire sprinklers as per code, generally 1 or more to cover every 200 sq. ft. __ Wet and dry standpipes, fire hose cabinets, etc. all as per code and preferably in excess of code minimums __ Employee drinking fountain and restrooms __ Janitorial maintenance closet with mop sink	__ Fire sprinklers and other fire protection as per code __ Employee restrooms with janitorial mop sink

DESIGN STANDARDS -- SUPERMARKETS

HVAC	Recommended	Minimum
__ **Occupancies**	__ As per program	__ As per program
__ **Heating**	__ Temperatures 68° to 72° F -- forced air	__ Unit heaters
__ **Ventilation**	__ 35 - 50 cfm outdoor air per occupant __ Extra ventilation at high-heat lighting, displays, and equipment	__ Outside air: 15 - 30 cfm per occupant
__ **HVAC System & Controls**	__ Package HVAC units OK __ Positive air pressure to block outside air __ Air lock vestibule to preserve air temperatures and buffer air pressure changes as people enter and leave the building __ Central thermostat control	__ As per Recommended

ELECTRICAL POWER	Recommended	Minimum
__ **Power Outlets**	__ Outlets as required for janitorial service __ Generous distribution of junction box outlets for floor-mounted and wall-mounted display cases __ Checkout stand wiring as per program and manufacturer's requirements __ Lighted exit signs at exit doors	__ As per Recommended and client's program for display cases and special fixtures

LIGHTING	Recommended	Minimum
__ **Lamps**	__ Surface mounted, recessed, or flush recessed fluorescent fixtures for general illumination (4'x4' units at 12' spacing is common) __ Supplementary display lights: Stage lights, track lights, swivel spots, pin spots, cove lights, display case and accent lights	__ As per Recommended CAUTION: Even at low budget, the primary rule is to concentrate on lighting the merchandise, in a complementary fashion -- meat and produce require special lighting and color
__ **Switching**	__ Lockable switches, lighting control panel, dimmers on accent lights	__ Standard switches and dimmers, central light control panel

ILLUMINATION	Recommended	Minimum
__ **Sales areas**	__ Self service areas 150-200 f.c.	__ 70 f.c.
__ **Product displays**	__ 100 to 500 f.c. (highest light on small items)	__ 300 f.c.
__ **General merchandise**	__ 100 f.c. minimum, higher in showcases	__ 70 f.c.
__ **Non display space**	__ 30-40 f.c. (showcase light 2 x ambient lighting)	__ 20 f.c.

COMMUNICATIONS	Recommended	Minimum
__ **Communications**	__ Fire and smoke detectors and alarms __ Cash register area phone lines and intercom __ Security alarms __ Surveillance systems, remote controlled video cameras and monitors	__ As per Recommended

257

THEATERS

DESIGN STANDARDS -- THEATER AUDITORIUMS

GENERAL	Recommended Standards	Minimum Standards
__ Occupancies & Floor Areas	__ 8 to 10 sq. ft. per person for average 700 to 1,200 person occupancy (includes aisles)	__ 7.5 sq. ft. per person
__ Depth of Auditorium	__ 50' to see gestures clearly, 80' to see large motions	__ 65' maximum to see gestures, 110' maximum to see large motions
__ Depth to Width Ratio	__ Depth of auditorium = 3 x proscenium width	__ Depth of auditorium = 3.5 x proscenium width
__ Sight Lines	__ 60° angle of viewer sightline to screen or subject on stage is maximum for horizontal viewing __ 30° is maximum vertically from center of screen or head height of performers, which determines lowest front row seating and highest balcony seating	__ Sight line angles as per Recommended Standards with some seats at up to 65° horizontal and 35% vertical viewing angles if absolutely necessary
__ Aisle Widths	__ As per Code, typically start at 36" and widen 1-1/2" per 5' to 45" at cross aisles	__ As required by code
__ Seats Per Row	__ 7 seats to aisle is maximum unless there is generous space in front of each seat (follow seating company recommendations)	__ As required by code
__ Seat Spacing	__ Conventional = 14" clear at front of seats __ Continental = 21" clear at front of seats __ 36"+ for back-to-back, conventional seating __ 22"+ o.c. side-by-side spacing	__ Conventional = 13" clear at front of seats __ Continental = 18" clear at front of seats __ 32"+ for back-to-back, conventional seating __ 20" o.c. side-by-side spacing

FINISHES	Cost Categories		
	A	B	C
__ Floors & Sub-structure	__ Concrete slab, raised above HVAC plenum at ground floor, stepped at balconies __ Heavy duty carpet at aisles, stain resistant, glued	__ Concrete slab	NOTE: Theater auditorium and stage requirements are so important to successful utilization of the building, that the lowest cost economies of construction, materials, and fixtures should not normally be considered
__ Wainscot/Walls at Side Aisles	__ Sound reflective or absorbant walls as required for acoustic control __ Highly resistant to abrasion and damage by moving crowds	__ Materials to meet acoustic requirements as specified by consultants	
__ Seating	__ As per requirements and recommendations of seating manufacturer __ Built-in A/V cabinet, projection booth	__ As per program	
__ Walls & Substructure	__ 1-hour fire rating or more, as per building code __ Finish material flame spread ratings as per code __ Sound-isolated construction __ Plaster or gypsum board with acoustic control structure and treatments	__ Materials and shaping to meet acoustic requirements as specified by consultants	
__ Ceiling & Sub-structure	__ Theater ceiling engineered for acoustic control, stage lighting supports, and fire and seismic safety	__ Materials and shaping to meet acoustic requirements as specified by consultants	
__ Acoustics -- Auditorium shaping, baffles, materials	__ As per professional theater acoustical engineer	__ As per professional theater acoustical engineer	

259

DESIGN STANDARDS -- THEATER AUDITORIUMS

DOORS & WINDOWS	Recommended	Minimum
__ **Doors**	__ 1-3/4" solid core steel auditorium doors, fire rated as required by local fire code __ Vision panels __ Sound proofing gaskets	NOTE: Quiet and effective door operation is so important to proper theater operation that all minimum door standards are as per Recommended.
__ **Frames**	__ 14 gauge steel at fire exit doors and doors to corridors __ Fire rated assembly as required by local code	
__ **Hardware**	__ Quiet, concealed automatic closers, sound gasketing __ Heavy duty panic bar and related exit hardware __ Quiet panic bar operation __ Wall grabs to hold doors open during intermissions and exiting	
__ **Windows / Glazing**	__ Glazing at projection and spotlight and sound control booths __ Projection or control booth glazing must be as approved by acoustic consultant in materials, location, and angular orientation	__ As per Recommended

FIXTURES/EQUIPMENT	Recommended	Minimum
__ **Audio-Visual**	__ Projection, lighting, and sound control equipment all as per program and as recommended or required by engineering and theater consultants __ Locked security access to all control rooms and spaces	__ As per program

PLUMBING	Recommended	Minimum
__ **Fixtures**	__ Sprinklers as required by local fire code __ Fire hose cabinets as required by local fire code	__ As per code

DESIGN STANDARDS -- THEATER AUDITORIUMS

HVAC	Recommended	Minimum
__ Occupancies	__ As per program (programming for full use of these facilities requires expert consultation)	__ As per program
__ Ventilation	__ 25 - 30 cfm outdoor air per occupant	__ 20 cfm outdoor air per occupant
__ HVAC System & Controls	__ Central HVAC system __ Under floor HVAC plenum recommended for large volume, slow air speed heating and ventilation	
__ HeatinG Temperature WARNING: A common source of complaints about auditoriums is fluctuating temperatures and excessive air movement . . . top-quality equipment and engineering is mandatory for public auditorium design	__ Temperatures at seating levels controlled at 68 to 72F with equipment adequate to quietly handle quick adjustment to rapidly changing occupancies	__ Temperatures at seating levels at 68 to 72F. __ Even at minimum construction cost, provide generous fresh air supply and quiet, quick response system

ELECTRICAL POWER	Recommended	Minimum
__ Power Outlets	__ Concealed floor outlets for building maintenance __ All stage and control booth outlets as per theater consultant and electrical engineer	__ As per Recommended or as per program

LIGHTING	Recommended	Minimum
__ Lamps	__ Variable ceiling house lighting __ Variable and decorative wall washer lighting __ Subdued floor lighting at aisles and all steps and ramps	__ As per Recommended
__ Switching	__ Controls at secure master switch control room	

ILLUMINATION WARNING: Inadequate floor and aisle lights are a common cause of accidents, especially at steps	Recommended	Minimum
	__ Totally variable as per theater consultant recommendations	__ As per Recommended

COMMUNICATIONS	Recommended	Minimum
__ Communications	__ Speakers as per acoustic and sound engineering consultants	__ As per Recommended or as per program

DESIGN STANDARDS -- THEATER STAGE & BACKSTAGE

GENERAL	Recommended Standards	Minimum Standards
__ **Floor Areas**	__ 3,600 sq. ft. stage for average 700 to 900 audience capacity theater	__ 3,200 sq. ft. for average 700 to 900 audience
__ **Sizes of Stage Areas**	__ Proscenium width = 45' - 60' __ Stage depth = 2.5 to 3 x proscenium width __ Proscenium height = 2.5 x width __ Total stage width = 2 x proscenium width (total 90' for 45' wide proscenium) __ Stage height = 30" to 36" above first row floor	__ Proscenium width = 40' with total side stages of 24' on each side minimum __ Proscenium depth = 2 x proscenium width __ Proscenium height = 20' minimum __ Total stage width = 2 x proscenium width (88' for 40' wide proscenium) __ Max. stage height = 44" above first row floor
__ **Gridiron Height**	__ Gridiron height = 2.5 to 3 x stage picture height (full width and depth extends from proscenium to back stage wall)	__ Gridiron height = 2.5 x proscenium height
__ **Sight Lines**	__ Allow for 60° angle of audience sightline to screen or subject on stage as maximum for horizontal viewing __ Allow for 30° as maximum vertically from center of screen or head height of performers, which determines lowest front row seating and highest balcony seating	__ Sight lines as per Recommended Standards
__ **Other backstage areas for average community theater -- 700 to 900 audience**	__ Workshop = 1,600 to 2,000 sq. ft. __ Scenery storage = 1,200 to 1,600 sq. ft. __ Costume sewing and storage = 800 to 1,000 sq. ft. __ Conference room = 600 sq. ft. __ Green room = 200 sq. ft. __ Six dressing and makeup rooms, 2 occupants or 1 "star" performer each = 140 sq. ft. each __ Two chorus dressing rooms = 300 sq. ft. each __ Restrooms = 160 sq. ft. each __ Stage manager = 160 sq. ft. __ Office space(s) for directors = 200 sq. ft. each.	__ Workshop = 1,200 to 1,400 sq. ft. __ Scenery storage = 1,000 to 1,200 sq. ft. __ Costume sewing and storage = 700 sq. ft. __ Conference room = 400 sq. ft. __ Green room = 140 sq. ft. __ Six dressing and makeup rooms, 2 occupants or 1 "star" performer each = 100 sq. ft. each __ Two chorus dressing rooms = 240 sq. ft. each __ Restrooms = 120 sq. ft. each __ Stage manager = 120 sq. ft. __ Director's office and additional office spaces as per program or 140 sq. ft. each

FINISHES	Cost Categories		
	A	B	C
__ **Floors & Sub-structure** NOTE: All finishes as approved by professional theater design and acoustic consultants and fire marshall	__ Concrete slab ground floor support for stage structure __ Traps beneath stage as per theater consultant __ Effective stage area: hardwood floor on sleepers __ Surface for mounting neoprene cushioned dance floor, if required __ Concrete slab at work areas __ Vinyl at occupied spaces	__ Concrete slab base floor with sleepers and hardwood floor above __ Concrete slab at work and storage areas __ Vinyl or asphalt tile at occupied backstage rooms such as dressing rooms	NOTE: Theater auditorium and stage requirements are so important to successful utilization of the building, that the lowest cost economies of construction, materials, and fixtures should not normally be considered
__ **Walls** NOTE: Dressing room mirrors with makeup lights	__ Backstage utility space walls: gypsum board, etc. -- 2-hour fire rating	__ Backstage utility space walls: concrete block, unfinished gypsum board	
__ **Ceiling**	__ Stage and fly loft ceiling engineered for acoustic control, lighting supports, and fire and seismic safety __ Equipment and fixtures as per stage equipment manufacturer	__ As per theater consultant and equipment manufacturer	

262

DESIGN STANDARDS -- THEATER STAGE & BACKSTAGE

DOORS & WINDOWS	Recommended	Minimum
__ **Doors**	__ 10' x 14' exterior wall doors for moving scenery, traveling show sets, etc.	__ 8' x 12' scenery and equipment access doors
	__ 8' x 12' to 10' x 14' stage workshop door	__ 8' x 12' stage workshop door
	__ Security entry door for cast and crew	
	__ 1-3/4" solid core steel doors to backstage rooms, fire rated as required by local fire code	__ 1-3/4" solid core doors
	__ Vision panels	
	__ Sound proofing gaskets at all edges of back-stage doors	__ As per Recommended
__ **Frames**	__ 14 gauge steel at fire exit doors and doors to corridors	
	__ Fire rated assembly as required by local code	__ Automatic closers at entry doors
__ **Hardware**	__ Quiet, concealed automatic closers, sound gasketing	__ Panic bar and related exit hardware
	__ Heavy duty panic bar and related exit hard-ware	
__ **Windows / Glazing**	__ Glazing as per theater consultant or equip-ment manufacturer details at projection and spotlight and sound control booths	__ As per Recommended
	__ Projection or control booth glazing must be as approved by acoustic constultant in materials, location, and angular orientation	
	__ No exterior wall glazing except in peripheral backstage rooms such as costume, shop, and possibly some dressing rooms	

FIXTURES/EQUIPMENT	Recommended	Minimum
__ **Audio-Visual**	__ Projection, lighting, and sound control equip-ment all as per program and as recommend-ed or required by engineering and theater consultants	__ As per program and Recommended -- primarily a factor of elaboration and sophis-tication of staging and lighting effects and programmed variable uses of the theater
	__ Locked security access to all lighting, switch-ing, and sound control rooms	

PLUMBING	Recommended	Minimum
__ **Fixtures**	__ Sprinklers as required by local fire code	__ As per program and fire code
	__ Fire hose cabinets as required by local fire code	
	__ Standard restroom fixtures	
	__ Janitor's closet with mop sink	
	__ Work sink in workshop	
	__ Two lavatories in each dressing room, 5 lavs in chorus dressing rooms	
	__ Lav, toilet, and shower in "star" dressing room	

263

DESIGN STANDARDS -- THEATER STAGE & BACKSTAGE

HVAC	Recommended	Minimum
__ Occupancies	__ As per program	__ As per program
__ Ventilation	__ Shared with auditorium __ Large smoke vent and emergency vent fan at roof above fly loft	__ As per Recommended
__ HVAC System & Control	__ Central HVAC system, shared with auditorium __ Because of the critical nature of thermal and air comfort for performers and audience, this work requires expert theater and HVAC engineering consulting	__ As per Recommended
__ Temperature	__ Temperatures range 68 to 72F -- lower range in stage area for dance performances	__ Temperatures range 68 to 72F

ELECTRICAL POWER	Recommended	Minimum
__ Power Outlets	__ Outlets at columns and perimeter walls for building maintenance __ All stage and control booth outlets as per theater consultant and electrical engineer	__ As per Recommended or as per program

LIGHTING	Recommended	Minimum
__ Lamps	__ Spot and flood lighting as per theater and electrical engineeing consultants __ Emergency exit lights __ Battery operated emergency exit lamps	__ As per Recommended or as per program
__ Switching	__ Master control room and spotligtht booth consoles as per theater and electrical engineering consultants	__ As per Recommended or as per program

ILLUMINATION	Recommended	Minimum
	__ Stage lighting as per theater consultants and stage production designers	__ As per Recommended or as per program

COMMUNICATIONS	Recommended	Minimum
__ Communications	__ Cross-stage and stage to spot booth and control booth intercoms __ Outside phone lines __ Fire call system	__ As per Recommended or as per program

264

DESIGN STANDARDS -- THEATER FOYER

GENERAL	Recommended Standards	Minimum Standards
__ Occupancies and Floor Area	__ As per program, typically 1,400 sq. ft. foyer or gallery for average 700 to 900 audience capacity theater	__ As per program
__ Ceiling Height	__ 14' and up with low soffits at entry or alcove	__ 12' ceiling in smaller theaters with low (8') soffits at entrance and side alcoves
__ Auxiliary Spaces	__ Bar or concession alcove = 200 sq. ft. __ Checkroom = 300 sq. ft. for average 700-900 capacity theater __ Box office with two windows = 60 sq. ft., plus 100 sq. ft. for adjacent business office	__ Bar or concession, as per program __ Checkroom may be optional __ Box office with two windows = 50 sq. ft. plus 80 sq. ft. for business office
__ Special Plan Considerations	__ Double-door air lock vestibule in hot or cold climates __ Clear signage for aisle numbers, restrooms	__ As per Recommended Standards __ Planning should emphasize clarity and ease of movement in and out of theater auditorium and lobby

FINISHES	Cost Categories A	B	C
__ Floors WARNING: Smooth, hard surface materials sometimes used at entrances -- such as terrazzo, marble, smooth tile, or polished travertine are safety hazards -- even those treated to be non-slip are a problem when wet and when in contact with certain shoe sole materials	__ Recessed floor mat for rainy/snowy climates at vestibule __ Non-slip rubber or vinyl tile at entry vestibule __ Nylon or other synthetic fabric carpet near entry should be rated for heavy wear, stain resistant and reasonably dark tone, glued to floor __ Carpet may be a different, complementary color and fabric than at other spaces to allow easier replacement of the more heavily trafficked entry floor area __ Avoid light-tone reflective floor surfaces	__ Vinyl or asphalt tile at entry vestibule __ Synthetic fabric carpet rated for heavy wear near entry, glued to floor __ Complementary heavy to medium wear carpet at adjacent areas __ Other flooring considerations as per Cost Category A	__ Non-slip rubber or vinyl at entry vestibule __ Synthetic fabric carpet near entry, glued __ Vinyl or asphalt tile
__ Fixtures	__ Public phones __ Handicap access allowing for handicapped and elderly __ Lighted fire exit signs __ Wall poster or art displays	__ Fixtures as per Cost Category A and/or program	__ Fixtures as per Cost Category A and/or program
__ Walls & Substructure	__ Full-height store-front entry __ Interior wall finish typically plaster or gypsum board with heavy weight vinyl or fabric __ Exit wall fire ratings as per code __ May include mirror, polished stone, or wood decorative panels or wainscot	__ Foyer and exit area wall fire ratings as per code __ Gypsum board with heavy weight vinyl or fabric __ Plaster with sound absorbant treatment __ Protective or decorative hard surface paneling where walls are subject to abrasion by crowd movement	__ Fire ratings as per code __ Gypsum board, painted
__ Ceiling	__ Plaster __ Baffle, metal, wood or other decorative ceiling __ Gypsum board with acoustic treatment __ Suspended decorative acoustic tile __ Fire resistive treated wood	__ Suspended decorative acoustic tile __ Gypsum board	__ Suspended acoustic tile, exposed grid __ Gypsum board

DESIGN STANDARDS -- THEATER FOYER

DOORS & WINDOWS	Recommended	Minimum
__ **Doors**	__ Automatic doors as needed for heavy traffic and for most convenient handicap access __ Heavy-duty, glazed public entry doors with quiet operating hardware and automatic closers __ Double door air-lock vestibule to control indoor-outdoor temperature differences and outside noise	__ Glazed public entry doors
__ **Frames**	__ 14 gauge steel or heavy duty aluminum store front detailing	__ 16 gauge steel or as per store front manufacturer
__ **Hardware**	__ Quiet, concealed automatic closers	
__ **Related Fixtures**	__ Lighted exit signs at exit doors as per code __ Controlled locking with security alarm system __ Side panel glazing or safety vision panels at non-glazed doors to auditorium	
__ **Windows**	__ Floor to ceiling front glazing with glass entry doors __ Floor base and extremely conspicuous horizontal bars or barriers to prevent adults and children from walking into full-height glazing	__ No minimum requirements but views to the exterior are desirable __ Safety barriers at full-height glazing as per Recommended

FIXTURES/EQUIPMENT	Recommended	Minimum
__ **Special Furnishings**	__ Box office equipment __ Event announcement boards __ Display and exhibit cabinets __ Checkroom shelving, coat racks, tag hooks __ Bar, back bar and concession counters, refrigerator, ice maker, shelving, bar sink	__ As per program and Recommended

PLUMBING	Recommended	Minimum
__ **Fixtures**	__ Drinking fountains near entry and/or near restrooms __ Fire sprinklers as required by code __ Fire hose cabinets as required __ Bar sink at refreshment counter	__ As per Recommended

266

DESIGN STANDARDS -- THEATER FOYER

HVAC	Recommended	Minimum
__ Occupancies	__ As per program -- allowing for large variations in traffic prior to performances and during theater intermissions	__ As per program
__ Ventilation	__ 20 - 30 cfm outdoor air per occupant __ Air lock vestibule in extreme climate areas to preserve indoor air temperatures and buffer air pressure changes as people enter and leave the building	__ 20 cfm outdoor air per occupant
__ HVAC System & Controls	__ As per primary adjacent public spaces __ Localized heating may be provided in waiting area of vestibule	__ As per main public areas

ELECTRICAL POWER	Recommended	Minimum
__ Power Outlets	__ Outlets at information/registration desk __ Wall clock outlet __ Outlets as required for janitorial service __ Lighted fire exit signs as per code __ Battery powered emergency lights	__ Outlets at information desk __ Outlets as required for janitorial service __ Lighted fire exit signs as per code __ Battery powered emergency lights

LIGHTING	Recommended	Minimum
__ Lamps	__ Overall incandescent pendants and/or recessed fluorescent ceiling fixtures __ Downlights and accent lights __ Chandelier decorative lighting __ Spotlights and wall wash lights for displays and artwork	__ Fluorescent ceiling fixtures __ Spotlights and wall wash lights for displays and artwork
__ Switching	__ Central control, dimmers, and timers near theater manager or security office	__ Standard lockable dimmer switch controls near entry

ILLUMINATION	Recommended	Minimum
	__ 20 - 30 f.c. at entry vestibule __ 50 - 70 f.c. at information desk area	__ 15 - 20 f.c. at entry vestibule __ 30 - 70 f.c. at information desk area

COMMUNICATIONS	Recommended	Minimum
	__ Fire/security alarms __ Generous number of public phones __ PA system	__ Alarms as required by code __ Public phones __ PA system

WAREHOUSES

DESIGN STANDARDS -- WAREHOUSES

GENERAL	Recommended Standards	Minimum Standards
__ Occupancies	__ As per program	__ As per program
__ Floor Area and Spans NOTE: One-story, long-span construction is almost universally preferred over two- or more story construction	__ Floor area as per program but should provide generous allowance for expansion of at least 100% over time __ One story clear spans from 80' to 120' __ Two-story construction will virtually always be reinforced concrete with very limited spans and bay sizes __ Minimum aisles but each main aisle with two-way fork lift or other loading vehicle traffic __ Aisle widths determined by vehicles, pallet types and sizes, and stored materials sizes	__ As per program __ Clear spans 40' to 80'
__ Storage Systems	__ Pallet rack and other systems as per warehouse planning engineer, consultants, and manufacturers' recommendations	__ Systems as per storage system manufacturer
__ Ceiling Height	__ 20' to 24' for high stacking storage systems __ Allow for 24" clear space under fire sprinklers	__ 16'-18' minimum __ Allow for 18" clear space under fire sprinklers
__ Loading Docks	__ Loading docks 18' wide with side ramps __ Floor height 4'-4" for truck loading docks __ Floor height 3'-7" for train loading docks __ Confirm heights, clearances, other specifics with local controlling transport agencies	__ Loading docks 16' wide __ Heights as per Recommended Standards

FINISHES	Cost Categories		
	A	B	C
__ Floors & Sub-structures	__ Portland cement concrete __ Asphaltic concrete with light broom finish __ Trowel finish where applied must have non-slip surface __ Floor drainage slopes at 1/4" per lin. ft., 1/2" per lin. ft. to slab drains at loading doors	__ Concrete slab, light broom texture finish NOTE: __ Higher cost warehousing may entail special refrigeration, HVAC, security, structural, and finish standards, but otherwise there won't be much cost differential between A, B, and C cost categories	__ Asphalt paving
__ Walls & Structure	__ Concrete, tilt-up __ Concrete masonry units __ If clear spans not used, structural bays typically 20' to 40' __ Light color paint finish recommended to improve lighting and safety __ Interior fire walls as per fire code		__ Corrugated sheet metal
__ Ceiling & Sub-structure	__ Exposed truss and joist or beam and joist system __ Corrugated metal		__ Metal or wood pole framing with corrugated sheet metal
__ Acoustics	__ As per OSHA and state industrial safety standards	__ As per OSHA and state industrial safety standards	__ As required by code

269

DESIGN STANDARDS -- WAREHOUSES

DOORS & WINDOWS	Recommended	Minimum

__ Doors
 	
__ Frames
 	
__ Hardware
	__ Steel roll-up doors
	__ Overhead doors
	__ Actual sizes as per program, otherwise:
	  __ 12' wide x 12' high nominal size
	  __ 18' to 20' wide x 18' high, motor operated
	    for larger or unpredictable size storage
	    items
	
	__ Heaviest-gauge steel frames, channels and
	  corner guards as recommended by door
	  manufacturers
	
	__ Door spacing 15' centers for trucks, 45' cen-
	  ters for trains
		__ Horizontal sliding doors
		__ Vertical lift doors (if head room permits; see
		  door manufacturer's literature)
		__ 10' wide x 10' to 12' high nominal size
		__ 16' x 16' for larger size storage items
		
		__ As per door manufacturer's minimum require-
		  ments
		
		__ As per program or Recommended

__ Windows	__ Side-wall windows aren't usually effective
	__ High-level protected factory sash or fixed
	  glass with small lights for easy replacement
		__ None required except for administrative office
		  space

__ Skylighting	__ Roof skylights -- pyramid wire glass or plastic
	  bubble -- spaced for maximum utility and
	  even distribution
	__ Monitors and sawtooth roofs if maximum
	  interior daylight is required
		__ None required if the required overall lighting--
		  natural or artifical--is minimal

FIXTURES/EQUIPMENT	Recommended	Minimum

__ Special Equipment	__ Heaviest gauge corner guards at all interior
	  corners, door frames, and columns
	__ Column guards to 5' height
	__ Guards, bollards, and mesh protection at:
	  __ Electrical panels and switchboards
	  __ Water or steam supply lines
	  __ Sprinkler risers
	  __ Plumbing valves
		__ Corner, wall guard, and utility protection in
		  general as per Recommended

__ Conveyor Equipment	__ Selection as per warehouse planning engi-
	  neer, consultants, and manufacturers' re-
	  commendations:
	  __ Conveyor systems
	  __ Stacker cranes
	  __ Robotic vehicles
	  __ Straddle fork trucks
	  __ Overhead bridge crane
	  __ Robotic/fully automated systems
		__ As per program

PLUMBING	Recommended	Minimum

__ Fixtures	__ Sprinklers
	__ Fire hose cabinets
	__ Color code painting of major plumbing units
	__ Floor drains at each structural bay
	__ Floor drains or troughs at large loading dock
	  doors to catch rain/melted snow
	__ Washroom cluster sink and other washroom
	  fixtures as per program
		__ Sprinklers and other fire protection equipment
		  as per code

DESIGN STANDARDS -- WAREHOUSES

HVAC	Recommended	Minimum

__ Ventilation	__ Roof ventilators:
	    __ Motorized rotary units
	    __ Continuous ridge ventilation
		__ Roof ventilators:
		    __ Wind powered rotary units
		    __ Ridge vents

__ HVAC System &
   Controls
	__ Central system with thermostat controls
	    as per climate and special requirements of
	    materials in storage
	__ Any central HVAC facilities should allow for
	    at least 100% expansion of the warehouse
	    space
		__ Unit heaters and ventilators, thermostat
		    controlled

ELECTRICAL POWER	Recommended	Minimum

__ Power	__ Dependent on lighting and need for motor
	    power such as for conveyors
	    __ 480/277-volt, 4-wire -- for larger buildings,
	      all-purpose service
	    __ 120/240-volt, 3-wire for basic lighting
	      types
	    __ 208/120 3- phase for motor power and
	      electrical heating
		__ 120/240-volt, 3 wire

__ Power Outlets	__ As per program:
	    __ Office outlets
	    __ Building maintenance outlets
	    __ Battery recharge outlets for electric
	      vehicles
		__ As per Recommended

LIGHTING	Recommended	Minimum

__ Lamps	__ Surface mounted or suspended fluorescent
	__ Suspended mercury vapor lamps
	__ Color-corrected lighting if necessary to read
	    color-coded packaging
	__ Exterior mercury vapor lamps at loading
	    docks, security lights at entrances and exits
		__ Fluorescent or mercury vapor lamps
		__ Task lights at inspection and paperwork
		    areas

__ Switching	__ Master switchboard near main entry and administration or maintenance office	__ As per Recommended

ILLUMINATION	Recommended	Minimum

	__ 10-15 foot-candles overall
	__ 60-100 foot-candles for office work, paper-
	    work, supervisory areas
	__ 3-6 foot-candles loading dock night lights
		__ 5-10 foot-candles overall
		__ 50 foot-candles for office work, paperwork,
		    supervisory areas
		__ 1-3 foot candles loading dock night lights

COMMUNICATIONS	Recommended	Minimum
__ Communications	__ Intercoms __ Time buzzers for breaks, lunch, shift changes __ Warning sirens __ Fire alarms and fire department call __ Security systems and police call	__ As per program

ROOM DESIGN CHECKLIST

CONTENTS

ROOM DESIGN CHECKLIST

DESIGN DECISIONS RECORD LOG

PROJECT NAME AND NUMBER:

_____

_____

Project Architect or Manager: _____

Principal in Charge: _____

MEETING DATES AND PARTICIPANTS:

Phase	Date	Participants (initials)
_____	_____	_____
_____	_____	_____
_____	_____	_____
_____	_____	_____
_____	_____	_____
_____	_____	_____
_____	_____	_____
_____	_____	_____
_____	_____	_____

Legend for Coded Decisions:
(Revise as required)

D	Design/Aesthetic Requirement
CL	Client Requirement
B	Building Code Requirement
ZP	Zoning or Planning Dept. Requirement
$	Cost Requirement
S	Standard Practice
CN	Contractor Recommendation
SC	Security Protection
SF	Safety Requirement

Other regulations/agency requirements, etc.:

_____

_____

_____

Names and Initials of Project Participants

_____

_____

_____

_____

_____

_____

_____

_____

_____

_____

ROOM DESIGN CHECKLIST

DIVISION 3--CONCRETE   (INTERIOR)

__ **CONCRETE FLOOR**   NOTES
       (Other flooring, see:
        DIVISION 9--FINISHES)
__ Concrete Slab   03300   _____

__ Concrete Topping   03320   _____
__ Concrete Slab Steel
       Trowel Finish   03356   _____
__ Concrete Slab Float
       Finish   03357   _____
__ Concrete Slab Broom
       Finish   03358   _____
__ Concrete Slab Nonslip
       Finish   03359   _____

Date/Who/Why: Changed (Date/Who/Why):

Coord check: ___structural ___cross sections ___finish schedule ___drains

__ **CAST-IN-PLACE CONCRETE WALLS**   NOTES

__ Exposed Aggregate
       Concrete   03351   _____

__ Tooled Concrete   03352   _____

__ Sand Blasted Concrete 03353   _____
__ Grooved Surface
       Concrete   03354   _____

__ Colored Concrete   03355   _____
__ Formwork Board
       Pattern Concrete   03356   _____

Date/Who/Why: Changed (Date/Who/Why):

Coord check: ___structural ___cross sections ___interior elevations ___finish schedule

__ **PRECAST CONCRETE WALLS AND DECK**   NOTES

__ Precast Concrete   03400   _____
__ Precast Concrete
       Pane   03411   _____

__ Precast Concrete Deck 03412   _____

__ Tilt-up Concrete   03430   _____
__ Decorative Precast Concrete
       Wall Panel   03451   _____

Date/Who/Why: Changed (Date/Who/Why):

Coord check: ___structural ___cross sections ___interior elevations ___finish schedule

ROOM DESIGN CHECKLIST

DIVISION 3--CONCRETE (INTERIOR) continued

__ **CEMENTITIOUS DECKS**

NOTES

__ Gypsum Concrete   03310   _____

__ Precast Gypsum Plank 03515   _____
__ Wood Fiber Plank/
      Deck   03530   _____
__ Composite Concrete
      and Insulation   03540   _____
__ Asphalt and Perlite
      Concrete Deck   03550   _____

Date/Who/Why: Changed (Date/Who/Why):

Coord check: ___structural ___cross sections

ROOM DESIGN CHECKLIST

DIVISION 4--MASONRY   (INTERIOR)

__ BRICK   NOTES

__ Brick Wall	04210	_____
__ Freestanding Brick Wall	04210	_____
__ Adobe Wall	04212	_____
__ Structural Glazed Tile	04213	_____
__ Brick Cavity Wall	04214	_____
__ Face Brick	04215	_____
__ Brick Veneer	04215	_____
__ SCR Brick	04216	_____

Date/Who/Why: Changed (Date/Who/Why):

Coord check: ___structural ___cross sections ___interior elevations ___finish schedule

__ CONCRETE BLOCK   NOTES

__ Concrete Block Wall	04220	_____
__ Glazed Concrete Block	04221	_____
__ Exposed Aggregate Concrete Block	04222	_____
__ Split-Face Concrete Block	04223	_____
__ Fluted Concrete Block	04224	_____
__ Molded Face Concrete Block	04225	_____
__ Freestanding Concrete Block Wall	04229	_____

Date/Who/Why: Changed (Date/Who/Why):

Coord check: ___structural ___cross sections ___interior elevations ___finish schedule

__ MISC. UNIT MASONRY WALLS AND FINISHES   NOTES

__ Clay Facing Tile	04245	_____
__ Ceramic Tile Veneer	04250	_____
__ Terra Cotta Veneer	04251	_____
__ Glass Unit Masonry	04270	_____
__ Gypsum Unit Masonry	04280	_____
__ Sound Absorbing Unit Masonry	04285	_____

Date/Who/Why: Changed (Date/Who/Why):

Coord check: ___structural ___cross sections ___interior elevations ___finish schedule

ROOM DESIGN CHECKLIST

DIVISION 4--MASONRY (INTERIOR) continued

__ **STONE WALLS**

NOTES

__ Stone Wall	04400	_____
__ Rough Stone	04410	_____
__ Cut Stone	04420	_____
__ Marble	04422	_____
__ Limestone	04423	_____
__ Granite	04424	_____
__ Sandstone	04425	_____
__ Slate	04426	_____
__ Cast Stone	04435	_____
__ Flagstone	04440	_____
__ Blue Stone	04441	_____
__ Stone Veneer	04450	_____
__ Natural Stone Veneer	04450	_____
__ Marble Veneer	04451	_____

Date/Who/Why: Changed (Date/Who/Why):

Coord check: ___structural ___cross sections ___interior elevations ___finish schedule

277

ROOM DESIGN CHECKLIST

DIVISION 5--METALS   (INTERIOR)

NOTES

__ **METAL DECKING** 05300 _____

Date/Who/Why: Changed (Date/Who/Why):
Coord check: ___structural ___cross sections

__ **METAL FABRICATIONS/ORNAMENTAL METAL**   NOTES

__ Metal Stair   05510   _____
__ Ornamental Metal
        Stair   05710   _____
__ Prefab Metal Spiral
        Stair   05715   _____

Date/Who/Why: Changed (Date/Who/Why):

Coord check: ___structural ___anchors ___interior elevations ___finish schedule

ROOM DESIGN CHECKLIST

DIVISION 6--WOOD AND PLASTIC   (INTERIOR)

__ **FINISH CARPENTRY**   NOTES

__ Decorative Millwork   06220   _____

__ Laminated Plastic   06240   _____

Date/Who/Why: Changed (Date/Who/Why):

Coord check: ___interior elevations ___finish schedule

__ **ARCHITECTURAL WOODWORK**   NOTES

__ Wood Cabinetwork   06410   _____

__ Wood Shelving   06412   _____

__ Wood Paneling   06420   _____

__ Wood Stairwork   06431   _____

__ Wood Workbenches   06453   _____

Date/Who/Why: Changed (Date/Who/Why):

Coord check: ___wall anchors ___interior elevations ___finish schedule ___furnishings ___electrical

ROOM DESIGN CHECKLIST

DIVISION 7--THERMAL AND MOISTURE PROTECTION   (INTERIOR)

__ **INSULATION**   NOTES

__ Rigid Insulation   07212   _____
__ Batt Thermal
           Insulation   07213   _____
__ Foamed-In-Place
           Insulation   07214   _____

__ Sprayed Insulation   07216   _____

__ Granular Insulation   07216   _____

Date/Who/Why: Changed (Date/Who/Why):

Coord check: ___code ___hvac ___cross sections

ROOM DESIGN CHECKLIST

DIVISION 8--DOORS AND WINDOWS   (INTERIOR)

__ **METAL DOORS AND FRAMES**   NOTES

__ Steel Door   08110   _____

__ Custom Steel Door   08112   _____

__ Aluminum Door   08120   _____

__ Stainless Steel   08130   _____

__ Bronze Door/Frame   08140   _____

Date/Who/Why: Changed (Date/Who/Why):

Coord check: ___interior elevations ___frame schedule ___hardware schedule ___finish schedule

__ **WOOD AND PLASTIC DOORS**   NOTES

__ Wood Door   08210   _____

__ Flush Wood Door   08211   _____

__ Wood Panel Door   08212   _____

__ Plastic Faced Door   08213   _____

__ Steel Faced Door   08214   _____

Date/Who/Why: Changed (Date/Who/Why):

Coord check: ___interior elevations ___frame schedule ___hardware schedule ___finish schedule

ROOM DESIGN CHECKLIST

DIVISION 8--DOORS AND WINDOWS (INTERIOR) continued

__ **SPECIAL DOORS**   NOTES

__ Access Door	08305	_____
__ Manual Sliding Fire Door	08310	_____
__ Powered Sliding Fire Door	08311	_____
__ Blast-Resistant Door	08315	_____
__ Security Door	08316	_____
__ Kalamein (Metal Clad)	08320	_____
__ Metal-Clad Door	08320	_____
__ Lead Lined Door	08325	_____
__ Coiling Door	08330	_____
__ Overhead Coiling Door	08331	_____
__ Side Coiling Door	08332	_____
__ Coiling Grille	08340	_____
__ Overhead Coiling Grille	08341	_____
__ Side Coiling Grille	08342	_____
__ Folding Door	08350	_____
__ Panel Folding Door	08351	_____
__ Accordion Door	08353	_____
__ Flexible Door	08355	_____
__ Overhead Door	08360	_____
__ Vertical Lift Wood Door	08366	_____
__ Vertical Lift Metal Door	08366	_____
__ Sliding Glass Door	08370	_____
__ Sound Retardant Door	08380	_____

Date/Who/Why: Changed (Date/Who/Why):

Coord check: ___structural ___interior elevations ___frame schedule ___hardware schedule

ROOM DESIGN CHECKLIST

DIVISION 8--DOORS AND WINDOWS (INTERIOR) continued

ENTRANCES AND STOREFRONTS
(See Exterior Design and Construction) 08400

__ **INTERIOR GLAZING**   NOTES

__ Fixed Glass   08800   _____

__ Plate/Float Glass   08811   _____

__ Tempered Glass   08813   _____

__ Wire Glass   08814   _____

__ Obscure Glass   08815   _____
__ Laminated Safety
        Glass   08822   _____

__ Mirror   08830   _____

__ Mirror Glass   08830   _____
__ Two-Way Surveillance
        Mirror   08835   _____

__ Plastic Glazing   08840   _____

Date/Who/Why: Changed (Date/Who/Why):

Coord check: ___code ___interior elevations ___cross sections ___finish schedule

283

ROOM DESIGN CHECKLIST

DIVISION 9--FINISHES   (INTERIOR)

NOTES

__ **METAL SUPPORTED CEILING**
    SYSTEM   09120   _____

Date/Who/Why: Changed (Date/Who/Why):

Coord check: ___structural ___electrical ___cross sections ___finish schedule ___reflected ceiling

__ **LATH AND PLASTER**   NOTES

__ Gypsum Lath and Plaster
    Partition   09202   _____
__ Gypsum Lath and
    Plaster Ceiling 09202   _____
__ Metal Lath and Plaster
    Partition   09203   _____
__ Metal Lath and Plaster
    Ceiling   09203   _____

__ Gypsum Plaster   09210   _____

__ Veneer Plaster   09215   _____
__ Portland Cement
    Plaster   09220   _____

Date/Who/Why: Changed (Date/Who/Why):

Coord check: ___code ___cross sections ___interior elevations ___reflected ceiling ___finish schedule

__ **GYPSUM WALLBOARD**   NOTES

__ Gypsum Wallboard
    Walls   09250   _____
__ Gypsum Wallboard
    Ceiling   09250   _____

Date/Who/Why: Changed (Date/Who/Why):

Coord check: ___code ___cross sections ___interior elevations ___reflec ceiling ___finish schedule

__ **TILE**   NOTES

__ Ceramic Tile   09310   _____

__ Ceramic Mosaic   09320   _____

__ Quarry Tile   09330   _____

__ Slate Tile   09332   _____

__ Marble Tile   09340   _____

__ Glass Mosaic   09350   _____

__ Metal Tile   09380   _____

Date/Who/Why: Changed (Date/Who/Why):

Coord check: ___cross sections ___floor drain ___interior elevations ___finish schedule

284

ROOM DESIGN CHECKLIST

DIVISION 9--FINISHES (INTERIOR) continued

__ TERRAZZO   NOTES

__ Portland		
__ Cement Terrazzo	09410	_____
__ Terrazzo Bonded to		
Concrete	09411	_____
__ Precast Terrazzo	09420	_____
__ Terrazzo Tile	09421	_____
__ Conductive Terrazzo	09430	_____
__ Plastic Matrix		
Terrazzo	09440	_____

Date/Who/Why: Changed (Date/Who/Why):

Coord check: ___cross sections ___floor drain ___finish schedule

__ ACOUSTICAL TREATMENT   NOTES

__ Acoustical Ceiling	09510	_____
__ Acoustical Wall Panel	09511	_____
__ Acoustical Ceiling		
Panel	09511	_____
__ Acoustical Wall Tile	09512	_____
__ Acoustical Ceiling		
Tile	09512	_____
__ Acoustical Metal		
Ceiling	09513	_____
__ Acoustical Plaster	09520	_____
__ Acoustical Insulation	09530	_____
__ Sound Isolation Wall	09530/	_____
	13080	
__ Acoustical Barriers	09530	_____

Date/Who/Why: Changed (Date/Who/Why):

Coord check: ___hvac ___cross sections ___finish schedule ___reflected ceiling

ROOM DESIGN CHECKLIST

DIVISION 9--FINISHES (INTERIOR) continued

__ WOOD FLOORING

NOTES

__ Wood Floor	09550	_____
__ Perim. Expansion Strip	09550	_____
__ Wood Strip Floor	09560	_____
__ Gym Hardwood Floor	09561	_____
__ Gym Steel Spline Floor	09562	_____
__ Wood Parquet Floor	09570	_____
__ Wood Block Floor	09595	_____

Date/Who/Why: Changed (Date/Who/Why):

Coord check: ___cross sections ___finish schedule

__ STONE AND BRICK FLOORING

NOTES

__ Flagstone Floor	09611	_____
__ Slate Floor	09612	_____
__ Marble Floor	09613	_____
__ Granite Floor	09614	_____
__ Brick Floor	09620	_____

Date/Who/Why: Changed (Date/Who/Why):

Coord check: ___structural ___cross sections ___finish schedule ___drains

__ RESILIENT FLOORING

NOTES

__ Resilient Tile Floor	09660	_____
__ Resilient Sheet Floor	09665	_____
__ Conductive Resilient Floor	09675	_____

Date/Who/Why: Changed (Date/Who/Why):

Coord check: ___finish schedule

__ CARPETING

NOTES

__ Carpet	09682	_____
__ Bonded Cushion Carpet	09683	_____
__ Carpet Tile	09690	_____

Date/Who/Why: Changed (Date/Who/Why):

Coord check: ___finish schedule

ROOM DESIGN CHECKLIST

DIVISION 9--FINISHES (INTERIOR) continued

__ SPECIAL FLOORING

NOTES

__ Resinous Flooring	09701	_____
__ Elastomeric Floor	09731	_____
__ Heavy Duty Concrete Topping	09740	_____
__ Armored Floor	09741	_____
__ Laminated Plastic Flooring	09755	_____

Date/Who/Why: Changed (Date/Who/Why):

Coord check: ___finish schedule

__ WALL COVERING

NOTES

__ Vinyl-Coated Fabric	09951	_____
__ Vinyl	09952	_____
__ Cork	09953	_____
__ Fabric	09955	_____
__ Wood Sheet/Veneer	09960	_____
__ Prefinished Panels	09970	_____

Date/Who/Why: Changed (Date/Who/Why):

Coord check: ___finish schedule ___furnishings

ROOM DESIGN CHECKLIST

DIVISION 10--SPECIALTIES   (INTERIOR)

__ **CHALKBOARDS/TACKBOARDS**   NOTES

__ Chalkboard   10110   _____

__ Tackboard   10120   _____

Date/Who/Why: Changed (Date/Who/Why):

Coord check: ___anchors ___interior elevations

                                                 NOTES
__ **SERVICE WALL**
       SYSTEMS   10250   _____

Date/Who/Why: Changed (Date/Who/Why):

Coord check: ___structural ___mechanical

                                                 NOTES

__ **ACCESS FLOORING** 10270   _____

Date/Who/Why: Changed (Date/Who/Why):

Coord check: ___mechanical ___electrical ___finish schedule

__ **FIREPLACES AND STOVES**   NOTES

__ Prefab Fireplace   10301   _____

__ Stove   10320   _____

Date/Who/Why: Changed (Date/Who/Why):

Coord check: ___code ___structural ___interior elevations

__ **IDENTIFYING DEVICES**   NOTES

__ Directory   10411   _____

__ Bulletin Board   10415   _____

__ Plaque   10420   _____

__ Architect's Plaque   10420   _____

__ Illuminated Sign   10430   _____

__ Sign   10440   _____

__ Fire Exit Sign   10455   _____

Date/Who/Why: Changed (Date/Who/Why):

Coord check: ___code ___electrical ___anchors ___interior elevations

288

ROOM DESIGN CHECKLIST

DIVISION 10--SPECIALTIES (INTERIOR) continued

__ **LOCKERS**   NOTES

__ Workbench Locker   10500   _____

__ Wardrobe Locker   10501   _____

__ Box Lockers   10502   _____

__ Basket Lockers   10503   _____

__ Coin Lockers   10505   _____

__ Locker Bench   10510   _____

Date/Who/Why: Changed (Date/Who/Why):

Coord check: ___anchors ___interior elevations

__ **FIRE EXTINGUISHER CABINETS/ACCESSORIES**   NOTES
    (Also see Fire Protection 15500)

__ Fire Extinguisher
    Cabinet   10522   _____

__ Fire Blankets   10523   _____

Date/Who/Why: Changed (Date/Who/Why):

Coord check: ___code ___anchors ___interior elevations

__ **POSTAL SPECIALTIES**   NOTES

__ Mail Chute   10551   _____

__ Mail Box   10552   _____

Date/Who/Why: Changed (Date/Who/Why):

Coord check: ___anchors ___interior elevations

__ **PARTITIONS**   NOTES

__ Mesh Partition   10601   _____
__ Demountable
    Partition   10610   _____
__ Stud Type Movable
    Partition   10613   _____
__ Movable Gypsum
    Partition   10616   _____
__ Movable Metal
    Partition   10617   _____

Date/Who/Why: Changed (Date/Who/Why):

Coord check: ___structural ___interior elevations ___reflec ceiling ___finish schedule

ROOM DESIGN CHECKLIST

DIVISION 10--SPECIALTIES (INTERIOR) continued

__ FOLDING PARTITIONS   NOTES

__ Folding Partition   10620   _____
__ Accordion Folding
        Partition   10623   _____

__ Folding Gate   10624   _____

Date/Who/Why: Changed (Date/Who/Why):

Coord check: ___structural ___interior elevations ___reflec ceiling ___finish schedule

__ STORAGE SHELVING   NOTES

__ Metal Storage Shelf   10671   _____

__ Wire Shelf   10673   _____

Date/Who/Why: Changed (Date/Who/Why):

Coord check: ___anchors ___interior elevations

__ TELEPHONE ENCLOSURES   NOTES

__ Telephone Booth   10751   _____

__ Telephone Shelf   10753   _____

Date/Who/Why: Changed (Date/Who/Why):
Coord check: ___electrical ___anchors ___interior elevations

                                                          NOTES

__ WARDROBE   10900   _____

Date/Who/Why: Changed (Date/Who/Why):

Coord check: ___interior elevations ___finish schedule

ROOM DESIGN CHECKLIST

DIVISION 11--EQUIPMENT (INTERIOR)

NOTES

__ **MAINTENANCE EQUIPMENT** 11010 _____

__ **SECURITY AND VAULT EQUIPMENT**

NOTES

__ Vault Door/Day Gates 11021 _____

__ Service/Teller Window Unit 11022 _____

__ Package Transfer Unit 11023 _____

__ Security/Emergency System 11024 _____

__ Automatic Teller 11025 _____

__ Depository Slot 11026 _____

__ Depository Box 11026 _____

__ Wall Safe 11028 _____

__ Floor Safe 11028 _____

Date/Who/Why: Changed (Date/Who/Why):

Coord check: ___electrical ___structural ___anchors ___interior elevations

NOTES

__ **CHECKROOM EQUIPMENT** 11030 _____

Date/Who/Why: Changed (Date/Who/Why):

Coord check: ___electrical ___interior elevations

NOTES

__ **LIBRARY EQUIPMENT** 11050 _____

Date/Who/Why: Changed (Date/Who/Why):

Coord check: ___electrical ___interior elevations

NOTES

__ **THEATER/STAGE EQUIPMENT** 11060 _____

Date/Who/Why: Changed (Date/Who/Why):

Coord check: ___code ___structural ___electrical ___interior elevations

ROOM DESIGN CHECKLIST

DIVISION 11--EQUIPMENT (INTERIOR) continued

NOTES

__ **MUSICAL
     EQUIPMENT** 11070 _____

Date/Who/Why: Changed (Date/Who/Why):

Coord check: ___electrical ___interior elevations

__ **MERCANTILE EQUIPMENT**   NOTES

__ Display Cases   11101 _____

Date/Who/Why: Changed (Date/Who/Why):

Coord check: ___anchors ___electrical ___interior elevations

                                        NOTES

__ **VENDING
     EQUIPMENT** 11120 _____

Date/Who/Why: Changed (Date/Who/Why):

Coord check: ___electrical ___plumbing ___interior elevations

__ **AUDIO-VISUAL EQUIPMENT**   NOTES

__ Projection Screen   11131 _____

__ Projector   11132 _____

__ Projector Booth   11133 _____

Date/Who/Why: Changed (Date/Who/Why):

Coord check: ___electrical ___interior elevations

__ **PARKING EQUIPMENT**   NOTES

__ Parking Gate   11151 _____

__ Ticket Dispenser   11152 _____
__ Key/Card Control
       Unit   11153 _____

__ Coin Machine Unit   11154 _____

Date/Who/Why: Changed (Date/Who/Why):

Coord check: ___electrical ___interior elevations

                                        NOTES

__ **LOADING DOCK
     EQUIPMENT** 11160 _____

Date/Who/Why: Changed (Date/Who/Why):

Coord check: ___electrical ___interior elevations

ROOM DESIGN CHECKLIST

DIVISION 11--EQUIPMENT (INTERIOR) continued

__ **WASTE HANDLING EQUIPMENT**   NOTES

__ Waste Compactor   11172   _____

__ Pulping System   11174   _____
__ Waste Collector/
      Chute   11175   _____

Date/Who/Why: Changed (Date/Who/Why):

Coord check: ___code ___structural ___electrical ___plumb

__ **FOOD SERVICE EQUIPMENT**   NOTES

__ Cooking Equipment   11410   _____

__ Washing Equipment   11411   _____

Date/Who/Why: Changed (Date/Who/Why):

Coord check: ___code ___electrical ___plumbing ___drains ___hvac/vent ___interior elevations

__ **RESIDENTIAL EQUIPMENT**   NOTES

__ Kitchen   11451   _____

__ Laundry   11452   _____

__ Disappearing Stairs   11454   _____

Date/Who/Why: Changed (Date/Who/Why):

Coord check: ___electrical ___plumbing ___drains ___vent ___interior elevations

                                                   NOTES
__ **UNIT KITCHEN/
      CABS**   11460   _____

Date/Who/Why: Changed (Date/Who/Why):

Coord check: ___electrical ___plumbing ___drains ___vent ___interior elevations

__ **DARKROOM EQUIPMENT**   NOTES

__ Revolving Door   11471   _____

__ Transfer Cabinet   11472   _____

__ Processing Equipment   11474   _____

Date/Who/Why: Changed (Date/Who/Why):

Coord check: ___electrical ___plumbing ___drains ___interior elevations

ROOM DESIGN CHECKLIST

DIVISION 11--EQUIPMENT (INTERIOR) continued

__ **ATHLETIC, RECREATIONAL/THERAPEUTIC
    EQUIPMENT**   NOTES

__ Gymnasium Equipment 11486 _____

__ Therapy Equipment   11490 _____

Date/Who/Why: Changed (Date/Who/Why):

Coord check: ___electrical ___plumbing ___interior elevations

                                                   NOTES
__ **INDUSTRIAL AND PROCESS
    EQUIPMENT**   11500 _____

Date/Who/Why: Changed (Date/Who/Why):

Coord check: ___structural ___electrical   ___plumbing ___hvac ___interior elevations

                                                   NOTES
__ **LABORATORY
    EQUIPMENT**   11600 _____

Date/Who/Why: Changed (Date/Who/Why):

Coord check: ___structural ___electrical   ___plumbing ___hvac/vent ___interior elevations

                                                   NOTES
__ **MEDICAL
    EQUIPMENT**   11700 _____

Date/Who/Why: Changed (Date/Who/Why):

Coord check: ___electrical   ___plumbing ___hvac/vent ___interior elevations

                                                   NOTES
__ **TELECOMMUNICATIONS
    EQUIPMENT**   11800 _____

Date/Who/Why: Changed (Date/Who/Why):

Coord check: ___electrical

ROOM DESIGN CHECKLIST

DIVISION 12--FURNISHINGS   (INTERIOR)

__ ARTWORK   NOTES

__Mural   12110   _____

__Sculpture   12140   _____

__Statuary   12140   _____

__Bas-Relief   12150   _____

__Stained Glass   12170   _____

Date/Who/Why: Changed (Date/Who/Why):

Coord check: ___electrical ___anchors ___interior elevations

__ MANUFACTURED CABINETS AND CASEWORK   NOTES

__ Metal Casework/
      Cabinets   12301   _____
__ Wood Casework/
      Cabinets   12302   _____

__ Built-in Table   12303   _____

__ Display Casework   12380   _____

Date/Who/Why: Changed (Date/Who/Why):

Coord check: ___anchors ___furnishings ___interior elevations ___finish schedule

__ WINDOW TREATMENT   NOTES

__ Drape/Blind Valance   12503   _____

__ Blinds   12510   _____

__ Vertical Louver Blinds 12511   _____
__ Horizontal Louver
      Blinds   12512   _____

__ Shades   12513   _____

__ Interior Shutters   12527   _____

Date/Who/Why: Changed (Date/Who/Why):

Coord check: ___anchors ___interior elevations ___finish schedule

ROOM DESIGN CHECKLIST

DIVISION 12--FURNISHINGS (INTERIOR) continued

__ **FURNITURE AND ACCESSORIES**   NOTES

__ Landscape Partition   12610   _____

__ Room Divider   12615   _____

Date/Who/Why: Changed (Date/Who/Why):

Coord check: ___electrical   ___interior elevations ___finish schedule

__ **RUGS AND MATS**   NOTES

__ Foot Grille   12672   _____
__ Recessed Frame for
        Floor Mat   12673   _____

__ Floor Mat   12675   _____

Date/Who/Why: Changed (Date/Who/Why):

Coord check: ___finish schedule

__ **MULTIPLE SEATING**   NOTES

__ Auditorium/Theater
        Seating   12710   _____
__ Multi-use Fixed
        Seating   12750   _____

Date/Who/Why: Changed (Date/Who/Why):

Coord check: ___code ___anchors ___interior elevations ___cross sections

                                                NOTES
__ **INTERIOR
    PLANTERS**   12815   _____

Date/Who/Why: Changed (Date/Who/Why):

Coord check: ___electrical   ___plumbing ___drains ___interior elevations ___furnishings

ROOM DESIGN CHECKLIST

DIVISION 13--SPECIAL CONSTRUCTION   (INTERIOR)

NOTES

__ **CLEAN ROOMS**   13040 _____

Date/Who/Why: Changed (Date/Who/Why):

Coord check: ___hvac ___electrical ___interior elevations ___finish schedule

NOTES

__ **INSULATED ROOMS**
__ Cold Storage   13061 _____

Date/Who/Why: Changed (Date/Who/Why):

Coord check: ___hvac ___electrical ___interior elevations ___finish schedule

NOTES

__ **INTEGRATED
     CEILING**   13070 _____

Date/Who/Why: Changed (Date/Who/Why):

Coord check: ___hvac ___electrical ___reflec ceiling ___cross sections ___finish schedule

__ **SOUND, VIBRATION AND SEISMIC CONTROL**   NOTES

__ Isolation Slab   13080 _____

Date/Who/Why: Changed (Date/Who/Why):

Coord check: ___structural ___hvac ___cross sections

NOTES

__ **RADIATION
     SHIELDING**   13090 _____

Date/Who/Why: Changed (Date/Who/Why):

Coord check: ___electrical ___cross sections ___reflec ceiling ___interior elevations

__ **SPECIAL PURPOSE ROOMS/BUILDINGS**   NOTES

__ Prefab Steam Bath   13131 _____

__ Prefab Sauna   13131 _____

Date/Who/Why: Changed (Date/Who/Why):

Coord check: ___electrical ___plumbing ___drains ___interior elevations ___finish schedule

NOTES

__ **VAULTS**   13140 _____

Date/Who/Why: Changed (Date/Who/Why):

Coord check: ___structural ___electrical ___hvac ___interior elevations ___cross sections

ROOM DESIGN CHECKLIST

DIVISION 12--FURNISHINGS   (INTERIOR)   continued

__ **POOLS**   NOTES

__ Swimming Pool   13151   _____

__ Aquaria   13152   _____

__ Jacuzzi   13153   _____

__ Hot Tub   13154   _____

Date/Who/Why: Changed (Date/Who/Why):

Coord check: ___plumbing ___electrical   ___cross sections ___finish schedule

ROOM DESIGN CHECKLIST

DIVISION 14--CONVEYING SYSTEMS   (INTERIOR)

NOTES

__ **DUMBWAITERS**   14100   _____

Date/Who/Why: Changed (Date/Who/Why):

Coord check: ___structural ___electrical   ___cross sections

NOTES

__ **ELEVATORS**

__Elevator   14210   _____

__Freight Elevator   14220   _____

Date/Who/Why: Changed (Date/Who/Why):

Coord check: ___structural ___electrical   ___mechanical ___cross sections ___interior elevations

NOTES

__ **HOISTS/CRANES**

__Hoist   14300   _____

__Crane   14300   _____

Date/Who/Why: Changed (Date/Who/Why):

Coord check: ___structural ___electrical   ___cross sections ___interior elevations

__ **LIFTS**   NOTES

__People Lift   14410   _____

__Wheelchair Lift   14415   _____

__Vehicle Lift   14450   _____

Date/Who/Why: Changed (Date/Who/Why):

Coord check: ___structural ___electrical   ___cross sections ___interior elevations

__ **MATERIAL HANDLING SYSTEMS**   NOTES

__Chute   14560   _____

__Laundry Chute   14560   _____

__Pneumatic Tube   14581   _____

Date/Who/Why: Changed (Date/Who/Why):

Data source(s):   Who finds data:

Coord check: ___structural ___electrical   ___cross sections ___interior elevations

299

ROOM DESIGN CHECKLIST

DIVISION 14--CONVEYING SYSTEMS (INTERIOR)

NOTES

__ **TURNTABLE**   14600   _____

Date/Who/Why: Changed (Date/Who/Why):

Coord check: ___structural ___electrical ___cross sections

__ **MOVING STAIRS/WALKS**   NOTES

__ Escalator   14710   _____

__ Moving Walk   14720   _____

Date/Who/Why: Changed (Date/Who/Why):

Coord check: ___structural ___electrical ___cross sections ___interior elevations

300

ROOM DESIGN CHECKLIST

DIVISION 15--MECHANICAL (INTERIOR)

__ PLUMBING FIXTURES

NOTES

__ Water Cooler	15455	_____
__ Wash Fountain	15456	_____
__ Shower	15457	_____
__ Tub Enclosure	15459	_____
__ Shower Enclosure	15459	_____
__ Drinking Fountain	15461	_____
__ Lavatory	15471	_____
__ Floor Sink	15475	_____
__ Janitor's Sink	15476	_____
__ Work Sink	15481	_____

Date/Who/Why: Changed (Date/Who/Why):

__ LIQUID HEAT SYSTEMS

NOTES

__ Radiant Panel	15745	_____
__ Baseboard Unit	15751	_____
__ Finned Tube	15752	_____
__ Convector	15733	_____
__ Radiator	15754	_____
__ Unit Heater	15760/ 16850	_____
__ Fan Coil Unit	15761	_____
__ Unit Ventilator	15762/ 16850	_____
__ Humidifier	15781	_____

Date/Who/Why: Changed (Date/Who/Why):

ROOM DESIGN CHECKLIST

DIVISION 16--ELECTRICAL   (INTERIOR)

__ **COMMUNICATIONS**   NOTES

__ Burglar Detector	16720	_____
__ Fire Detector	16721	_____
__ Fire Alarm	16721	_____
__ Smoke Detector	16725	_____
__ Burglar Alarm	16727	_____
__ Clock	16730	_____
__ Telephone Switching Closet	16740	_____
__ Telephone Panelboard	16740	_____
__ Telephone Wiring Chase	16740	_____
__ Speaker	16770	_____
__ Annunciator	16770	_____
__ Closed Circuit TV Monitor	16780	_____
__ Surveillance TV Camera	16780	_____

Date/Who/Why: Changed (Date/Who/Why):

__ **HEATING AND COOLING**   NOTES

__ Electric Heating Coils	16860	_____
__ Electric Baseboard	16865	_____
__ Packaged Room Air Conditioner	16870	_____
__ Radiant Heater	16880	_____
__ Electric Heater	16890	_____

Date/Who/Why: Changed (Date/Who/Why):

ROOM DESIGN CHECKLIST

DIVISION 16--ELECTRICAL   (INTERIOR)   continued

__ **LIGHTING**   NOTES

__ Fluorescent Fixture	16501	_____
__ Egg Crate Light		
Diffuser	16501/	_____
	09120	
__ Light Diffuser	16501/	_____
	09120	
__ Spotlight	16501	_____
__ Chandelier	16501	_____
__ Surface-Mounted		
Light Fixture	16510	_____
__ Recessed Light		
Fixture	16510	_____
__ Lighting Track	16510	_____
__ Luminous Ceiling	16515/	_____
	09120	

Date/Who/Why: Changed (Date/Who/Why):

__ **ELECTRICAL FIXTURES AND SYSTEMS**   NOTES

__ Electromagnetic		
Shielding	16650	_____
__ Ceiling-Hung Clock	16730	_____
__ Ceiling-Mounted		
TV Camera	16780	_____
__ Ceiling-Mounted		
TV Monitor	16780	_____

Date/Who/Why: Changed (Date/Who/Why):

303

INTRODUCTION

The pages that follow are outline technical specifications and specifications checklists pertaining to room design and construction.

These specifications name generic products, workmanship standards, materials checklists and construction preparation and clean-up instructions. Although written in an abbreviated checklist format, you'll find them to be comprehensive guides to completing your own in-house specifications in your future projects.

NOTE THAT CSI MASTERFORMAT NUMBERS AT THE START OF EACH SECTION ARE ACCORDING TO CONSTRUCTION SPECIFICATIONS INSTITUTE SI MP-2-1, 1978.

ROOM MATERIALS SPECIFICATIONS CHECKLIST

CONTENTS

ROOM MATERIALS SPECIFICATIONS CHECKLIST
DIVISION 3 -- CONCRETE

These are items to check in working drawings, specifications, and during construction to assure best use of interior construction materials and finishes.

03100   FORMWORK

__ Formwork free of defects that would affect appearance of finish concrete surfaces.

__ Place, align, fasten, and protect formwork strips:
    __ Chamfers   __ Nailers   __ Rustication strips

__ Install movement joints as detailed:
    __ Locations   __ Widths   __ Secure fillers   __ Free movement isn't blocked
    __ No reinforcement or fixed metal continue through joints

__ Install construction joints as detailed:
    __ Locations   __ Widths   __ Keys   __ Waterproofing

__ Construct form joints plumb and tight to prevent seepage.

__ Provide for:
    __ Depressed slab areas   __ Cutouts   __ Curbs   __ Inserts

__ Provide sleeves for piping, conduit, and ducts.

__ Construct forms that provide for and are removable for:
    __ Doors __ Windows __ Vents __ Access panel openings

__ Repair and recondition reused formwork so that strength, joint tightness, and surface quality match original.

__ Set floor components in coordination with finish floor elevations:
    __ Drains   __ Equipment anchors   __ Boxes   __ Cleanouts   __ Flanges   __ Pipe sleeves

__ Provide consistently aligned sleeves for plumbing and conduit at column forms on each floor.

__ Clean formwork immediately prior to pour:
    __ Clear of debris   __ Clear of organic matter   __ Clear of loose dirt
    __ Clear of mud and water

__ Treat formwork:
    __ Seal   __ Wet wood forms   __ Oil metal forms   __ Remove excess oil

__ Where finish concrete will be exposed, verify that form boards are free of stains from mortar droppings or other contamination.

__ Protect newly poured concrete surfaces from damage during and after stripping of forms.

__ Remove loose nails and other metals that might leave rust.

__ After form removal, promptly patch and repair concrete surfaces that will remain visible:
    __ Honeycombs __ Form marks __ Fins __ Holes __ All other surface defects

03200 REINFORCEMENT--MATERIALS CHECKLIST

__ Reinforcement:
    __ Bars: Deformed steel, ASTM A 615, Grade 60.
    __ Mesh: Welded steel wire fabric, ASTM A 185.
    __ Spacing __ Ties __ Laps __ Chairs/stirrups/supports

03200 REINFORCING--CONSTRUCTION

__ Install reinforcing:
    __ Secure against dislocation during pour __ 2" clear from sides or bottom of forms
    __ Free of loose rust __ Clean of dirt and grease

__ Where final surfaces will be exposed, use rust-free chairs and other rust-free formwork
    materials.

03300 CONCRETE --MATERIALS CHECKLIST

__ Concrete materials:
    __ Cement: Portland cement, ASTM C 150, Type 1.
    __ Aggregate: Normalweight aggregates, ASTM C 33.

__ Admixtures with less than 1% chloride ions:
    __ Water reducing type and superplasticizer for workability.
    __ Air-entraining type for concrete exposed to freezing temperatures.

__ Miscellaneous Materials:
    __ Vapor barrier at grade under, 6 mil polyethylene.
    __ Hardener, non-metallic, quartz-silica, interior/exterior type
    __ Grout, non-metallic, non-shrink type.
    __ Waterstops, dumbbell shaped, rubber or PVC.
    __ Non-slip finish, aluminum oxide grit.

__ Concrete Mixes:
    __ 3000 psi for slabs on metal deck
    __ 3000 psi for paving and paving base.

__ Concrete mix:
    __ Mix proportions __ Cement type __ Aggregate __ Admixtures
    __ Compressive strength

__ Formwork: APA rated B-B Plyform forms

03300 CONCRETE--PREPARATION

__ A preconstruction meeting will be held with all concerned parties, to review concrete work and coordination between trades during concrete work.

__ Install related work before concrete pour, and protect from damage:
    __ Anchors for fixtures and equipment __ Base plates __ Bolts
    __ Sleeves for bollards __ Utility boxes __ Drains __ Electrical conduit
    __ Pipe and plumbing

__ Make all necessary arrangements for continuous inspection of concrete during:
    __ Batching __ Mixing __ Conveying __ Placing __ Compacting
    __ Finishing __ Curing

03300 CAST-IN-PLACE CONCRETE

__ Verify concrete requirements before delivery and placement:
    __ Tests __ Mix design __ Ingredients __ Inspections

__ Provide site sample test materials:
    __ Cylinders __ Slump cone __ Measuring equipment

__ Concrete cylinders:
    __ Mix and fill __ Rodding __ Strike off and tap __ Curing under job conditions

__ Check test results at 3 or 7 days, and confirm at 28 days.

__ Prepare previously placed concrete for new work.

__ Ready-mix concrete:
    __ Allowable time of transport __ Mixing time
    __ Certified as tested and/or inspected at the plant __ Allow no unauthorized watering
    __ Allow no overwatering __ There must be no sign of mix segregation
    __ Slump must pass visual inspection

__ Job-mixed concrete:
    __ Keep cement in dry storage __ Sample sand and course aggregate for compliance
    __ Protect all materials from contamination

03300 JOINTS IN SLABS AND WALLS

__ Construction joints with keyways with reinforcement continued through joint.

__ Isolation joints between slabs and vertical elements such as columns and structural walls.

__ Control joints sawn or tooled joints or cast with removeable insert strips
    __ Depth equal to 1/4 slab thickness.
    __ Spacing as per engineer's specifications.

03350/03370 FINISHING AND CURING MATERIALS CHECKLIST

__ Concrete mixes as per design criteria and as required for specified:
   __ Abrasive blast finish with brasive grit in air blast.
   __ Bushhammer finish.
   __ Scrubbed finish with brush scraping and partial removal of concrete surface.

__ Curing compounds application as per manufacturer's instructions.
   __ Compatible with other finishes.

__ Sealants application as per manufacturer's instructions.
   __ Compatible with other adjacent materials and finishes.

__ Sealing application as per manufacturer's instructions.
   __ Compatible with other finishes.

__ Paint application as per manufacturer's instructions.
   __ Colors and textures as per samples.

03350/03370 CONCRETE FINISHING AND CURING--APPLICATION

__ Floating, troweling, and texture finishes:
   __ Do not trowel until bleed water is gone   __ Do not overtrowel
   __ Do not dust cement to expedite troweling start time

__ Provide slopes for required floor drains.

__ Match up finish work to adjacent or nearby surfaces at:
   __ Joints __ Edges __ Corners

__ Remove marks left by finishing tools.

__ Coordinate sawn joints so all are straight and continuous.

__ Keep joint lines uniform and free of damage.

__ Start curing procedures promptly after pour.

__ Use spray or moist curing methods as needed to control curing to meet climate conditions.

__ Apply waterproof paper or other covers with ample laps and seals, for protection during curing.

__ Use covers on top of special concrete finishes or colored work as necessary to prevent stains.

__ Protect fresh slab work from foot or traffic damage.

__ Wall finishes: As-cast and patched for concealed work; rubbed smooth, filled and cement paste coated for exposed work.

__ Slab finishes as per approved sample:

    __ Scratch finish -- surfaces to receive mortar setting beds or cementitious flooring.

    __ Trowel finish -- hard, smooth, uniform surface for exposed finished floors or slabs
        for resilient flooring, carpet, or other thin finish flooring applied directly to slab.

    __ Broom finish -- roughened surface after troweling with fine texture brooming
        across traffic direction at steps and ramps (usually for exterior work, not interior).

__ Non-slip aggregate:
    __ After trowel finishing, add and smoothly trowel 25 lbs per100 s.f. of damp non-slip
        aggregate into surface.

    __ Lightly rubbed to expose aggregate after curing (usually for for interior exposed
        concrete stairs and ramps).

__ Exposed aggregate:
    __ Chemical retarder or
        __ Tamp aggregate into wet concrete and expose by brushing with water.

__ Hardener finish: For exposed interior concrete floors.
    As per manufacturer's instructions

__ Concrete floor topping:
    __ Portland-cement based topping mix.
    __ Minimum compressive strength of 3,500 psi

03450 ARCHITECTURAL PRECAST CONCRETE

__ Concrete units for exposed architectural applications:
    __ Smooth-faced units.
    __ Exposed aggregate units with integral aggregate exposed.
    __ Special formed and textured units.

__ Applied at:
    __ Interior wall panels.
    __ Column covers.
    __ Sills.

__ Concrete Materials:
    __ Portland cement as per ASTM C150, Type I or II, non-staining, no efflorescence.
    __ Fine aggregate as per ASTM C33.
    __ Coarse aggregate for exposed aggregate to match project sample.
    __ Water potable, non-staining.
    __ Pigment non-fading, inorganic pigments for use in concrete.

__ Concrete mix:
    __ 5000 psi   __ Air entrained   __ Pigmented portland cement concrete
    __ Design mix to match color and texture of approved sample.

__ Joints:
    __ Mortar, ASTM C 270.
    __ Sealant.

__ Reinforcing:
    __ Bars: ASTM A615, grade 40, deformed.
    __ Welded wire: ASTM A185.
    __ Hot-dipped galvanized.

__ Accessories, stainless steel:
    __ Clip angles   __ Bolts   __ Anchors   __ Fasteners   __ Stainless steel.

__ Quality standard:
    __ PCI MNL 117, Architectural Precast Concrete.

ROOM SPECIFICATIONS CHECKLIST
DIVISION 4 -- MASONRY

04000 MASONRY--PRECONSTRUCTION PROJECT PREPARATION

__ Maintain and use all up-to-date construction documents onsite.

__ Maintain and use up-to-date trade standards.

__ A preconstruction meeting will be held at the site with all concerned parties, including varied subcontractors whose work will be coordinated with masonry and related interior wall work.

__ Confirm that there are no conflicts between masons' local customs, building codes, and construction document requirements.

__ Do not begin to install masonry without approval of design firm.

__ Use agreed schedule for installation and for field observation by a representative of the design firm, of masonry preparation, tests, sample panel or wall, and masonry installation.

04050 MASONRY--MATERIALS, TESTS, AND SAMPLES CHECKLIST

__ Match masonry units to approved samples for:
   __ Types __ Grades __ Sizes __ Shapes __ Colors __ Textures __ Curing

__ Clips, angles, straps, and other anchors and attachments:
   __ Materials __ Sizes and shapes __ Metal gauges __ Connectors
   __ Corrosion protection coatings

__ Certify mortar:
   __ Tests __ Types __ Colors __ Mix and ingredients

04050 MASONRY--TESTS AND SAMPLES

__ Store masonry materials to be installed off the ground, and protect from dirt, ground moisture, contaminants, and weather:
   __ Unit masonry __ Cement __ Lime __ Sand __ Aggregate __ Admixtures
   __ Reinforcing __ Connectors __ Expansion/contraction joint materials

__ Schedule tests and inspections prior to construction.

__ Provide mill test certifications from suppliers.

__ Certify mortar is as specified as regards:
   __ Tests __ Types __ Colors __ Mix and ingredients

04050 MASONRY--TESTS AND SAMPLES

__ Confirm positive results of laboratory tests:
    __ Unit masonry   __ Mortar mix ingredients   __ Grout ingredients   __ Reinforcing

__ Use several approved masonry samples to establish acceptable range of variation.

__ Match masonry units to approved samples for:
    __ Types   __ Grades   __ Sizes   __ Shapes   __ Colors   __ Textures   __ Curing

__ Reject defective masonry units:
    __ Cracks   __ Kiln marks   __ Size variation   __ Bends   __ Chips   __ Patches
    __ Spalling   __ Flaking   __ Lime nodules

__ Conduct mortar tests to match site and work conditions.

__ Protect water supply:
    __ From freezing   __ Maintain clean and free of contaminants

__ Clips, angles, straps, and other anchors and attachments:
    __ Materials   __ Sizes and shapes   __ Metal gauges   __ Connectors
    __ Corrosion protection coatings

__ Construct sample wall panel of full depth and adequate height to show compliance with
    construction documents:
    __ Coursing   __ Joint sizes   __ Bonding   __ Uniform layering __ Patterning
    __ Weep holes   __ Cleanouts   __ Ties   __ Reinforcing   __ Parging   __ Grouting

04050 MASONRY--PLANNING AND COORDINATION WITH OTHER WORK

__ Prepare a work layout to establish and assure correct:
    __ Coursing   __ Patterns   __ Elevation of base course   __ Opening sill and header heights

__ Level shelf angles, and provide with bond breaks as necessary, to allow differential movements
    between building frame and masonry wall.

__ Put in place, anchor, plumb, and level metal work that will be embedded in masonry:
    __ Angles   __ Bucks and frames   __ Lintels

__ Provide flashing and openings for materials and fixtures to be installed.

__ Install appurtenances such as piping and conduit, ductwork, and sleeves.
    __ Insulate appurtenancees protected from impact damage, abrasion, or chemical corrosion.

__ Install bond-break felts, flashing, or other movement separators as detailed.

04270 GLASS BLOCK MATERIALS CHECKLIST

__ Glass block masonry units:

    __ Hollow block, 8" square.

    __ Solid block, 4" square.

__ Mortar, Portland cement lime mortar, Type S.

__ Ties minimum at 24" o.c. in both directions

__ Provide expansion strips.

__ Galvanized steel double wire mesh reinforcing.

__ 20 gauge perforated galvanized steel strip anchors.

04400 CUT STONE MATERIALS CHECKLIST

    __ Limestone:
        __ Select grade.
        __ Textured finish.

    __ Granite:
        __ Architectural Grade granite, ASTM C 615.
        __ Textured and polished finishes.

    __ Marble:
        __ Domestic marble, ASTM C 503
        __ Polished finish 1.

    __ Slate:
        __ Uniform color, even grain, ASTM C 629.

    __ Mortar:
        __ ASTM C 270; Portland cement-lime mortar, ASTM C 150.
        __ Color for pointing mortar as selected by design firm.

__ Anchors and fasteners, stainless steel, AISI alloy 302/304.

04400 CONSTRUCTION

__ Dress joints straight and at exact degree angles

__ Provide miter corners and 3/8" joints or as indicated.

__ Provide mortar joints, color as approved.

__ Install interior veneer with stainless steel strap anchors and dowels at structural supports.

__ Install stone paving in mortar setting bed over concrete slab.

__ Provide mortar joints, color as approved.

__ Install finished cut stone work plumb, aligned and level at tolerance of plus or minus 1/8" in 20'.

ROOM SPECIFICATIONS CHECKLIST -- MASONRY continued
GROUTING, ACCESSORIES AND REINFORCING

04100 GROUTING, PARGING, AND WATERPROOFING

__ Complete required regulatory agency inspection of masonry before grouting.

__ Complete grout mix testing and certification before grouting.
__ Use accurate job grout mixing measuring units.
    __ Measure by shovel load is not allowed.

__ Install inserts, anchor bolts, straps, dowels and bars as per detail drawings.

04150 MASONRY ACCESSORIES AND REINFORCING--MATERIALS CHECKLIST

__ Reinforcing:
    __ Ties and reinforcing, hot-dipped galvanized, ASTM A 153.
    __ Horizontal reinforcing, welded truss type, 9 gauge wire, deformed side rods.
    __ Reinforcing bars, deformed, ASTM A 615, Grade 60.

04150 MASONRY ACCESSORIES AND REINFORCING--CONSTRUCTION

__ Install metal ties for bonding as per details and referenced trade standards:
    __ Types __ Sizes __ Horizontal spacing __ Vertical spacing __ Staggering pattern
    __ Depth of anchoring __ Corrosion resistance

__ Install reinforcing as per details and referenced trade standards:
    __ Types __ Grades __ Sizes __ Spacing __ Clearances between bars
    __ Clearances from surfaces __ Coursing __ Laps and splicing
    __ Laps staggered in bond beams __ Door and window jamb hooks
    __ Lintel reinforcing for poured headers __ Pier and column ties
    __ Ties at top and bottom of vertical bars __ Bracing

__ Provide extra reinforcement at corners of openings and intersections.

__ Do not deform reinforcing bars to force fit.

04100/04200 MASONRY UNIT CONSTRUCTION AND MORTAR APPLICATION

__ Use wall thickness-to-height ratios as detailed.

__ Follow lateral structural support requirements as detailed.

__ Use mortar mix components according to trade standards, laboratory or site testing, and as detailed:
__ Cement __ Sand __ Cleanliness __ Fineness __ Moisture __ Aggregate
__ Lime __ Plasticizing agents __ Admixtures

__ Construct mortar joint sizes as detailed.

__ Provide full head and bed joints.

__ Properly butter masonry unit edges.

__ Completely fill all joints--bed, cross, end, and head.

__ Do not tool joints prematurely before initial mortar set.

__ Promptly point holes, such as for line nails, as work proceeds.

__ Remove wedges as work progresses.

__ Repair defective units as work progresses.

__ Align and plumb vertical joint lines in alternate courses.

__ Keep caulking spaces at window and door frames uniform and of detailed size.

__ Keep spaces for expansion/contraction control jointsuniform and of detailed size.

__ Recess window and door lintels from face of wall.

__ Keep wythes and other wall spaces even and of correct size.

__ Clean out masonry refuse that accumulates within the building at each work shift.

__ Protect tops of uncompleted wall sections at end of each full work shift.

__ Late-day work shall match quality of early-day work.

__ Carefully lay parapets and fire walls, and completely bed joints.

__ Tightly mortar fire wall flashing into walls.

__ Don't allow any mortar to enter expansion/contraction joints.

04200   MASONRY UNITS--MATERIALS CHECKLIST

__ Brick:
    __ Standard modular.
    __ 2-1/4" by 3-3/4" by 7-5/8"
    __ ASTM C 216.

__ Concrete block:
    __ Normalweight.
    __ 7-5/8" by 15-5/8" face size.
    __ ASTM C 145 and C 90 Type1, Grade N.

__ Facing block:
    High-density, low-absorption concrete block.

__ Mortar:
    __ ASTM C 270, portland cement-lime mortar, Type N.
    __ Other mortar as required for special applications.
    __ Inorganic oxide mortar pigments.

04200   CONSTRUCTION--MASONRY UNITS

__ Install masonry as detailed and as per approved samples:
    __ Base course   __ Coursing   __ Joint sizes   __ Bonding   __ Uniform layering
    __ Patterning   __ Weep holes   __ Cleanouts

__ Saturate bricks prior to bricklaying.

__ Determine that broken brick samples show the required moisture penetration:
    __ Core and perimeter are wet   __ Surface is dry   __ Brick isn't oversaturated

__ Observe installation temperature limits.

__ Provide heat to warm materials as necessary prior to installation, as necessary to prevent freezing.

__ Protect concrete masonry units from moisture, and keep them dry during installation.

ROOM SPECIFICATIONS CHECKLIST -- METALS
HANDRAILS AND RAILINGS

05521 - HANDRAILS AND RAILINGS

__ Provide handrails and railings:
      __ Aluminum pipe.
      __ Stainless steel pipe.
      __ Bronze pipe.
      __ Engineered ornamental aluminum rails.
      __ Engineered glass supported rails.

05521 MATERIALS AND FINISHES CHECKLIST

__ Aluminum:
      __ Mechanical finish.
      __ Clear anodized finish, Class 1.
      __ Color anodized finish, Class 1.
      __ Fluorocarbon coating, 2-coat.

__ Stainless Steel,18-8 Type 302/304:
      __ AISI No. 4, bright directional polish.
      __ AISI No. 6, satin directional polish.
      __ AISI No. 8, mirror-like reflective finish.

__ Bronze, ASTM B455 architectural bronze:
      __ Satin mechanical finish.
      __ Smooth specular.
      __ Statuary finish.

__ Glass:
      __ Tempered safety glass
      __ 1/2" thick for glass supported rails
      __ 3/8" thick for non-structural panels.

__ Fasteners and anchors, stainless steel or other non-corrosive concealed connectors.

05520 CONSTRUCTION

__ Confirm actual field measurements prior to fabrication.

__ Form to required shapes and sizes with true, straight edges, lines and angles.

__ All metal miters and joints to be solid for intended purpose and light-tight.

__ Install materials and systems in coordination with adjacent construction.

__ Provide all necessary backing plates, blocking, and concealed structural supports for rails.

__ All work in true alignment and uniform in appearance.

__ Repair damaged work and protect it from further damage.

ROOM SPECIFICATIONS CHECKLIST -- METALS
SHEET METAL FABRICATIONS

05580 SHEET METAL MATERIALS CHECKLIST

__ Sheet metal fabrications for:
    __ Cabinets __ Closures __ Trim __ Sills __ Panels __ HVAC unit enclosures

__ Aluminum: 0.125" with color anodized finish.

__ Stainless steel, 16 gauge:
    __ AISI No. 6 satin directional polish.

__ Carbon steel, 16 gauge:
    __ Thermoset acrylic enamel primer and topcoat.

__ Hardware:
    __ Hinges __ Handles and pulls __ Locking devices

CONSTRUCTION

__ Confirm actual field measurements prior to fabrication.

__ Form to required shapes and sizes with true, straight edges, lines and angles.

__ All metal miters and joints to be solid for intended purpose and light-tight.

__ Install materials and systems in coordination with adjacent construction.

__ Provide all necessary backing plates, blocking, and concealed anchors and supports.

__ All work plumb, level, and uniform in appearance.

__ Repair damaged work and protect it from further damage.

ROOM SPECIFICATIONS CHECKLIST
DIVISION 6 -- WOOD

06000 WOOD FRAMING--PRECONSTRUCTION PREPARATION

__ Cross-coordinate all related disciplines with framing:
  __ Plumbing __ HVAC __ Electrical
  __ Complete rough plumbing before starting framing.

__ Identify all required rough opening sizes in framing:
  __ Doors __ Windows __ Access panel openings __ Other framed openings

__ A preconstruction meeting will be held with all concerned parties, to review framing and coordination between trades during frame construction.

06050 FASTENERS, CONNECTORS, AND SUPPORTS--MATERIALS CHECKLIST

__ Nailing as per NFPA Recommended Nailing Schedule or local building code.

__ Metal connectors:
  __ Types __ Sizes __ Materials __ Gauges __ Corrosion protection
  __ Matching connectors

__ Metal crossbridging:
  __ Materials __ Sizes __ Gauges __ Corrosion protection __ Connection design

__ Joist hangers:
  __ Types __ Materials __ Sizes __ Gauges __ Spacings __ Set straight
  __ Aligned __ Completely secured at all connection points
  __ Secured with correct size and type fastenings

06050 FASTENERS, CONNECTORS, AND SUPPORTS--CONSTRUCTION

__ Install joist hangers as per details and manufacturer's instructions:
  __ Spacings __ Set straight __ Aligned
  __ Completely secured at all connection points
  __ Secured with correct size and type fastenings

__ Install bridging as per details and manufacturer's instructions:
  __ Placed so as to provide full bearing
  __ Set at joist midpoints or otherwise correctly spaced
  __ Bottoms are not nailed until the roof sheathing is laid
  __ Secured with correct size and type fastenings

__ Provide anchors, brackets, frames, hangers, and other supports, to support ceiling-hung or supported:
  __ Piping __ Plumbing __ Conduit __ Light fixtures
  __ Miscellaneous electrical fixtures __ Ducts __ Miscellaneous HVAC equipment
  __ Kitchen or shop equipment __ Suspended shelving __ Suspended storage units

321

06100   WOOD FRAMING MATERIALS CHECKLIST

__ Lumber, finished 4 sides, 19% maximum moisture content:
    __ Light framing, Construction grade Douglas Fir or Southern Pine
    __ Structural framing and timbers, No. 1 grade Douglas fir or southern pine
    __ Boards, Construction grade.

__ Framing as per NFPA National Design Specifications for Wood Construction

__ Wood for nailers, blocking, furring and sleepers:
    __ Construction grade.
    __ Finished 4 sides.
    __ 19% maximum moisture content.
    __ Pressure preservative treatment for wood in contact with flashing, masonry, concrete.

__ Provide blocking for all mounted items, including:
    __ Casework   __ Shelving   __ Handrails and railings   __ Bath accessories
    __ Window blind drape supports

__ Plywood, APA rated:
    __ Subfloor/underlayment: APA Sturd-I-Floor, Exposure 1.
    __ Subflooring, APA sheathing.
    __ Wall sheathing, APA sheathing, C-D plugged, Exterior.
    __ Backing panels, APA C-D plugged interior
        __ Exterior glue
        __ Fire-retardant
        __ 3/4" thick
    __ Underlayment.

__ Plywood as per APA Design and Construction Guide

__ Building paper, asphalt saturated felt, ASTM D 226, Type 1.

__ Preservative:
    __ Pressure-treated with waterborne preservatives as per AWPB LP-2 for above-
        grade wood
    __ Kiln dry after treatment to 19% maximum moisture content for lumber, 15%
        for plywood.
    __ Treat above-ground wood exposed to moisture such as framing at shower and tub rooms,
        commercial kitchens, etc.

__ Fire-retardant:
    __ Pressure-treated, as per AWPA C20 for lumber and AWPA C27 for plywood.
    __ No ammonium phosphates.

06100 WOOD FRAMING--MATERIALS HANDLING AND STORAGE

__ Reject framing lumber that is not grade-stamped.

__ Verify that delivered lumber is certified by a bona fide grading agency.

__ Do not accept delivery or attempt to use lumber that deviates from grade standards or is defective and inappropriate to its intended use, such as wood with:
   __ High moisture content __ Loose knots __ Decay streaks __ Rot __ Insect damage
   __ Splits __ Pitch pockets __ Wanes __ Crooks __ Warps __ Twists __ Bends

__ Test and certify moisture content.

__ Reject special, required lumber that is not marked and certified:
   __ Preservative-treated __ Fire-resistant __ Kiln-dried

__ Provide all tests, certificates, and affidavits necessary to verify quality of materials.

__ Do not accept delivery, or attempt to use plywood that deviates from grade standards or is defective and inappropriate to its intended use, such as plywood with:
   __ Marred surfaces __ Cracks __ Defective patches __ Loose knots __ Split edges
   __ Delaminations

__ Handle lumber with care to avoid damage during:
   __ Transport __ Unloading __ Moving __ Stacking

__ Store framing lumber and plywood to prevent damage and moisture absorption:
   __ Off the ground __ Protected from weather __ Protected from all sources of water
   __ Neatly stacked to prevent warping __ Stacked with cross pieces for ventilation
   __ Secure from leaning or toppling

__ Store chemically treated lumber and plywood outside until installation.

__ Keep chemically treated lumber and plywood well ventilated if it has to be stored indoors.

06100   INTERIOR WOOD FRAMING--PREPARATION

__ Verify that materials are stored so as to not overload existing construction in terms of:
__ Quantities and weights   __ Locations   __ Machine traffic:
__ Fork lift   __ Crane   __ Trucks   __ Buggies   __ Other machines

__ Provide completely secure temporary bracing:
__ Nailing and stop plates at floors and slabs   __ Double-sided prop bracing at walls
__ Diagonal horizontal cross bracing at plates of intersecting walls
__ Braced walls won't move, waver, or shake when force is applied to them

06100   WOOD FRAMING--INTERIOR WALLS

__ Install stud framing as per framing sections, details, and building code requirements:
__ Material species and grades   __ Sizes   __ Spacings   __ Plumb   __ Square
__ Aligned   __ Substantially braced   __ Secured with correct size and type fastenings

__ Install fire stops so as to provide complete, snug blocking between studs.

__ Special framing:
__ Double walls at chases   __ Separate plates and framing at party walls
__ Separate plates and staggered studs at soundproof walls
__ Secure with correct size and type fastenings

__ Position studs at corners to provide ample nailing backing for interior and exterior panels.

__ Provide blocking and double top plate headers for wall openings.

__ Lap top plates and set butt joints so they don't occur over openings.

__ Install top plates so as to provide uninterrupted and ample nailing backing for interior and exterior panels.

__ Install headers and lintels as per details and building code requirements:
__ Materials   __ Wood grades   __ Metal gauges   __ Header widths and depths
__ Ample bearing   __ Secure connection to supports

__ Install furring as per details and design firm instructions:
__ Materials   __ Sizes of furring strips   __ Spacing of furring strips or members
__ Alignment   __ Connectors to support surface   __ Connectors to finish surface

__ Prepare stud framing for soundproofing as detailed.

__ Prepare stud framing for waterproof finishes as detailed.

__ Construct stud framing and blocking to allow for installation of wall-mounted fixtures and equipment.

06100   WOOD FRAMING--CEILING

__ Install ceiling and roof framing members as per framing plans, details, and building code
      requirements:
      __ Framing lumber grades   __ Sizes   __ Spacings   __ Bracing
      __ Minimal notching or drilling

__ Install ceiling soffits and furring as per drawings and design firm instructions:
      __ Materials   __ Sizes of soffit or furring supports
      __ Spacing of soffit or furring supports   __ Alignment
      __ Connectors to support surface   __ Connectors to finish surface

__ Prepare framing for soundproofing as detailed.

06100   WOOD FRAMING--COORDINATION WITH OTHER TRADES

__ Provide joints and connectors for non-wood construction to allow for movement such as:
      __ Lumber shrinkage   __ Concrete shrinkage   __ Masonry expansion and contraction
      __ Overall building thermal expansion and contraction

__ Provide clearances between framing and other construction that may be subject to:
      __ Differential movement   __ Noise transfer   __ Fire hazard such as:
      __ Chimneys and flues   __ Thru-building expansion joints   __ Elevator cores
      __ Other types of construction:
      __ Steel   __ Concrete   __ Masonry

__ Coordinate electrical stub-ups with the framing plan.

__ Align floor-mounted electric outlet boxes with finish wall lines.

__ Coordinate girders, floor joists, and stud walls with plumbing:
      __ Supply lines   __ Floor drains   __ Thru-building roof drains

__ Coordinate girders and floor joists with HVAC ducts and vents.

__ Do not allow HVAC ducts in wall framing to protrude beyond face of framing.

__ Recess floor joists to allow for:
      __ Underlayment   __ Tile flooring   __ Poured topping   __ Recessed matts
      __ Recessed grilles   __ Changes in floor surfaces

__ Prepare framing for soundproofing as detailed.

__ Prepare framing for waterproof finishes as detailed.

__ Supply and coordinate in-wall fixture and equipment supports:
      __ Anchors __ Brackets __ Grounds __ Chairs __ Frames

WOOD FRAMING--COORDINATION WITH OTHER TRADES continued

__ Provide as needed, in-wall blocking, anchors, brackets, grounds, chairs, frames, and other supports for wall-supported:
__ Plumbing fixtures __ Electrical fixtures __ HVAC equipment
__ Kitchen or shop equipment __ Bathroom accessories __ Handrails
__ Guards/protective rails __ Shelves __ Storage units __ Fire hose cabinets

__ Do not allow other trades to impair framing strength by cutting or drilling through members.

__ Do not change framing members without written consent of the designer.

__ Install plaster grounds as detailed and as per trade association standards:
__ Types __ Materials __ Attachments __ Level __ Plumb
__ Allowance for specified plaster thickness

__ Set and prepare framing as required for tile or other waterproof wall finishes.

__ Provide waterproofing sealing as detailed.

__ Combine water barriers with framing as detailed:
__ Materials __ Thicknesses/weights/gauges __ Laps __ Undamaged
__ Fastenings: __ Types __ Spacing

__ Combine vapor barriers with framing as detailed:
__ Materials __ Thicknesses/weight __ Laps __ Fastenings:
__ Types __ Spacing

__ Combine flashing with framing as detailed:
__ Materials __ Gauges __ Laps __ Connections __ Positive drainage to exterior

__ Combine thermal insulation with framing as detailed:
__ Materials __ Thicknesses __ Laps __ Fastenings:
__ Types __ Spacing

__ Combine soundproofing with framing as detailed:
__ Sound barrier materials __ Sound insulation gaskets __ Sound insulation clips
__ Separated framing members

__ Roof framing for concentrated roof loads:
__ Closer joist spacing __ Double or triple joists __ Girder supports __ Blocking

__ Provide curbs, anchors, brackets, pitch pockets, and other supports, to support roof-mounted:
__ Platforms __ Piping __ Plumbing vents __ Light fixtures __ Roof vents
__ Miscellaneous HVAC equipment __ Room enclosures __ Railings
__ Communications equipment __ Guy wires

__ Provide fire protection during construction.

__ Provide fireproofing before closing in.

06113 SUBFLOOR SHEATHING

__ Install plywood subflooring as per framing drawings and building code requirements:
  __ Grades __ Dimensions __ Staggered pattern __ Nailing pattern __ Blocking:
  __ Provide 100% support at all edges
  __ Blocking support as required at intermediate spans

__ Stagger subflooring butt joints.

__ Install subflooring panels so that edges have full bearing on framing members.

__ Glue or secure subflooring to floor joists with screw-type nails, to prevent squeaking.

__ Prepare framing for soundproofing as detailed.

__ Prepare framing for waterproof finishes as detailed.

__ Prepare framing for floor-mounted fixtures and equipment as detailed.

__ Verify that completed subflooring is:
  __ Level __ Free of depressions or humps __ Patched as required to repair:
  __ Holes __ Splits __ Construction damage

06113 SHEATHING AND FINISH UP WORK

__ Stagger wall sheathing butt joints.

__ Install wall sheathing panels so that edges have full bearing on framing.

__ Install plywood shear wall construction as per framing drawings and as required by building code:
  __ Thicknesses of plywood __ Nail types and sizes __ Nailing pattern

__ Install siding so that joints:
  __ Are square __ Are staggered in alternate pieces if so designed
  __ Include expansion joint space between panels

__ Prepare finsh plywood wall surfaces for paint or stain according to manufacturer's instructions:
  __ Preservatives __ Patching __ Sanding __ Cleaning __ Priming

06200   FINISH CARPENTRY AND MILLWORK--MATERIALS CHECKLIST

__ Woodwork standards as per Architectural Woodwork Institute Quality Standards
    __ Premium grade unless noted otherwise.

__ Interior finish woodwork:
    __ Wood for transparent finish:
        __ Plain sawn red oak or comparable.
        __ Sequence matched veneers for plywood.
    __ Wood for opaque finish, softwood if not subject to abrasion and wear.
    __ Millwork for transparent finish:
        __ Plain sawn red oak for solid wood or comparable.
        __ Rift cut for plywood.
    __ Millwork for opaque finish, closed-grain hardwood as suited to application and wear.
    __ Prefinished hardwood paneling, 1/2" thick red oak or comparable.
    __ Softwood panel board with clip mounting, 1/2" thick redwood or comparable.
    __ Plastic laminate:
        __ NEMA LD-3, 0.050" thick horizontal grade
        __ For counters, glue to 3/4" plywood substrate.
    __ Synthetic countertops: Corian or comparable product.

__ Service and closet shelving, medium density particleboard with hardwood edge bands.

__ Millwork finishes:
    __ Wood for transparent finish:
        __ AWI Premium grade
        __ AWI finish system No. 5, premium polyurethane.
    __ Wood for opaque finish
        __ AWI Custom grade
        __ AWI finish system No. 11, premium opaque polyurethane.
    __ Plastic laminate finish, AWI Premium grade.

__ Millwork hardware:
    __ Steel and/or brass pulls and handles with chromium plate finish.
    __ Inside-mounted hinges, self-closing.
    __ Ball-bearing side-mount drawer slides.

__ Wood Treatment:
    __ Preservative, waterborne pressure-treated.
    __ Kiln dry after treatment:
        __ 19% maximum moisture content for lumber
        __ 15% for plywood.
        __ Treat all interior wood exposed to prolonged moisture such as in bath rooms and
            kitchens.
    __ Fire-retardant treatment:
        __ Pressure impregnated, as per AWPA C20 for lumber and AWPA C27 for plywood.
        __ No ammonium phosphates.
        __ Vehicle for preservative must be compatible with finish material

FINISH CARPENTRY AND MILLWORK--MATERIALS CHECKLIST continued

__ Provide materials as per detail drawings, applicable trade standards, or approved samples:
    __ Types   __ Grades   __ Shapes   __ Sizes   __ Finishes   __ Preservatives
    __ Quality of surfaces   __ Moisture content   __ Grade stamp requirement
    __ Matching appearance of grain and pattern

__ Provide wood free of significant defects or deviations from grade standards:
    __ Moisture content   __ Loose knots   __ Splits   __ Pitch pockets   __ Wanes
    __ Crooks   __ Warps   __ Twists   __ Bends   __ Raised grain   __ Defective finish

__ Plywood and finish wood panels:
    __ Sizes   __ Types   __ Thicknesses   __ Grades (plywood is grade stamped)
    __ Waterproofing   __ Preservatives   __ Surface finishes
    __ Size and number of patches

__ Fastenings and hardware:
    __ Types   __ Materials   __ Sizes   __ Stainless fastenings at exterior work
    __ Concealed types where required

__ Millwork materials:
    __ Preservative treatment   __ All-heart lumber

__ Finish nails and nailing:
    __ Types of nails and nail heads   __ Nailing pattern   __ Setting   __ Puttying

06200 FINISH CARPENTRY AND MILLWORK--PREPARATION

__ Reject any wood not certified as to grade.

__ Test and certify moisture content.

__ Obtain all tests, certificates, and affidavits as required to verify quality of materials.

__ Do not have finish materials delivered until after the building is closed in.

__ Verify that special wood is marked and certified:
    __ Preservative-treated   __ Fire-resistant   __ Kiln-dried

__ Do not install finish panels with defects or deviations from grade standards:
    __ Marred surfaces   __ Cracks   __ Defective patches   __ Loose knots   __ Split edges
    __ Delaminations

06200 FINISHED CARPENTRY AND MILLWORK--STORAGE AND HANDLING

__ Handle wood with care to avoid damage during:
   __ Transport   __ Unloading   __ Moving   __ Stacking

__ Store wood as required to prevent damage and moisture absorption:
   __ Off the floor   __ Protected from weather   __ Protected from all sources of water
   __ Neatly stacked to prevent warping   __ Stacked with crosspieces for ventilation
   __ Secure from leaning or toppling   __ In clean enviroment free of construction dust

__ Properly ventilate wood treated with preservatives; store away from work areas.

__ Store special kiln-dry materials as required to assure compliance with temperature and
   humidity restrictions.

__ Add preservative treatment or backpriming to wood that will be exposed to potential rot
   conditions.

06200 FINISHED CARPENTRY AND MILLWORK--CONSTRUCTION

__ Coordinate with finish carpentry, furnishings, fixtures, and equipment to be installed by
   others:
   __ Coordinate scheduling of deliveries and installation
   __ Coordinate backing materials and blocking
   __ Protect finish work from damage by other trades

__ Prepare sub-surfaces to receive finish materials.

__ Keep working environment:
   __ Clean, free of airborne construction dirt and dust
   __ Dry as required to maintain proper wood moisture content
   __ At comfortable working temperature

__ All work per details and applicable trade standards:
   __ Make saw cuts straight and clean   __ Make tight fits, without gaps
   __ Make splices tight and staggered (never side by side)

__ Align and exactly match miter joints at edges and corners.

__ Install running trim in maximum lengths; do not use short pieces or splicing of scraps.

__ Wood joints:
   __ Keep number of joints to a minimum by consistently using maximum size material
   __ Install tight joints without gaps

__ Finish work:
   __ Thoroughly sand smooth __ Smooth edges

FINISHED CARPENTRY AND MILLWORK--CONSTRUCTION continued

___ Reject work as nonconforming due to:
    ___ Substandard material   ___ Hammer or other tool marks   ___ Dents   ___ Nailing splits
    ___ Unmatched grains or patterns   ___ Uneven or over-sanding

___ Support shelves and closet poles so they will not sag when loaded.

___ Securely attach wood handrails to meet load tests.

___ Set finish nails before painting or staining.

___ Re-sand any unfinished or unsmooth surfaces.

___ Make repairs so they are undetectable.

___ Thoroughly clean and finish surfaces.

___ Protect finish work from construction damage.

07200 THERMAL INSULATION--MATERIALS CHECKLIST

__ Blanket or batt glass fiber blanket insulation:
    __ Unfaced   __ Paper-faced (vapor barrier)   __ Foil-faced (vapor barrier)

__ Extruded polystyrene board.

__ Loose granular perlite or vermiculite fill insulation.

__ Vapor barrier: 6 mil clear polyethylene.

07200 CONSTRUCTION

__ Provide full thickness of insulation:
    __ At exterior walls.
    __ Under floors at crawl spaces.
    __ At attics and roof slabs.
    __ At rooms with different temperature and humidity requirements from other rooms.

__ Tightly packed and fit at all penetrations.

__ Pour loose fill insulation into cavities with care for uniform density and thickness.

__ Apply vapor barrier over inside face of exterior walls and elsewhere as required.

__ Seal all seams and edges of vapor barrier with approved tape to form an uninterrupted barrier.

__ Coordinate with work of all other trades.

__ Repair damaged areas.

__ Protect finished work from damage by others.

07250 FIREPROOFING--MATERIALS CHECKLIST

__ Mineral fiber fireproofing.

__ Cementitious fireproofing.

__ Portland cement type fireproofing (high-density or medium density type as required by code).

__ Intumescent mastic fireproofing.

07250 CONSTRUCTION

__ Provide spray fireproofing at structural steel and metal deck as required by code.

__ Coordinate work with other trades to prevent damage.

__ Allow for adequate testing and inspection before work is covered over.

__ Examine, repair, clean, and prepare substrates as per fireproofing manufacturer's instructions.

__ Reinforce fireproofing at potential points of stress and movement.

__ Provide ample material thickness -- more than code requirements where possible.

__ Use independent testing agency to verify work.

__ Repair damaged areas.

__ Protect finished fireproofing from damage by other trades.

07600 FLASHING MATERIALS

__ Verify that materials are as per details and samples:
   __ Material types __ Gauges or weights __ Coatings or primers __ Shapes
   __ Materials free of damage or corrosion
   __ Fastenings are of specified materials, types, and sizes

__ Recommended flashing materials standards are:
   __ Stainless steel - 28 gauge AISI Type 302/304, ASTM A 167.
   __ Steel - 20 gauge galvanized steel, G90 galvanizing, ASTM A 525.
   __ Copper - 16 oz./sq.ft. cold-rolled copper, ASTM B 370.
   __ Aluminum Sheet - 20 gauge alloy 3003 clear anodized aluminum, ASTM B 209.
   __ Lead-coated copper - 16 oz./sq.ft. cold-rolled copper, ASTM B 370, 0.06 psf lead
        coating both sides.
   __ Laminated copper/fabric flashing for masonry flashing -- 5 oz. copper sheet laminated
        between 2 sheets bituminous saturated fabric.

07600 CONSTRUCTION

__ Follow manufacturers's instructions.

__ Follow standards of the SMACNA SHEET METAL MANUAL.

__ Coordinate with other trades.

__ Keep dissimilar metals separated to avoid corrosion.

__ Fastenings will be noncorrosive.

__ Lap and lock seams.

__ Allow for thermal movement of flashing materials and adjacent materials.

__ Solder seam joints where necessary, to guarantee watertightness.

__ Create flashing widths and laps as detailed.

__ Caulk and paint exposed flashing as required.

__ Use plastic cement or other adhesive to cover edge laps.

__ Install flashing inserts into walls adequate in depth; secure well, and caulk.

ROOM SPECIFICATIONS CHECKLIST
THERMAL & MOISTURE PROTECTION -- JOINT SEALANTS

07900 JOINT SEALERS--MATERIALS CHECKLIST

__ Seal all joints subject to expansion, contraction, or other movement:
    __ Ceramic tile, toilet fixture joints -- silicone rubber.
    __ Interior glazing joints, joints at mirrors -- acrylic latex.
    __ Exterior joints on vertical surfaces -- polyurethane (non-sag).
    __ Horizontal paving joints -- polyurethane (self-leveling).
    __ Precompressed expanding sealant tape.
    __ Pavement joint filler: Resilient, premolded asphalt impregnated fiberboard.

    __ Primers, bond breakers, and backing material:
        __ As directed and approved by sealant manufacturers.
        __ Safe and compatible with adjacent surfaces.

07900 CONSTRUCTION

__ Provide complete sealing of joints in or between materials subject to penetration by air or water.

__ Coordinate with work of other trades.

__ Use sealants of colors suited to adjacent materials as directed by designer.

__ Examine, repair, clean, and prepare substrates as per sealant manufacturer's instructions.

__ Install materials as per manufacturer's instructions and approved samples.

__ Depth of joints:
    __ Equal to the width up to 1/2" wide
    __ Equal 1/2 width for joints over1/2" wide.

__ Cure and protect sealants as per manufacturer's instructions.

__ Replace or restore damaged sealants.

__ Clean adjacent surfaces to remove spillage.

__ Repair damaged areas.

__ Protect finished work from damage by others.

07810 SKYLIGHTS--MATERIALS CHECKLIST

__ Prefab plastic skylight units:
  __ Plastic:
    __ Double-layer, factory-sealed insulating units with cast acrylic or cast polycarbonate rated for skylight loads and weather exposure.
    __ Clear inner layer.   __ Gray tint outer layer.

  __ Frame and trim:
    __ Extruded aluminum with insulating curb
      __ Self-flashing.   __ Integral condensation control.   __ Baked enamel finish.

__ Metal framed skylights:
  __ Engineered glass and metal frame units rated for skylight loads and weather exposure.
  __ Extruded aluminum with gaskets and accessories.

  __ Glazing:
    __ Single-glazed.
    __ Insulated glass.
    __ Plastic glazing.

  __ Glazing application:
    __ Cap glazing.
    __ Two-sided structural silicone glazing.
    __ Four-sided structural silicone glazing.

  __ Finishes:
    __ Clear or color anodized aluminum, Class 1.
    __ Polyester baked enamel coating.
    __ Fluoropolymer coating, 2 coat or 3 coat.

07810 SKYLIGHTS--CONSTRUCTION

__ Provide proven detailing and application instructions to assure watertight fit.

__ Coordinate with roofers to assure watertight flashing and sealant application.

__ Provide and install all flashings and counterflashings needed for weathertight construction.

__ Don't allow contact between dissimilar metals.

__ Don't allow contact between metal and treated wood.

__ Repair or replace damaged components and finishes.

__ Keep work clean after installation and protect from damage.

ROOM SPECIFICATIONS CHECKLIST
DIVISION 8 -- DOORS AND WINDOWS -- STEEL DOORS

08100/08200 STEEL DOORS AND FRAMES --MATERIALS CHECKLIST

__ Steel Doors and Frames:

     __ Doors, 1-3/4" thick, flush:
         __ Interior doors, SDI-100 grade II, heavy duty.
            __ Model 3 or 4 seamless.
            __18 gauge ASTM A 366 or A 568 cold-rolled steel.
         __ Exterior doors, SDI-100 grade III, extra heavy-duty.
            __ Model 3 or 4 seamless.
            __ 16 gauge ASTM A 526 steel.
            __ ASTM A 525 G60 galvanizing.
            __ Insulated

     __ Frames, cold-rolled sheet steel:
         __ Interior frames, 16 gauge up to 5' wide.
         __ Interior frames, 14 gauge over 5' wide.
         __ Exterior frames, 14 gauge ASTM A 526 steel.
         __ ASTM A 525 G60 galvanizing.
         __ Frame - fully welded, mitered corners or:
            __ Knock-down type, mitered corners.
         __ Asphalt emulsion sound deadening coating on concealed frame interiors.

     __ Louvers, 24 gauge cold rolled steel in 20 gauge frame.

     __ Finish, rust-inhibiting primer.

     __ Fire rating, UL labeled, fire-rated assembly as required by code.

     __ Thermal doors with maximum U-value of 0.24 btu/hr/sq.ft./degree F (ASTM C236) for exterior doors and elsewhere as required.

     __ Acoustically insulated doors with minimum STC 33 (ASTM E90 and ASTM E413) as required.

08100/08200 CONSTRUCTION

__ Install doors and frames in compliance with SDI-100, NFPA 80, and requirements of code

__ Grout frames during construction.

__ Caulk frames for complete seal.

__ Hardware:
         __ Prepare doors and frames to receive hardware on final schedule.
         __ Three silencers on single door frames
         __ Two silencers on double door frames.

__ Repair damaged coating as required to receive finish painting.

08100/08200 WOOD DOORS --MATERIALS CHECKLIST

__ Wood Doors:
    __ Solid core flush:
        __ AWI PC-5 or PC-7 particleboard core.
        __ AWI premium grade.
        __ Transparent finish, rift cut red oak veneer or comparable, book matched.
        __ Painted finish, birch veneer or comparable.
        __ Painted finish, MDO over hardwood veneer.

    __ Hollow core flush wood door:
        __ Closed-grain hardwood face for paint finish.
        __ AWI SHC or IHC, custom grade.

    __ Laminate finish doors:
        __ Solid core flush door with particleboard core (interior use)
        __ AWI premium grade
        __ Plastic laminate face, 0.050" thick, NEMA LD-3.

    __ Fire rating - UL labeled, fire-rated assembly
        __ As required by code
        __ As per NFPA 80 for rated assembly.

    __ Prefit to frames.

    __ Prefit for hardware.

__ Wood construction and finish for wood doors:
    __ Grade __ Species __ Veneer cut/match __ Edge banded __ Factory bevel

__ Reject doors and accessories that are not as specified:
    __ Fire ratings __ Types __ Gauges __ Sizes __ Straightness
    __ Factory-applied components __ Joints __ Hardware locations __ Prebracing
    __ Anchors __ Reinforcement at heads and corners __ Sound-deadening
    __ Silencers __ Finishes __ Glazing __ Provisions for finish hardware

__ Provide door glazing with:
    __ Stops as required __ Safety glass labeled:
    __ Tempered __ Safety
    __ Glass as per door schedule:
    __ Types __ Patterns __ Thicknesses

__ Factory-applied hardware:
    __ Hinge types __ Closure channels __ Reinforcing and backing plates
    __ Lock blocks, other blocks required for hardware
    __ Stile edges and astragals for paired doors

08100/08200 DOORS--DELIVERY AND STORAGE

__ Store delivered doors:
    __ Consistently vertical or flat __ Supported off floor
    __ Protected from weather and moisture __ Protected from construction damage

__ Provide doors that are straight, free of defects and marred surfaces, and that have:
    __ Smooth edges __ Clean joints __ Consistent, blemish-free finishes
    __ Correct finish material thicknesses

__ Provide fire-rated doors that include:
    __ Correct identification labels and/or certification __ Wire glass lights
    __ Fusible links for louvers __ Correct factory-applied hardware
    __ Automatic closure hardware

__ Provide fire-rated doors that follow all requirements to maintain fire rating:
    __ Openings/glass are as required __ Hinges are as required
    __ Undercut does not exceed the allowable code maximum.

__ Verify that factory preparation and prefitting follow required hardware templates

08100/08200 DOORS--CONSTRUCTION

__ Door installation as per NWMA I.S.-1 and AWI quality standards.

__ Provide jambs for doors:
    __ Plumb __ Square __ Block for hinges and other hardware
    __ Securely anchor to rough bucks

__ Hang doors:
    __ Straight __ Level __ Plumb __ Smooth in opening __ Smooth and secure in closing
    __ Maximum of 1/8" clearance at top and sides
    __ Maximum of 1/4" clearance at bottom

__ Provide clearances below doors as necessary to allow for:
    __ Thresholds __ Weatherstripping __ Gasketing __ Carpet

__ Do not allow door swings to conflict with:
    __ Electrical switches or outlets __ Wall guards or rails

__ Do not cut fire-rated doors so as to negate fire rating.

__ After installation:
    __ Seal or reseal doors whenever they are cut.
    __ Seal doors at tops and bottoms after installation.
    __ Repair and retouch any damaged factory coat.
    __ Make undetectable repairs before applying final finish.
    __ Apply first coats of paint or sealer at both sides of doors during the same operation.
    __ Seal, stain, or paint exterior doors before or immediately after installing them.
    __ Thoroughly clean installed doors as per instructions of manufacturer.

08200   WOOD SLIDING GLASS DOORS--MATERIALS CHECKLIST

__ Preservative-treated teak or mahogany.
    __ Solid stock at commercial applications.

__ Preservative treated fine-grained lumber.
__ Finishes:
    __ Factory primed, white.
    __ Oiled finish.

__ Glass and auxilary materials:
    __ Tempered insulating safety glass.
    __ Compression weatherstripping.
    __ Plastic-coated glass fiber screen fabric.

08370   ALUMINUM SLIDING GLASS DOORS--MATERIALS CHECKLIST

__ Extruded aluminum:
    __ As per AAMA 402.9 SGD-BD for residential applications.
    __ As per SGD-BA for commercial applications .

    __ Finish:
        __ Color anodized, Class 1.
        __ Baked acrylic or polyester enamel.
        __ Fluoropolymer, 2-coat.

__ Glass and auxilary materials:
    __ Tempered insulating glass.
    __ Thermal break.
    __ Insect screen.

WOOD AND ALUMINUM SLIDING DOORS--CONSTRUCTION

__ Install assemblies complete with all required:
    __ Hardware   __ Anchors and supports   __ Inserts   __ Accessories

__ Install all work plumb, level, and with uniform appearance throughout.

__ Coordinate with work of other trades.

__ Repair damaged areas.

__ Clean and protect finished work from damage by others.

08350 FOLDING DOORS--MATERIALS CHECKLIST

__ Accordian-fold doors and grilles:
    __ Top-supported, manually-operated units without floor track or guide.
    __ Acoustical construction af required for STC rating.
    __ Wood folding doors and partitions, prefinished oak veneer.
    __ Wood folding doors and partitions, 4 mil vinyl fabric.
    __ Fabric folding doors and partitions: Vinyl coated cotton or glass fabric.

__ Bi-fold closet doors.
    __ Panels hinged together in pairs
    __ Suspended from overhead tracks with guide slots at bottom
    __ Mirrored doors - steel panels with applied mirror
    __ Wood doors - flush hollow wood panels with prefinished oak veneer face.

08350 CONSTRUCTION

__ Install assemblies complete with all required:
    __ Hardware   __ Anchors and supports   __ Inserts   __ Accessories

__ Install all work plumb, level, and with uniform appearance throughout.

__ Coordinate with work of other trades.

__ Repair damaged areas.

__ Clean and protect finished work from damage by others.

08410 ALUMINUM ENTRANCES AND STOREFRONT--MATERIALS CHECKLIST

__ Stile-and-rail door:
      __ 1-3/4" thick.
      __ Medium stile (3" width) with secured and reinforced joints.
      __ Compression and sliding weatherstripping.

__ Framing System fabricated from:
      __ Aluminum extrusions, ASTM B 221
      __ Sheet, ASTM B 209
      __ With thermal break

__ Finishes:
      __ Color anodized, Class 1.
      __ Fluoropolymer finish, 2-coat.

__ Glazing:
      __ Single-glazing - tempered glass.
      __ Insulating-glass - tempered insulating glass units.

__ Hardware:
      __ Center pivots __ Overhead-concealed closers __ Stops __ Threshold
      __ Deadlocks and keyed cylinders __ Push/pull bars or panic hardware and pull bar

CONSTRUCTION

__ Anchor securely in place:
      __ Plumb, level and in true alignment.
      __ Weathertight.

__ Isolate dissimilar materials to prevent corrosion.

__ Coordinate with other glass and glazing work.

__ Install glass to avoid direct metal-to-glass contact.

__ Adjust operating hardware for smooth, proper operation.

__ Repair damaged areas.

__ Clean and protect finished work from damage.

08450 ALL-GLASS ENTRANCES--MATERIALS CHECKLIST

__ Metals:

    __ Stainless Steel - Sheet and roll formed members AISI Type 302/304 alloy.
    __ Architectural Bronze; sheet alloy C28000, Muntz metal; castings ASTM B 584.
    __ Bronze - extrusions ASTM B455, alloy C38500
    __ Aluminum - extrusions ASTM B221, alloy 6063-T5.

__ All-glass doors:

    __ 1/2" thick tempered safety glass with metal top and bottom rails and fittings; penciled at exposed edges; butting edges flat-ground with arrised corners.

__ Exposed metal components:

    __ Heads and shoes.
    __ Rails and patch fittings from extrusions or clad aluminum extrusions;

__ Metal Finishes:

    __ Bronze:
    __ Stainless Steel:
    __ Aluminum:

__ Butt glazing with clear silicone structural sealant.

__ Hardware:

    __ Pivoted doors:

        __ Center pivots   __ Overhead-concealed closers   __ Stops   __ Threshold
        __ Deadlocks and keyed cylinders   __ Push/pull bars or panic hardware and pull bar

    __ Balanced doors:

        __ Top and bottom ball bearing pivots with cast bronze pivot arms.
        __ Full height adjustable spring closing hinge concealed in casing.
        __ Concealed hydraulic checking device.
        __ As per pivoted doors.

08450 GLASS ENTRANCES--CONSTRUCTION

__ Anchor securely in place:

    __ Plumb, level and in true alignment.

    __ Weathertight.

__ Isolate dissimilar materials to prevent corrosion.

__ Coordinate with other glass and glazing work.

__ Install glass to avoid direct metal-to-glass contact.

__ Adjust operating hardware for smooth, proper operation.

__ Repair damaged areas.

__ Clean and protect finished work from damage.

08450 ALL-GLASS ENTRANCES--MATERIALS CHECKLIST

__ Metals:
    __ Stainless Steel - Sheet and roll formed members AISI Type 302/304 alloy.
    __ Architectural Bronze; sheet alloy C28000, Muntz metal; castings ASTM B 584.
    __ Bronze - extrusions ASTM B455, alloy C38500
    __ Aluminum - extrusions ASTM B221, alloy 6063-T5.

__ All-glass doors:
    __ 1/2" thick tempered safety glass with metal top and bottom rails and fittings; penciled at exposed edges; butting edges flat-ground with arrised corners.

__ Exposed metal components:
    __ Heads and shoes.
    __ Rails and patch fittings from extrusions or clad aluminum extrusions;

__ Metal Finishes:
    __ Bronze:
    __ Stainless Steel:
    __ Aluminum:

__ Butt glazing with clear silicone structural sealant.

__ Hardware:
    __ Pivoted doors:
        __ Center pivots __ Overhead-concealed closers __ Stops __ Threshold
        __ Deadlocks and keyed cylinders __ Push/pull bars or panic hardware and pull bar

    __ Balanced doors:
        __ Top and bottom ball bearing pivots with cast bronze pivot arms.
        __ Full height adjustable spring closing hinge concealed in casing.
        __ Concealed hydraulic checking device.
        __ As per pivoted doors.

08425 AUTOMATIC ENTRANCE DOORS

__ Doors, frames for sidelights and transoms, controls and accessories:
    __ One-way swing   __ Single sliding   __ Bi-parting sliding

    __ Aluminum extrusions, ASTM B 221
    __ Aluminum sheets, ASTM B 209
    __ Color anodized aluminum finish, Class 1

__ Operation: Pneumatic or electro-mechanical operation; self-contained.

__ Sensors at both sides of doors to prevent door swinging into people or objects:
    __ Overhead motion detecting control for sliding doors.
    __ Switch mat detection control for swinging doors.

08470 REVOLVING DOORS

__ 4-leaf revolving doors:
    __ Weatherstripped   __ Concealed steel supports   __ Speed control
    __ Panic-collapsing mechanism

__ Metals:
    __ Bronze   __ Aluminum   __ Stainless Steel

__ Clear tempered glass at wings.

__ Enclosure walls:
    __ Laminated glass.
    __ Metal sheet as per stiles and rails.

__ Ceiling:
    __ Tempered glass.
    __ Metal; same as stiles and rails.

__ Coordinate with work of other trades.

__ Repair damaged areas.

__ Clean and protect finished work from damage by others.

08100 DOORS--METAL BUCKS

__ Provide and verify that materials are as per samples and drawings.
    __ Sizes __ Shapes __ Gauges __ Welding __ Reinforcement
    __ Shop fabrication details __ Finish __ Free from defects

__ Install bucks:
    __ Plumb __ Square __ Securely anchored
    __ Touched up where shop coat is damaged
    __ Protected from damage from other construction

08710 DOOR CLOSERS--MATERIALS

__ Low frequency doors: LCN 4030/4130 series or approved equal.

__ High frequency doors (fire-labeled doors, toilet room doors, tenant entry doors, stair doors):
    LCN 4010/4110 series or approved equal.

__ Door closers match samples:
    __ Types __ Sizes __ Materials __ Finishes __ Accessories
    __ As required for fire-rated doors

08710 DOOR CLOSERS--CONSTRUCTION

__ Install per manufacturer's instructions, with special attachments as required for:
    __ Wood doors __ Metal doors

__ Install closer fasteners straight, true, and undamaged.

__ After adjustment, verify that door closers operate:
    __ Smoothly at correct speed __ Without noise __ Firmly to close and latch doors

__ Verify that door arms of closers are straight out when doors are closed.

08710 LOCKSETS, LATCHES, AND KEYS--MATERIALS CHECKLIST

__ Locksets and latchsets:
    __ Standard duty (residential) - Comparable to Schlage A Series or comparable.
    __ Heavy duty (commercial and institutional) - Comparable to Schlage D Series.
    __ Heavy duty mortise type (commercial) - Comparable to Schlage L 9000 Series.

__ Lock cylinders and keying:
    __ Interchangeable-core pin tumbler lock cylinders.
    __ Nickle silver keys.

__ Provide all master keying.

08710   LOCKSETS, LATCHES, AND KEYS--CONSTRUCTION

__ Install locksets as per manufacturer's instructions:
    __ Jig bore or predrilling.
    __ Mortise for strike allows latchbolt to project fully.
    __ Install cylinder cores with tumblers set upward.
    __ Backsets:
        __ Straight   __ Clear stops

__ Carefully guard master keys during construction.

__ Remove construction locks, and install permanent locks.

__ Match up locks and tagged keys after installing all units.

__ Verify that all keys and locks operate smoothly without effort.

__ Deliver keys and instructions to owner:
    __ With permanent tags   __ Checked with door locks   __ Indexed   __ With key cabinet

08715   PANIC BARS AND FLUSH BOLTS--MATERIALS

__ Exit devices as required and approved by the fire code and the NFPA.

__ Exit hardware components:
    __ Types __ Sizes __ Materials __ Finishes __ Accessories
    __ As required for fire-rated doors   __ Match samples

08715   PANIC BARS AND FLUSH BOLTS--CONSTRUCTION

__ Install exit hardware as per manufacturer's instructions:
    __ Exit cross bars:
        __ Are level __ Both arms securely attached
        __ Move simultaneously when pressed and released
    __ Top and bottom bolts:
        __ Seat properly   __ Are straight
        __ Stabilized as necessary as with mullion stabilizers
        __ Have correct depth of bolt throw in strike

ROOM SPECIFICATIONS CHECKLIST -- WINDOWS
GLASS & GLAZING PRODUCTS

08400-08900 WINDOWS MATERIALS AND PRODUCTS CHECKLIST

__ Glass schedule:
    __ Metal windows - 1" thick insulating frame, clear glass.
    __ Wood windows - 5/8" thick insulating frame, clear glass.
    __ Storefront - 1" thick clear insulating frame.
    __ Entrances - 5/8" thick clear insulating frame.
    __ Skylights - 1-1/16" thick insulating frame.
        __ Cear laminated interior pane.
        __ Tinted exterior pane

__ Glazing:
    __ Window glass, ASTM C1036:
        __ Clear and tinted float glass.
        __ Figured/pattern glass.
        __ Wire glass.

    __ Heat treated glass, ASTM C1048:
        __ Heat-strengthened glass.
        __ Tempered glass.

    __ Coated glass.
    __ Laminated glass.

    __ Plastic glazing:
        __ Acrylic.
        __ Polycarbonate.

__ Insulating sealed glass units:
    __ 2 panes with air space
    __ Double sealing system:
        __ Spacer   __ dessicant   __ Corner reinforcement

__ Glass thicknesses and heat strengthening as per manufacturer to resist wind load.

__ Glazing sealant, gaskets, accessories:
    __ Silicone glazing sealants.
        __ Weather seal   __ Structural sealant
        __ Acrylic glazing sealant (interior)

    __ Glazing gaskets:
        __ Lock-strip gaskets   __ Preformed gaskets.
        __ Preformed glazing tape.
        __ Setting blocks, shims, and spacers.

08400-08900 CONSTRUCTION

__ Install glazing as per FGMA "Glazing Manual" and manufacturer's instructions.

__ Apply sealants for complete bond.

__ Shape sealants to wash water away from glass.

__ Grout frames, sills, jambs, and heads completely full and solid.

__ Put in place and tightly secure frame braces and anchors.

__ Construct sash free of bends, warps, and dents.

__ Place windows into openings without forcing.

__ Provide barriers or clear separations between dissimilar metals.

__ Window dimensions and alignments are according to drawings:
    __ Heads and sills are at correct elevations   __ Heads and sills are level
    __ Jambs are at correct locations   __ Opening sizes are correct
    __ Jambs are plumb and aligned with other facade elements

__ Tolerances:
    __ Openings of 6 feet or less within plus or minus 1/16" tolerance in each direction.
    __ Openings larger than 6 feet within plus or minus 1/8" tolerance in each direction.
    __ Maintain diagonal dimensions of openings within 1/8" of each other.

__ Cleaning and protection:
    __ Protect aluminum frames and other materials from contact with mortar or other sources
        of chemical damage.
    __ Protect shop coat treatment from damage.
    __ Touch up damaged shop coats before final painting.
    __ Keep hardware clean.
    __ After installation, protect finishes from physical and chemical damage.
    __ Make repairs to damaged materials or finishes as directed by the design firm.
    __ Clean and protect metal and glass after installation.

08400-08900 WINDOW ADJUSTMENTS AND TESTING

__ Install windows to be weathertight and so as to allow no air infiltration.

__ Install ventilator hardware to operate easily and without sticking.

__ Use closures that are uniform and tight when units are closed and locked.

__ Install windows that open and close smoothly, without rattling or sticking.

09110 METAL STUD PARTITIONS--MATERIALS CHECKLIST

(This is often specified under the CSI designation: 05400 COLD-FORMED METAL FRAMING)

__ Metal studs, channels, and accessories:
     __ Loadbearing metal studs.
     __ C-shaped studs.
     __ Punched channel type studs.

     __ Steel - ASTM A 446, A 570, or A 611.
        __ 16 gauge and heavier - 40,000 psi yield strength.
        __ 18 gauge and lighter - 33,000 psi yield strength.
        __ Galvanized light weight framing components - ASTM A 525, G90.

     __ Miscellaneous accessories as provided by stud system manufacturer:
        __ Standard runners   __ Clip angles   __ Shoes __ Reinforcements   __ Fasteners
        __ Blocking   __ Lintels

09110 (05400) METAL STUD PARTITIONS--CONSTRUCTION

__ Coordinate work with other trades.

__ As per Metal Lath & Steel Framing Association LIGHTWEIGHT STEEL FRAMING SYSTEMS MANUAL
     and ASTM C1007 for installation of steel studs and accessories.

__ Install metal stud partitions per plans or details:
     __ Partition locations   __ Stud spacings   __ Make framing surfaces flush
     __ Align holes for attached materials   __ Install studs plumb to specified tolerance
     __ Align studs vertically and horizontally   __ Install double studs at jambs
     __ Install reinforced/heavy gauge studs at stress points
     __ Galvanize metal where subject to moisture or fumes
     __ Allow top plate space for slab deflection/movement
     __ Stagger with plate separations for soundproofing   __ Caulk for soundproofing

__ Partition and furring anchors as detailed and as required by manufacturer:
     __ Top plates to ceiling or slab   __ Floor plates

__ Provide backing and anchors for:
     __ Door frames   __ Opening frames   __ Wall-mounted fixtures
     __ Wall-mounted counters and cabinets   __ Shelves   __ Lockers   __ Recessed fixtures
     __ Attached equipment   __ Rails and grab bars   __ Toilet room partitions
     __ Chair rails   __ Acoustical separation for noisy fixtures and equipment

__ Repair, restore, or replace damaged components as required.

__ Protect work from damage.

09200   LATH AND PLASTER--MATERIALS CHECKLIST

__ Gypsum plaster, interior:
    __ 2 coat gypsum plaster with gauging plaster.
    __ Lime finish coat for painting.

__ Portland cement plaster:
    __ 3 coat white, ASTM C 926.
    __ Smooth troweled base.
    __ Prepared finish coat for sand float finish.

__ All materials:
    __ Unopened, labeled containers.
    __ Mix proportions as per manufacturer's instructions.
    __ Mixing tools & equipment as per manufacturer's instructions.

__ Metal lath and furring:
    __ Screw-attached self-furring diamond-mesh steel lath.
    __ Rust-inhibitive finish.

__ Metal lath and furring as detailed:
    __ Stagger butt joints at wall and ceiling junctures.
    __ Nest ribbed lath sections together at joints.
    __ Provide butt joints only where supported.
    __ Spacings of backing and frames to support finish materials

__ Install gypsum lath:
    __ Dry   __ Staggered joints; absolutely no continuous joints from panel to panel

__ Furring and lathing accessories:
    __ Studs as per 09110, previous page).
    __ Channels   __ Stiffeners   __ Base anchors   __ Top anchors   __ Fasteners   __ Hangers
    __ Clips   __ Galvanized steel corner beads   __ Grounds   __ Screeds   __ Control joints
    __ Expansion joints   __ Tie wires

__ Gypsum lath fastenings as per manufacturer's instructions.

__ Bonding agent for plaster patching must be compatible with substrate.

09200 PREPARATION AND CONSTRUCTION FOR PLASTERING

__ Grounds and screeds as detailed:
    __ Level   __ Align   __ Match to specified thickness of plaster
    __ Install in maximum lengths   __ Minimal, carefully done splices
    __ Install wood grounds where required
    __ Align top and bottom grounds vertically in same plane

__ Size grounds to match combined thickness of lath plus plaster.

__ Install diagonal lath reinforcing at stress points:
    __ Window openings   __ Door openings   __ Unframed openings

__ Provide relief joints at edges of small and large openings.

__ Tightly install and secure lath accessories:
    __ Trim __ Casings __ Corner beads __ Control joints __ Vent screeds
    __ Channels __ Runners __ Stiffeners __ Anchors __ Ties

__ Install separation joints where work adjoins other materials and finishes.

__ Provide metal corners or edge strips to protect all exposed edges, such as at plaster corners.

__ Install metal trims at perimeters and joints.

__ Set corner beads exactly, to assure equal plaster thickness at both sides.

__ Securely nail corner beads:
    __ With required type and size nails   __ Starting 2 inches from each end
    __ Spaced and staggered as required by applicable trade standard

__ Provide and securely anchor frames for:
    __ Access panels __ Large openings

__ Recheck frames and backing for wall-mounted equipment, fixtures, and specialties.

__ Complete and secure rough plumbing adjacent to plaster work.

__ Electrical outlets and switch boxes:
    __ Complete __ Position __ Anchor __ Not too far in or out relative to finish wall surface

__ Prepare concrete or masonry surfaces to be plastered:
    __ Wire brush __ Abrade __ Clean __ Moisten
    __ Add bonding materials or coatings.

__ Protection of other work:
    __ Protect adjacent wall surfaces.
    __ Protect adjacent work from plaster:
        __ Fixtures __ Vents __ Bucks __ Sash __ Trim __ Tile __ Woodwork
    __ Thoroughly cover flooring to prevent stains.
    __ Plug drains and open piping.

09200 PLASTERING APPLICATION

__ Provide and maintain work space adequate for good work:
    __ Closed in, not exposed to weather   __ Clean   __ Dry   __ Protected from moisture
    __ Well-ventilated   __ Well-lighted   __ Heated to required working temperature

__ Install portland cement plaster as per ASTM C 926, 3-coat plaster.

__ Install gypsum plaster as per ASTM C 842, 3-coat plaster.

__ All plastering as per ASTM, trade standards, and manufacturer's instructions:
    __ Form full keys at scratch coat.
    __ Follow all procedures to assure tight adhesion between coats at second and third coats.
    __ Tool in small V joints at edges of doors, windows, and other openings.
    __ Strictly observe required application sequence, setting time, and curing time.
    __ Do not over-sand the mix.
    __ Verify that smoothly troweled plaster looks even and true from side views.
    __ Keep textured plaster consistent across surface, and match it with sample.
    __ Keep colored plaster consistent across surface, and match it with sample.
    __ Recheck work for necessary repairs before beginning painting or other added work.

09215 VENEER PLASTER--MATERIALS AND APPLICATION

__ Veneer plaster over gypsum board:
    __ One coat veneer plaster - ASTM C 587.
    __ Two coat veneer plaster - ASTM C 587.

__ Gypsum board for veneer plaster:
    __ ASTM C 588, 5/8" thick regular gypsum board.
    __ Fire-resistance as required by code.
    __ Foil-backed as required.

__ Gypsum board for muli-layer applications:
    __ ASTM C 588, 5/8" thick regular gypsum base or ASTM C 442 backing board.
    __ Fire-resistance as required by code.
    __ Foil-backed as required.

__ Application as per ASTM C 754, ASTM C 843, ASTM C 844 and manufacturer's instructions.

__ Machine mix.

__ Troweling must be consistently smooth and dense.

__ Complete all finishes behind movable furnishings, fixtures, and equipment.

__ Clean spillage and protect plaster work from damage.

09200   PLASTERING--CLEANUP

__ Immediately wipe clean, plaster spills on adjacent materials.

__ Do not track materials to other floors.

__ Thoroughly clean.

__ Promptly remove all plastering debris from site:
   __ Do not permit long-term debris storage   __ Do not bury debris
   __ Do not store plastering debris at scrap piles

09200   PLASTERING--PATCHING AND REPAIR

__ Replace or repair nonconforming work before starting other room finishes.

__ Make final checks for damage at close of construction, prior to final patch and repair.

__ Complete repairs when and as required.

__ Make final patching and repair work indetectable.

09202   GYPSUM LATH

__ Install gypsum lath:
   __ Dry   __ Staggered joints; absolutely no continuous joints from panel to panel

09203   METAL LATH

__ Stagger butt joints at wall and ceiling junctures.

__ Nest ribbed lath sections together at joints.

__ Provide butt joints only where supported.

__ Use foil covered lath; face foil toward framing.

09250   GYPSUM WALLBOARD--MATERIALS CHECKLIST

__ Gypsum board:
    __ Interior - ASTM C 36, 5/8" thick regular.
    __ Water resistant in moisture exposure rooms.
    __ Fire resistant as required by code.
    __ Foil-backed as required.

__ Backer boards - glass mesh reinforced portland cement backer board.

__ 25 gauge screw-type steel studs, ASTM C 645 (heavier as required).

__ Fasteners:
    __ ASTM C 514 and ASTM C 646.
    __ Type S bugle head screws at interior, cadmium plated at humid areas or areas exposed to moisture.

__ Gypsum drywall shaft systems:
    __ Gypsum wallboard for exposed finish, ASTM C 36, Type X.
    __ Shaftwall board, ASTM C 442, Type X.
    __ Water resistant backing board, ASTM C 630, Type X.
    __ Shaftwall framing - C, H, or E studs, shape and gauge as required.
    __ Adhesive for multi-layer applications.

__ Ceiling and furring materials:
    __ Steel runners and galvanized hanger wire.
    __ Stainless steel hanger wire in areas exposed to moisture or high humidity.

__ Joint reinforcement:
    __ ASTM C 587 tape   __ Ready-mix vinyl compound.

__ Accessories:
    __ Galvanized steel corner beads   __ Casing beads   __ Control joints.

__ Acoustical insulation - unfaced mineral fiber batt to fit full stud spacing.

__ Acoustical sealant - concealed acoustical sealant.

__ Provide seals for sound and thermal insulation at:
    __ Floor plates   __ Top plates   __ Connection to adjacent walls/pilasters/columns
    __ All cutouts

09250 GYPSUM WALLBOARD--PRECONSTRUCTION

__ Put blocking and backups in place, and position them to support all edges of wallboard.

__ Verify that wood framing to receive wallboard is dry; not subject to shrinkage and nail popouts.

__ Keep wallboard materials dry and protected from moisture.

__ Store wallboard materials so they are protected from damage to surfaces and edges.

__ Do not overload floor construction with stored wallboard. (Estimate stored material weights, and compare allowable dead load.)

__ Interior work environment:
   __ Closed in, not exposed to weather __ Clean __ Dry __ Protected from moisture
   __ Well-ventilated   __ Well-lighted   __ Comfortable in temperature

__ Keep work of other trades clear of inside faces of wall panels:
   __ Conduit __ Piping __ Ducts

09250 GYPSUM WALLBOARD--CONSTRUCTION

__ Follow applicable trade standards--ASTM C 840 and GA 216 - RECOMMENDED SPECIFICATIONS FOR THE APPLICATION AND FINISHING OF GYPSUM BOARD--and manufacturers' instructions throughout:
   __ Hold wallboard 3/8 inch to 1/2 inch up from floor.
   __ Install wall panels horizontally unless otherwise required.
   __ Joints must occur over framing members.
   __ Stagger panel joints vertically.
   __ Stagger panel joints back-to-back if using double-layered panels.
   __ Keep long joints of ceiling joints straight and aligned.
   __ Stagger short joints of ceiling panels at halfway long dimensions of panels.
   __ Keep joints to a minimum.
   __ Align door jambs and vertical joints.
   __ Keep piecing and use of odd sizes to an absolute minimum.
   __ Remove damaged sheets as scrap.
   __ Use moisture-resistant wallboard in damp environments.
   __ Seal edges and cuts of wallboard in damp environments.
   __ Install metal corners or other protection where edges of work might be subject to damage.
   __ Securely nail corner beads:
      __ With required type and size nails __ Starting 2 inches from each end
      __ Space and stagger nailing as required by wallboard system manufacturer.
   __ Install trim and 3-coat joint treatment as per trade standards
   __ Joint treatment at all fasteners and edges between boards.
   __ Fill all surface defects.
   __ Sand between and after joint treatment coatings.
   __ Protect all affected surfaces and spaces from dust from sanding.
   __ Leave ready for finish painting or wall treatment.

__ Extend non fire-rated partitions at least 3" above ceilings.

09250 GYPSUM WALLBOARD--CONSTRUCTION continued

__ Provide blocking for grab bars, fixtures, accessories, etc.

__ Fill wall cavities with insulation as required.

__ Tolerances of workmanship:
    __ Maximum 1/16" difference in true plane at joints between adjacent boards after nailing.
    __ After finishing, joints shall be not be visible.
    __ Maximum deviation of 1/8" in 10' from true plane
    __ All finish work lumb, level and aligned with adjacent finishes.

__ Fire rated construction:
    __ Provide fire-rated systems as required by code and as per ASTM E 119.
    __ Extend fire-rated partitions to underside of decks above ceilings.

__ Nailing as per trade standards and manufacturer's instructions:
    __ Start nailing from centers of panels, and proceed outward to edges.
    __ Avoid paper damage in nailing.
    __ Where paper damage occurs, add another nail within about 2 inches.
    __ Do not position conduit and piping where it can be damaged by nailing.

__ Fire and acoustical sealants:
    __ Acoustical sealant:
        __ At both faces at top and bottom runner tracks
        __ At wall perimeters
        __ At openings
        __ At expansion and control joints.

    __ Thoroughly seal penetrations in fire-rated walls to match fire resistance of walls.
    __ Box in recesses in fire-rated walls to match wall fire resistance
    __ Cut openings for electrical outlets, switch boxes, pipe, etc., tightly to size, and seal completely.

__ Taping and spackling as per trade standards and manufacturer's instructions:
    __ Keep temperature above specified minimum (usually 55 degrees).
    __ Do not allow any bumps, bubbles, or dimples in taping and spackling.
    __ Allow 24 hours between spackling coats.
    __ Final spackle coat:
        __ Sand smoothly __ Feather outward from 12 inches to 16 inches, each side of joint
    __ Sand and spackle wallboard as required, as base for final specified texture or finish.
    __ Do not track gypsum and spackle dust to clean areas.

__ Cleaning and repair:
    __ Thoroughly clean work space and remove all debris from site.
    __ Make final check to determine that there are no unsealed penetrations in fire-rated walls.
    __ Recheck work for necessary repairs that may be required before beginning painting or other added work.
    __ Complete repairs so they are undetectable.

09300   CERAMIC TILE, WALLS AND FLOORS--MATERIALS CHECKLIST

__ Tiles:
    __ Unglazed porcelain ceramic mosaic tile:
        __ 2" by 2" by 1/4"
        __ Factory mounted, plain face.
        __ Square edges except cushion edge at corner.
        __ Floor tile with slip resistant finish.

    __ Glazed wall tile:
        __ 4-1/4" by 4-1/4" by 5/16"
        __ Factory mounted, plain with modified square edges.

    __ Quarry tile:
        __ 6" by 6" by 1/2"
        __ Unglazed slip-resistant square edged tile.

    __ Trim - coved base, edge pieces, etc. to match field tile.

__ Thresholds - Group A marble, ASTM C 503.

09300 CERAMIC TILE PREPARATION AND CONSTRUCTION

__ Preparation and installation as per Tile Council of America and ANSI STANDARD SPECIFICATIONS
    FOR INSTALLATION and as per manufacturer's instructions.

__ Setting:
    __ Floors:
        __ Mortar setting bed (over waterproof membrane in "wet" rooms).
        __ Thin set latex portland cement mortar (over waterproof membrane in "wet"
           rooms).
        __ Epoxy mortar.

    __ Walls:
        __ Thin set latex portland cement mortar.
        __ Mortar setting bed over metal lath.
        __ Organic adhesive.

__ Grout - colored latex portland cement grout.

__ Provide tile materials that match approved samples:
    __ Types __ Shapes __ Sizes __ Thicknesses __ Patterns __ Colors __ Glazing
    __ Undamaged __ Consistent in sizes and appearance __ Certified

__ Provide grout and sealant materials as per:
    __ Applicable trade standards/tile manufacturer's instructions
    __ New unopened containers __ Correct color additives

09300 CERAMIC TILE PREPARATION AND CONSTRUCTION continued

__ Provide non-corrosive lath:
    __ Zinc-coated   __ Lapped   __ Tied with zinc-coated wires

__ Install waterproofing and backing that will absolutely block water leakage:
    __ Primer   __ Felt   __ Waterproof membrane   __ Sealant
    __ Waterproof sheet metal work   __ Underlayment

__ Perfectly match tile pieces with other tile work:
    __ Trim   __ Tile accessories   __ Bases

__ Install all support framing, furring, and backing:
    __ Plumb   __ Square   __ Aligned
    __ Well secured so surfaces will not move or deflect

__ Prepare floors to receive tile so the finish floor will be either perfectly level, or slope properly to drains.

__ Put in place and properly position, work of related trades:
    __ Electrical outlet and switch boxes   __ Stub ups   __ Drains   __ Wall plumbing

__ Provide supports for fixtures and related construction:
    __ Wall blocking   __ Backing   __ Inserts   __ Anchors

__ Premark and doublecheck locations for accessories to be installed.

__ Set accessories in place before beginning tile work.

__ Install control joints and edge strips:
    __ Securely fastened   __ Sized and shaped exactly to fit finish tile work

__ Set layout start points to achieve tile patterning that is:
    __ Symmetrical and complete
    __ Planned for minimal and balanced tile cutting

__ Fit special border tiles squarely without cuts.

__ Install wall tiles before floor tiles.

__ Include trim, edge, and base shapes with materials that:
    __ Match other tiles in all regards   __ Are free of irregularities

__ Keep work surfaces and working environment:
    __ Clean   __ Dry   __ Well-lighted   __ Well-ventilated
    __ Free of airborne construction dust
    __ At comfortable working temperature, minimum 60 degrees

__ Prepare tile according to manufacturer's instructions:
    __ Presoak   __ Dry surfaces before application   __ Clean

09300 CERAMIC TILE PREPARATION AND CONSTRUCTION continued

__ Plan and install correct patterning:
    __ Symmetrical   __ Complete   __ Square to floor or wall

__ Apply tile surface smoothly and free of:
    __ Irregularities   __ Humps   __ Dips

__ Install tile joints:
    __ Straight   __ Level horizontally   __ Aligned and exact vertically
    __ Uniform in size   __ With extra care at difficult areas:
    __ Corners   __ Fixture locations   __ Around wall openings and recesses
    __ At penetrations such as floor drains   __ Door trim

__ Lay tile in grid pattern with alignment grids.

__ Layout to provide uniform joint widths and to minimize cutting

__ Provide sealant joints where recommended by TCA and approved by Architect.

__ Make tile cuts:
    __ Minimal   __ Uniform   __ Not smaller than half a tile

__ Complete grouted or thinset adhesion so no tiles can be pulled loose.

__ Do not allow tile at door thresholds to interfere with closure.

__ Do not use broken or cracked scrap tiles.

09300 CERAMIC TILE--REPAIR AND CLEANUP

__ Reject tiles and replace if:
    __ Chipped   __ Scratched   __ Crazed   __ Popped up   __ Loose

__ Repair or replace all defective and nonconforming work.

__ Make undetectable repairs.

__ Use cleaning solutions and materials per manufacturer's instructions.

__ Do not use acidic cleaners near finish metal or other vulnerable surfaces.

__ Remove excess corrosive cleaning solutions from site; do not empty into building drains.

09400   TERRAZZO--MATERIALS CHECKLIST

__ Cementitious terrazzo:
    __ Bonded cast-in-place terrazzo, 1-1/2" - 2" thick.
    __ Sand cushion cast-in-place terrazzo, 2-3/4" - 3" thick.
    __ Monolithic cast-in-place terrazzo, 1/2" thick.
    __ Precast terrazzo for stair treads, bases, etc.

__ Thinset terrazzo - modified cementitious or resinous matrix.

__ Accessories:
    __ Isolation membrane   __ Setting bed reinforcement   __ Curing compounds
    __ Brass or zinc divider strips   __ Control strips

09400   TERRAZZO--PREPARATION AND CONSTRUCTION

__ Preparation and construction as per National Terrazzo and Mosaic Association GUIDE
    SPECIFICATIONS, TERRAZZO DESIGN DATA, and TERRAZZO TECHNICAL DATA.

__ Terrazzo substrate per manufacturer's instructions or applicable trade standards:
    __ Prepare surface as required for terrazzo bonding   __ Clean
    __ Wet prior to application

__ Position joint materials of correct height:
    __ Beads   __ Temporary screeds   __ Expansion strips

__ Line up terrazzo joints with adjacent construction.

__ Apply materials and allow them to set and cure exactly as per manufacturer's instructions and
    standards of the National Terrazzo and Mosaic Association.

__ Cure exactly as per manufacturer's instructions or applicable trade standards.

__ Properly equip for grinding operation:
    __ Adequately staffed, well-trained work crew   __ Correct equipment
    __ Grinder dust control system

__ Finish terrazzo surface:
    __ Level, except as sloped to drain   __ Do not allow humps or depressions
    __ Do not allow irregularities   __ Keep smooth and true throughout

__ Provide nonslip surfaces where required for pedestrian safety.

__ After curing and grinding, verify that finish work is:
    __ Completely cleaned   __ Finish sealed   __ Protected from construction work

09530 ACOUSTICAL INSULATION

__ Acoustical insulation material as detailed:
    __ Types   __ Thicknesses   __ Backing materials   __ Stored dry

__ Completely fill all batt spaces.

__ Repack any cutouts made through insulation.

__ Tightly attach edges to surfaces.

09120/09500 SUSPENDED CEILING SYSTEMS--MATERIALS CHECKLIST

__ Acoustical panels, exposed suspension: 3/4" thick, molded, medium fissured mineral tile:
    __ Panel size, 24" by 48"
    __ Panel size, 24" by 24"
    __ Panel edge, square edge; flush mount with grid.
    __ Panel edge, reveal edge; panel partly below grid.

__ Acoustical panels, exposed suspension, 5/8" thick, felted, medium fissured mineral tile.
    __ Panel size 24" by 48"
    __ Panel edge, square edge; flush mount with grid.

__ Acoustical tiles, concealed, 12" by 12" by 3/4" thick medium natural fissured mineral tile.

__ Match new materials with existing acoustical ceilings and suspension as required.

__ Exposed grid suspension system:
    __ T-grid   __ Reveal grid   __ Painted steel

__ Exposed grid system for kitchens and wet areas:
    __ T-grid   __ Painted aluminum

__ Concealed grid system:
    __ Concealed spline   __ Medium weight steel

__ Ceiling acoustical tiles and boards fire resistant and rated as required by fire code.

__ Special attachments:
    __ Extra intermediate hanger wire   __ Sway bracing   __ Turnbuckles   __ Isolators
    __ Hold-down clips on fire-rated ceilings

__ Provide hanger ties--three twists per tie--close to each anchor.

__ Provide undamaged, uninterrupted, and tightly sealed through-ceiling fire barriers.

__ Install through-ceiling sound walls undamaged and tightly sealed.

__ Acoustical treatment above ceiling as required for extra acoustical control:
    __ Material   __ Thickness   __ Application

09120/09500 SUSPENDED CEILING SYSTEMS--PREPARATION AND CONSTRUCTION

__ Install suspension systems as per manufacturer's instructions and ASTM C636.

__ Coordinate installation with mechanical and electrical trades.

09120/09500 SUSPENDED CEILING SYSTEMS--CONSTRUCTION

__ Follow ceiling grid space pattern as per reflected ceiling plans.

__ Measure and lay out work to avoid less than half panel units in grid.

__ Firmly attach hangers with special anchors as required for support by:
    __ Concrete   __ Metal deck or frame   __ Wood frame

__ Install and adjust ceiling to be level and aligned within 1/8" in 10' in both directions.

__ Provide hanger ties--three twists per tie--close to each anchor.

__ Do not permit extra loads on ceiling system.

__ Do not allow ceiling to brace or support mechanical or electrical equipment other than designed fixtures and loads.

__ Label ceiling maintenance and inspection access panels.

__ Provide undamaged, uninterrupted, and tightly sealed through-ceiling fire barriers.

__ Install through-ceiling sound walls undamaged and tightly sealed.

__ Sound treatment above ceiling:
    __ Material   __ Thickness   __ Application

__ Do not apply paint or other coatings at tiles or boards that would affect acoustical properties.

__ Adjust, repair, clean, and touch-up all system components.

MISCELLANEOUS FLOORING--MATERIALS CHECKLIST

__ Primers, sealers, cements, adhesives:
  __ Types   __ Manufacture   __ New, in unopened containers
  __ Special application requirements

__ Waterproofing:
  __ Type   __ Material   __ Fastening   __ Thorough cover   __ Undamaged

__ Flooring materials per manufacturer's instructions or applicable trade standards:
  __ Types __ Sizes   __ Thicknesses   __ Cove shapes   __ Colors   __ Patterns
  __ Quality of finish   __ Undamaged   __ Consistent in sizes and appearance

__ Supplementary subfloor construction:
  __ Underlayment   __ Felt or other moisture barrier   __ Vapor barrier:
  __ Types   __ Materials   __ Thicknesses   __ Fastenings   __ Thorough cover
  __ Undamaged

__ Nails and other fasteners:
  __ Types   __ Materials   __ Sizes   __ Coatings

MISCELLANEOUS FLOORING--PREPARATION

__ Subfloor:
  __ Make level, without humps or depressions
  __ Nail well, and secure against moving and squeaking
  __ Patch, repair, and sand smooth   __ Tighten and seal at joints   __ Clean

__ Concrete slab:
  __ Make level, without humps or depressions
  __ Dry (test moisture content if required)   __ Trowel smooth
  __ Patch and repair as required for smooth surface   __ Seal smoothly at joints
  __ Non-powdery   __ Clean

__ Verify that materials are delivered undamaged; store:
  __ Protected from weather and moisture
  __ Protected from construction dirt or damage

__ Store materials securely, and protect from:
  __ Weather   __ Moisture   __ Cold   __ Dirt   __ Construction damage

__ Verify that work of related trades is in place and properly positioned:
  __ Electrical floor outlets   __ Stub ups   __ Floor drains

__ Keep work environment:
  __ Clean   __ Dry   __ Well lighted   __ Well ventilated
  __ Free of airborne construction dust   __ At comfortable working temperature

09550   WOOD FLOORING--MATERIALS CHECKLIST

__ Wood strip flooring:
    __ Select grade plain-sawn white oak, 25/32" thick
    __ 3-1/4" face width with standard random lengths
    __ Tongue and groove edges.
    __ Field finish: Sand to level using successively finer sandpaper.
    __ Filler as recommended by flooring manufacturer.
    __ Stain as recommended by flooring manufacturer.
    __ Varnish as recommended by flooring manufacturer.

__ Hardwood parquet flooring:
    __ Prime grade quarter-sawn white oak
    __ Solid stock strips pre-assembled into 9" square units
    __ 5/16" thick, tongue and groove edges
    __ Eased edges
    __ Factory stain and polyurethane varnish finish
    __ Mastic application as recommended by flooring manufacturer.

__ Teak parquet flooring:
    __ Prime grade teak
    __ Solid stock strips pre-glued into 12" x 12" square units
    __ 5/16" thick, square edges
    __ Factory finished
    __ Mastic application as recommended by flooring manufacturer.

__ Plastic-impregnated parquet flooring:
    __ Solid oak slat parquet flooring impregnated with acrylic plastic
    __ Tongue and groove edges
    __ 5/16" thick
    __ Factory finished
    __ Mastic application as recommended by flooring manufacturer.

__ Match existing wood flooring with new materials.

__ Trim and accessories: Provide wood trim, saddles, nosing, thresholds matching wood flooring.

09550   WOOD FLOORING--PREPARATION

__ Store wood flooring materials in dry, protected work space 72 hours prior to installation.

__ Do preconstruction review with subcontractor to confirm:
    __ Materials   __ Strip direction   __ Patterning   __ Bordering
    __ Nailing, types and spacing   __ Scheduling of sanding and finish

09560 WOOD FLOORING--CONSTRUCTION

__ Install material as detailed:
    __ Type __ Sizes __ Species __ Grade __ Pattern
    __ Reject warped or bent material __ Match with samples

__ Install sleepers as detailed:
    __ Sizes __ Spacings __ Fastening __ Ventilation

__ Nails and nailing:
    __ Drive diagonally __ Space as required __ Nail at ends of each strip
    __ Predrill as necessary to prevent splits __ Nail type as instructed by manufacturer:
    __ 8d __ Screw __ Spiral

__ Do not allow end joints to occur side by side; separate by at least two strips.

__ Construct tight joints.

__ Do not damage tongues and grooves before or during application.

__ Use small or varied strips sparingly and never near one another.

__ Provide expansion joint space at all walls (1/2 inch min.)

09565 WOOD FLOORING--REPAIR AND CLEANUP

__ Keep work area thoroughly clean:
    __ Clear all nails away __ Remove all scrap

__ Sand promptly after cleaning:
    __ Schedule to avoid contaminating other work __ Consistently smooth
    __ Without lumps __ Without depressions __ Without burns

__ Vacuum all sanding dust.

__ Final finish:
    __ Filler __ Stain __ Wax and buffing

__ Do final finish right after sanding and cleaning.

__ Fasten baseboards at walls only, not at floors, with gap

__ Cover and protect floor surfaces from:
    __ Construction equipment __ Materials storage and movement __ Foot traffic
    __ Paint and other spills/droppings __ Temperature extremes
    __ Weather intrusion through open doors and/or windows
    __ Any other sources of moisture

__ Verify that tiles fit with door thresholds and do not interfere with door closure.

09570   WOOD FLOORING--PARQUET

__ Adhesives and application per manufacturer's instructions or applicable trade standards:

    __ Type __ Manufacture __ New __ Unopened containers
    __ Special application as per manufacturer's instructions
    __ Keep work space well ventilated

__ Construct joints within tolerances required by manufacturer.

09595   WOOD FLOORING--BLOCK

__ Application per manufacturer's instructions or applicable trade standards:

    __ Apply fully bedded __ Do not butter edges
    __ Provide prefinished blocks free of raised edges

09660 ASPHALT AND VINYL TILE FLOORING--APPLICATION

TILE FLOORING:

___ Vinyl tile: 12" by 12" by 1/8".

___ Vinyl composition tile: 12" by 12" by 1/8".

___ Rubber tile: 12" by 12" by 1/8".

___ Raised profile rubber tile: Round raised low-profile rubber tile, 18" by 18" by 1/8".

___ Match existing tile flooring with new materials.

SHEET FLOORING:

___ Vinyl sheet flooring: 0.085" overall gauge, 0.050" vinyl wear layer.

___ Rubber sheet flooring: 1/8" thick sheet flooring, 36" wide rolls.

___ Match existing tile flooring with new materials.

ACCESSORIES:

___ Wall base: 2-1/2" high, 1/8" thick.

___ Wall base: 4" high, 1/8" thick.

___ Wall base profile: Straight at carpet, coved at resilient tile.

___ Stair treads, stair skirt, risers, edge strips as required.

___ Corners are formed at the job.

09660 ASPHALT AND VINYL TILE FLOORING--APPLICATION

__ Set tile layout start points that result in an even, balanced tile pattern, as directed by designer

__ Lay special border tiles that fit squarely without cuts.

__ Do not mix material lots for any single floor area without design firm's approval.

__ Do not use broken, damaged, or marred tiles.

__ Apply adhesive:
    __ Quantity   __ Coverage   __ Allow to reach correct dry tack before laying tiles
    __ Completely adhere so no tiles can be moved or loosened

__ Tile cuts:
    __ Minimal   __ Uniform   __ Not smaller than half a tile

__ Tile joints:
    __ Straight   __ Aligned   __ Tight, without gaps   __ Carefully done at difficult areas:
    __ Corners   __ Fixture locations   __ Around wall openings and recesses
    __ At penetrations such as floor drains   __ Around door trim

09665 RESILIENT FLOORING--APPLICATION

__ Install resilient sheet flooring so that:
    __ All portions are laid in one uniform direction   __ Seams are minimal
    __ Seam joints are:
    __ Cleanly cut   __ Straight   __ Matched   __ Aligned
    __ Level, without humps or depressions

__ Perfectly match color and pattern throughout installation.

__ Unroll rolled material 24 hours ahead of installation, if
    required by manufacturer's instructions.

__ Start compression rolling over sheet flooring in middle,
    and move outward to press out all air bubbles.

09665 RESILIENT SHEET AND TILE FLOORING--COMPLETION, REPAIR, AND CLEANUP

__ Thoroughly adhere base materials; do not spot glue.

__ Do not allow scrap for base work; use maximum piece lengths.

__ Remove all stains and excess adhesive immediately after installation.

__ Replace work:
    __ Chipped   __ Scratched   __ Marred   __ Wrinkled   __ Cracked   __ Blistered
    __ Edges or corners are raised   __ Joints are not completely tight
    __ There are gaps at: __ Walls   __ Jambs   __ Trim

__ Repair or replace all defective and nonconforming work.

__ Make undetectable repairs.

__ Leave factory finish unless otherwise required.

__ Do new finishing such as waxing strictly according to manufacturer's instructions.

__ Provide temporary required coverings, to protect floor from traffic or further construction
    work.

__ Verify level joining at flush floor electrical cover plates, cleanouts, etc.

09680   CARPETING--MATERIALS CHECKLIST

__ Match existing carpets with new material as approved.

__ Carpet will be selected by Allowance amount.

__ Provide carpet:
    __ Manufacturer and Style:
    __ Yarn
    __ Weave:
    __ Pile:
    __ Face yarn:
    __ Face weight:
    __ Gauge:
    __ Stitches per 6":
    __ Pile height:
    __ Primary backing:
    __ Secondary backing:
    __ Static control:
    __ Flame spread:
    __ Width of roll:
    __ Color system (dye, natural, etc.)
    __ Color: As selected.
    __ Smoke-density factor:

__ Mounting:
    __ Tackless on pad: __ Firm: Slab rubber. __ Soft: Virgin urethane, medium density.
    __ Direct glue down: Waterproof, strippable adhesive.

__ Accessories:
    __ Edge guard: Heavy-gauge aluminum.   __ Reducer strip: Vinyl or rubber.

__ Provide carpet and pad as required by manufacturer's warranty or applicable trade standards:
    __ Fabric __ Thickness __ Weave __ Color __ Pattern
    __ Consistency in weave, pattern, and color   __ Flame resistance
    __ Antistatic treatment   __ Square yardage with overage

09680 CARPETING--PREPARATION

__ Order carpet in ample time for scheduled installation.

__ Verify that materials are delivered undamaged; store:
   __ Protected from weather and moisture
   __ Protected from construction dirt and damage

__ Plywood subfloor is ready for finish flooring:
   __ Level, without humps or depressions
   __ Nail well, and secure against moving and squeaking
   __ Patch, repair, and sand smooth   __ Tighten and seal at joints   __ Clean

__ Concrete slab is ready for finish flooring:
   __ Level, without humps or dips   __ Dry (test moisture content if required)
   __ Trowel smooth   __ Patch and repair as required for smooth surface
   __ Seal smoothly at joints   __ Non-powdery   __ Clean

__ Prepare joints and coordinate with carpet installation:
   __ Thresholds   __ Carpet strips   __ Borders with other flooring materials
   __ Trench duct cover plates   __ Floor access panels
   __ Cuts at openings and edges such as balcony or stair   __ Cuts at:
   __ Stub ups   __ Steps   __ Platforms   __ Curbs

09680   CARPETING--APPLICATION

__ Apply carpet pad per manufacturer's instructions:
  __ Protect from moisture before installation   __ Install perfectly dry
  __ Adhere thoroughly   __ Adhere with materials required by manufacturer

__ Prepare carpet and pad prior to installation:
  __ Unroll 24 hours in advance   __ Check for defects and moisture

__ Plan seam layout in detail prior to installation.

__ Install carpet so that:
  __ All portions are laid in one uniform direction   __ Seams are minimal
  __ There are no seams in heavy traffic areas
  __ There are no seams in high visibility areas   __ There are no cross seams
  __ Cuts for seams are made only on the weave line
  __ Cuts are not visible at lines of walls, door jambs,
     floor-mounted cabinets, etc.
  __ Straight   __ Matched   __ Aligned   __ Level, without humps or depressions

__ Coordinate carpet installation with other trades:
  __ Baseboard installation   __ Floor-mounted fixtures
  __ Floor-mounted cabinets and furnishings

__ Finish carpeted areas:
  __ Thoroughly clean scraps, threads, and dust
  __ Secure from further construction traffic
  __ Protect from foot traffic in work traffic areas
  __ Do not expose to weather or moisture

__ Save large scraps for owner's maintenance.

__ Return for credit or otherwise utilize for benefit of owner, any remaining substantial
   amount of excess material.

__ Provide temporary cover if required, to protect carpet.

__ Repair or replace all defective and nonconforming work.

__ Make repairs so they are undetectable.

09900 PAINTING MATERIALS CHECKLIST

__ Match color chips selected.

__ Exterior paint systems:
    __ Concrete, stucco and masonry: Primer, 1 coat; acrylic latex (flat finish), 2 coats.
    __ Concrete masonry units: Block filler, 1 coat; acrylic latex (flat finish), 2 coats.
    __ Wood for opaque finish (walls): Exterior primer, 1 coat; latex (flat finish), 2 coats.
    __ Wood for opaque finish (trim): Alkyd primer, 1 coat; alkyd enamel (gloss finish), 2 coats.
    __ Wood for semi-transparent finish: Semi-transparent stain (flat appearing finish), 2 coats.
    __ Ferrous metal: Zinc chromate primer, 1 coat; alkyd enamel (gloss finish), 2 coats.
    __ Ferrous metal (high performance): Epoxy primer, 1 coat; epoxy, 1 coat; catalyzed urethane (gloss finish), 1 coat.
    __ Galvanized metal: Galvanized metal primer, 1 coat; alkyd enamel (gloss finish), 2 coats.
    __ Galvanized metal (high performance): Epoxy primer, 1 coat; catalyzed urethane (gloss finish), 1 coat.

__ Interior paint systems:
    __ Concrete, stucco and masonry: Primer, 1 coat; interior latex (flat finish), 2 coats.
    __ Concrete masonry units: Block filler, 1 coat; interior latex (flat finish), 2 coats.
    __ Drywall and plaster: Latex primer, 1 coat; interior latex (flat finish), 2 coats.
    __ Drywall and plaster (heavy duty): Latex primer, 1 coat; water-based epoxy (semi-gloss finish), 2 coats.
    __ Drywall and plaster (high performance): Latex primer, 1 coat; polychromatic vinyl copolymer (multi-color finish)
    __ Drywall and plaster (for wallcovering): 1 coat oil-based sealer or enamel undercoater.
    __ Wood for opaque finish (walls): Latex primer, 1 coat; interior latex (flat finish), 2 coats.
    __ Wood for opaque finish (trim): Alkyd enamel undercoater, 1 coat; alkyd enamel (semi-gloss finish), 2 coats.
    __ Wood for transparent finish: Oil stain, 1 coat; sanding sealer, 1 coat; alkyd varnish (gloss finish), 2 coats.
    __ Ferrous metal: Alkyd metal primer, 1 coat; alkyd enamel (semi-gloss finish), 2 coats.
    __ Ferrous metal (high performance): Epoxy primer, 1 coat; catalyzed urethane (gloss finish), 2 coats.

__ Paints, stains, and enamels:
    __ Types   __ Manufacturers   __ Grades   __ Colors   __ Texture additives

09900   PAINTING MATERIALS--STORAGE

__ All paint materials shall be delivered:
    __ New   __ In labeled, unopened containers   __ Certified

__ Material quality shall be:
    __ Verified as necessary by onsite tests   __ Verified as necessary by laboratory tests

__ Do not use mixed brands or partial substitutions.

__ Have materials delivered in a timely sequence as required to expedite the work flow.

__ Store all paint materials:
    __ With ample ventilation   __ In fire-protected space   __ Secure from damage

__ Keep paint storage areas clean and clear of:
    __ Spilled material   __ Empty containers   __ Rags and scrap

09900   PAINTING PREPARATION

__ Colors and application:
    __ Keep color samples on hand, and use them continuously for comparisons
    __ Use completed color schedule

__ Test areas with paint, and match dried paint to approved color and texture samples.

__ Prepare surfaces to be painted as per manufacturer's instructions or applicable trade
        standards:
    __ Clean   __ Dry   __ Smooth, free of bumps or depressions
    __ Correctly repair, fill, and sand as necessary   __ Treated   __ Sealed   __ Primed

__ Confirm dryness of surfaces before painting by moisture meter testing of new:
    __ Plaster   __ Concrete   __ Masonry

__ Thoroughly clean surfaces of construction droppings or stains:
    __ Rust   __ Mortar   __ Sealants   __ Waterproofing

09900   PAINTING

__ Painting procedures:
    __ Texturing   __ Mixing   __ Thinning   __ Application tools:
    __ Brush   __ Spray   __ Roller

__ Paint coats:
    __ Thicknesses   __ Curing time between coats   __ Numbers of coats
    __ Varied tints for each coat   __ Paint thickness meter testing

__ Apply paint to thoroughly cover undercoat, and do not allow:

09900   PAINTING continued

__ Maintain a painting log to control schedule and completeness of painting.

__ Maintain a proper work environment:
   __ Dry   __ Clean   __ Well ventilated   __ Free of airborne construction dust
   __ Well lighted   __ In temperature range required by paint manufacturer

__ Keep working temperatures and humidity adequate to prevent moisture condensation on work
   surfaces.

__ Maintain thorough dust and dirt control throughout the painting process.

__ Thoroughly protect all surfaces that won't be painted with:
   __ Clean drop cloths   __ Masking tape   __ Masking plastic

__ Totally cover work areas with drop cloths that are free of gaps or rips.

__ Immediately clean any spilled materials.

__ Do not allow dirt or spilled materials to be tracked from one work area to another.

__ Coordinate painting with adjacent or related work such as:
   __ Hardware   __ Electrical and plumbing fixtures   __ Outlets and switch boxes   __ Trim

__ Remove adjacent or related work that might be marred by painting, or provide complete
   protection.

__ Do not allow paint gaps or overlaps at edges of hardware, fixtures, or trim.

__ Periodically sample paint for tests directly from paint containers being used.

__ Do not allow paint to dry in cans that are being used or on applicators.

__ Paint remote and out-of-reach places:
   __ Inside cabinets   __ Under shelves and drawers   __ Hinge edges of doors
   __ Top edges of high trim   __ Undersides of low trim
   __ Behind fixtures and equipment

__ Allow absolutely no paint smears or splatters to remain on adjacent surfaces.

__ Replace or repair all nonconforming work.

__ Do repairs and touch-ups so they are undetectable.

ROOM SPECIFICATIONS CHECKLIST
DIVISION 10 -- SPECIALTIES

10000--SPECIALTIES

__ Chalkboards and Tackboards:
    __ Porcelain-on-metal markerboards: Enameling grade sheet steel with porcelain finish with gloss finish for use with liquid chalk markers.
    __ Painted finish chalkboards: 1/4" thick treated hardboard panel surfaced with organic coating for chalk-receptive finish.
    __ Plastic impregnated cork tackboards: 1/4" thick seamless sheet with washable vinyl finish with cork in resinous binder.
    __ Vinyl fabric-faced cork tackboards: 1/4" cork backing sheet with mildew-resistant vinyl fabric face.

__ Compartments and Cubicles:
    __ Metal partitions:
        __ Steel with baked enamel finish; ASTM A 591, Class C, galvanized and bonderized.
        __ Steel for porcelain enamel finish: ASTM A 424, Commercial Quality, 18 gauge minimum.
        __ Stainless steel, AISI No. 4 finish, bright directional polish, ASTM A 167, Type 302/304.

    __ Plastic laminate faced partitions: Pressure-laminated one-piece face sheets, 0.062" thick.

    __ Fittings: Door latches and coat hook on inside face of door.

__ Louvers and Vents:
    __ Extruded aluminum louvers: Stationary, horizontal drainable blade louvers, minimum extrusion 0.081", insect screen.
    __ Provide the following finish:
        __ Clear anodized finish, Class 1. __ Color anodized, Class 1.
        __ Baked enamel. __ Fluoropolymer, 2-coat

    __ Formed sheet metal louvers: Stationary, horizontal drainable louvers, 16 gauge galvanized steel minimum, insect screen.
        Provide the following finish:
        __ Baked enamel. __ Fluropolymer, 2-coat

    __ Vents: Extruded or bent aluminum louvers and frames, clear anodized finish.

__ Service Wall Systems.

__ Wall and Corner Guards:
    __ Stainless steel: 18 gauge 4" by 4" stainless steel with AISI No. 4 bright directional polish finish.

    __ Plastic: High impact molded plastic corner guards.

__ Access Flooring:
 __ Die-cast aluminum panels: One-piece panels in stringerless system;.

 __ Steel-covered wood core panels: High-density particleboard core with perimeter steel channel and steel top sheet.

 __ Formed steel panels: All steel panels with die-cut flat top sheet.

 __ Concrete panels: Reinforced concrete panels.

 __ Floor covering:
  __ Vinyl composition tile.   __ Plastic laminate.   __ Carpet tile.

__ Pest Control

__ Fireplaces and Stoves

__ Flagpoles:
 __ Flagpoles with cone taper designed for site and wind conditions:
  __ Aluminum, ASTM B 241, color anodized finish.
  __ Stainless steel, AISI Alloy 302/304, No. 4 bright directional polish finish:
  __ Bronze, CDA No. 230 bronze alloy, statuary finish:

__ Identifying Devices (Directories/Plaques/Signs):
 __ Directories, component system with extruded aluminum frame, back, letterboard, mounting:
  __ Rear-illuminated type.   __ Non-illuminated type.   __ Reveal-type frame.
  __ Frameless. __ Laminated glass. __ Bronze acrylic sheet.
  __ Film-type name strips.   __ Engraved-type name strips.
  __ Silkscreened name strips.

 __ Bulletin boards, component system with extruded aluminum housing, tackable surface, perimeter frame and back:
  __ Non-illuminated type.   __ Top-illuminated type.   __ Hinged cover.
  __ Sliding cover.   __ Laminated glass.   __ No glazing.

 __ Aluminum finish:
  __ Anodized.   __ Baked enamel.

__ Pedestrian Control Devices:
 __ Panel signs; Vomar Products or approved equal:
  __Framed type.   __ Unframed type.   __ Plastic laminate fabrication.
  __ Acrylic plastic fabrication.   __ Metal fabrication.
  __ Engraved copy graphics.   __ Subsurface printing graphics.
  __ Raised letter graphics.   __ Applied vinyl letter graphics.
  __ Metal letters and numbers:
   __ Aluminum, color anodized finish.   __ Bronze, smooth specular finish.
   __ Stainless steel, AISI No. 8, reflective finish.
   __ Cast (aluminum or bronze) type.   __ Cut-out type.   __ Fabricated units.

 __ Cast plaques:
  __ Aluminum, color anodized finish.   __ Bronze, statuary finish.

379

__ Lockers

    __ Steel locker units with baked enamel finish, interior shelf and hooks, number plates, latching mechanism, filler panels, and legs where raised base not provided; baked enamel finish:

        __ Wardrobe lockers, 24 gauge steel fabrication.

        __ Athletic lockers, 16 gauge steel fabrication.   __ Single tier type.

        __ Double tier type.   __ Multi-tier type.   __ Sloped tops.

        __ Flat tops with closure panels.

__ Fire Extinguishers, Cabinets, and Accessories:

    __ Fire extinguishers: UL listed and labeled units:

        __ Stored-pressure water type.   __ Dry chemical type.   __ Halon type.

    __ Cabinets: Enamelled steel box with trim, frame, door, and accessories:

        __ Recessed mounting.   __ Semi-recessed mounting.   __ Surface-mounted.

        __ Trimless.   __ Trimless with hidden flange.   __ Exposed trim.

        __ Enamelled steel door, baked enamel finish.

        __ Aluminum door, color anodized finish.

        __ Stainless steel door, AISI No. 4 bright directional polish finish.

        __ Solid panel door style.   __ Duo-panel door style.

        __ Full-glass panel door style.

__ Protective Covers   (Walkways/Car Shelters/Awnings)

__ Postal Specialties:

    __ Mail chutes:

        __ Aluminum, with satin anodized finish.

        __ Stainless steel, with AISI No. 4 directional polish finish.

        __ Bronze, with statuary finish.

    __ Collection and receiving boxes:

        __ Aluminum, with satin anodized finish.

        __ Stainless steel, with AISI No. 4 directional polish finish.

        __ Bronze, with statuary finish.

    __ Indoor mail boxes:

        __ Horizontal type.

            __ Front loading type.   __ Rear loading type.

            __ Aluminum, with satin anodized finish.

            __ Steel, with baked enamel finish.

        __ Vertical type.

            __ Front loading, bottom hinged type.

            __ Aluminum, with satin anodized finish.

    __ Neighborhood delivery and collection box units:

        __ Aluminum unit with satin anodized finish   __ Pedestal mounted

        __ Master loading door and individual compartment doors.

__ Partitions
    __ Wire Mesh Partitions:
        __ Partitions: 10 gauge crimped steel wire woven into 1-1/2" mesh, with stiffening bars, posts, floor shoes, and shop-applied enamel finish.

    __ Accessories:
        __ Hinged door with lock and hardware   __ Service window with shelf.

    __ Demountable Partitions:
        __ Pre-engineered systems with gypsum panels.

    __ Pre-engineered system with 20 gauge metal faced panels.

    __ Operable Partions
        __ Accordian folding: Vinyl faced accordian folding partition; Modernfold or approved equal.
        __ Manually operated.   __ Electrically operated.

    __ Sliding partitions: Vinyl faced sliding partition; Hufcor or approved equal.
        __ Manually operated.   __ Electrically operated.   __ Single panel.
        __ Double panel.   __ Mechanical top and bottom seals.

__ Storage Shelving

__ Sun Control Devices

__ Telephone Enclosures

    __ Outdoor units: Fully-enclosed, folding-door unit; safety glass doors, stainless steel writing shelf, overhead light.

    __ Indoor enclosed units: Full-enclosed, folding-door unit; safety glass doors, writing shelf, overhead light, and fan.

    __ Indoor shelf units: Overhead illumination, with stainless steel shelf and acoustical panel walls.

    __ Materials:
        __ Stainless steel, Type 302/304 with AISI No. 4 finish.
        __ Aluminum extrusions and plate, color anodized finish.
        __ Galvanized steel panels, with baked-on enamel finish.

__ Toilet and Bath Enclosures:

    __ Stainless steel fabrication with NAAMM No. 4 bright directional polish finish.

    __ Surface and recessed mounting as indicated.

    __ Types and quantities:

        __ Towel dispenser; 1 per toilet room.

        __ Waste dispenser; 1 per toilet room.

        __ Combination towel/waste dispenser; 1 per toilet room.

        __ Toilet tissue dispenser, double roll; 1 per stall.

        __ Sanitary napkin dispenser; 1 per ladies room.

        __ Sanitary napkin disposal, through partition type; 1 per two stalls.

        __ Soap dispenser; 1 per basin.
          __ Deck-mounted.   __ Surface-mounted.

        __ Grab bars; 1 pair per handicapped stall.

        __ Shelf, 1 per toilet room.

        __ Janitor's utility unit; 2 per janitor's closet.

        __ Shower curtain rod; 1 per shower stall.

        __ Shower curtain and hooks; 1 per shower stall.

        __ Hinged shower seat; 1 per handicapped shower.

        __ Towel bars; 2 per toilet room.

        __ Soap dish; 1 per lavatory.

        __ Mirror units; 1 per lavatory and as indicated.

        __ Ash urn; 1 per toilet room.

11000 EQUIPMENT

__ Security and Vault Equipment

__ Mercantile Equipment

__ Vending Equipment

__ Audio-Visual Equipment:
   __ Electrically operated, remote control units.
      __ Surface-mounted on ceiling.   __ Surface-mounted on wall.
      __ Recessed, ceiling mounted.
      __ Recessed, ceiling mounted with automatic closure.

   __ Manually-operated pull-down units.
      __ Surface-mounted on wall.   __ Surface-mounted on ceiling.

   __ Screen fabric, glass-beaded type.

   __ Screen fabric, non-gloss matt white, for wide shallow rooms.

__ Parking Equipment:
   __ Automatic barrier gates.

   __ Vehicle detectors: Automatic vehicle sensing device in pavement.

   __ Ticket dispensers: Dispenser with clock, cabinet, and control mechanism.

   __ Card control units: Card access units, cabinet, and automatic gate arm control.

   __ Cashier's clock: Ticket-controlled fee system clock.

__ Loading Dock Equipment:
   __ Dock bumpers: Molded rubber bumpers and bumper risers.

   __ Dock levelers: Mechanical or hydraulic operation, permanent pit installation, with automatic vertical and lateral compensation, hinged lip, safety devices, with capacity rated for intended use.

   __ Dock seals: Fabric-covered compressible foam pads, adjustable head pad, nylon cover pad, and steel support frame.

   __ Dock shelters: Flexible side and head polyurethane-coated nylon curtain system with translucent fabric and metal framing.

___ Waste Handling Equipment:
    ___ Incinerator units: Packaged units; Atlas Incinerators, Inc or approved equal.

    ___ Paper shredder units: Packaged units; Industrial Shreader and Cutter Co or approved equal.

    ___ Waste compactor units, bins and hoppers: Packaged units; Compackager, Inc or approved equal.

___ Food Service Equipment:
    ___ Equipment: Stainless steel equipment with AISI No. 4 bright directional polish finish, NSF and UL approved. Fabricated products and equipment suitable for operational food service facilities.

___ Residential Equipment: ___ Kitchen ___ Laundry
    ___ Utility service as available at the building.

    ___ Appliances:
        ___ Ranges. ___ Cooktops. ___ Self-vented cooktop units. ___ Wall ovens.
        ___ Microwave ovens. ___ Refrigerator/freezers.
        ___ Undercounter refrigerators. ___ Hot water dispensers.
        ___ Food waste disposers. ___ Trash compactors. ___ Dishwashers.
        ___ Clothes washers. ___ Clothes dryers. ___ Exhaust hood for range.
        ___ Exhaust system for dryer.

___ Unit Kitchens and Cabinets:
    ___ Factory-fabricated and assembled units with stainless steel counter, baked enamel on steel cabinets and built-in appliances and accessories; Dwyer Products Corp or approved equal. Width as indicated on the Drawings.
        ___ Oven. ___ Cooktop, 3 burner. ___ Cooktop, 4 burner. ___ Refrigerator.
        ___ Sink and faucet. ___ Ice maker. ___ Hot water dispenser.
        ___ Microwave oven. ___ Range hood. ___ Under-cabinet light.
        ___ Dishwasher. ___ Trash compactor. ___ Cabinets, below counter.
        ___ Cabinets, above counter. ___ Metal splash below cabinets. ___ Finished ends.

___ Darkroom Equipment

___ Athletic Equipment
    ___ Basketball backstop and steel support: Ceiling suspended unit with rectangular clear view backboard; forward-folding crank-operated type for manual winch operation; steel ring, net goals with no-tie clips, twine net.

    ___ Basketball scoreboard:
        ___ Indoor scoreboard with solid state operation on low voltage two-wire cable.
        ___ Display possession, bonus indicator lights, and horn.

___ Laboratory Equipment

___ Medical Equipment

___ Telecommunication Equipment

ROOM SPECIFICATIONS CHECKLIST
DIVISION 12 -- FURNISHINGS

06400/12300 CABINETS AND FIXTURES--MATERIALS AND PRODUCTS

__ Materials must be as per shop drawings, applicable trade standards and/or approved
      samples:
      __ Types __ Finishes __ Wood species and grades __ Surface materials
      __ Internal construction __ Joints __ Fastenings and/or adhesives
      __ With grade stamps __ Certified __ Hardware:
      __ Types __ Materials __ Finishes

__ Provide cabinets complete with preassembled accessories and hardware:
      __ Shelf holders __ Magnetic or other catches __ Pulls and handles

06400/12300 CABINETS AND FIXTURES--PREPARATION

__ Order materials and provide for storage in ample time for delivery before building occupancy.

__ Have materials shipped and delivered:
      __ After building is closed in __ Securely padded and cushioned
      __ On skids to prevent damage at bases
      __ With internal bracing to prevent wracking and weakening of joints
      __ With protective covers to prevent shipping and handling damage

__ Provide and install hardware with:
      __ Consistent appearance in hardware sets and types __ Secure fasteners
      __ Smooth and precise operation

__ Have furnishings, cabinets, and fixtures delivered complete with all required accessories,
      including:
      __ Preattached hardware __ Job-mounted hardware __ Trim __ Moldings
      __ Scribes

__ Store furnishings and fixtures:
      __ In clean storage area __ Secure from weather or moisture
      __ Secure from possible construction damage __ At comfortable room temperature
      __ Logged and accounted for

__ Provide supports for floor-, wall-, and ceiling-mounted furnishings and fixtures, and
      coordinate with:
      __ Wall furring __ Ceiling soffits __ Blocking __ Backing materials __ Bases
      __ Anchors __ Inserts __ Hangers __ Brackets

06400/12300 CABINETS AND FIXTURES--CONSTRUCTION

__ Cabinet doors:
     __ Hang straight   __ Mount with uniform clearance at all edges
     __ Make smoothly operating in opening and closing

__ Drawer guides:
     __ Mount straight   __ Attach securely
     __ Make smoothly operating in opening and closing

__ Install and anchor base cabinets level and securely.

__ Align base cabinet toe spaces with adjacent bases and coves.

__ Prepare countertop and other surfaces as required:
     __ For additional final finish materials
     __ Coordinated with sinks and other added fixtures and equipment

__ Install countertops as per shop drawings, applicable trade standards and/or approved
     samples:
     __ Types   __ Materials   __ Finishes   __ Clean
     __ Protect from construction damage

__ Cut openings for sinks and other fixtures evenly for close fit of added fixtures.

__ Repair, job-finish, and clean materials as per manufacturer's instructions:
     __ Make undetectable repairs of damaged or nonconforming work
     __ Do not allow cleaning or finishing materials and operations to damage adjacent
         materials
     __ Protect all surfaces from dirt and damage until final occupancy

12500 WINDOW TREATMENT

MATERIALS:

__ Horizontal blinds, raising and tilting, wand and cord operation:
    __ Slat width: 1".   __ Slat width: 2".

__ Vertical blinds, traversing and rotating, cord and chain operation:
    __ Blades, 3-1/2" wide pvc.   __ Head and sill track, 0.025" thick blades.
    __ Head track only, 0.030" thick blades.

__ Drapery tracks:
    __ Anodized aluminum single channel for hand traverse.
    __ Anodized aluminum dual channel for cord traverse.
    __ Painted steel channel, C-shaped for either hand or cord traverse.

__ Solar control shades:
    __ Vinyl coated fiberglass fabric.   __ Electric operation.   __ Manual operation.

__ Provide secure blocking and backing.

__ Provide required stacking.

__ Provide supports for rods as required to prevent sagging.

__ Coordinate locations and heights of controls with other required furnishings.

__ Use required flameproof material.

__ Provide non-rusting weights.

__ Provide ample carriers.

__ Provide bypassing arms for bi-parting types.

__ Verify required fullness (usually 2-1/2 times).

__ Provide required types and lengths of batons.

__ Allow carriers to run freely, especially on curved rack.

13000 SPECIAL CONSTRUCTION

__ Integrated Ceilings

__ Pre-Engineered Structures:
    __ Metal Building Systems   __ Greenhouses   __ Portable and Mobile Buildings

        __ Primary components:
            __ Frames: Hot rolled structural steel, ASTM A36.
            __ Roofing: Zinc-coated steel sheets, ASTM A 446, Grade C with ASTM A 525 G90 galvanizing.
            __ Insulated wall panels: Steel faced panels with interlocking design, closure strips and Kynar 500 finish.

__ Special Purpose Rooms and Buildings:
    __ Prefab Rooms

    __ Saunas
        __ Pre-engineered units.
        __ Walls, ceilings, floors, and doors: Redwood or western red cedar, tongue and groove construction; insulated perimeter.
        __ Ventilation, heaters, and lighting; capacity required for size of sauna.
        __ Controls, thermometers, and clock timers.
        __ Backrests and seats.

__ Vaults

__ Pools

PRODUCTS/MATERIALS SPECIFIED IN THIS SECTION

__ Product or Trade Name(s). (Write the product required, or the list of acceptable choices. If writing generic specifications, write the standards of performance separately as a checklist.)

__ Model or Catalog Order Number(s)

Catalog Number/Date/Page(s) _____

__ Manufacturer(s) Name/Address/Phone/Contact Name(s)

__ Supplier(s) Name/Address/Phone/Contact Name(s)

__ Applicable Trade and Reference Standards

ROOM SPECIFICATIONS CHECKLIST
DIVISION 14 -- CONVEYING

SOURCES

__ ANSI Safety Code for Elevators, Dumbwaiters, Escalators, and Moving Walks.
  (ANSI) American National Standards Institute, 1430 Broadway, New York, NY, 10018

14000 CONVEYING

__ Dumbwaiters:
  __ Components:
      __ Materials and finishes:
          __ Enamelled steel cab.   __ Stainless steel doors and hoistway entrances.
      __ Control system: Fully automatic operation; signal equipment; operating
          system.
      __ Countertop level access.   __ Floor level access.   __ Building supported.
      __ Self-supporting.   __ Machine location at top of hoistway shaft.
      __ Machine location at bottom of hoistway shaft.

__ Elevators: __ Electric   __ Hydraulic

    __ Components and features:
        __ Geared traction type operation (up to 400 fpm.)
        __ Gearless traction type operation (400 fpm and over).
        __ Hoistway entrances, stainless steel, No. 4 bright directional polish.
        __ Hoistway entrances, bronze, alloy 220 commercial bronze, mirror polished.
        __ Hoistway entrances, enameled steel.
        __ Hoistway entrances, plastic laminate, 0.050" thick.
        __ Door panels, stainless steel, No. 4 bright directional polish.
        __ Door panels, bronze, alloy 220 commercial bronze, mirror polished.
        __ Door panels, enameled steel.
        __ Door panels, Plastic laminate, 0.050" thick.
        __ Handrail, bronze, mirror polished finish.
        __ Handrail, stainless steel, No. 4 bright directional polish.   __ Handrail, wood.

    __ Control and cab features:
        __ Key controlled car light switch and fan switch.
        __ Alarm/emergency stop button.
        __ Car position and direction indicators.   __ Audible signals.
        __ Automatic leveling.   __ Key switches to lockout every floor individually.
        __ Door nudging feature to discourage holding door open.   __ Ceiling hatch.
        __ Liner blanket hooks and blankets.

__ Hoists and Cranes

__ Lifts:
    __ Wheelchair lifts: Pre-engineered wheelchair lift.
        __ Capacity: 500 pounds. __ Speed: 10 feet per minute.
        __ Motor: Minimum 1/3HP, 120V AC, 60 Hz, 1 phase.
        __ Switches: Key operation requiring constant pressure to operate.

    __ Vertical wheelchair lift.

    __ Stair rail following wheelchair lift.

__ Material Handling Systems

__ Turntables

__ Moving Stairs and Walks:
    __ Escalators:
        __ Components and Features:
            __ Tread width, 48". __ Tread width, 32".
            __ Balustrades, transparent tempered glass.
            __ Balustrades, opaque.
            __ Trim, decks, skirts, panels fabricated of stainless steel, AISI No. 4
                bright directional polish.
            __ Trim, decks, skirts, panels fabricated of bronze, mirror polished finish.
            __ Trim, decks, skirts, panels fabricated of porcelain enamel on steel, 4 mil.
            __ Floor plates: Cast aluminum.
            __ Handrails: Black neoprene.

14000 CONVEYING SYSTEMS

PRODUCTS/MATERIALS SPECIFIED IN THIS SECTION

__ Product or Trade Name(s). (Write the product required, or the list of acceptable choices. If writing generic specifications, write the standards of performance separately as a checklist.)

__ Model or Catalog Order Number(s)

Catalog Number/Date/Page(s) _____

__ Manufacturer(s) Name/Address/Phone/Contact Name(s)

__ Supplier(s) Name/Address/Phone/Contact Name(s)

__ Applicable Trade and Reference Standards

ROOM SPECIFICATIONS CHECKLIST
DIVISION 15 -- MECHANICAL

SOURCES

__ (ANSI) American National Standards Institute, New York, NY, 10018

__ (ASHRAE) American Society of Heating, Refrigerating, and Air-Conditioning Engineers
345 E. 47th St., New York, NY 10017

__ Basic Plumbing Code, Building Officials and Code Administrators International, Inc., 17926
S. Halsted St., Homewood, IL 60430

__ National Plumbing Code, American Society of Mechanical Engineers, 345 E. 47th St., New York,
NY 10017

15000 MATERIALS AND CONSTRUCTION SPECIFICATIONS CHECKLIST

__ GENERAL PROVISIONS 15000/15050
__ Work Included __ Related Requirements __ Coordination with Other Trades
__ Permits and Inspections __ Codes and Standards
__ Submittals and Review of Materials, Samples, and Drawings
__ Guarantees and Warranties __ Operations and Maintenance Data
__ Labels and Identification __ Product Delivery, Storage, and Handling
__ Tolerances for Installation __ Temporary Services

__ MATERIALS AND PRODUCTS
__ Pipe __ Water __ Refrigerant __ Soil, Waste, and Vent __ Gas
__ Pipe Fittings __ Pipe Specialties __ Valve Boxes __ Shock Absorbers
__ Hose Bibbs __ Pipe Hangers and Supports __ Valves and Cocks
__ Motors and Motor Starters

__ EXECUTION
__ Excavation, Trenching, and Backfilling __ Openings, Cutting, and Patching
__ Caulking and Flashing __ Cleaning and Sterilization __ Piping Installation:
__ Without air pockets __ Expansion/Contraction Joints __ Sleeves and Plates
__ Pipe Supports __ Pipe Joints __ Unions
__ Testing of Piping __ Mounting Heights __ Motors, Starters, and Electrical Work
__ Start-up Instructions

__ INSULATION--GENERAL PROVISIONS 15250
__ Work Included __ Related Requirements

__ INSULATION--MATERIALS AND PRODUCTS
__ Piping Insulation __ Duct Insulation __ Duct Liner

__ INSULATION--EXECUTION
__ Preparation __ Installation __ Acoustic Lining and Joints

__ PLUMBING SYSTEMS/PLUMBING FIXTURES--GENERAL PROVISIONS 15400/15450
      __ Work Included   __ Related Requirements
      __ Work Installed but Furnished by Others   __ Reference Standards   __ Submittals
      __ Product Delivery, Storage, and Handling

__ PLUMBING SYSTEMS/PLUMBING FIXTURES--PRODUCTS

      __ Provide plumbing systems components and all required accessories including shut-offs and clean-outs
      __ Provide components which prevent back-siphonage or cross-connections.

      __ Sanitary, waste and vent piping: Service weight cast iron with load and oakum fittings or no-hub pipe with MG joints or clamp-all couplings for pipe 2-1/2" and larger.
      __ Service weight cast iron or Type DWV copper pipe and copper fittings for 2" and smaller waste pipe, except provide cast iron pipe on urinal waste.

      __ Hot and cold water piping: Type L seamless hard drawn copper tubing assembled with solder fittings. Support piping with grade to drain to drainoff cocks.

      __ Hangers: For cast iron, provide heavy wrought iron pipe hangers, brackets or clamps at 5' intervals. Fasten with lag screw or with expansion shields as applicable. For water piping, provide adjustable wrought iron copper plated hangers at 6' intervals maximum. Provide hangers to allow for full thickness of insulation.

      __ Sleeves and escutcheons: Galvanized wrought iron. Where uncovered pipes pass through finished areas, provide heavy chromium escutcheons.

      __ Covering and insulation: For domestic hot and cold water piping provide 1/2" flexible foamed tubing. Seal joints vapor tight. Insulate valves and fittings including water service piping with equal thickness of pipe insulation. Provide 18 gauge protection saddles between insulation and pipe hangers. Comply with fire hazard regulations.

      __ Valves and shut-offs: Full size bronze gate valves for hot and cold water branches.
      __ Provide drainage valves.

      __ Hose bibbs: Anti-siphon hose bibbs.

      __ Floor drains and cleanouts: Units with bronze strainer and copper flashing.

      __ Shock absorbers.

      __ Domestic water mixing valve: Self-contained thermostatic type including hot water temperature limit, check valves, stainers and stop valves.

__ PLUMBING SYSTEMS/PLUMBING FIXTURES--PRODUCTS continued

    __ Water heater: Glass lined storage type for utility service at site. Provide baked enamel steel jacket, fiberglass insulation, and UL flame retention burner; 10 year warranty.

    __ Water cooler: Stainless steel dual drinking fountain.

    __ Sewage ejector: Size and automatic controls to meet project requirements.

    __ Pool systems: Complete system including filters, recirculating pumps, chlorination equipment, water heaters, and deck drain.

    __ Access panels:
        __ Metal units with locks.
        __ Configuration and trim as required by finish wall surface.

    __ Fixtures and Accessories Schedule

    __ Fixtures and Accessories Product Manufacturers

__ PLUMBING SYSTEMS/PLUMBING FIXTURES--EXECUTION
    __ Inspection Prior to Installation   __ Rough-in   __ Installation
    __ Traps and Cleanouts   __ Water Heater Relief Valve   __ Testing
    __ Cleaning   __ Protection of Finished Work

FIRE PROTECTION SPRINKLER SYSTEM 15500

__ FIRE PROTECTION SPRINKLER SYSTEM--GENERAL PROVISIONS
    __ Work Included   __ Related Requirements
    __ Work Installed but Furnished by Others   __ Reference Standards   __ Submittals
    __ Product Delivery, Storage, and Handling

__ FIRE PROTECTION SPRINKLER SYSTEM--MATERIALS AND PRODUCTS

    __ Provide sprinkler systems components including standpipes, backflow preventers, hose cabinets, fire pump, jockey pump, starter, fire department connection, test valves, horns, signals, and all required accessories.

    __ Provide zoned electrically-supervised fire detection and fire alarm system components including equipment, photoelectric and thermal detectors, duct smoke detectors, and control equipment. Comply with NFPA 72B.

    __ Pipe and fittings: Schedule 40 steel with threaded ends meeting NFPA requirements.

    __ Valves: Bronze construction; 2" and small with bronze bodies and bonnets with screwed ends; 2-1/2" and larger flanged.

    __ Sprinkler heads: Style as approved.

    __ Fire department connection: Free-standing polished brass with threads as per local fire department requirements.

    __ Fire pump: Size and configuration per NFPA requirements. Horizontal split case, single stage, double suction pump.

    __ Pipe   __ Pipe Fittings   __ Pipe Specialties   __ Sprinkler Heads
    __ Pipe Hangers and Supports   __ Valves and Cocks   __ Alarm Connection

__ FIRE PROTECTION SPRINKLER SYSTEM--EXECUTION
    __ Openings, Cutting, and Patching   __ Caulking and Flashing   __ Piping Installation
    __ Without air pockets   __ Expansion/Contraction Joints   __ Sleeves and Plates
    __ Pipe Supports   __ Pipe Joints   __ Unions   __ Mounting Heights and Slopes
    __ Certificates   __ Tests and Approval

__ FIRE PROTECTION--FIRE HOSES AND CABINETS
    __ Pipe   __ Valves/Fittings   __ Hose   __ Cabinet

ROOM SPECIFICATIONS CHECKLIST -- MECHANICAL continued

HEATING AND AIR CONDITIONING--REFRIGERATION

__ REFRIGERATION/LIQUID HEAT TRANSFER--GENERAL PROVISIONS 15650/15700
  __ Work Included   __ Related Work Specified Elsewhere   __ Reference Standards
  __ Work Installed   __ Submittals and Review of Materials, Samples, and Drawings
  __ Job Conditions   __ Sequence of Work   __ Coordination with Other Trades
  __ Products Delivery, Storage, and Handling

__ REFRIGERATION/LIQUID HEAT TRANSFER--MATERIALS AND PRODUCTS

  __ Piping: Schedule 40 seamless black steel, ASTM A 53, Grade A; Type L copper pipe ASTM B 88; Schedule 40 PVC with solvent joints as applicable to class of service required and applicable regulations.

  __ Valves: Provide valves required by service intended including gate, globe, check, and ball valves.

  __ Hangers and supports: Comply with ANSI B31.1.

  __ Convectors: Copper tubes with aluminum fins, 16 gauge steel front and top panels.

  __ Unit heaters: Copper tube coils with aluminum fins, baked enamel steel enclosure.

  __ Components: Automatic air vents, thermometers, pressure gauges, expansion joints, regulating valves, air separators, expansion tanks, and pumps as required.

  __ Sheet metal work and accessories: Comply with SMACNA Duct Manual and Sheet Metal Construction for Ventilating and Air Conditioning Systems.

  __ Fans and air handling units: Rated by manufacturer for service intended.

  __ Grilles and registers: Units with approved face and frame design, gaskets, and baked enamel finish.

__ Fan coil units: 22 gauge galvanized steel with seamless copper tube and aluminum fin coil.

__ Controls: Automatic temperature control system with thermostats and aquastats as required.

__ Boilers: Cast iron hot water boiler with utility service as available at the site. Comply with ASME Code including operating and high limit control, burner, and low water cutoff and relief valve. Provide double-walled preinsulated sheet metal chimney. Provide 16 gauge sheet metal insulated breeching.

__ Access panels:
    __ Metal units with locks.
    __ Configuration and trim as required by finish wall surface.

__ Equipment:
__ Heat Pump Units __ Coils __ Condensing Units __ Furnace __ Fans
__ Firestats __ Gas Vents __ Gravity Vents

__ REFRIGERATION/LIQUID HEAT TRANSFER--EXECUTION
    __ Installation __ Balancing

HEATING AND AIR CONDITIONING--AIR DISTRIBUTION

__ AIR DISTRIBUTION--GENERAL PROVISIONS 15800
    __ Work Included __ Related Work Specified Elsewhere __ Reference Standards
    __ Submittals and Review of Materials, Samples, and Drawings __ Job Conditions
    __ Sequence of Work __ Coordination with Other Trades
    __ Materials Delivery, Storage, and Handling

__ AIR DISTRIBUTION--MATERIALS AND PRODUCTS
    __ Sheet Metal __ Duct Types and Sizes __ Dampers __ Louvers
    __ Flashing/Counterflashing __ Diffusers __ Grilles--Supply/Return/Door

__ AIR DISTRIBUTION--EXECUTION
    __ Installation __ Flashing __ Caulking __ Balancing

__ CONTROLS AND INSTRUMENTATION--GENERAL PROVISIONS 15900
    __ Work Included __ Related Work Specified Elsewhere __ Reference Standards
    __ Submittals and Review of Control Diagrams __ Job Conditions
    __ Sequence of Work __ Coordination with Other Trades

__ CONTROLS AND INSTRUMENTATION--PRODUCTS
    __ Control Systems __ Thermostats __ Interlocking

__ CONTROLS AND INSTRUMENTATION--EXECUTION
    __ Interlocking __ Control Sequence--Heat Pumps
    __ Control Sequence--Furnace Coils

15000 MECHANICAL

PRODUCTS/MATERIALS SPECIFIED IN THIS SECTION

__ Primary Construction Materials and Manufacturer/Supplier(s). (Write the items and a list of acceptable sources. If writing generic performance specifications, write the standards of performance separately as a checklist.)

(For reference, include contact names/phone numbers.)

__ Type/Grade/Standard   Applicable Trade and Reference Standards

__ Preparation Materials and/or Accessory Materials/Products

(For reference, include contact names/phone numbers.)

__ Type/Grade/Standard   Applicable Trade and Reference Standards

ROOM SPECIFICATIONS CHECKLIST
DIVISION 16 -- ELECTRICAL

SOURCES

__ National Electrical Code, National Fire Protection Association, Inc., Batterymarch Park, Quincy, MA 02269.

16000   MATERIALS AND CONSTRUCTION SPECIFICATIONS CHECKLIST

__ GENERAL PROVISIONS
    __ Work Included   __ Related Requirements   __ Coordination with Other Trades
    __ Permits and Inspections   __ Codes and Standards
    __ Submittals and Review of Materials, Samples, and Drawings
    __ Gurantees and Warranties   __ Operations and Maintenance Data
    __ Labels and Identification   __ Product Delivery, Storage, and Handling
    __ Wiring for Equipment by Others   __ Tolerances   __ Temporary Utilities

__ MATERIALS AND PRODUCTS
    __ Conduit: Rigid galvanized metal conduit, intermediate metallic conduit, electrical metallic tubing for concealed interior raceways, flexible metal conduit, and rigid nonmetallic conduit as required.

    __ Exposed metal raceways by Wiremold, Walker Parkersburg or approved equal where wiring cannot be concealed.

    __ Boxes: Provide galvanized steel outlet, junction and pull boxes sized to meet requirements of National Electrical Code. Provide outlet boxes for 48 volt emergency lights with blank covers painted yellow.

    __ Conductors and wiring: 600 volt insulation type THWN or THHN copper wiring for branch circuits. Conductors AWG No. 12 shall be solid. Conductors AWG No. 10 and larger stranded. Minimum conductor size AWG No. 12. Green ground conductor in all raceways. Other sizes as required by service intended.

    __ Wiring devices: Receptacles, lighting switches, ground fault receptacles, dimmers, and coverplates as required.

    __ Panelboards as required by National Electrical Code.

    __ Fixtures: Fluorescent fixtures with ETL/CBM approved high power factor with quiet energy-saving rapid-start ballasts. Provide wattmiser lamps and acrylic prismatic lenses.

    __ Occupancy sensors: Ceiling-mounted occupancy sensors by Unenco or approved equal to control light fixtures in designated areas such as toilet and utility rooms.

__ Emergency generator: Engine generator set rated for project requirements. Provide starting batteries, automatic transfer switch, annunciator panel, overcurrent protection.

__ Transformers: High voltage transformers suitable for building requirements.

__ Conductors __ Conduit __ Branch Circuit Panelboards __ Outlet Boxes
__ Outlet Cover Plates __ Wiring Devices __ Weatherproof Receptacles

__ EXECUTION
    __ Color Coding and Identification __ Wiring Splices and Terminations
    __ Motor and Control Wiring __ Panelboards __ Branch Circuits __ Grounding
    __ Conduit Installation: __ Underground __ In Slab
    __ Mounting Heights __ Openings, Cutting, and Patching
    __ Excavation, Trenching, and Backfilling

__ SERVICE AND DISTRIBUTION 16400
    __ Products:
    __ Service Entry __ Safety Switches __ Meters __ Grounding Devices
    __ Panelboards __ Branch Circuit Panelboards __ Fuses/Circuit Breakers
    __ Conductors and Conduit
    __ Execution:
    __ Service Entry and Feeder Circuits __ Supports __ Meters __ Grounding
    __ Panelboards

__ LIGHTING 16500
    __ General Provisions __ Work Included __ Related Work Specified Elsewhere
    __ Submittals and Review of Materials, Samples, and Drawings __ Job Conditions
    __ Sequence of Work __ Coordination with Other Trades

__ LIGHTING FIXTURES 16500
    __ Materials __ Inspection __ Supports __ Installation __ Cleaning __ Testing

__ COMMUNICATIONS 16700
    __ Alarms and Detection Systems __ Clock and Program Systems
    __ Telecommunications __ Television Systems __ Computer Communications

__ HEATING AND COOLING 16850
    __ Snow Melting __ Electric Heating Coils __ Electric Baseboard
    __ Air Conditioners __ Radiant Heaters __ Electric Heaters

16000 ELECTRICAL

PRODUCTS/MATERIALS SPECIFIED IN THIS SECTION

__ Primary Construction Materials and Manufacturer/Supplier(s). (Write the items and a list of acceptable sources. If writing generic performance specifications, write the standards of performance separately as a checklist.)

 (For reference, include contact names/phone numbers.)

__ Type/Grade/Standard   Applicable Trade and Reference Standards

__ Preparation Materials and/or Accessory Materials/Products

(For reference, include contact names/phone numbers.)

__ Type/Grade/Standard   Applicable Trade and Reference Standards

__ Rewrite in checklist format the data you select to use from previous specifications, reference texts, and product catalogs.

__ For more information on the checklist format and how to create your own customized office master specifications, see the ROOM MATERIALS SPECIFICATIONS INTRODUCTION AND INSTRUCTIONS